ARCHBISHOP

# The Archbishops of Canterbury Series

*Series Editor*: Andrew Chandler, University of Chichester, UK

*Series Advisory Board*: Katy Cubitt, University of York, UK; Nicholas Brooks, University of Birmingham, UK; Anne Duggan, King's College London, UK; Sally Vaughn, University of Houston, USA; Julia Barrow, University of Nottingham, UK; Christopher Harper-Bill, University of East Anglia, UK; Robert Swanson, University of Birmingham, UK; Diarmaid MacCulloch, University of Oxford, UK; Alexandra Walsham, University of Cambridge, UK; Judith Maltby, University of Oxford, UK; Jeremy Gregory, University of Manchester, UK; Stephen Taylor, University of Reading, UK; Arthur Burns, King's College, London, UK; David Hein, Hood College, Maryland, USA

Developed in association with Lambeth Palace Library archives, this series presents authoritative studies on the Archbishops of Canterbury. Each book combines biographical, historical, theological, social and political analysis within each archiepiscopacy, with original source material drawn from the Archbishop's correspondence, speeches and published and unpublished writings. The *Archbishops of Canterbury* series offers a vital source of reference, of lasting importance to scholars, students and all readers interested in the history of the international Church.

**Other titles in this series:**

*Archbishops Ralph d'Escures, William of Corbeil and Theobald of Bec*
*Heirs of Anselm and Ancestors of Becket*
Jean Truax

*Archbishop Anselm 1093–1109*
*Bec Missionary, Canterbury Primate, Patriarch of Another World*
Sally N. Vaughn

*Archbishop Fisher, 1945–1961*
*Church, State and World*
Andrew Chandler and David Hein

This fresh exploration of the life, work and writing of Archbishop Pole, focuses particularly on Pole's final years (1556–58) as Archbishop of Canterbury. Fully integrating Pole's English and Continental European experiences, John Edwards places these in their historical context and signposts lessons for contemporary issues and concerns.

Stressing the events and character of Pole's 'English' life, up to his exile in the 1530s, as well as in his final years in England (1554–58), this book explores his close relationship, both genealogical and emotional, with Henry VIII and Mary I. Portraying Pole as a crucial figure in the Catholic–Protestant division, which still affects Britain today, this book details the first, and so far last, attempt to restore Roman Catholicism as the 'national religion' of England and Wales. It tells the life-story of the hinge figure in forging English religious and political identity for several centuries. The final section of this book draws together important and illuminating source material written by Pole before and during his years as Archbishop of Canterbury.

# Contents

# Preface

The seventieth archbishop of Canterbury, Reginald Pole, might, at a superficial glance, seem fairly insignificant, and is largely ignored by the modern 'Tudor industry'. He only did the job for two years and eight months, though he had been papal legate in England for about the same amount of time before that, to begin with based abroad. Also, coming immediately after Thomas Cranmer and before a long series of 'Anglican' archbishops, from Matthew Parker to the present day, he might seem, like the queen whom he served, Mary I, to be a Catholic throwback and anomaly in an inevitable English Protestant progress. In fact, Pole was one of the most remarkable of all occupants of St Augustine's chair. To begin with, he was of royal, Plantagenet, descent. He had a stronger claim to the throne of England than any of what has come, anachronistically but apparently ineradicably, to be known as the 'House of Tudor'.[1] During many years in Italy, first as a student and then an exile, he witnessed and formed part of the eventful and colourful period in which Renaissance turned to Protestant and Catholic Reformation. Though he had little formal theological training, he became an accomplished humanist author and Church reformer. He included Michelangelo Buonarroti and Ignatius of Loyola among his friends, became a cardinal of the Roman Church, was a joint president of the first epoch of the Council of Trent, and helped to supervise the Roman Inquisition, yet ended his life as one of its suspects, a supposed crypto-Lutheran. But, as legate and archbishop in England, he presided over what might have been, had Queen Mary reigned as long as her half-sister Elizabeth would do, the re-construction and development of a Catholic Church of England, in full communion with Rome, that combined tradition with innovation. Such a man is clearly worthy of being thoroughly considered and well-known, but can the biography of a sixteenth-century prelate be written? In his own lifetime, Pole, or 'Poole', defied and contradicted many of the political and ideological currents of his native land, and the history of his age can indeed be written around him, to a significant extent. His last four years, back in England, were spent on the hinge of a secular change in its history. Only after he and his queen had died, both on 17 November 1558, did England gradually, and often painfully, settle into its pattern for the succeeding four centuries, as a conquering and colonising

---

[1] Clifford S.L. Davies, 'The "Tudors": or not?', *The Oxford Historian*, 9 (2011), pp. 6–10; Davies, 'Tudor: what's in a name', *History*, 97 (2012), pp. 24–42.

Protestant power, with an independent and proudly Protestant national Church at the heart of its political and social life. Efforts to reconnect with the European continent, and with Catholicism, have struggled ever since.

Pole lived in a period of Renaissance in the West, when churchmen, scholars and members of the political and social elite self-consciously wrote voluminously, for public as well as private consumption.[2] A notable feature of his life and character was his delight in committing his ideas to paper. Although his output could in no way compare with that of one of his favourite Church Fathers, Augustine of Hippo, he did produce more than 2,000 letters, counting only those that survive, as well as a series of lengthier works, some of which may be described as sermons, and others as treatises, tracts or books. His convoluted writing habits, and the problems of establishing the proper sequence and status of his texts, are considered in the chapters that follow, and in the Appendix. It is clear that the modern reader can know a great deal about how Pole, or 'Poole', wanted to be viewed, and this may indicate some pitfalls that lie in the way of one who seeks to write his 'life'. Also, in his case, it is not possible to avoid psychological questions. He lived an intense spiritual life, as a disciple of Christ, and inevitably, at least to some extent, shared his experience, as a cardinal, scholar, legate and archbishop, with his private circle, with popes and monarchs, and with the educated public in general. With careful use of the sources, generally but not universally in chronological order, it will be possible to say a great deal about Pole's character, and about his spiritual life, though less about his physical health, which seems not to have been good.[3] It is clear that Pole was far more than an administrator, though he did a great deal of that kind of work, in Italy and in England. Most of his writings, and particularly some of his letters, his 'books' and treatises, and his sermons and sermon notes, explore deep matters of the Christian soul. This is the personal aspect of the English cardinal, but as he lived, worked and wrote in a period that saw a turning point in the history of the Western Church, with implications for life far beyond Europe, he is also a guide, though rather an idiosyncratic one, to the true nature of Christian reform in his day. In reading Pole's life, it should always be remembered that, even when he died, in November 1558, the division between 'Catholic' and 'Protestant', on the European continent as well as in England, was not fixed and set. In what follows, there will therefore be times when what today would be called 'Protestant' or 'Evangelical' views come from the pens of Roman cardinals, even though some of them, including Pole himself, came under Inquisition suspicion as a result.

---

[2]  For a stimulating general survey of this subject, in relation to England, see Stephen Greenblatt, *Renaissance self-fashioning: from More to Shakespeare* (Chicago: Chicago University Press, [1980] 2005).

[3]  Michael Prestwich, 'Medieval biography', *Journal of Interdisciplinary History*, 40 (2010), pp. 325–346, at pp. 334–335.

The case of Pole was well set out by one of his close Italian friends, Pietro Carnesecchi, who was himself tried by the Roman Inquisition: '[Pole] has been considered a Lutheran in Rome, in Germany a papist, in the [Habsburg] court of Flanders French, and in that of France, Imperial.'[4] This is the fascination of the man. Today, it has something to say to anyone who is engaged in ecumenism among the still-divided churches.

As is natural when describing a 'life', the approach in the following chapters is basically chronological. Although there is a natural, and proper, stress on the cardinal's achievement in his homeland, it is impossible to understand him without full recognition of his formative years in Italy, and of his very extensive Continental interests and network. Also, given Pole's preoccupation, during his periods of exile, with the history and politics of England, and his own role within them, it is necessary to start with the tormented history of his family up to year of his birth, which began the sixteenth century. To conclude, his two legacies are described, one as a 'backward-looking' Catholic who failed to prevent the triumph of Protestantism in England, and the other as a saintly Catholic reformer, almost a martyr, whose loyal and reforming ideas would influence the Catholic Church up to the present day.

The story begins with traumas that occurred in the Pole family even before Reginald's birth, and the first chapter also includes what is known of his youth and education. The second chapter covers the 1520s, during which Pole was 'the King's servant', taking part, as a scholar, in the intellectual life of Italy and observing its politics. This chapter ends with Pole's work on behalf of King Henry VIII, in trying to gain the support of the Paris theologians for the divorce of Queen Catherine. After this came Pole's quarrel with Henry, and the third chapter covers his great polemic against his master's religious policies in the 1530s, known as *De unitate*, as well as the king's subsequent violent pursuit of Reginald and his family. In the 1540s, discussed in the fourth chapter, Pole, now as a cardinal of the Roman Church, became a leading Catholic reformer, particularly in his household at Viterbo. The chapter concludes with the first phase of the Council of Trent, in which he took an active role, before leaving amidst theological controversy. Chapter 5 covers the years between 1547, beginning with the death of King Henry, and Pole's appointment as legate to England, once Mary I was on the throne. The next two chapters overlap in chronology, as they recount Pole's efforts to restore and embed the Catholic Church in Mary's kingdom, while the eighth chapter records Pole's difficult last months, before his death on 17 November 1558, in which Pope Paul IV seemed to want to undermine all his work. The final chapter offers two very different accounts of his legacy, one from his Protestant enemies, including Queen

---

[4]  Giacomo Manzoni, ed., 'Il processo Carnesechi', *Miscellanea di storia italiana*, 10 (1870), pp. 189–573, at p. 301; *PPP*, pp. 1–2.

Elizabeth, who did their best to dismantle his work in the English Church, and his Continental Catholic legacy, in which he was seen as a saintly prelate who had a major influence on what came to be called the Counter-Reformation.

Just as Pole and Mary were cousins, and became friends and colleagues in the 1550s, so this biography of the cardinal has, for several years, moved in step with my 'life' of his Queen, *Mary I: England's Catholic Queen* (Yale English Monarchs, 2011). Research on the two of them went in parallel, involving debts to the staff of the same libraries and archives. Thus honourable mention should be made of the Bodleian Library at Oxford, and particularly its digital services, now including the History Faculty Library, as well as the Modern Languages Faculty Library. Also valuable have been Cambridge University Library, as well as the British Library and its digital services. Early work on Pole was done, using Vatican Library manuscripts on film, in the Vatican Film Library at Saint Louis Library, where I held a visiting fellowship in the autumn of 2007. Also essential have been the Archivo General de Simancas, where Isabel Aguirre is unfailingly helpful, and the Royal English College of St Alban the Martyr in Valladolid, where Javier Burrieza has offered a warm welcome and valuable aid.

Finally, I must pay tribute to two great scholars who provide an example, and offer a possibility, for effective work on the life and achievement of Cardinal Pole. José Ignacio Tellechea Idígoras first identified the importance of the friendship between the main subject of his researches, Bartolomé Carranza, and Pole. Both were devout Catholic archbishops, who had their lives blighted by destructive criticism, not least from the Inquisition. Secondly, and above all, I owe an immense debt to Professor Thomas Mayer, who over many years made the study of Pole his own. Sadly, he died soon after this book was completed. It would not be possible to make a serious study of the cardinal without absorbing what he has written, and this work is dedicated to his memory.

*Oxford, 4 November 2013,*
*Feast of St Carlo Borromeo*


**Notes**

The footnotes to this book, when referring to primary manuscript sources, offer, in the vast majority of cases, firstly, an original manuscript source, secondly, where possible, the most readily available printed version of the document concerned, and thirdly, also wherever possible, one or more printed calendar references, always including *CRP*. Where the textual history of a document is particularly complicated (this frequently being the case with Pole's own works), the reader is referred, as appropriate, to Mayer's scholarly work.

# List of Abbreviations

| | |
|---|---|
| Add. | Additional |
| AGS | Archivo General de Simancas |
| *APC* | *Acts of the Privy Council*, ed. J.R. Dasent, 32 vols (London: HMSO, 1890–1907) |
| BAV | Biblioteca apostolica vaticana, Rome |
| BL | British Library, London |
| Bod. | Bodleian Library, Oxford |
| CCCC | Corpus Christi College, Cambridge: Parker Library |
| *CMT* | Eamon Duffy and David Loades, eds, *The Church of Mary Tudor* (Aldershot: Ashgate, 2006) |
| *CP* | José Ignacio Tellechea Idígoras, *Fray Bartolomé Carranza y el Cardenal Pole. Un navarro en la restauración católica de Inglaterra (1554–1558)* (Pamplona: Diputación Foral de Navarra and others, 1977) |
| *CPEC* | Thomas F. Mayer, *Cardinal Pole in European Context. A* Via Media *in the Reformation* (Aldershot: Variorum, 2000) |
| *CPR* | *Calendar of the Patent Rolls preserved in the Public Record Office*, ed. H.C. Maxwell, 6 vols (London: HMSO, 1924–9) |
| *CPRPM* | *Calendar of Patent Rolls: Philip and Mary*, 4 vols (London: HMSO, 1936–9) |
| *CRP* | Thomas F. Mayer, ed., *The Correspondence of Reginald Pole: A Calendar*, 3 vols (Aldershot: Ashgate, 2000–4) |
| *CSP Dom* | *Calendar of State Papers, Domestic Series, 1547–1580*, ed. Robert Lemon (London: Longman, Brown, Green, Longman and Roberts, 1856) |
| *CSP Dom rev* | *Calendar of State Papers, Domestic Series of the Reign of Mary, 1553–1558, revised*, ed. C.S. Knighton (London: Public Record Office, 1998) |
| *CSP For* | *Calendar of State Papers, Foreign Series, of the Reign of Mary, 1553–1558*, ed. W.H. Turnbull (London: Longman, Green, Longman and Roberts, 1861) |
| *CSP Milan* | *Calendar of State Papers and Manuscripts in the Archives and Collections of Milan, 1385–1618* (London: HMSO, 1912) |
| *CSP Rome* | *Calendar of State Papers ... Rome*, ed. J.M. Rigg, 2 vols (London: HMSO, 1916, 1926) |

CSP Span *Calendar of Letters, Despatches and State Papers relating to the Negotiations between England and Spain*, ed. Gustav A. Bergenroth and others, 20 vols (London: Longman and Company, and others, 1864–98)

CSP Ven *Calendar of State Papers and Manuscripts relating to English Affairs in the Archives and Collections of Venice*, ed. Rawdon Brown, 9 vols (London: Longman and others, 1864–98)

CT *Concilium tridentinum*, ed. Stephan Eses and others, 13 vols (Freiburg-im-Breisgau: Herder, 1901–67)

CUL Cambridge University Library

Dwyer Joseph G. Dwyer, ed. and trans., *Pole's Defense of the Unity of the Church [De Unitate]* (Westminster MD: The Newman Press, 1965)

ERP *Epistolarum Reginaldi Poli ... Libri V*, ed. Angelo Maria Querini, 5 vols (Brescia: Rizzardi, 1744–57)

Foxe, *A&M* John Foxe, *Actes and Monuments of these Latter and Perilous Dayes ...* (commonly known as the *Book of Martyrs*) (London: John Day, 1563, 1570, 1576, 1583). Full online edition at johnfoxe.org

Gasquet Adrian Gasquet, *Cardinal Pole and his Early Friends* (London: George Bell and Sons, 1927)

HMSO Her or His Majesty's Stationery Office, London

LP *Letters and Papers, Foreign and Domestic, of the Reign of Henry VIII*, ed. J.S. Brewer, James Gairdner and R.H. Brodie, 21 vols (London: HMSO, 1862–1932)

LPL Lambeth Palace Library, London

Lutz Heinrich Lutz, ed., *Fridenslegation des Reginald Pole zu Kaiser Karl V und König Heinrich II (1553–1556). Nuntiatur-berichte aus Deutschland nebst ergänzenden Akten stücke. Erste Abteilung* (Tübingen: Niemayer, 1981)

MS(S) Manuscripts

ODCC *Oxford Dictionary of the Christian Church*, ed. F.L. Cross and E.A. Livingstone, 3rd edn (Oxford: Oxford University Press, 1998)

ODNB *Oxford Dictionary of National Biography*, ed. H.G.C. Matthew and Brian Harrison (Oxford: Oxford University Press, 2004–) and online

OEE *Opus epistolarum Desiderii Erasmi Roterodami*, ed. P.S. Allen, H.M. Allen and H.W. Garrod, 12 vols (Oxford: Clarendon Press, 1905–58)

OUA Oxford University Archive

PL *Patrologia latina*, ed. J.-P. Migne, 221 vols (Paris, 1844–64)

| | |
|---|---|
| *PPP* | Thomas F. Mayer, *Reginald Pole: Prince and Prophet* (Cambridge: Cambridge University Press, 2000) |
| *RCEMT* | *Reforming Catholicism in the England of Mary Tudor: The Achievement of Friar Bartolomé Carranza*, ed. John Edwards and Ronald Truman (Aldershot: Ashgate, 2005) |
| *Rot. Parl.* | *Rotuli Parliamentorum et petitiones et placita in Parliamento*, 6 vols (London: Houses of Parliament, 1707–77) |
| Rymer, *Foedera* | *Acta regia, or an Account of the Treaties, Letters and Instruments between the Monarchs of England and Foreign Powers*, ed. Thomas Rymer (London: For J. Darby and others, 1726–7) |
| *SP* | State Papers |
| TNA | The National Archives, Kew |
| WAM | Westminster Abbey Muniments Room |

# Chapter 1
# Family and Upbringing

Reginald Pole was born in March 1500, the third son of Sir Richard Pole (1458/9–1504) and his wife Margaret, née Plantagenet (1473–1541). It is virtually certain that the birth took place at Stourton Castle, in Staffordshire, the use of which had been granted to the future cardinal archbishop's parents by King Henry VII, so that his mother could remain fairly close to her husband's operations in the government of Wales and the Marches. The fortified manor house stood on the banks of the river Stour, about half a mile north-east of the village of Kinver, and about a day's ride from the seat of Prince Arthur of Wales' council at Ludlow.[1]

Much of Reginald's character and future life would be strongly influenced by his mother's Plantagenet descent, and by the violent events that befell the family, both before his birth and during his early years. She had been born at Farleigh Castle near Bath, on 14 August 1473, to George, duke of Clarence and Isabel, née Neville, her father then being third in the line of succession. Clarence was a son of Richard, duke of York, and brother of King Edward IV and Richard, duke of Gloucester, the future Richard III. He received his dukedom in 1461, when Edward seized the throne, and the turbulence of his life would set the tone for that of his grandson Reginald, involving high political status and ambition, along with deep insecurity. Eventually, on 18 February 1478, Cardinal Pole's grandfather was executed, on trumped-up charges of treason. The deed was done privately within the precincts of the Tower of London, perhaps to avoid any public demonstration in his favour, as Clarence had been quite popular. Whether the legendary butt of Canary wine (*malvasí*, or malmsey) was used cannot be known, but it is not impossible.[2]

After his wife's death, in December 1476, the duke had behaved in a foolish and provocative way, given his brother Edward's well-founded fears for the long-term security of his regime, and the effects of his actions on Margaret, the

---

[1]  Hazel Pierce, 'The life, career and political significance of Margaret Pole, countess of Salisbury (1473–1541)', PhD thesis, University of Wales, Bangor, 1997, pp. 63–64; Pierce, 'Pole, Margaret', *ODNB*.

[2]  J.R. Lander, 'The treason and death of the duke of Clarence', *Canadian Journal of History*, 2(2) (1967), pp. 1–28; Charles Ross, *Edward IV* (London: Eyre Methuen, 1974), pp. 239–245; Jonathan Hughes, *Arthurian myths and alchemy: the kingship of Edward IV* (Stroud: Sutton Publishing, 2002), pp. 289–290. William Shakespeare has the duke of Clarence die by drowning in a butt of malmsey (wine) (*Richard III*, act 1 scene 4).

mother of the future Cardinal Pole, were rapid and severe. In her earliest years, she had lived in a large household, in which her father and mother between them had over 300 servants, and where the traditional liturgy of the Church was scrupulously and devoutly observed.[3] Now, at the age of just five, she was the daughter of a convicted and executed traitor, who was believed to have plotted to overthrow his own brother. Under the treason legislation of the time, after their father's death, Margaret and her brother Edward became wards under the protection of the king, and completely dependent upon him. Also, while Edward was allowed to inherit the Neville estates of his mother, including the earldom of Warwick, which were not affected by the Act of Attainder against Clarence, his sister's prospects, in February 1478, appeared to be grim. King Edward subsequently granted the wardship of the young earl of Warwick to Thomas Grey, marquess of Dorset, and Margaret was entrusted to his care as well. If anything unfortunate happened to her brother, which was hardly unlikely in the circumstances which prevailed in the England of the 1480s, her impressive royal pedigree might still produce a good marriage for her in the future.

In the event both Edward and Margaret outlived Edward IV, and on 9 April 1483, Margaret became a ward of the new king, her uncle Richard of Gloucester. The deaths in the Tower of London of Edward IV's two sons, Edward V and Richard of York, ironically raised the status of Clarence's son and daughter. Although Margaret's claim to the throne remained more distant than that of her brother, Edward, earl of Warwick, she now had a considerable amount to offer a future husband, but Richard III was all too aware and fearful of this. Although Earl Edward and Margaret escaped death at this stage, the new king used his own interpretation of the law against them, declaring that they were both barred from the succession by their father's attainder, although the relevant act of parliament required no such thing.[4] While Princes Edward and Richard were still alive in the Tower, Earl Edward and Margaret were sent to Sheriff Hutton Castle, 10 miles from York, to live under the supervision of their cousin John de la Pole, earl of Lincoln. This castle had once belonged to the Neville side of the children's family, though it was now in royal hands. In March or April 1484, with Edward's sons already dead, King Richard's own son, Edward, died too. Under the hazy English succession law of the period, this should probably have made the earl of Warwick next in line to the throne, but that never happened in legal form, since Richard was all too aware that, if Warwick's position was thus formalised, he himself would have to admit that the young earl should in fact be king already. In these circumstances, given

---

[3]    *Collection of ordinances and regulations for the government of the royal household* (London: John Nichols, 1790), pp. 89, 91, 99, 100–101, 166.

[4]    Mortimer Levine, *Tudor dynastic problems, 1460–1571* (London: Allen & Unwin, 1973), p. 137.

Richard's record in government to date, it looked, when 1485 began, as though Earl Edward and Margaret would be lucky to survive to adulthood. At best, they were going to be closely watched.[5]

In fact, on 22 August 1485, Henry Tudor, earl of Richmond, defeated Richard's superior forces in battle near Bosworth, in Leicestershire, the king died during the battle, and Henry replaced him. This situation created new threats to Clarence's offspring. Earl Edward was especially vulnerable under the new, insecure and fearful regime of Henry VII, because the series of recent royal and noble deaths had left him as the only surviving direct and legitimate male descendant of Edward III, through his fourth son, Edmund, duke of York, and also by a female line from that king's third son, John of Gaunt. In contrast, Henry VII could only claim descent from Edward III through his mother, Lady Margaret Beaufort, also from John of Gaunt, but by an illegitimate line. Earl Edward thus better represented the claim which the Tudors would later make for themselves, to combine the Yorkist and Lancastrian inheritances, and bring to an end the series of conflicts known to history as the 'Wars of the Roses'. An even more intriguing possibility was that Margaret herself, rather than the Tudor Mary I, might have been England's first sovereign and reigning queen. Henry VII was generally worried about his position, at home and abroad, but he was rightly anxious in particular about Warwick and Margaret. Indeed, immediately after the battle of Bosworth, he headed straight for Sheriff Hutton, and even before that, while still in Leicester, he sent his servant Robert Willoughby to secure the young earl, in case he became a focus of immediate rebellion.[6] The new king's fear was entirely realistic, given that Warwick, as Isabel Neville's son, might have called upon considerable political and military support in the north.

On top of that, when Henry came to the throne, Isabella of Castile and Ferdinand of Aragon were already seeking marriage alliances for their children which would both secure their own Trastamaran dynasty and enhance Spain's position in Europe. In this context, Diego de Valera, a military man and political commentator who frequently advised the Spanish rulers, wrote to them, on 1 March 1486, about the current situation in England. In this letter he reported that Edward of Warwick was a major threat to Henry VII's rule, in part because he had the backing of the highly influential Henry Percy, earl of Northumberland.[7] Indeed, as early as October 1485, some in the English garrison in Calais had apparently believed for a while that Henry was already dead, and that he would

---

[5]  Hazel Pierce, *Margaret Pole, countess of Salisbury, 1473–1541: loyalty, lineage and leadership* (Cardiff: University of Wales Press, 2003), pp. 2–9.

[6]  *The* Anglica Historia *of Polydore Vergil, A.D. 1485–1537*, ed. and trans. Denys Hay, *Camden Society*, 3rd series, 74 (1950), p. 3.

[7]  Anthony Goodman and Angus MacKay, 'A Castilian report on English affairs in 1486', *English Historical Review*, 88 (1973), pp. 92–99, at pp. 93, 95, 97.

be succeeded by the earl of Warwick.[8] In view of all this, as well no doubt as his own imaginary fears, Henry Tudor moved Earl Edward and Margaret well away from the potentially rebellious north, placing them as 'guests' with his mother, Lady Margaret Beaufort, along with other royals and nobles, including Henry's own wife, Elizabeth of York, and her sisters, as well as the earl of Westmoreland and the duke of Buckingham. He no doubt thought it would be better if they were under Lady Margaret's eagle eye, rather than travelling the country as potential focuses, or even fomentors, of trouble for him. Such measures will have seemed all the more justified and necessary when two minor uprisings did indeed occur in March and April 1486 respectively. The second of these, led by a former servant of Richard III, Humphrey Stafford, was apparently precipitated by a rumour that the earl of Warwick had escaped to the Channel Islands, with the intention of following Henry VII's earlier example by mounting an invasion from abroad, probably with French help.

Before this tumult subsided, Humphrey Stafford's supporters apparently mounted a demonstration in the earl of Warwick's heartland, crying out 'A Warwick! A Warwick!' in Birmingham.[9] Henry no doubt hoped that the semi-hostages lodged with his mother, including Clarence's heirs, would renounce their claims to the throne, as she had done for him. Given that Earl Edward and Margaret were clearly legitimate, while some doubt was cast on his own wife's legitimacy, as there were indeed questions in some quarters over King Edward's marriage to Elizabeth Woodville, the Clarence children would have to be closely watched for the foreseeable future. Despite this, and perhaps with the purpose of incorporating her into the Tudor establishment, Margaret now received particular honours from the king. In September 1486, she headed the list of ladies who attended Henry and Elizabeth's son, Prince Arthur, at his baptism and confirmation in Winchester Cathedral, and in the following year she was a prominent attendant at Elizabeth of York's coronation as queen, in Westminster Abbey.[10] She herself would soon be married to the future cardinal archbishop's father.

In an account of Elizabeth of York's coronation, which took place in November 1487, it is said that Margaret watched the ceremony with Henry VII and Lady Margaret Beaufort, and she is referred to there as the wife of Richard Pole.[11] There is a possibility that this document, being a late sixteenth-

---

[8]   C.S.L. Davies, 'Bishop John Morton, the Holy See, and the accession of Henry VII', *English Historical Review*, 102 (1987), pp. 2–30, at p. 27.

[9]   David Loades, *Politics and the nation, 1450–1660*, 3rd edn (London: Fontana, 1988), p. 97 n. 18.

[10]   Pierce, *Margaret Pole*, pp. 10–12.

[11]   BL Egerton MS 985, fol. 19; Thomas Hearne, ed., *Joannis Lelandi antiquarii de rebus Britannicis collectanea*, 4 vols (London, 1770, reprinted Farnborough: Gregg International, 1971), 4, p. 225.

century copy, contains a subsequent amendment of Margaret's surname, and her marriage to Richard has commonly been dated, in modern historiography, to about 1491–4.[12] Hazel Pierce, on the other hand, has argued strongly for 1487 as the correct date, saying that the arrangement of the Pole marriage may well have been a response by Henry VII to the dangerous threat which had just been posed to him by the young man, known subsequently as Lambert Simnel, who had claimed to be the earl of Warwick, raised troops in Ireland, invaded England as 'King Edward VI', and was only defeated by a major military effort on the Tudor king's part, at the battle of Stoke, on 16 June 1487. Simnel's enterprise could fairly be described as a Yorkist plot, and involvement in it came dangerously close to Margaret and her brother, in that one of those who fled to Flanders, after it was discovered, was none other than John de la Pole, earl of Lincoln, who had once guarded the pair at Sheriff Hutton.[13] In the circumstances in which she found herself in 1487, under effective house-arrest in the charge of Lady Margaret Beaufort, and facing the additional danger of being linked with Simnel's rebellion, it is perhaps not surprising that Cardinal Pole's mother accepted as her husband someone who was neither of royal nor of noble descent, at least in England.

Richard Pole was born in Buckinghamshire, in 1458 or the following year, as the eldest son of Geoffrey Pole, esquire, and Edith St John, of Bletsoe.[14] Geoffrey came originally from Wales, and was a staunch supporter of Henry VI, to whom he was an esquire of the body from 1440. His main governmental and other offices were located in South Wales, and he was a councillor of Jasper Tudor, earl of Pembroke. Richard Pole's mother, Edith St John, was also a solid Lancastrian supporter in the Tudor connection, being a half-sister of the future Henry VII's mother, Lady Margaret Beaufort, countess of Richmond, and widowed sister-in-law of Jasper Tudor. Perhaps not surprisingly, given this background, Geoffrey Pole held himself aloof from Edward IV's regime, remaining largely on his Buckinghamshire manors of Ellsborough, Medmenham and Stoke Mandeville, and dying in that county in 1479. Thus his son Richard's childhood was spent in relative obscurity, until Henry Tudor successfully invaded Wales and England in 1485. In response to her son's victory, Lady Margaret Beaufort quickly rallied the known Tudor supporters in England, and on 22 October of that year, Richard Pole was appointed esquire to the new king's body. In 1486, he was made constable of Harlech Castle, and sheriff of Merioneth, both offices being

[12]  Michael Jones and Malcolm Underwood, *The King's matter* (Cambridge: Cambridge University Press, 1992), p. 82.

[13]  S.B. Chrimes, *Henry VII* (New Haven and London: Yale University Press, [1972] 1999), pp. 75–77.

[14]  Hazel Pierce, 'The king's cousin: the life, career, and Welsh connection of Sir Richard Pole, 1458–1504', *Welsh History Review*, 19 (1998), pp. 187–225.

for life, a strong sign of Henry's personal trust in him.[15] To cement his reputation
with the king, he fought for him against Simnel in the battle of Stoke, being
knighted on the field, and his marriage to Margaret Plantagenet seems to have
been an extra reward, with far-reaching and unforeseen consequences.[16] When
the council and household of Henry and Elizabeth's son Arthur, Prince of Wales,
were established in Ludlow Castle in 1493, Richard Pole became his chamberlain,
acting for him in his proxy betrothal to Princess Catalina of Spain, at Tickhill
near Bewdley, in May 1499. On St George's day of that year, 23 April, Richard
had been installed in Windsor as a knight of the Garter.[17] If a supposed family
tree is reliable, it was entirely appropriate that Richard Pole should have taken
such a prominent role in the government of Wales, during the reign of Henry
VII. According to this account, his father Geoffrey was the son of David Fychan
and Margaret Griffith, the latter being a descendant of the princes of Powys.[18]
It is also probable, though not possible to establish absolutely, that Owen Pole,
a leading cleric in Wales, whose offices included a canonry of St David's and
who certainly was a descendant of the royal house of Powys, was a close relative
of Geoffrey Pole, and hence an ancestor of Cardinal Archbishop Reginald.[19] In
any case, Geoffrey left artistic testimony of his loyalty to the Tudors in a screen
which he had installed in Aberconwy parish church, at the foot of the walls of
Conway Castle. Carved by craftsmen from Ludlow, it displays Tudor roses, the
Prince of Wales' feathers, the Beaufort portcullis, the dragon of Cadwaladr, and
Catherine of Aragon's personal emblem, the pomegranate, or 'Granada apple'.[20]
When Prince Arthur, who had been Henry and Elizabeth's white hope, died in
Ludlow Castle on 2 April 1502, Richard and Margaret Pole's son Reginald was
just over two years old. He had never had a chance to see his uncle, Edward, earl
of Warwick, who was executed in 1499 (see below). Reginald would, however,
retain pride in his Welsh ancestry. His first biographer, Ludovico Beccadelli,
whose work was revised by another of the cardinal's servants, Andras Dudic,
stressed that his work was based on his master's own words. Dudic, as well as

---

[15]   *CPR*, 1485–94, nos 5, 78.

[16]   Pierce, *Margaret Pole*, pp. 12–16.

[17]   Chrimes, *Henry VII*, p. 303 n. 1.

[18]   Pierce, 'Richard Pole', pp. 188–190.

[19]   Pierce, 'Richard Pole', pp. 188–190.

[20]   Steven Gunn, 'Prince Arthur's preparation for kingship', in *Arthur Tudor, prince of Wales: life, death and commemoration*, ed. Steven Gunn and Linda Monckton (Woodbridge: The Boydell Press, 2009), pp. 7–19, at pp. 11, 13–15; John Morgan-Guy, 'Arthur, Hari Tudor and the iconography of loyalty in Wales', in Gunn and Monckton, *Arthur Tudor*, pp. 50–63, at pp. 54–55 and Figure 9.

stressing Pole's English royal descent, asserts that, through his father, the cardinal was descended from the British line of King Arthur, he of the Round Table.[21]

While the earl of Warwick's sister, Margaret, was allowed by Henry VII to marry the trusted Richard Pole, he found himself caught up, through no fault of his own, in the European politics which surrounded the proposed marriage of Arthur of Wales and Catherine of Spain. Central to what happened to him was the activity of Edward IV's sister Margaret, dowager duchess of Burgundy, whose husband, Charles the Bold, had been killed in battle against the French in 1477. Margaret never accepted Henry VII as king of England and supported the claims of Lambert Simnel as 'Edward VI' in 1487. Then, in 1491, she saw another opportunity to subvert the Tudor regime when a new pretender appeared, claiming to be Edward IV's son Richard, duke of York, who was generally believed to have been murdered in the Tower of London, on the orders of Richard III, probably in 1483. The monarchs of western Europe were forced to come to a decision as to whether or not the claim of 'Richard IV' was genuine, and Margaret of York did not hesitate to accept it, though no one at the time seems to have believed that his brother, Edward V, was still alive. In November 1491, 'Richard IV', or 'Perkin Warbeck' as he has become known to history, landed at Cork, and attempted to raise a rebellion in Ireland against Henry's rule. Between 1491 and October 1497, when he was at last captured by Henry's servants, the pretender received support from a wide range of the king's enemies, including some Anglo-Irish nobles, James IV of Scotland, and Charles VIII of France, as well as Margaret of York and Burgundy. Once captured, 'Perkn Warbeck' joined Reginald Pole's uncle in the Tower of London, where they apparently spoke to each other, from one floor to another, by means of a hole that Warwick had made with a file. Inevitably, there was suspicion that they were conspiring against Henry VII. The young earl seems to have been innocent and clueless throughout, anxious for friendship and very apt to confide in the wrong people, but the dénouement was brutal.

Charges of treason against Warwick were read by Chief Justice Fineux, before the king in council, on 12 November 1499, while Margaret was pregnant with the future Cardinal Pole. The judge urged that the earl and Warbeck should both be indicted, and the next day, under a commission of oyer and terminer, the sheriff of London was ordered to empanel a London jury to hear the case, which it duly did, in the Guildhall, on 18 November. The fact that Warbeck, if Ferdinand and Isabella's ambassador had correctly identified him back in 1496, was not Henry's subject did not prevent him from being convicted of treason and dragged to Tyburn for hanging, drawing and quartering. Warwick was tried

---

[21] Ludovico Beccadelli, revised by Andras Dudic, with Giovanni Battista Binardi, *Vita Reginaldi Poli, Britanni S. R. E. cardinalis, et cantuariensis archiepiscopi* (Venice: Ex oficina Dominici Guerrei et Joannis Baptistae fratrum, 1563), sig. Bi.

for treason by his peers, on 21 November, convicted and given a similar sentence, but as he was a nobleman, he was beheaded instead, in an unobtrusive manner on Tower Green, within the walls, on 28 November.[22] The young Reginald no doubt heard, not too many years afterwards, of the spectacular meteorological events which apparently accompanied his uncle's violent death (Appendix 2C).

As she prepared for the birth of her child, documentary references suggest that Margaret Pole was happily married to Richard, who was 14 years older than her. Involved in the government of Wales and the Marches since 1488, Richard Pole had followed the courtier's custom of living beyond his means, but was well enough in the king's favour, despite the dubious political history of his wife's family, to receive additional support. With typical Tudor wit, this help took the form of the manors of Fifield and Long Wittenham in Oxfordshire, which had previously been confiscated from Margaret and Edward's former guardian at Sheriff Hutton, John de la Pole, who had since fallen out of favour with the king, as a suspected rebel. Even so, Reginald's father felt financially constrained, in 1491, to sell the manor of Stoke Mandeville and mortgage that of Ellsborough. He must have feared for his own future, as well as that of his wife, and their children, Henry, Jane, Arthur and Ursula, when he heard of the earl of Warwick's execution. Nevertheless, at the time of Reginald's birth, in March 1500, his father was still Prince Arthur's chamberlain, and his mother was certainly in the household of Princess Catherine at Ludlow in 1501–2, as a lady in waiting. Margaret seems to have remained close to her husband in the Marches, when the widowed princess returned to London, though she continued to exchange letters with Catherine until the latter married Henry VIII, in 1509.

This was the situation into which Reginald began his life at Stourton Castle, and the next major change in the family's life was the death of his father Richard, in October 1504. The loss caused both political and economic insecurity for Margaret and her now six children, since Geoffrey was born to her soon after her husband's death. Her jointure in her late husband's Buckinghamshire and Oxfordshire manors produced some income, but his royal salaries of course disappeared, and her Plantagenet pride had to submit to the receipt of loans and gifts from servants, notable among them being John Evans, bailiff of Medmenham. Thus it may well have been sheer economic pressure, as much as religious devotion, which led her to direct Reginald into the Church, though this was in any case quite a normal course for a younger son who had no prospect of inheriting family estates. In the remaining years of Henry VII's reign, Reginald's older brother Henry was a king's ward, but never appeared at court, perhaps because he had a stronger claim to the throne than its current occupant,

---

[22]   Anne Wroe, *Perkin: a story of deception* (London: Jonathan Cape, 2003), pp. 72, 417–418, 423–439.

and Margaret Pole's friendship with Catherine of Aragon grew in a situation of shared political and social limbo, with both struggling as impoverished widows.[23]

Reginald's mother found her prospects transformed, along with those of Catherine, when Henry VIII succeeded his father in April 1509. Once Henry and Catherine were married, Margaret joined the new queen's household, having attended their joint coronation, on 24 June 1509.[24] The economic situation of the Pole family improved rapidly, and its members appear to have benefited from the new king's notorious desire to demonstrate the remarkable difference between his reign and that of his father. Now Henry Pole did come to court, and by 1512 he was 'sewer', or waiter in the privy chamber, to the king, and in the same year, perhaps through the intercession of his mother and of the then up-and-coming cleric, Thomas Wolsey, the 12-year-old Reginald was sent to Oxford with royal support.[25] At about the same time, Henry VIII made Margaret countess of Salisbury in her own right, which would prove to be a precedent, in very different circumstances, for his second wife Anne Boleyn, when she received a peerage as 'marquess' of Pembroke, in 1532. Reginald's mother entered the Salisbury estates in January 1514, as the fifth- or sixth-richest woman in England.[26] Meanwhile, the future cardinal archbishop's early formal education seems to have taken place in the precincts of the Carthusian priory of Sheen, to which the reforming dean of St Paul's in London, John Colet, had retired, though the young Pole may also, or instead, have been connected with Christ Church, Canterbury.[27] Beccadelli and Dudic were clear that Reginald received his first education from his mother, went to the Carthusians at Sheen as a young adolescent (*adolescentulum*), and from there proceeded to Magdalen.[28] In March 1511, he received from the king £12, 'for his exhibition at school', and in the following year entered Magdalen College, Oxford, receiving in April 1513 an additional 'pension', or scholarship, which bound him to the prior of St Frideswide's, the house of Augustinian canons which would later become first Cardinal College, then King Henry VIII College and finally Christ Church. This arrangement suggests that, at least by the age of 13, Reginald was definitely intended for an ecclesiastical career, as the prior was supposed to provide him eventually with a suitable benefice.[29]

When he arrived at Magdalen, young Reginald entered one of the most dynamic academic institutions in Oxford at the time. The college had been founded in around 1460, by William Waynflete, bishop of Winchester, on the

23    Pierce, *Margaret Pole*, pp. 17–18, 23–31.
24    *LP* I (i) p. 1442.
25    TNA C.82/38 (i); *LP* I (i) no. 158.
26    Pierce, *Margaret Pole*, pp. 31–37.
27    T[homas] F. Mayer, 'Pole, Reginald', *ODNB*.
28    Beccadelli and Dudic, *Vita*, sig. Bii.
29    Pierce, *Margaret Pole*, pp. 32–33.

model of his predecessor William of Wykeham's colleges at Winchester and Oxford (St Mary of Winchester or 'New' College). It consisted of a president and 70 scholars, including 40 clerks training for the priesthood and 30 students on half-stipends, hence known as 'demyes'. When young Reginald arrived in the college, it was still, as its founder intended, a centre for arts teaching with a humanistic bent, and for the preparation of priests for the Church. Unlike many other colleges, Magdalen gave priority to graduate studies in theology, rather than civil and canon law and, at both undergraduate and graduate levels, the college provided teaching for the rest of the university, as well as for its own members. Demyes could be admitted from the age of 12, and often came, though not apparently in Pole's case, from the grammar school still known as Magdalen College School. For his first four years, Pole will have studied logic and philosophy with masters known as *informatores*, who were on the lowest rung of a hierarchical system in which the dean of arts supervised the senior fellows, who were mostly theologians with a few lawyers and medics, while these fellows in turn taught their juniors, who would teach the other scholars and demyes. This formal teaching consisted partly of lectures and partly of the formal disputations which were the staple of the medieval European universities.[30] Reginald does not seem to have thought this part of his life important enough to be recorded in detail, so that only the outward structure of his time at Magdalen can be described, though it is thought that he was taught by the great physician Thomas Linacre, and the Classicist William Latimer, among others.[31] In 1515, Pole was granted a dispensation to enter the university library in lay dress, perhaps because of his royal rank.[32] The other Oxford college with which Pole was associated, Corpus Christi, shines further light on his academic development and his future scholarly interests, but that came later. In 1521, again with financial support from Henry VIII, Reginald left Oxford to pursue his studies in Italy, not long before, on 17 May 1521, one of his mother's relatives and friends, Edward Stafford, duke of Buckingham, was executed on charges of treason. But before the consequences of that action for his own immediate family could become clear, the lands of the Most Serene Republic of Venice beckoned to Pole.[33]

---

[30] James McConica, 'The rise of the undergraduate college', in *The history of the University of Oxford*, 3, *The collegiate university*, ed. McConica (Oxford: Clarendon Press, 1986), pp. 3–7; *Statutes of the colleges of Oxford*, 3 vols (London: Royal Commission on the Universities, 1859), 2 pt 8 (Magdalen College); Nicholas Orme, 'Latimer, William (c. 1487–1545)', *ODNB*.

[31] William Schenk, *Reginald Pole, cardinal of England* (London: Longman, Green, and Co., 1950), p. 5.

[32] Elizabeth Russell, 'The influx of commoners into the University of Oxford before 1581: an optical illusion?', *English Historical Review*, 92 (1977), pp. 721–745, at p. 723 n. 1.

[33] Pierce, *Margaret Pole*, pp. 11, 87.

# Chapter 2
# The King's Servant

It is not entirely certain when young Reginald Pole arrived in Padua, to begin what turned out to be a long and formative involvement with Italy. But on or about 1 March 1521, the then Venetian ambassador in London, Marin Sanudo, reported to the city's Signoria that Henry VIII was about to send a relative (*nepote*) to Padua, a city which had been governed by Venice since its conquest in 1405. In another dispatch, in May of that year, Sanudo reported to his masters that the English king had asked him to warn them not to make too much fuss of Pole, lest he become another duke of Buckingham. The threat cast a shadow over the royal student from the start of his education abroad.[1]

Edward Stafford, third duke of Buckingham, had had a plausible claim to the English throne through his descent from Edward III's fifth and youngest son, Thomas of Woodstock, duke of Gloucester. In view of this, young Buckingham, while still a minor, had been one of those placed by Henry VII, for security, in the care of his mother, Lady Margaret Beaufort, by means of a warrant issued on 24 February 1486.[2] Despite this, the duke continued to be seen as a threat to the very existence of the Tudor dynasty, and in 1506, one John Flamant reported to the king some gossip which had been overheard in Calais from the treasurer there, Sir Hugh Conway, while Henry lay ill at Wanstead: 'Some of them spoke of my lorde of Buckingham, saying that he was a noble man and would be a royal ruler.'[3] When Henry VIII came to the throne, Buckingham had seemed to be restored to favour, like many who had been regarded as suspects by his father, and it was in this difficult context that his son, Henry Stafford, married Reginald Pole's sister Ursula. The alliance appeared to be highly advantageous to the Pole family, since Henry was heir to the leading peer of England, who possessed 124 manors, 12 castles, 11 boroughs, nine whole hundreds of land, nine forests, 24 parks, the right of presentation of clergy (advowson) of 58 churches and 65 other properties.[4] Ursula Pole was not the third duke of Buckingham's initial choice as a wife for his son, but after her mother had approached the earl of Shrewsbury, without success, in 1518 the duke accepted her marriage to young

---

[1]   *I diarii di Marino Sanudo*, 30, cols 176, 297; *CSP Ven*, III, no. 204; *CRP* 1 p. 50.

[2]   TNA E 404/79, nos 45, 337.

[3]   *LP* I p. 233.

[4]   Barbara J. Harris, *Edward Stafford, third duke of Buckingham, 1478–1521* (Stanford: Stanford University Press, 1986), p. 104.

Henry, with the direct involvement of Thomas Wolsey, now lord chancellor, and surely at least the tacit support of the king. It may well be that, since Henry VIII still hoped, at that time, that his wife Catherine would produce a son and heir to follow and replace Princess Mary, who had been born in February 1516, he was prepared to overlook, at least for the time being, the strong dynastic claims of the Stafford and Pole families. In the marriage contract, Buckingham was able to force a hard bargain on Margaret Pole for her daughter, demanding a dowry of up to 4,000 marks, as long as Ursula subsequently received an additional grant of certain lands from the king, though the duke also agreed to settle lands and rents worth £500 on her after his death, and sooner if Henry Stafford predeceased her.[5]

Up until about the time of Reginald Pole's departure for Italy, Buckingham lived in high royal favour, and relations between the now closely related Staffords and Poles were apparently cordial. The duke evidently did not regard Margaret, countess of Salisbury, as a political rival or threat, even though she occupied the crucial position of governess to Henry and Catherine's only child, Mary.[6] Buckingham was not a regular attender of the royal council, but he lived in a grand style, and happily became a grandfather when Ursula and his son produced a son, another Henry, who was the first of a dozen offspring. The couple remained in Buckingham's household after their wedding, and were so frequently visited by Ursula's brothers, Arthur and Henry, that the Venetian ambassador, Antonio Suriano, mistakenly thought that the young Poles were the duke's nephews.[7] But in April 1521 everything changed: the duke of Buckingham was executed as a traitor, Margaret Pole was sacked as Princess Mary's governess, her second son, Arthur, was expelled from court, and her eldest son, Henry Pole, Baron Montagu, was imprisoned in the Tower of London, with his father-in-law, Lord Bergavenny. It seems that Buckingham brought about his own downfall, at the hand of a suspicious king, by a series of indiscreet statements, particularly on the subject of the succession, which hung upon the thread of the five-year-old Princess Mary's life. Edward Stafford was not the humblest of men, and he was given to rages, during one of which he was reported to have actually threatened to kill the king.[8] Henry seems to have been genuinely afraid, and lashed out at both the Staffords and the Poles. On 8 April 1521, he summoned Buckingham to London, and by 16 April the duke's servants, in particular his confessor and chancellor, were being interrogated, no doubt with little subtlety, in the Tower of London. Finally, on 13 May, the duke went to trial for treason, and just four days later he was executed, Montagu and Bergavenny having also been lodged in the Tower since 7 May. Thus the third duke suffered the fate which had befallen

---

[5]   *HMC Report* 7, 1879, p. 584.

[6]   Harris, *Edward Stafford*, p. 61.

[7]   *CSP Ven*, 1520–6 no. 204.

[8]   Harris, *Edward Stafford*, p. 209.

his father, Duke Henry of Buckingham, in 1483, as a result of attainder for rebellion against Richard III.[9]

It was in the midst of the turmoil surrounding his uncle Edward Stafford's final days, and with these events in England already well known in Venice, that Reginald wrote to Henry VIII, from Padua, on 27 April 1521, asking for more money. Pole told the king that he had used up most of the royal funds with which he had been provided, during his long and arduous journey to that flourishing northern Italian city. The Paduan magistrates and their governor, the Venetian *podestà*, knew very well whose relative he was, and the young exhibitioner was sure that he in turn would have to entertain as lavishly as he himself was already being received. The preparations which had been made locally, before his arrival, included setting aside as his residence the late fifteenth-century Palazzo Roccabonella. He had been warmly welcomed, amidst praise of the English king which suggested that news of the Buckingham fiasco had not yet arrived. Young Pole concluded his letter with a declaration that, if Henry did not send more money, he might have to leave Padua for somewhere cheaper, thus wasting all the goodwill there towards England.[10] It should be noted, however, that the 'King's Exhibitioner' had in addition been supported by crown patronage, in the form of the income from the deanery of Wimborne Minster, which was a collegiate church, and prebends, or canon's stalls in Salisbury cathedral, representing Ruscombe Southbury and Yetminster Secunda, the latter replacing the former in April 1519.[11] Pole's student friend, Richard Pace, brought him the resulting, much-needed revenues.[12] In a subsequent letter, sent from Padua and dated 31 May, Reginald indicated to the king that he was still being very well received, and in another, dated 31 July and apparently addressed to Cardinal Wolsey, he suggested that this happy situation was continuing, despite Henry's warning to the Venetians.[13] In the meantime, he had taken his first steps towards joining and further developing a network of Italian contacts which would stay with him for the rest of his life.

Reginald Pole was far from being the first Englishman to benefit from the resources of the University of Padua, and the Italian scholarly community of which it was part. Indeed, one of his Oxford tutors, William Latimer, a noted scholar of Latin and Greek, had been there in about 1498, before taking an MA degree at Ferrara in 1502.[14] It was natural for enthusiasts of humanism in Henry

---

[9]   Pierce, *Margaret Pole*, pp. 11–12, 30, 42, 52–54, 63–64, 86–89; Chrimes, *Henry VII*, p. 56 n. 13, 248.

[10]   BL Nero B.VI, fol. 122r; *LP* III (i) no. 198; *CRP* 1 no. 5; *PPP*, pp. 50–51.

[11]   Thomas F. Mayer, 'Cardinal Pole's finances: the property of a reformer', *CPEC*, XV, p. 2.

[12]   Beccadelli and Dudic, *Vita*, sig. Bii.

[13]   BL Harleian 6989, fols 78r–79v, *CRP* 1 no 6; BL Vespasian F.XIII, fol 285r; *LP* IV (i) no. 1529, *CRP* 1 no. 9.

[14]   Orme, 'Latimer, William', *ODNB*.

VIII's court to gravitate towards the homeland of the Renaissance, and many English nobles, clerics, students and royal agents did so for varying lengths of time. Their quest for the true sources (*fontes*) of knowledge ranged widely over the Latin and Greek classics of philosophy, history, poetry and drama, as well as the study of law and medicine, for both of which Padua was noted in the period. They also sought the roots of the Christian religion, recognising, like the Fathers of the Church in the earlier centuries after Christ, that Roman and Hellenic knowledge and scholarship were by then intimately bound up with Jewish and Christian belief and practice.[15] As a result of his career in Oxford, Pole no doubt came well-equipped to profit from the opportunities which Padua offered. Although, when he was a student at Magdalen College, the university statutes of the baccalaureate of arts, unlike those of many Continental universities, had not been reformed so as to accommodate the 'new learning' of the Renaissance, there had been some changes in teaching practice, which provided for the study of Greek grammar and classical rhetoric.[16] As well as his membership of Magdalen, Pole had also benefited from his association with the Oxford college, Corpus Christi, which was most closely involved in the new classical scholarship and with Christian humanism of the kind espoused by Erasmus of Rotterdam, and enthusiastically adopted by Henry VIII, his wife Catherine, and their court and government. Founded by Bishop Richard Fox of Winchester, and beginning operations, under royal licence, in November 1516, the new college combined humanistic and Christian studies, though with the latter always having precedence.[17] On 14 February 1523, Corpus elected Pole, *in absentia*, to what was in effect a three-year research fellowship, since he would never return to teach in Oxford, but his earlier academic training there would stand him in good stead during his years abroad.[18]

Reginald's institutional connection with the University of Padua is not entirely clear. However, he quickly became part of an active network of humanistic scholars in and around that city, and the tuition which he received did not necessarily come from university tutors, though among the latter was the nearest he had to a personal tutor, Niccolò Leonico Tomeo. Leonico represented two of the main strands in Paduan legal and political thought: Aristotelian philosophy and Venetian constitutional ideas.[19] In religious and philosophical terms, he was

---

[15]   Jonathan Woolfson, *Padua and the Tudors. English students in Italy, 1485–1603* (Cambridge: James Clark, 1998); Anne Overell, *Italian reform and English reformations, c. 1535–c. 1585* (Aldershot: Ashgate, 2008), pp. 6–8, 17–20.

[16]   J.M. Fletcher, 'The faculty of arts', in McConica, *History of the University of Oxford*, 3, pp. 157–199, at pp. 157–160.

[17]   McConica, 'The rise of the undergraduate college', pp. 17–23.

[18]   *OEE*, 6, pp. 191–192; Mayer, *PPP*, p. 425.

[19]   M.L. King, *Venetian patriotism in an age of patrician dominance* (Princeton: Princeton University Press, 1986), p. 182.

strongly influenced by Erasmus, and this would have given him an intellectual affinity with young Pole, in terms of Platonic thought and classical erudition.[20] In the Paduan circle which included Leonico, the Plantagenet Reginald also came into contact with Italian republican ideas, both from Venice and from Florence. The Venetian oligarchy, with its elected duke (*doge*), governed Padua, while the city also provided a home for Florentine republican refugees from the Medici dukes of their home state, who were satellites of Habsburg power in the peninsula. In this context, Pole met Donato Gianotto, who wrote in Padua an anti-Medicean tract entitled *Della Repubblica*, as well as a work on the Venetian political system in which he especially praised Leonico.[21] It would not in future be possible for Pole to regard monarchy as the only possible form of government, but even more important for his future development were the Platonic ideas which Leonico and others espoused, particularly in relation to religion and theology. In 1524, Leonico published a set of dialogues in the Platonic style, which reveal his yearning for contemplation and the divine, rather than the active public life which had been so prized by fifteenth-century Florentine humanists. In this work the Paduan humanist expressed the view that every man has two essences within him, one of which is always in God, while the other perpetually longs to return to Him. Typically, among Italian scholars of the period, Leonico was equally at home with the works of Aristotle, including those on the natural sciences, which were the staple of medieval university syllabuses and had traditionally been taught at Padua.[22] Pole was one of a number of English students who were taught by Leonico, and he seems to have learnt from him, and no doubt others, the Renaissance art of making friends and writing elegantly and effusively to them and about them.[23] Some evidence of this may be found in Reginald's early correspondence, which constantly cross-references his contacts, in Italy, England and elsewhere. In particular, whenever he was away from Padua, for example retreating from the city heat in the villa of Rovolon, or else in Venice, he corresponded with Leonico.[24] He also wrote to Cardinal Giulio de' Medici, to congratulate him on his election, as Pope Clement VII, on 18 November 1523, receiving a personal reply dated 31 January 1524.[25]

---

[20]   Luca d'Ascia, 'Un erasmiano italiano. Note sulla filosofia della religione di Niccolò Leonico Tomeo', *Rivista di storia e letteratura religiosa*, 26 (1990), pp. 242–264.

[21]   Mayer, 'Nursery of resistance: Reginald Pole and his friends', *CPEC*, II, pp. 54–55.

[22]   Niccolò Leonico Tomeo, *Dialogi* (Venice, 1524); Mayer, 'Marco Mantova and the Paduan religious crisis of the early sixteenth century', *CPEC*, IX, p. 51.

[23]   Mayer, 'When Maecenas was broke: Cardinal Pole's "spiritual" patronage', *CPEC*, XIV, p. 425.

[24]   *CRP* 1 nos 7 (trans. Gasquet, pp. 24–27), 8 (*ERP* 1 no. 3), 10 (trans. Gasquet, p. 20), 11 (trans. Gasquet, p. 20), 15 (*LP* IV (i) no. 79), 16 (trans. Gasquet, pp. 65–67), 19–22 (trans. Gasquet, pp. 65–68, 71–72), letters dated between June 1521 and 1 August 1524.

[25]   *CRP* 1 no. 15 p. 46.

One of the earliest core members of Pole's Italian circle and household, apparently by July 1521, was Christophe de Longueil (Longolius), a disciple and correspondent of Erasmus.[26] On the 11th of that month, the noted humanist and papal official Pietro Bembo wrote to Pole from Noniano, mentioning that Longolius would be carrying the letter to him, but by the following year Longolius' health had apparently deteriorated greatly. In a letter probably sent on 20 August 1522, he referred to an earlier illness and said that he was now avoiding travel and remaining in Padua. Three days later, however, he reported to Pole that his efforts had been unsuccessful, and he was now suffering from a raging fever. He feared death and asked the Englishman to look after his library in such a case, his appeal to the Englishman to preserve his memory being evidently more heartfelt than rhetorical.[27] There is some doubt as to what Pole actually did to help Longolius during his lifetime, and the young man died alone, his premature death being much lamented by Erasmus.[28] After this, it does appear that Pole indeed produced a biography of Longolius.[29] The short anonymous work appeared in print as the preface to an edition of two *orationes* by Longolius and said by its editor and publisher, Bernardo Giunti, to have been written by someone who had been the author's friend and familiar, and almost certainly this was Pole, though some have argued against this. In any case, the preface mentions that Longolius had indeed made Pole his executor, with a charge to keep his fame and reputation alive.[30] It has proved quite difficult to trace Reginald's precise whereabouts in the tumultuous years between 1524 and 1529, when the threat of schism in the Church became ever stronger, being realised in parts of both Germany and Switzerland, and in addition the Ottoman Turks advanced far into central Europe, conquering much of Hungary and in 1526 killing its king. Although Pole kept his links with Padua during this period, it appears nevertheless that he spent much of 1525 in Venice, and was thus in an ideal position to monitor the traumatic political events which unrolled in western Europe, and particularly in Italy, during that year.[31]

Throughout Pole's life, France and the Habsburgs fought for control of the papacy in particular, and the Italian peninsula in general. The conflict culminated in the battle of Pavia, in February 1525, which saw the greatest slaughter of French nobles since the English victory at Agincourt in 1415, and

---

[26]   *CRP* 1 no. 8 p. 43; *OEE*, 6, no. 1675 pp. 281–283, at p. 282.

[27]   *CRP* 1 nos 13 (*ERP* 1 no. 1), 14 (*ERP* 1 no. 2, partly trans. Gasquet, p. 31).

[28]   Mayer, 'Cardinal Pole's "spiritual" patronage', *CPEC*, XIV, p. 425; *OEE*, 6, nos 1675, 1706 pp. 281–283, 335–337 (8 March 1526, and c. 6 May 1526).

[29]   *Christophori Longolii orationes duae [Vita Longolii]* (Florence: Heirs of F. Giunti, 1524, reprinted Farnborough: Gregg Reprints, 1967).

[30]   For a comprehensive discussion of this text see Mayer, 'Reluctant author', pp. 91–96.

[31]   *CRP* 1 nos 27 (*ERP* 1 no. 5), 28–31 (trans. Gasquet, pp. 75–76, 77–78, 82–83, 78–79), 32 (trans. Gasquet, pp. 79–81), 34–36, 39 (trans. Gasquet, pp. 81–82, 87–88, 89, 90); *PPP*, p. 48.

the capture of King Francis I.[32] While these dramatic events were taking place in north-west Italy, Pole was further east, in Venice, where he was evidently kept well informed. For one thing, the peace envoy sent by Clement VII, in November 1524, to the French and Imperial camps was one of Pole's Italian circle, the datary, Gianmatteo Giberti.[33] Then in February 1525, as the action at Pavia hotted up, Pole's former tutor in Padua, Leonico, was in correspondence with him about what was happening. From this and subsequent letters from Leonico to Pole, it appears that the latter was actually an eyewitness of the siege of Pavia. On 11 February, Leonico acknowledged a long report on the fighting which he had received from Pole. In this letter, Leonico said that he regarded Pole as his most reliable source, but other Englishmen were also monitoring the Pavian situation, which would inevitably affect Henry VIII's England, their native country which they were clearly dedicated to serving. On 18 February, Leonico mentions a map of the military action, which had been prepared for him by Thomas Lupset, who appears to have been there with Pole. According to an undated letter sent by Leonico to Pole from Padua, there were already rumours there by 20 February that the French had been routed by the Pavia garrison, and a reply, three days later, shows that the Englishman had an intimate knowledge of the layout around that city, and its military significance. Leonico himself was mainly concerned that peace should be achieved, but Pole and his friends seem to have been quite happy to follow the course of the fighting, always with English interests in mind.[34]

In the latter part of 1525, Reginald Pole seems to have been back in England, and away from the centre of European political events. According to Beccadelli and Dudic, he had returned to Dean Colet's former residence at Sheen.[35] Nevertheless, he must have been aware, with his recent Italian experience in mind, of at least some of the twists and turns of Henry and Wolsey's foreign policy.[36] Things at home were about to become even more interesting. By the end of 1525, Queen Catherine was 40 years old, was past child-bearing, and had produced no son to continue the Tudor dynasty. Her husband seems not to have considered their daughter Mary to be a proper successor, and he also had an illegitimate son, Henry Fitzroy, born to Elizabeth Blount. As he seems never to have considered the dynastic possibilities of the Scottish royal family, through his sister Queen Margaret, he had clearly come, by the beginning of 1526, to regard the house of Tudor as being in a dynastic crisis. By then, Henry's new love,

---

[32] Alfonso de Valdés, 'Relación de la batalla de Pavia', in Valdés, *Obra completa* (Madrid: Fundación José Antonio de Castro, 1996), pp. 37–44.

[33] R.J. Knecht, *Renaissance warrior and patron: the reign of Francis I* (Cambridge: Cambridge University Press, 1994), p. 216.

[34] *CRP* 1 nos 28–33.

[35] Beccadelli and Dudic, *Vita*, sig. Bii.

[36] *CRP* 1 no. 42 (*ERP* 1 no. 11).

Anne Boleyn, was at court. Henry, with Wolsey's advice and support, had been trying to employ Mary as a dynastic pawn, betrothing her at different times to the houses of Valois and Habsburg, but neither project had come to fruition, so that in the winter of 1525–6 he felt that he was facing three options. He could legally recognise Mary as heir to the throne, and accept her future husband, whoever that might be, or he could choose Henry Fitzroy as his heir, despite his illegitimate status, or else he could repudiate Catherine and marry again. Whether at this stage he already had Anne in mind as his second wife is not entirely clear.[37]

While these events were unfolding, Reginald Pole seems to have remained on the margin of public life. According to a letter written to him, on 10 May 1527, by his former Paduan tutor, Leonico, he had earlier paid a brief visit to France but had then been recalled to England, presumably by the king.[38] At this stage, he appears still to have been in royal favour, since in late July 1527 he was successively elected, *in absentia*, as first a canon and then dean of Exeter cathedral.[39] During the autumn of 1527, Cardinal Wolsey tried to exploit his Roman contacts in order to secure Henry's annulment, which was commonly described at the time as a divorce. Those involved were the main English representatives at the Curia, Girolamo Ghinucci, bishop of Worcester, the papal nuncio to England, Uberto de Gambara, bishop of Tortona, and the English king's faithful diplomatic servant Gregorio Casale. A problem which quickly arose was Wolsey's determination to link Henry's quest to be rid of Catherine with his own remarkable ambitions concerning the papacy. He urged his collaborators in Rome not to reveal to Pope Clement, who had suffered the sack of the city, by unpaid Imperial troops, in May 1527, that Henry wanted a divorce, until the pope had appointed him, Wolsey, as papal administrator on his behalf. He even expected Clement to validate all his future actions in that capacity.[40] In parallel with these efforts by Wolsey, on or about 10 December 1527, Henry's own agent, William Knight, had arrived in Rome, after being attacked outside the city, and found Pope Clement still, for a short time at least, in the Castel Sant'Angelo. The English secretary at once approached Clement in writing, and initially received what appeared to be an encouraging reply, though this was probably due to no more than the pope's well-justified feeling of isolation and friendlessness at that

[37]   J.J. Scarisbrick, *Henry VIII* (New Haven and London: Yale University Press, 1999), pp. 149–150; John Edwards, *Mary I: England's Catholic queen* (New Haven and London: Yale University Press, 2011), pp. 18–86.

[38]   *CRP* 1 no. 46 (trans. Gasquet, pp. 93–96).

[39]   *CRP* 1 nos 47 (25 July), and 48 (29 July).

[40]   Scarisbrick, *Henry VIII*, pp. 202–203; Anne Reynolds, 'The papal court in exile: Clement VII in Orvieto, 1527–28', in *The pontificate of Clement VI: History, politics, culture*, ed. Kenneth Gouwens and Sheryl E. Reiss (Aldershot: Ashgate, 2005), pp. 143–161 at p. 145; *LP* IV no. 3400.

time.[41] In the event, Henry of England would struggle for nearly three more years after that, before he finally gave up hope of having his desires validated by the pope, and instead opted for schism and for his own supremacy over the English Church. Meanwhile, once he reached Orvieto, Clement felt more secure, and able to adopt an independent line. He decided that Henry's documents, which had been brought to him by Knight, would have to be perused by one of his own experts, Lorenzo Pucci, cardinal of Sancti Quattuor Coronati. In his draft bull, Henry had tried to slip the invalidation of his marriage to Catherine into a general dispensation for him to remarry, but Pucci's expert eye quickly spotted this subterfuge, which he regarded as unworthy of a king, and the cardinal duly surrounded the submitted text with highly critical glosses.[42] Henry's cause was clearly stalled.

It had always been inevitable that English concerns, in this as in all other matters, would become entangled with Continental politics. The very existence of the papacy had been threatened by the sack of May 1527, and its future largely depended on the attitude of the Emperor Charles V. Thus when Clement held a secret consistory in Orvieto, on 18 December 1527, at which eight new cardinals were appointed, the revenues received from four of them, as routine payments for obtaining their offices, went directly to Habsburg coffers. However, Clement also needed to secure his own position, as far as possible, with France and England. Thus on 2 January 1528, talks began in Bologna, between Uberto Gambara on behalf of the pope, and Odet de Foix, Seigneur de Lautrec, representing Francis I. Clement's aims at this time were to gain French and English support for a general European peace, in order to obtain the release of Francis I's captive sons, held in Madrid since the battle of Pavia, and above all to ensure his own escape from dependence on Charles V. Given their desperate need for papal support in obtaining the divorce, Henry and Wolsey were happy to do what they could to help the pope. English efforts were weakened, however, by the increasing lack of full, working co-operation between the king and his chief minister. Thus Knight, who was still acting solely for Henry, left Orvieto on 1 January with the partial dispensation for the king's proposed remarriage.[43] Then, in March 1528, Gregorio Casale, who had stayed on in Orvieto, wrote to Wolsey that Lautrec was trying to persuade Clement VII to join the French and Italian alliance against Charles V, but in the meantime Henry had decided, on the basis of what he had heard so far, to pursue his divorce more vigorously with Clement. Thus in late March, his new ambassadors, Stephen Gardiner, master of Trinity Hall, Cambridge, and Edward Fox, fellow of King's College, Cambridge, arrived in Orvieto and found the pope living in poor conditions. They had taken

---

[41]   *LP* IV no. 3458.

[42]   *LP* IV no. 3686.

[43]   Reynolds, 'Papal court in exile', pp. 154–156; Scarisbrick, *Henry VIII*, p. 204.

with them a 'book' of collected documents in support of Henry's case, which had been compiled, during the previous autumn, by the king himself, Wolsey, and other English bishops and scholars. Perhaps surprisingly, the royal case, as expounded by Gardiner and Fox, as well as in the written documentation, initially received some support from Cardinals Lorenzo Pucci and Antonio Ciocchi del Monte, but nevertheless the matter continued to progress slowly. Clement VII finally left Orvieto for Rome on 1 June 1528, and in the following month he granted a commission for a full legatine court to Wolsey and Cardinal Lorenzo Campeggio, in order to hear King Henry's plea for the annulment of his marriage to Queen Catherine.[44]

After a long and painful journey, during which he suffered severely from gout, Campeggio arrived in London in May 1529. The legatine court opened in the London Dominican house, Blackfriars, on 28 May. It proved to be a remarkable process, in which the king and queen confronted each other personally, but finally, on 31 July, Campeggio referred the case to Rome for decision, much to the frustration of Henry and his supporters. In reaction, Henry left Greenwich Palace, at the beginning of August, for a progress to the north and west of London. At this time, Thomas Cranmer, who was then a tutor in theology at Jesus College, Cambridge, and had fled from an outbreak of the plague in that town, was staying at Waltham Cross with some relatives, the Cressy family, and tutoring their two sons. On 2 August, Stephen Gardiner and Edward Fox dined with the Cressys. They told Cranmer about the current state of the divorce process, and he suggested that theologians all over Europe should be canvassed for their opinions on the subject. This was not an original idea of Cranmer's, since a similar method had previously been advocated, as a way of solving intractable problems in Church and religion, by authorities as diverse as the Catholic theologian Johannes Eck, the Dutch Christian humanist Desiderius Erasmus, and the Swiss reformer Hyldrich Zwingli. Indeed, back in October 1528, the highly prestigious Paris theology faculty had already voted on the validity or otherwise of Henry's marriage to Catherine, finding in the king's favour by a bare majority. Now, with this precedent in mind, and desperate to satisfy their royal master, Gardiner and Fox seized upon Cranmer's suggestion. On or about 4 August, they reported their discussion at Waltham Cross to Henry, and the idea was taken up, in a manner that would have an irrevocable effect on the life of Reginald Pole.[45] It was probably at some time in 1528, not long after his return from Italy, that the royal secretary, Thomas Cromwell, canvassed Pole as a potentially active supporter of the annulment of King Henry's marriage to Queen Catherine. Reginald's subsequent attempts to

[44]    Reynolds, 'Papal court in exile', pp. 157–160.
[45]    Diarmaid MacCulloch, *Thomas Cranmer: a life* (New Haven and London: Yale University Press, 1996), pp. 44–46.

re-write and reinterpret his own conduct, in the last years before his permanent split with the king, make it impossible to establish a reliable and complete account of his actions at this time.[46]

Pole created problems for later historians by crafting, deliberately or not, his developing interpretation of his own conduct, and his feelings towards Henry's proposed divorce from Catherine. His first attempt is to be found in his lengthy and much redrafted response to the king's urgent request to him to express his views on the divorce, which he wrote in 1535–6, under the title *Pro ecclesiastiae unitatis defensione* ('For the defence of church unity'), generally known as *De unitate* ('On unity', see Chapter 3 and Appendix 2). In it he told Henry that there was nothing more bitter in his memory than the Paris legation, which his sovereign had given him. He claimed that he had gone to Paris as a student, with the explicit intention of not becoming involved in the Paris theology faculty's debates on the divorce. When he received the message directing him to Paris, he claimed that 'grief robbed me not only of my voice, but almost even of thought'. He had asked to be excused from this mission, in favour of someone more experienced and Henry had 'saved' his life by agreeing to send with him a more expert companion, even though he would not dispense him from what was in effect an embassy. At the distance of about five years, Pole portrayed himself as an actor or role-player: 'That office, plainly, I never accepted, although I suffered the part to be played by me for that occasion', but only on the basis that someone more experienced was with him, in charge of the whole enterprise. He claimed that he was unaware, in mid-1529, of the 'equity' of the divorce case, but added that the more he learned about it, the less sure he became that Henry was acting rightly, and the more convinced he was that he was not the man to represent the king in Paris.[47] This may well be true. On 16 February 1537, Pole wrote a lengthy letter to Henry's council, in which he did not refer directly to the Paris mission, but nonetheless gave some insight into his mental processes in the matter of the divorce. In it he claimed, while calling on the duke of Norfolk to bear witness to the truth of what he was saying, that, by the time of an interview which he had with the king towards the end of 1530, after his return from Paris, it had dawned on him that the only way in which he could hope to retain Henry's favour 'was by favoring the mattier off dyvorce'. Even so, despite the efforts that were made by his friends to persuade him, he could never in his heart accept it. In any case, many of these friends also had reservations, but were too afraid to express them. In these circumstances, Pole had reluctantly decided that the best way in which he could serve his king and country, which was all he wanted to

---

[46]   Mayer, 'Fate worse than death', *CPEC*, XI, pp. 870–871.

[47]   Mayer, 'Fate worse than death', *CPEC*, XI, p. 874; *Pro ecclesiastiae unitatis defensione* (*De unitate*), fols lxxviii, verso, to lxxix, recto (translation by Mayer).

do, was to support Henry in his suit to the pope for divorce from Catherine. As a result, he stated that, while in Paris:

> I suffered my selfe to be per[suad]yd, [and] that I remember I sayd then to doctour [Edward Fox], whiche had been wythe me for the kyngis matter, that I truste I had founde a waye to satysfye hys grace.[48]

About a year later, in his so-called 'Apologia' to the Emperor Charles V, in fact a preface to *De unitate*; Pole claimed that he had always been a clear opponent of Henry's divorce, but that he had been bullied by Thomas Cromwell into appearing to hold the opposite view, and hence being sent on the mission to Paris.[49]

Nonetheless, by going to sources other than Pole's own writings, it is possible to identify some of the pressures which he felt upon him, his reactions to them, and at least a partial narrative of his activities in 1529–30, years which were so crucial to England's relationships with Continental powers and with the See of Rome. One indication of Pole's state of mind, at the time of his return from Italy, may be found in a work by his friend Thomas Starkey, who had been with him in Padua. This took the form of an imaginary dialogue, in a form derived from Plato and much favoured by Erasmus and his associates and followers, between Pole and Thomas Lupset, who had drawn the siege of Pavia for Leonico.[50] In it, Pole is portrayed as one preparing for a lifetime in Henry's service, though he was also imbued with the republican ideas that all three men had absorbed during their sojourn in Venetian territory. It is also possible that, in 1528, Pole was learning Hebrew from the Cambridge scholar Robert Wakefield, whose knowledge would actively assist the royal campaign for the divorce, given that the correct interpretation of texts from Leviticus and Deuteronomy were crucial to it. It cannot be proved that the king was grooming Pole for a mission to secure the divorce, but there is also a suggestion, in subsequent writing by Charles V's ambassador to London, Eustache Chapuys, that Henry considered Pole to be a possible future archbishop, replacing either William Warham at Canterbury or Thomas Wolsey at York.[51] Whatever the truth of this, there is every indication that, when Henry sent Pole on this mission to Paris, he regarded him as an ideal man for the job, both well-qualified and loyal.

In his efforts to reconstruct Pole's activity in Paris during 1529–30, Mayer has assembled some difficult fragments of evidence, which support this

---

[48]    *CRP* 1 no. 155 (TNA *SP* 11/116, fols 57 r–v; *ERP* 1 pp. 179–187); *LP* XI (i), no. 449 (1–2), *LP* Addenda I (i) no. 1196; Mayer, *CPEC*, XI, pp. 874–875.

[49]    *CPEC*, XI, p. 875 (Reginald Pole, 'Apologia ad Carolum Quintum', in *ERP* 1 136).

[50]    Thomas Starkey, *A dialogue between Pole and Lupset*, ed. T.F. Mayer, *Camden Society*, 4th series, no. 37 (1989); Mayer, 'Starkey, Thomas', *ODNB*; Mayer, 'Lupset, Thomas', *ODNB*.

[51]    *PPP*, pp. 54–55; *CSP Span* IV (ii) no. 888 (*LP* V no. 737).

interpretation of Pole's mind on the subject of the divorce. They were, of course, produced at a time when the king's determination to rid himself of Catherine, with its enormous implications for Church and country, was forcing many people in the royal service to re-examine their ideas and attitudes, and Pole was no exception. Firstly, an unfortunately undated manuscript letter, which was apparently written at court on the orders of the duke of Norfolk, states that Pole was to be 'heartily congratulated' on his service in Paris, in the cause of the divorce, particularly as it was done 'unasked by the king's command'. The anonymous writer, apparently a royal secretary, added that he had himself heard Henry rejoice that Pole had become 'a patron of his cause'.[52] In a second, undated, letter to Thomas Boleyn, earl of Wiltshire, who had also gone to France in the cause of the king and of his own daughter Anne, Henry set out his case for the divorce, and ordered the earl to deliver it to the Paris theology faculty, as long as this was agreed by Pole, which indicates that the king's cousin, and theological exhibitioner, was crucial to the entire enterprise.[53] Pole had been granted a royal exhibition of £100 on 16 October 1529.[54]

When Henry VIII started to seek the opinions of theologians and canon lawyers, in England and the rest of Europe, on the merits of his case for ending his marriage with Catherine, he will have known that the decision of the Paris theologians would be the most important, after that of Pope Clement himself. At that time, the university of Paris had about 40 colleges, out of which faculty members were drawn, each of them a doctor of theology with at least 20 years of study behind him. Theology faculty meetings were presided over by the dean or sub-dean, and since 1520 there had in addition been a syndic. This was technically an annual appointment, which involved keeping good order in faculty meetings and debates, drawing up agendas, keeping the minutes, and ensuring that the university's statutes were observed and that faculty decisions were carried out. In 1529–30, the post of syndic was held, as it had been from the start, by the conservative theologian Noël Béda, who was principal of the Collège de Montaigu, where Erasmus, Ignatius of Loyola, Rabelais and Calvin all studied. Béda would play a vital role in the fate of the English mission about the divorce.[55] When Henry's ambassadors arrived in Paris, in December 1529, there was already great tension between the theology faculty of Paris and King Francis I. The Paris faculty mistrusted its own king's theology. They believed that he was protecting, and perhaps even supporting and agreeing with, scholars and preachers with reforming views. In their efforts to uphold orthodoxy, and

---

52    BL Cotton Vitellius V, XIV, fol. 279r; *LP* IV (iii) no. 6252; Mayer, 'A fate worse than death: Reginald Pole and the Paris theologians', *CPEC*, XI, p. 878.
53    BL Cotton Vitellius B.XIV, fol. 278r; *LP* IV (iii) 6253; *CPEC*, XI, p. 878.
54    Mayer, 'Fate worse than death', *CPEC*, XI, p. 880.
55    Knecht, *Renaissance warrior*, p. 144.

punish and suppress those whom they believed to be deviating from it, the Paris
theologians often acted in alliance with the lawyers, both in the university itself
and in the senior legal body in Paris, the Parlement. While the king was away
in captivity in Madrid, efforts were made by these theologians and lawyers to
regain lost ground, but when he returned from Spain, arriving in Paris on 14
April 1527, Francis immediately set out to regain control over the French Church,
which he regarded as part of his right as monarch, though in communion with
Rome.[56] The resulting heated atmosphere in the Paris theology faculty would
not help Pole and his colleagues to obtain a decision favourable to Henry, in his
'great matter'.

Equally important was the state of relations between the two sovereigns,
Henry and Francis, which had had some ups and downs in the preceding years.
Wolsey, when negotiating the treaty of Amiens between them, in August 1527,
made no mention to the French king of Henry's desire to rid himself of his wife. He
seems to have thought that news of this would sabotage the treaty negotiations,
and reported back to Henry that he intended instead to speak to Francis about
the matter informally, and in a deliberately obscure manner, so that he would not
realise that Henry was utterly determined to achieve his desire in this respect.[57]
Between the end of 1527 and the summer of the following year, Francis tried to
regain his lost reputation for Catholic orthodoxy, but he continued to protect
some churchmen and scholars who had reformist tendencies. In March 1528
major controversy arose, involving the Paris theology faculty and the Parlement,
over one such reformer, the aristocratic Louis de Berquin. He had been tried
previously for heresy, in 1523, but although his books, which included works by
all the major reformers, were burned outside the cathedral of Nôtre Dame, on
the orders of the bishop of Paris, royal intervention enabled the man himself to
escape death by burning. Conservatives had not forgotten Francis's role in this
setback for their cause, and five years on they tested the king's self-proclaimed
Catholicity once more, by having Berquin arrested on heresy charges. The
young scholar was tried by a special commission, which had been named by
Pope Clement VII at the French king's request, but the Paris theology faculty
objected to some of the appointed members, on the grounds that they were
crypto-Lutherans. An angry Francis protested in turn to the papal nuncio,
Francesco Salviati, but the trial continued, and indeed resulted in the conviction
of Berquin, on 15 April 1528. He was sentenced to life imprisonment, and,
foolishly as it turned out, appealed to the Parlement two days later. The king
was away from Paris at the time and the conservative judges converted Berquin's
sentence to one of death by burning. To avoid any further royal interference, the

---

[56]   Knecht, *Renaissance warrior*, pp . 236, 260, 264.
[57]   *LP* IV no. 3350.

convict was dragged immediately to the Place de la Grève and executed.[58] None of this would help Henry VIII in his campaign to obtain approval of his divorce from the Paris theologians.

During 1528, in addition to these theological questions, relations between Francis I and Charles V caused renewed problems for the English king. By the end of that year, Francis was actively seeking renewed peace with the emperor, after the storm which had been caused by the battle of Pavia and its consequences. This process would culminate in the so-called 'Ladies' Peace' (*Paix des dames*), which was concluded at Cambrai, on 3 August 1529, by Charles V's aunt, Margaret of Austria, and Francis's mother, Louise of Savoy. The resulting treaty, which was ratified by Francis at Bordeaux on 20 October 1529, had been negotiated without any consultation with England or the major Italian powers, and was a bad omen for Henry's Paris mission, involving Pole, which was just about to begin. Even so, Francis seems to have been concerned about the English reaction, as on 16 August, soon after the Cambrai talks had finished, he dispatched as his ambassador to London Guillaume du Bellay, Sieur de Langey, who was to offer financial compensation to Henry for his bruised feelings over the Franco-Imperial agreement. Francis promised to pay his English 'brother' 185,000 gold *écus*, in instalments of 50,000, this money being owed to Henry by Charles V. He did not, however, offer to redeem the 'Fleur-de-lis' jewel, which had been pawned in England by Charles's grandfather, the Emperor Maximilian, in 1508, for 50,000 English crowns. Nor would he pay the English 'indemnity', which Charles had promised to Henry, while visiting him at Windsor in 1522, as compensation for the loss of his French pension at that time. In the circumstances, the English king quite reasonably demanded to see and read the treaty of Cambrai in full, before he would commit himself to any new financial arrangements with Francis. Through Du Bellay, the French king obliged, and on 31 August 1529, Henry duly agreed to remit the redemption charge for the 'Fleur-de-lis' jewel, and return it to Francis, also remitting the instalment of his French pension which was due that year. In return, Henry dropped a bombshell: he wanted Francis to help him secure the pope's consent for his marriage to Catherine to be annulled.[59] Following this policy through, Pole travelled to Paris in mid-October 1529, and Du Bellay innocently told his master that the purpose of the Englishman's visit was academic study.[60] At the same time, John Stokesley, later bishop of London, and George Boleyn, brother of Anne, were sent to Paris to replace the permanent ambassador there, Sir Francis Bryan. They were explicitly told to negotiate support for the divorce,

---

[58]    Knecht, *Renaissance warrior*, pp. 163, 282–283.
[59]    Knecht, *Renaissance warrior*, pp. 284–285.
[60]    *LP* IV (iii) no. 6003.

both from the king and from the Paris theologians.[61] In Stokesley's case, Rome was the ultimate destination, which he duly reached by 6 December 1529.[62]

In the winter of 1529–30, while Henry was becoming increasingly obsessed with the idea of ridding himself of his wife of 20 years, Francis was busy exploiting his peace with Charles to regroup for another attempt to regain Milan and its duchy. He saw the controversy over the divorce as an obstacle to his efforts to unite other powers against the Habsburgs, and therefore he decided to back Henry's attempt to gain a favourable opinion on the subject from the Paris theologians. Already, back in 1528, the faculty had discussed the validity of Julius II's brief of December 1502, which allowed Henry to marry his brother Arthur's widow, and debated whether any pope had the power to grant such a dispensation from the impediment of affinity in the first degree. On that occasion, they had decided in Henry's favour, but the faculty's discussions seem to have been academic rather than political in emphasis, and things would be very different the second time round. Now, the French king, with whom they had had such fractious relations in recent years, was supporting the propositions on which they had previously voted, and the emperor, now fully aware of the danger which faced his aunt, Catherine, was equally strongly against them. There may have been a military truce in place at this time, between France and the Habsburgs, but that certainly did not preclude a theological battle in faculty, over the interpretation of divine and natural law in Henry and Catherine's case. No doubt to provide accurate information on the English king's intentions, Francis recalled Guillaume du Bellay from London, and gave him the main responsibility for obtaining a verdict that was favourable to Henry. However, both Du Bellay, who was generally referred to in contemporary documents by his seigneurial title of 'Langey', and his king were limited in their desire to support Henry's cause. Langey was out for his own political advantage in France, while Francis, not yet being ready to invade the duchy of Milan again, had no wish to alienate Charles V totally. As a result, when the English ambassadors, led by George Boleyn, arrived in Paris, they found that the French king was unwilling to give open support to their mission, whatever his manoeuvres may have been behind the scenes. Yet he was also anxious not to appear unfriendly to the English, as he did not want to break the treaty of Cambrai, and he had found Henry's friendship and support useful in the recent past, first when he was a prisoner in Madrid and then when his sons were hostages in Spain, and he might need help from England again, at some point in the future.

Initially, George Boleyn had significant success in gaining theologians' signatures in favour of Henry's divorce, and denying the pope's power to refuse him. The matter came to a vote in faculty, and Henry's side won, but two Spanish

---

[61]    *LP* IV (iii) no. 5983.

[62]    *CSP Span* IV (i) p. 124.

theologians, Dr Pedro de Garay and Dr Álvaro de Moscoso, made objection on behalf of the Church and the Emperor, and they received the support of the syndic, Dr Noël Béda. Then, in late December 1529, the Grand Master, later Constable of France, Anne de Montmorency, formally rebuked Béda for failing to secure a formal faculty vote in favour of Henry, as King Francis wished. The syndic ignored this, however, and with Dr Garay continued to collect members' signatures in favour of Catherine. Amidst much controversy and turmoil, the opposing sides continued to round up supporters, until, on 4 February 1530, the faculty decided in a vote that it was only discrediting itself with this kind of horse-trading, and forbade such collecting of members' signatures in future. All the names of those in favour of allowing the divorce were handed for safe keeping to Gervais Wain, who was an agent of Guillaume du Bellay, and of his brother Jean, bishop of Bayonne. All the signatures against the granting of Henry's divorce, and in support of papal power to give dispensation in such cases, were entrusted to the president of the Paris Parlement, Pierre Lizet, and the clerk of the bishop of Paris's consistory court. Dr Garay, acting on behalf of his king, Charles V, tried hard to gain possession of the list of opponents, but without success.[63]

On 4 April, the duke of Norfolk wrote to Anne de Montmorency, thanking him for his efforts on King Henry's behalf.[64] On Catherine's side, Pedro de Garay, in a letter to the Emperor, dated 9 April, gave a detailed and somewhat pessimistic account of the situation. Garay had previously sent Charles a notarial copy of a statement in favour of Catherine, signed by 15 doctors of theology. He had also urged his master to obtain a brief from Clement VII, which would order the doctors to meet and give their individual written opinions on the case, each sealed secretly in an envelope. Garay also warned Charles of the power and intensity of Henry's campaign to secure the divorce: his fervour had the power to set the world on fire. At the same time, Guillaume du Bellay was holding regular dinner parties for faculty members, in groups of 10 or a dozen, at which, in addition to a good meal, they were being given a sight of a draft faculty resolution in favour of Henry having his divorce, and some money to help them make up their minds. As a result, 30 doctors signed up in support of Henry, some of whom had previously opposed the divorce but had no doubt been affected by Du Bellay's bribery and persuasion. In his fury, Garay even suggested that the emperor should have Clement send a representative to attend the Paris theology faculty, and punish those who took the English king's part.[65] In response, on 7 May, Charles wrote from Innsbruck to Michel Mai (May), in Brussels, asking him to send him copies of the correspondence that he had received from his

---

[63]   Knecht, *Renaissance warrior*, pp. 291–293.
[64]   *LP* IV (iii) no. 6306.
[65]   *LP* IV (iii) no. 6321.

ambassadors in Paris, concerning the question of Catherine's divorce, as well the letters which had been sent to him by Garay. The emperor said that he had also asked his Paris representatives to petition Francis I to obtain the list of signatures in Catherine's favour, about which Garay had written to him. He also warned Mai that it would be dangerous to place too much weight on the opinions of the Paris theologians, since Henry was highly respected in that city. Mai was also to tell the pope that his nuncio in Paris was doing everything he could to advance the common cause of Catherine and the emperor. On the same day, the University of Angers issued an opinion in favour of the validity of Catherine's marriage to Henry.[66] On 18 May, Thomas Boleyn, earl of Wiltshire, who was with Francis at Angoulême, wrote to tell his king that he was still not sure how things would turn out, and on 23 May, Garay sent a further report to Charles V.[67] In it, he stated that the faculty authorities had annulled the list of signatures in favour of Catherine which he had collected. Henry's side now had 35 signers, four or five of whom had previously signed for Catherine. Garay had hoped to obtain as many as 60 names for her, but now feared that the faculty would in the end vote for Henry's view. It was thus essential to make an immediate effort to rally support for the queen of England, with a strong hint that cash inducements would be required, since the emperor's name was not enough. Garay's letter was very probably occasioned by the fact that, on that same day, 23 May, the canon lawyers of Paris had voted in Henry's favour.[68]

The definitive vote of the Paris theology faculty took place on 7 June 1530. There was a large attendance, and Du Bellay spoke persuasively on Henry's behalf, claiming that he was only asking the faculty for advice on the subject, not a judgement. The main speaker for Catherine's cause was Bêda, who argued that to accede to Henry's wishes, even if this accorded with the will of their own King Francis, would be to sacrifice the eternal truth of Christian doctrine for the sake of friendly relations with England, which were a temporal and ephemeral concern. From the procedural debate which followed, three main opinions emerged. One was that the whole matter should be examined forthwith, the second that the pope, or at least King Francis, should be consulted before any action was taken, and the third was that Francis's opinion alone should be sought, with no faculty discussion of the subject until this had been received. The faculty bedel started listing speakers, according to which of these propositions they supported, but one doctor of theology snatched the paper from his hand and tore it up. The English representatives presumably saw all this, and protested strongly to Guillaume du Bellay, who duly reported events to King Francis, and asked him to order an immediate debate and vote on the divorce question.

---

[66]    *LP* IV (iii) nos 6369, 6370.
[67]    *LP* IV (iii) nos 6393, 6399.
[68]    *LP* IV (iii) no. 6400.

Francis was in Bordeaux at the time, and sent an order to Lizet, the president of the Paris Parlement to convey the royal anger to Noël Béda, who was to be told firmly that any attempt by the theology faculty to consult Pope Clement on the matter would breach the Most Christian King's rights and privileges. In fact, the faculty, as a body, had already held informal discussions on the subject, and now proceeded to a vote. On 2 July, it was resolved, by 53 votes to 47, that neither divine nor natural law allowed popes to issue a dispensation for a man to marry his brother's wife. On 6 July, a copy of this resolution was dispatched to England, but its opponents did not give up. Garay and Béda tried to prevent the written decision from receiving the faculty seal. They had already appealed against it on procedural grounds but failed to find a lawyer who would draw up the relevant document correctly. They also tried to gain possession of the register which contained the minutes of the meeting, but Guillaume Petit, who was bishop of Troyes and Francis's confessor, had by then abstracted it from the archive, on the king's orders. They also tried to obtain the opinions and signatures of those doctors who had not attended the meeting, but there was no escaping the fact that Catherine's cause had received a severe setback.[69] What was Pole's part in all this?

The surviving evidence leaves no doubt but that Reginald had had a central position in the attempt to secure support for the divorce from the theologians. On 13 May 1530 he had reported to Henry VIII that, according to Du Bellay, Francis I had sent letters to the University of Paris, urging it to come to a decision in Henry's favour, but that this correspondence was delayed.[70] Then, on 10 June, he wrote to the earl of Wiltshire, referring to copious correspondence on the divorce and make absolutely clear his own commitment to Henry's cause. He gave the earl a detailed report of the activities of Catherine's supporters. He and the other English envoys had visited both Du Bellay and Lizet that day, and at their meeting Lizet undertook to go in person to the theology faculty, on 11 June, with a letter from Henry which urged the theologians to come to a quick decision. Lizet also undertook to deal with Noël Béda, and Pole felt optimistic about developments.[71] Just over a week later, Henry wrote to Pole, under the signet, from Windsor. He was sorry that Du Bellay had failed to obtain a vote from the faculty on 12 June, as had been expected, and also that Pole, and another of Henry's servants, John Wellisburne, had not been allowed into the meeting, and that Pierre Lizet had failed to provide them with an adequate account of the proceedings. Increasingly worried and pessimistic, Henry told Pole that he now thought Du Bellay's estimate of the theologians' voting intentions had been over-optimistic, and that the strength of his opponents was increasing, while support

---

[69]  Knecht, *Renaissance warrior*, pp. 293–294.
[70]  *LP* IV (iii) no. 6383; *CRP* 1 no. 54.
[71]  *LP* Addenda I (ii) no. 638; *CRP* 1 no. 55.

for him was waning. As a result of what he had heard from Pole and others in Paris, he now regarded the president of the Parlement, Lizet, as an enemy rather than a friend, but evidently still had full confidence in Pole and Wellisburne.

Henry was obviously aware that Francis may have been reluctant to come out openly against Charles, since his two sons were still hostages in the Emperor's hands in Spain, and he felt that Du Bellay would still have to be treated as trustworthy. He was to receive 500–600 crowns to bribe the theologians, and thus the dinners, which have already been referred to, may well have been paid for by the English king. This was, of course, to be done with the utmost secrecy. While writing this letter, Henry received better news from Paris about his prospects, and his mood swung, characteristically, from depression to optimism, in his final words.[72] After this, it was Pole who reported to his king the outcome of the faculty meeting on 2 July, and the delayed official sealing of the decision on the 7th, after Garay and Béda's unsuccessful rearguard action. Evidently still fully committed to the annulment, Pole said that he was sending the written decision back to England, in the hands another member of the embassy, Edward Fox, who was in his own right an important propagandist for the king.[73] In an undated letter apparently written later in July, the duke of Norfolk wrote from court to congratulate Pole on his efforts, and emphasising that he had done all this for the king without being asked, thus showing real enthusiasm for the cause. Norfolk reported, as noted earlier, that Henry was now constantly talking about Pole, praising his learning, and saying that he was fully worthy of his royal descent.[74] In view of what would happen later, these sentiments seem ironical, but it does appear that, at least up to the end of 1530, Pole continued to support the divorce, and if he was really offered the archbishopric of York by Henry, this would surely confirm such an interpretation of his position. In any case, it seems probable that, after his return from Paris he went to the former Carthusian monastery at Sheen, near Richmond Palace, where he had been educated as a boy, to live once again in Dean Colet's former house.[75] At this time, Pole seems to have meditated on the issues and his own actions, and begun to change his view. By June 1531, Thomas Cranmer was reporting to the earl of Wiltshire that Pole had written to Henry, saying that 'he had *never* [this author's italics] pleasure to intromytte hymselfe in this cause'. Pole's mind seems not, however to have been entirely settled at this time. According to Cranmer, he had told Henry that, although he admitted he might be right in seeking divorce from Catherine, 'that

---

[72] *LP* Addenda I (ii) no. 688; *CRP* 1 no. 56.

[73] Pocock, *Records*, 1, no. 194, p. 563; *LP* IV (iii) no. 6505; *CRP* 1 no. 57.

[74] Pocock, *Records*, 1, appendix 21; *LP* IV (iii) no. 6252; *CRP* 1 no. 58.

[75] *LP* V no. 307 (= BL Cotton Nero B VI, fol. 169r, a letter from Edmund Harvel to Thomas Starkey, 18 June 1531).

he sholde not be a doer therin, and a setter forwarde therof, he cowde never fynde in hys harte'.[76]

It will probably never be possible to know fully Pole's mind on this vital subject, but one may suggest some factors that may have contributed to his change of heart, if that is what it was. His mission to Paris was, of course, just a part of a Europe-wide effort to secure the support of theologians and canon lawyers for Henry's request to Pope Clement for the annulment of his marriage to Catherine. To begin with, the campaign mainly involved England itself. The kingdom's two universities were naturally urged to vote in favour of the required dispensation, and efforts to persuade them were already under way while Pole and his colleagues were still in Paris. Cambridge was generally perceived as being more sympathetic than Oxford to reforming ideas in the Church, and men from that university were prominent in the efforts to gain approval from Clement VII for Henry's divorce. Then, on 25 October 1529, Thomas More had replaced Cardinal Wolsey as lord chancellor and, soon afterwards, the king sent a group of men, including the future Archbishop Thomas Cranmer, to present him with the latest version of the case for the annulment. This paperwork, which had been produced with the help of other Cambridge men including Cranmer and Thomas Goodrich, both of Jesus College, was taken and used by Stephen Gardiner and Edward Fox, also from Cambridge, when they went to their old university, in February 1530, to obtain its opinion on the subject. Meanwhile Cranmer, with the earl of Wiltshire, had gone on an embassy to Charles V and Clement VII at Bologna, where the emperor would be crowned by the pope in March. On 7 March, Clement cited Henry VIII to appear personally in Rome in his cause for divorce, and forbade him to remarry in the meantime. Thus it was that one future archbishop, Cranmer, was busy on royal business in Italy, while his successor, Pole, was on a similar mission in Paris. Neither led his respective mission, but both must have lived and breathed the divorce issue during the spring and summer of 1530. In charge of the English team in Italy was yet another Cambridge man, Richard Croke, who was a noted Greek scholar.[77]

Of course, by no means all of Henry's subjects were convinced that his scruples about his marriage to Catherine were justified. On 4 April 1530, the king wrote to the University of Oxford, urging its members to give a 'true' opinion in the case, in other words one favourable to him. They were to listen to John Longland, bishop of Lincoln, who as well as being Oxford's diocesan was Henry's representative, and they should not believe false arguments from the opponents of the divorce. The king complained that a large number of the young men in Oxford were opposing it, and behaving as though they were already

---

[76]  BL Lansdowne no. 115, fol. 2r (= Pocock, *Records*, 2, 130–131); Mayer, 'Fate worse than death', *CPEC*, XI, pp. 888–889.

[77]  MacCulloch, *Thomas Cranmer*, pp. 47–49, 51–52.

regent masters, and he compared the trouble and delay in Oxford unfavourably with Cambridge, which had given its opinion in favour of the divorce on 27 March. The royal admonition proved sufficient, and on the very same day, 4 April, the University of Oxford duly passed a decree in accordance with the king's wishes.[78] During the months of Pole's mission to Paris, most of the English bishops seem to have favoured, or at least accepted, the divorce, though John Fisher of Rochester famously resisted from the start, speaking boldly in support of Catherine.[79] Fisher's defiance showed that there was a serious case against as well as for Henry's proposed action, but all the king's servants were under immense pressure to conform to his will, and Pole could not have failed to observe the behaviour of the new lord chancellor in 1529–31. Early biographers of More, such as William Roper and Nicholas Harpsfield, whose work Pole would later support, see More as having been caught up at this time in Henry's campaign for divorce, but not implicated in it. Yet he did not oppose the king openly, as a few churchmen did, including Bishop John Clerk of Bath and Wells, and Princess Mary's chaplain, Thomas Abel, as well as Fisher. In private, More apparently told Henry what he really thought, in which case he did not deceive him, but as lord chancellor he nonetheless had to present formally to parliament the views of the English and Continental universities on the question. It would not be until 1532 that he resigned his office in protest against Henry's actions.[80] Perhaps even more influential on Pole's inner thought at this time were events in Italy, and the reactions of his friends and acquaintances there, and particularly in Venice and Padua.

On 16 March 1530, the Venetian ambassador in London, Lodovico Falier, informed the Signoria of the republic that Henry VIII had already received a favourable verdict on the divorce from the doctors of Leuven/Louvain University, in the Netherlands, and was now sending to Padua to obtain a similar verdict from the canon lawyers there. As that university was under Venetian authority, he naturally alerted the Signoria.[81] Falier's report was evidently accurate, as on 5 April, Giovanni Casale, an apostolic prothonotary who represented Henry in Venice, as his brother Gregorio did in Rome, informed the duke of Norfolk that he had undertaken to visit Padua, equipped with money, evidently for bribes to the lawyers and theologians there, which had been supplied by another of the English king's representatives in Rome, Girolamo Ghinucci, who was absentee bishop of Worcester.[82] On 13 April, Prothonotary Casale reported to Falier in

    [78]   *LP* IV (iii) nos 6303, 5308, 6320.
    [79]   *CSP Span* IV (ii) p. 241; *LP* IV (iii) no. 6596; *LP* IV (iii) no. 6757; *CSP Span* IV (ii) p. 547; Maria Dowling, *Fisher of men: a life of John Fisher, 1469–1535* (Basingstoke: Macmillan, 1999), pp. 144–147.
    [80]   John Guy, *Thomas More* (London: Arnold, 2000), pp. 146–152, 156–157.
    [81]   *CSP Ven*, IV, no. 568.
    [82]   *LP* IV (iii) no. 6310.

London that ambassadors from Henry had appeared before the Collegio, the senior governing body of Venice, requesting their authorisation for the doctors of Padua to rule on the divorce. Thus began a long and fairly mercenary process, in which academics were offered money, and the Venetian authorities tried to balance their contradictory desires to placate all the major powers – the emperor, the pope, and the French and English kings.[83] To make life even more difficult, Charles V had agents in Venice who were under orders to safeguard Catherine's interests, and remain alert for any moves made on her husband's behalf. Thus on 15 April the prothonotary Marco Antonio Caracciolo and Rodrigo Niño, who were the Imperial ambassadors to the Signoria, sent a detailed report to their master. They informed Charles that the English ambassadors in Venice were proposing that the University of Padua should give its opinion on the divorce, One of these men was still in Venice, while the other had gone to Rome, and it is at this point that a figure who would play a hugely important role in Reginald Pole's life makes his first appearance on the scene. Caracciolo and Niño reported that Henry's agents had been trying to persuade Gianpietro Carafa, bishop of Chieti and future Pope Paul IV, who was on a strict retreat in Venice, to intervene in the case on the English king's behalf. They had sent an unnamed Englishman to give him the details, and already there are signs here that the Habsburgs regarded Carafa as somewhat volatile. It is also clear that Imperial policy was not to intervene openly in Padua, for fear of offending Venetian susceptibilities.[84] Venice, ever anxious to secure and keep a balance of power in Europe, including England, as a means of assuring its own continuing independence, took the question of Henry's divorce extremely seriously. On 19 April the Collegio had a lengthy meeting, and as a result resolved to appoint a committee of the 'Sages of the Council' to consider the matter further.[85] On Henry's side, Carafa's view of his divorce was evidently important since, on 22 April, his envoy in Lucca, Pagnini, undertook to pass on the latest English documents on the subject to Carafa, and also to the bishop of Verona, Pole's friend, and papal datary, Gian Matteo Giberti.[86]

This was evidently true, since on the following day, in a long dispatch from Venice, Richard Croke told the king that Giberti had instructed his vicar, or deputy, to favour Henry's cause by assembling in Verona, in the bishop's absence, all available theologians to vote in favour of the divorce. Croke added that Giberti had written to Carafa on the subject, and was taking a cautious line. He had always respected Henry VIII, but he did not want to become involved in the divorce question. According to this account, Carafa, on the other hand,

---

[83]   *CSP Ven*, IV, no. 572.
[84]   *LP* IV (iii) no. 6338.
[85]   *CSP Ven*, IV, no. 573.
[86]   *LP* IV (ii) no. 6350.

thought the pope should authorise the discussion of the matter by any or all theologians, because he believed the English king to have a strong case. Carafa had, however, asked Giberti to write to Henry before he did, as he was diffident about approaching directly so great a prince. He wanted to act solely on the merits of the cause, and not just to support Henry. Croke reported that he had also made inroads in Padua. He claimed to have secured the support of Jacopo Simoneta, who was public reader in theology there and was highly respected by the Venetian Signoria. He himself was working hard in Venice, and had high hopes of gaining the support, in Henry's cause, of the minister of the Conventual Franciscans there, Gianfrancesco Marino. Croke had asked Ghinucci to write to Marino secretly from Bologna, in order not to alert the Venetian authorities, but in the hope that more Italian Franciscans might be enlisted. The manoeuvre was unsuccessful, since the Venetians found out what was going on and told Marino not to meddle in the matter, but the readiness of at least some Italian churchmen to deny the pope's right to dispense in such matters sheds an interesting light on Pole's own agonies.[87] Meanwhile, Rodrigo Niño reported on 28 April, to Charles V, that he had an audience of the most senior Venetian authorities, the doge and Senate, in which he had been assured that they would not allow Henry to obtain a formal opinion on the divorce from the University of Padua.[88] Despite this apparent setback, the English royal agents continued to work hard, and on 4 May, Gregorio Casale informed Henry, from Bologna, that he had enlisted in his cause a Dominican inquisitor, Master Crisostomo, as well as the minister of the Franciscan province of Bologna, a theology professor of Bologna University called Lorenzo, and several members of the Servite order. He also had hopes that at least some of the canon lawyers in the prestigious Bologna faculty would declare themselves on Henry's side.[89] The king does not, however, seem to have shared the optimism of his agents in Italy since the Venetian ambassador, Falier, reported to the Signoria, on 9 May, that Henry was already talking of using the English parliament to secure his divorce from Catherine, if he did not receive the longed-for papal dispensation.[90]

An important day in Venice, for Henry's hopes, was 12 May 1530. The republic's Council of Ten and the Giunta met together to discuss and vote on a motion to instruct Marco Dandolo, knight, who was a doctor of laws in Padua. The minutes of the meeting indicate that there was a conflict over whether to lean towards the English king, or towards the emperor, who supported Catherine. Dandalo was to have discussions with all lawyers and theologians who held teaching posts in the University of Padua. The talks were to be individual and

---

[87]   *LP* IV (iii) no. 6354.
[88]   *LP* IV (iii) no. 6359.
[89]   *LP* IV (iii) no. 6366.
[90]   *CSP Ven*, IV, no. 576.

secret, and Dandalo was to urge each man not to become involved in the matter of the English divorce, on either side. Some indication of the complexity of the affair, and perhaps also of the pliability of Italian academic consciences at the time, is given by the instruction to Dandolo that he should ask each lecturer whether he had already given an opinion on the matter to anyone else, on the English or the Imperial side. Anyone who had come to a private opinion was not to publish it. Dandalo was to stress to the Paduan professors that their actions, or inaction, must at all times appear to be 'voluntary', with no reference whatsoever to the Signoria, if they wished to receive any further favour from the Venetian republic. As an additional security, each man was to be put on oath not to tell anyone at all that these instructions had come from the Signoria. Each individual answer was to be put in a letter to the Council of Ten, and if they needed any further persuading, Dandalo was authorised to show this letter to them.[91] On the same day, Rodrigo Niño informed Charles V that he had received an assurance from the Signoria that no opinions on the divorce would be given by the University of Padua, but that Henry's agent, Richard Croke, had gone to Padua himself, in an attempt to circumvent the Venetian authorities. In this dispatch, Niño referred to a previous suggestion from the emperor that Gianpietro Carafa should come out of his retreat in Venice and go to England to try to persuade Henry to desist from seeking the divorce. Charles thought that Carafa was the right man to undertake the task because he knew Catherine well, from a visit to the kingdom earlier in the current reign.[92]

Also on 12 May, Charles received a report from Rome on the efforts of Henry's agents. His own agent said that he had not managed to organise resistance to Henry among the lawyers in Bologna, but wanted Charles to present to the pope the many precedents from recent Iberian and Italian history for the granting of the kind of dispensation that Henry had received to marry Catherine.[93] On 17 May, the Council of Ten and the Giunta met again to discuss the news that the Paduan professors had complied with their instructions, but still expressed concern that one of them, Mariano da Siena, was now demanding that all the individual opinions, and the reasons for them, should be published. Dandolo was instructed to tell Mariano, who was directly employed by the state, to remain silent.[94] On the same day, Rodrigo Niño reported to Charles V, from Venice, the recent happenings in the University of Padua. According to him, the Venetian authorities were aware that the king of Portugal, Manuel, had received a dispensation to marry a second of Ferdinand and Isabella's daughters, María, after the death of her older sister Isabel. They thought this case analogous to

---

[91]   *CSP Ven*, IV, no. 578.
[92]   *LP* IV (iii) no. 6378.
[93]   *LP* IV (iii) no. 6379.
[94]   *CSP Ven*, IV, no. 579.

that of Henry and Catherine, and wished to avoid annoying the pope by taking a public stance on the subject before he had made up his mind. As far as Padua was concerned, Niño said that five of the six Paduan professors had supported the policy of neutrality, as instructed, even though they had been spoken to by English representatives. Also, Carafa had been approached again by the English, on 13 May. They had asked him to undertake that, if he refused to support Henry's case, he would at least not support Catherine's either. As the English ambassadors complained that the Paduan academics had taken their money, but not delivered the votes, Niño reported that, on 15 May, Carafa had left Venice for Padua, purportedly to investigate and judge an unrelated case of heresy.[95]

Meanwhile, Pope Clement continued to vacillate over the English king's 'great matter', and on 21 May he issued an inhibition on all ecclesiastical judges from intervening in the case, or receiving money to do so, on pain of excommunication. [96] This mention of bribery was highly relevant as, on that same day, Bishop Ghinucci of Worcester wrote to Croke, asking for more of the king's money to help the Prothonotary Casale win votes.[97] By the time that he reported to Henry on 25 May, Croke appeared confident that there was overwhelming support for his master's case in Italy. Tommaso Omniboni had seven new signatures, and Simoneta had 20 more promised, while Croke himself had collected more in Vicenza, from Franciscan Observants. The pope was trying to stop these activities, but the important point in this dispatch, from Pole's perspective, is that Croke makes it clear that Reginald's former tutor, Leonico Tolomeo, was extremely active in Henry's cause, despite the official Venetian attitude. Significantly, Croke suggested to Henry that he should ask Bishop Cuthbert Tunstall and John Lambert about Leonico's qualities, as he had taught them both at Padua in earlier years. On the same day, Niño told Charles V that opposition to the English divorce was growing among the Paduans and at Vicenza.[98] A day later, Croke claimed to Edward Fox that he now had 36 doctors and 14 Franciscan Observants on his side, and that the Venetian senate was not interfering with his activities. On the other hand, on the same date he wrote separately to report to the king that the apostolic nuncio to Vicenza was collecting up and burning these signatures, while in Padua, Leonico tried to gain the support, in Henry's cause, of the provincial minister of the Conventual Franciscans there, Francesco Marino.[99] That Carafa was now clearly on Charles and Catherine's side is evident from a letter that he sent to the emperor on 1 June, but in other respects June saw each side sticking to its position, as Clement

[95]   *LP* IV (iii) no. 6392.
[96]   *LP* IV (iii) no. 6396.
[97]   *LP* IV (iii) no. 6398.
[98]   *LP* IV (iii) no. 6405.
[99]   *LP* IV (iii) nos 6406, 6407.

VII continued to avoid making a decision.[100] Pole's vacillations over the divorce were almost certainly influenced by these developments on the Continent, which saw Gianpietro Carafa take one side and Leonico the other, when the time of reckoning arrived.

---

[100]   *LP* IV (iii) nos 6421, 6422, 6423, 6445; *CSP Ven*, IV, nos 580, 583.

Chapter 3

# Rupture

At the beginning of the 1530s, Reginald Pole appeared to be an able scholar who was heading for a successful career in the service of Henry VIII. Yet by 1540, he had broken definitively with the king by condemning both his divorce of Queen Catherine and his separation from the Church of Rome. He had become a cardinal, had attempted to subvert Henry's regime, while acting as papal legate to England, and had seen some of his close relations executed on treason charges. In order to understand these extraordinary developments in the life of any Archbishop of Canterbury, it is necessary to piece together a narrative of events that do not always fully emerge at first sight, and require for their analysis a subtlety worthy of Pole himself.

The transformation seems to have begun with the much-disputed episode in which King Henry supposedly offered an English archbishopric to Pole, whom he evidently saw as loyal and reliable after his service in Paris. The Imperial ambassador, Eustache Chapuys, seems to have been right to report to his master that, in November and December 1530, Henry was in sole direction of English policy, both secular and ecclesiastical, and Pole was certainly an obvious man to recruit. The King needed a reliable prelate to replace Thomas Wolsey at York. If nothing came of Henry's attempts to gain a papal verdict favourable to him on his divorce from Catherine, it might well be possible for the new English archbishops to decide the case without further reference to the Roman Curia, in their *ex officio* capacity as legates (*legati nati*).[1] A willingness to dispense with Roman authority altogether, if necessary, had been building up, at least in the king's mind, since the previous summer. In an undated document, Henry had instructed his representatives in Rome, now Edward Carne, William Benet as well as Bishop Girolamo Ghinucci of Worcester, to assert as the custom of England that no one, whether ruler or subject, should be compelled to obey a summons to a court outside the kingdom.[2] Fearful of Pope Clement's likely reaction, the three men held back, thus incurring their royal master's wrath rather than that of the pope.[3] By the autumn of 1530, Henry was telling all around him

---

[1]  *LP* V no. 737; *CSP Span* IV (ii) 888.

[2]  On the historical justification for such royal claims in England see G.W. Bernard, *The late medieval English Church: vitality and vulnerability before the break with Rome* (New Haven and London: Yale University Press, 2012), pp. 17–36.

[3]  *CSP Span* IV (ii) no. 1873; *LP* IV (iii) nos 6307, 6513.

that he did not see how the pope could treat a king as he was being treated, since the succession to the English throne could not be decided in Rome. A king was supreme in his own kingdom, and therefore had the right to forbid his subjects to go to any court outside it.[4] Eventually, on 27 October 1530, Benet reported that he and his colleagues had at last put the king's views and arguments to Pope Clement, who had responded sharply that he would prove his jurisdiction over England, if Henry could prove the existence of the 'custom' that he was alleging.[5]

As the year 1531 began, Pole must still have appeared to be a tacit supporter of Henry's course of action, but his loyalty was soon to be severely tested. Although he had avoided becoming Wolsey's successor at York, the see being given instead to Edward Lee in September of that year, Pole was about to see Henry use parliament as a weapon against the papacy, with unforeseen and long-lasting consequences. Early in 1531, a draft bill was drawn up which, if it had actually been presented and enacted, would have empowered the two English archbishops, or if necessary just one of them, to pronounce on the king's marriage to Catherine. Reference was made in the text to the university opinions that had been collected on the subject, and the bill also stated that, if the archbishop(s) did annul the marriage, the pope and his agents would never again be allowed to intervene in the affairs of England.[6] It is impossible to know whether this draft was already in existence when Pole was involved with the succession at York, but in any case, it was the shape of things to come, even though it was never actually submitted to the two Houses in that form. Since the summer of 1530, with the verdict of the Paris theologians safely in the bag, Henry had begun to reward those churchmen who had been active for him in the cause, but Pole continued to keep a low profile. Very little of his correspondence in this period has come to light, and in a letter from Padua, dated 8 February 1531, Niccolò Leonico, who would die in the following month, professed himself even to be uncertain whether his former student was in England or France, and made no direct allusion to his own recent activity on King Henry's behalf in the case of the divorce.[7] In England, royal pressure on the clergy was mounting. In the autumn of 1530, 15 senior churchmen had appeared in King's Bench to answer charges, under the fourteenth-century statute of *praemunire*, of illegally accepting papal jurisdiction in England. Since Wolsey had earlier admitted his guilt in this respect, and, as legate and archbishop, had inevitably had dealings, direct or indirect, with most or all of the English clergy on behalf of the See of Rome, it was now clear that no one was safe from such charges.

---

⁴   *LP* IV (iii) no. 6667.

⁵   *LP* IV (iii) no. 6705.

⁶   *SP* 2/N 155–60; G.W. Bernard, *The King's Reformation: Henry VIII and the remaking of the English Church* (New Haven and London: Yale University Press, 2005), pp. 41–43.

⁷   *CRP* 1 no. 59 (trans. Gasquet, p. 110), 61 (*ERP* 1 no. 12; *OEE*, 9, no. 2526). Leonico died on 28 March 1531.

In the early months of 1531, Henry and his advisers began to deploy the opinions of the universities on the divorce in a parliamentary context. These were first collected together, in the original Latin, under the title *Censurae academiarum*, and then translated into English by Thomas Cranmer, as the *Determination of the universities*.[8] Henry's working parties also produced the suitably-named *Collectanea satis copiosa* ('A sufficiently ample collection'), and all these compilations consisted of extracts from the Bible and the Church Fathers, as well as other relevant documents.[9] Having replaced Wolsey as lord chancellor, Thomas More found himself having to present the universities' rulings to the House of Lords. Like Pole, and unlike Fisher, he did not, at this stage, oppose the divorce openly, and was allowed by Henry to keep his opinions to himself, and hence remain in office.[10] Pole, on the other hand, was beginning, at about this time, to formulate a view that was hostile to the divorce, though the surviving evidence for this is second-hand. When, in May 1531, 18 members of the convocation of Canterbury protested, also on behalf of many of their colleagues, against the king's recent ecclesiastical measures, and were quickly charged with offences mostly against the statute of *praemunire*, Pole was not among them. The implication is that, at this stage, he probably went along, at least externally, even with the royal headship of the English Church.[11] There is, however, evidence in a letter from Thomas Cranmer to the earl of Wiltshire, neither of them a friend of Catherine or Rome, that Pole did finally, at about the middle of 1531, commit to paper his opposition to Henry's proceedings. According to Cranmer, Pole had recently 'written a book much contrary to the king his purpose'.[12] He now argued that Henry should indeed submit the decision in the divorce case to Pope Clement, for various reasons both domestic and international. However, Pole apparently also explained in this document why he had up to then kept his views to himself. He was concerned about the succession to the English crown, and greatly feared civil war if it were to be disputed. He stated that he would never show anything but honour to the king, and therefore would not consent to the view that Henry's marriage to Catherine was 'so shameful, so abominable, so bestial and against nature' as his sovereign claimed. Perhaps disillusioned by the manner in which his own efforts in Paris had been treated since his return, he now criticised the use of the opinions of the universities in order to bolster the king's case. Cranmer may well have wanted to discredit Pole in the eyes not only of Wiltshire but also of the highly influential duke of Norfolk, but

---

[8]  *LP* V no. 171.

[9]  BL Cotton Cleopatra E.VI fols 16–135.

[10]  William Roper, *The life of Sir Thomas More*, in *The collected works of Sir Thomas More*, ed. R.S. Sylvester and D.P. Harding (New Haven: Yale University Press, 1962), pp. 210, 225.

[11]  Nicholas Pocock, ed., *The history of the reformation of the Church of England, by Gilbert Burnet* (Oxford: Clarendon Press, 1865), iv, 191, 353.

[12]  BL Lansdowne 115 fols 2r–3r; Pocock, *Records*, 2, 130–131; *CRP* 1 no. 60.

this account, if accurate, does suggest that a supporter of Henry was at least beginning to turn into the formidable opponent of divorce and schism which he would later become.[13]

Whatever unease he may have felt, Pole remained in England until the end of 1531, but he began, at some point during that year, to ask Henry for leave to return to Italy, once more on an academic pretext, and such permission was granted at the beginning of 1532. According to Chapuys, during these months Pole overtly threatened Henry that, if he stayed in England, he would attend 'Parliament' (in fact Convocation), in his capacity as dean of Exeter, and would speak according to his conscience if the subject of the divorce came up. Charles V's ambassador thought this was the reason why the king allowed Pole to go abroad, though he remained friendly enough to his protégé to allow him to retain his ecclesiastical benefices in England.[14] While it may be argued that Pole, by leaving for Italy, was evading the issue of the divorce, it might be that in fact he was already thinking of acting against Henry from there, even if he initially appeared thereby to make things easier for the king.[15] In any case, once back in his adopted land, Pole did indeed resume his studies, and he remained silent in public for the next three years, while Henry divorced Catherine and married Anne Boleyn, with the consent of the archbishop of Canterbury whom he had appointed, and the English Church of which he had been proclaimed Supreme Head by parliament.

During 1532, an act of parliament suspended the collection by the Roman See of annates, a tax on papal appointments to senior posts, and at the same time a campaign against the jurisdiction and status of the clergy was mounted in parliament, on the king's initiative. Meanwhile, the surviving fragments of Pole's correspondence give just a glimpse of his life in what appears to have been voluntary exile. According to a letter to him from Edward Wotton, dated 31 June 1532 and containing news from England, Pole was then in Avignon, pursuing his studies, but by October of that year, when his old friend Pietro Bembo wrote to him from Padua, he was evidently back in familiar Venetian territory.[16] What does seem clear from his correspondence between then and the end of 1534 is that his Italian friends, including Jacopo Sadoleto, Antonio Fiordibello and Cosmo Gheri, saw him as a bright scholar of the late Italian Renaissance, with not a mention either of the stormy events in his homeland or of the possibility of his becoming a member of the Catholic clergy. Around the end of October 1532, Pole wrote to Sadoleto, from Venice, about his recent discoveries in the works of Plato, Aristotle and Cicero. He told his friend that he had not read so much

---

[13]   *PPP*, pp. 56–57.
[14]   *CSP Span* IV (ii) no. 888; *LP* V no. 737.
[15]   Bernard, *King's Reformation*, p. 217.
[16]   *CRP* 1 nos 62 (*CSP Ven*, IV, no. 677), 63 (*ERP* 1 no. 9).

Latin for four years, that is, since he had left for England and become involved in the Paris mission. During that time, he says, he had concentrated on theological matters, and it seems quite likely that by this he meant the issues surrounding the divorce and Henry's religious policies.[17] On 3 December, Sadoleto replied from Carpentras, fully supporting Pole's philosophical studies and agreeing with the Church Fathers Basil and John Chrysostom's view that theology, which no one should tackle in any case before the age of 25, was just a part of philosophy.[18] A letter sent by Sadoleto to Pole from Carpentras, on 14 July 1533, indicates that Thomas Starkey, who would later turn against Pole, was still, at that stage, regarded by both men as a friend. Other letters show that Fiordibello was in the network, in the early months of 1534, and things seemed to be carrying on as normal.[19]

Probably at the end of February in that year, Pole wrote to Cosmo Gheri, still apparently on the basis that he himself would pursue a scholarly career. He made no mention of events in England, where Catherine and Mary were about to be deprived of their titles as queen and princess respectively, and had already been forbidden to see each other for nearly three years. In this letter, Pole discussed with Gheri his future plans for study, but said nothing in condemnation of King Henry's behaviour.[20] This continued to be the situation when Pole wrote again to Sadoleto, from Padua, on 17 September 1534. In this letter, as well as mentioning other members of his Italian circle, such as Pietro Bembo, Lazzaro Bonamico, Gianpietro Carafa and Gasparo Contarini, he continued their debate about the respective roles of philosophy and theology. He told Sadoleto that, after a period of intensive study since his return to Italy, he now wanted to revive the friendships of his youth, and had therefore brought Bonamico into his household. He criticised him for concentrating on the study of classical poets and orators rather than philosophy, which he regarded as a far more important subject. What followed was a clear and powerful statement of Pole's intellectual position, on the eve of his open conflict with Henry. Not only were teaching and ethics far more significant than poetry and oratory, but philosophy, for example the reading of Plato, led directly to God, a view which had considerable support in Renaissance Italy. Reliance on the human senses had to be abandoned, in favour of an acknowledgement that humans could, by their very nature, have no certain knowledge. In view of the subsequent development of Pole's theology (see Chapter 4), it is interesting to note that he already stresses, in September 1534, the need to reach and retain faith, in order

---

[17]   *ERP* 1 no. 13; *CRP* 1 no. 64 (with further textual details).

[18]   *ERP* 1 no. 14; *CRP* 1 no. 65.

[19]   *ERP* 1 pp. 499–500; *CRP* 1 no. 67 (with further textual details: letter dated 7 January 1534).

[20]   *CRP* 1 no. 68.

to receive benefit (*beneficium*) from God.[21] In the last letter of this surviving group, Sadoleto, writing from Carpentras on 23 November 1534, set out a defence of the superiority of theology as a study, asserting that all religious faith derived from the Gospels, and that only a select group of the Fathers should be read by Christians – Basil, Chrysostom, Augustine and Jerome.[22]

While this exchange between scholars was going on in Italy and southern France, Pope Clement VII died, on 25 September 1534. When he heard the news, King Henry was initially optimistic he would have a more amenable successor. Once again, he dispatched his regular agent, Gregorio Casale, to Rome, on a mission to support the preparations of the French cardinals for the forthcoming conclave, and he was initially pleased by the election, on 13 October 1534, of Cardinal Alessandro Farnese as Pope Paul III. The new pope had made friendly noises before his elevation, and within a week of it sent for Casale, in order to find out what he could do to help Henry, though his explicit purpose was to recover England for the Church. The new Pope Paul came to office with a strong desire to convene a general council, and at this stage still hoped that the English might participate in it.[23] Casale did his best as a diplomat, but Henry had no intention of submitting in any way to the pope, or reversing his policies.[24] By the beginning of 1535, however, he does seem to have come to suppose that some of Paul III's advisers were sympathetic to him.[25] Indeed, in June 1535, Casale reported to the king that the pope had apparently received well a proposal from Thomas Cromwell that the case of Catherine's marriage might be re-opened and considered by a new commission, not, as previously, by the auditors of the Rota, including Giacomo Simoneta, whom the English saw as particularly hostile to Henry.[26] By this time, however, the pope and Curia were more concerned with the fate of Bishop John Fisher than with making overtures to Henry.

In May 1535, Paul III had startled many by making the elderly bishop of Rochester a cardinal, but by the end of June the successor of Wolsey and predecessor of Pole as 'cardinal of England' was dead. As late as 15 June, Bernardino Sandino wrote from Padua to his friend, and Pole's, Thomas Starkey, then in Henry's entourage, to say that he must have heard of the latest creations of cardinals, including Fisher, who had, amazingly, obtained their red hats *senza dinari*, that is, without bribery. All of them, he said, were universally regarded as virtuous, learned and holy.[27] The new pope, when still Cardinal Farnese, seems

21   *ERP* 1 no. 16; *CRP* 1 no. 70.
22   *ERP* 1 no. 17; *CRP* 1 no. 71.
23   *LP* VII nos 1255, 1262, 1298; *CSP Span* V (i) no. 173; Scarisbrick, *Henry VIII*, p. 333.
24   *LP* VII nos 1397, 1483; *LP* VIII no. 176.
25   *LP* VIII nos 341, 399.
26   *LP* VIII nos 806–807; Scarisbrick, *Henry VIII*, p. 334.
27   *LP* VIII no. 875 (BL Cotton Nero B VII fol. 109).

to have been genuinely anxious for the reform of the Church, but he also had the traditional sense of duty to his family, and in his first creation of cardinals, in December 1534, he scandalised reformers by promoting two of his grandsons, both aged just 17. It thus appears that his next two creations, in May 1535 and December 1536, the latter involving Pole, were intended to restore his credibility as an opponent of abuses in the Church. It was still necessary, however, to balance political interests in choosing the successful candidates. Thus the archbishop of Capua received his hat as a pro-Imperialist, while Guillaume du Bellay, who had supervised the effort to obtain a favourable verdict on Henry's divorce from the Paris theology faculty, was elevated to please Francis I. John Fisher, and Pole's friend Gasparo Contarini, on the other hand, seem to have been appointed without any political motive, with great consequences for the former. Paul apparently imagined that the elevation of Fisher would actually help to bring Henry back into the bosom of the Church, but, even if that had been possible, the granting of a hat to Giacomo Simoneta, in the hope that he would use his expertise in canon law to reform the Curia and prepare for the general council, would in any case have prevented any rapprochement with England, given his role in the rejection of Henry's case for divorce. The true situation was not lost on Charles V's ambassador, and also Catherine's proctor, in Rome, Dr Pedro Ortiz, who reported to his master, on 31 May 1535, that while the pope should be praised for his idealism in the case of Fisher, he feared that the bishop of Rochester's blood-red hat would in fact betoken martyrdom, even though his appointment appeared to vindicate Catherine.[28]

Paul himself seems not to have been aware of the likely outcome of his elevation of Fisher until it was too late. In the event, Henry threatened to send Fisher's detached head to Rome to receive its cardinal's hat, and his fury was perhaps inevitable, while the behaviour of the main Continental powers, France and the Empire, certainly did not improve the situation. On 29 May, the bishop of Mâcon wrote to Francis I, asking him to intercede with Henry on Fisher's behalf, but he also said that Charles V and his advisers wanted to turn the French king against Fisher, because they supposed that Francis had been the chief mover of the bishop's promotion. Paul III declared his willingness to publish a denial of this, stating that he had been motivated by Fisher's learning and holiness and by a desire to please Henry, but events in England were entirely outside his control. Also on 29 May, a papal envoy, who had recently been in France, wrote to congratulate Guillaume du Bellay on his cardinalate, and urged him to beg Francis to intercede on Fisher's behalf. According to what he said to Casale, Paul III genuinely believed that he was pleasing Henry by honouring Fisher, and he even told the diplomat that Francis wanted him to settle the divorce

---

[28]  *CSP Span* V (i) no. 169.

case in the English king's favour.[29] Paul hoped to shame Henry into releasing
Fisher from the Tower of London, where he had been incarcerated since 16
April for refusing to agree to the 1534 Succession Act and the royal supremacy
over the English Church. The pope sent the cardinal's hat on 2 June, having
written placatory letters to both Henry and Francis, but Fisher was nonetheless
beheaded on Tower Hill on 22 June, the English king having promised both him
and Thomas More that they would die by St John the Baptist's day (24 June) if
they did not submit.[30] In response to these executions, on 30 August, Paul III
excommunicated King Henry once again, on paper, but the measure was not
implemented until it was approved in consistory in January 1536, by which
time Catherine, too, was dead.[31] In the meantime, the process of removing papal
authority from England had been speeded up, and Paul III had written to the
Catholic rulers of Europe, in July 1535, demanding action from them against
Henry's kingdom.[32] It was in this fraught situation that Pole worked on his great
tract against his former royal master.

It was in 1535 that he began, at long last, to put in writing his current views
on Henry's marital and ecclesiastical policies. Pole was probably staying at his
Venetian friend Alvise Priuli's villa in Treville, which he used as a refuge from the
summer heat of Padua, or else at Villottavia, in Rovolon. He had received more
than one request from London for his considered opinion on these matters,
Thomas Starkey having written to him on the subject on 15 February 1535.[33]
In that letter, his old friend, who was by then established in the royal service,
reported that he had recently been interviewed by the king on the subject of Pole
and his views. Starkey had said that Pole had never given him his opinion on the
divorce and the break with Rome, but he was sure that he, Pole, would serve his
king by helping him to distinguish clearly between divine and natural law in the
case. Henry had not been satisfied by this account, and had told Starkey to get
Pole to write to him on both subjects. Thomas Cromwell, too, was anxious that
Pole should clearly express his views on the divorce and schism. In this letter,
Starkey told his friend that, if he did what had been requested, he would help
his own family, and that Cromwell was being kind to him when he asked for
his views. Starkey then went on to set out the agenda that Pole should follow
when he composed his statement, in which he was evidently expected to come
down on Henry's side. He should argue that the Levitical law, in relation to a
man's not marrying his dead brother's wife, was part of natural, as well as divine,
law, and had been affirmed as such by numerous general councils of the Church.

[29]  *LP* VIII nos 779, 777.
[30]  Dowling, *Fisher of men*, pp. 159–163.
[31]  *LP* IX no. 207; *LP* X no. 82.
[32]  *LP* IX no. 15.
[33]  *LP* VIII no. 218; *CRP* 1 no. 73; *PPP*, p. 34.

Pole should also respond to the English view that successive popes had usurped the authority of the Mosaic law in such cases, having thus exploited the long-standing sufferance of Christian princes and the simplicity of the people. Being familiar with Pole's sphere of activity in Padua and Venice, Starkey suggested that his friend might well be away from what was happening in Rome, but he still had the Scriptures, as well as the laws and ceremonies of the Church, and should be aware that the separation of his native land from the papacy could become a reality, if Paul III continued to be hostile to Henry. The king and his council would act through parliament, and Starkey, for friendship's sake, urged Pole to realise that the state of the Church in England was not as it was being portrayed in Italy. Henry's kingdom was still Catholic, and Pole should support what he was doing there.

A week later, Starkey sent another letter to Pole, in which he repeated the king's demand for a written opinion on whether it was licit for a man to marry his dead brother's wife, on whether or not a pope might issue a dispensation to permit such an action, and finally on whether or not a pope might abrogate a decree made by a general Church council.[34] To spur Pole into action, Starkey set out the royalist case. On the question of whether the pope's authority derived from divine law, Starkey asserted that there was no proof of this proposition in Scripture, and noted that Jesus had condemned his disciples for seeking supremacy, one over another (Matthew 18:1–6), while Paul, in his epistle to the Romans (13:1), had asserted the headship of Christ alone over the Church. There was no evidence of the papal office in the Acts of the Apostles, and in the first centuries of the Church there was equivalency between the senior bishops, or patriarchs, in Jerusalem, Alexandria, Antioch and Rome, with Constantinople added later. Indeed the Greek Orthodox Church had split from the West over papal claims, and Starkey argued that Peter, who was regarded as the first bishop of Rome and pope, had had equally high status while he was previously bishop of Antioch. Now King Henry wanted Pole's specific answer, without prejudice, on the marriage question. The king was determined that Pole should be frank, and had apparently told Starkey, with his customary flamboyance and also ominously, that he would rather Pole were dead than that he should dissemble in stating his views, in order to curry favour. Perhaps influenced by the support for the divorce that Henry's envoys had initially gained in Italy, Starkey now suggested that Pole should consult Contarini and Gianpietro Carafa, before composing his text on the subject. In late May or early June 1535, Starkey wrote yet again to Pole, this time stating Henry's position on papal authority at greater length.[35] He also included the urgings of Henry himself, Thomas Cromwell, and the

---

[34]   BL Cotton Cleopatra E.VI, fols 375r–376r; *LP* VIII no. 219; *CRP* 1 no. 74 (22 February 1535).

[35]   BL Cotton Cleopatra E.VI, fols 372r–374r; *CRP* 1 no. 76.

privy councillor Andrew Baynton, that he should get down to writing without delay, and send the result within two months. By the time that Starkey wrote yet another letter to Pole, some time after 3 June, the cardinal had evidently told him that he was ready to start, and would base everything he said on Scripture alone. Starkey now suggested that he should read the work of the fourteenth-century pro-Imperial theorist Marsilius of Padua (c. 1275–1342), who had held a low view of papal jurisdiction. Starkey told Pole that England would not submit again to the pope, and would not have done so even if Contarini, who evidently had a reputation as a reformist, had been elected to succeed Clement VII, instead of Alessandro Farnese. Yet he concluded that Thomas Cromwell was still favouring Pole, despite his silence on the vital subject.

In the event, Pole seems to have begun the promised text in or about September 1535, after the deaths of Fisher and More. He claimed to be in poor health, suffering from eye and possibly heart problems, hence the delay. On 24 September, he wrote to Priuli from Venice, saying that he had now done nearly three weeks' work on his response to Henry, and made it clear to his friend and future secretary that he was defending the Roman Church ('St Peter's Barque'). However, he felt that he had lost impetus, and wanted to come and see Priuli in Padua, in the hope of reviving his own enthusiasm for the project.[36] By this time, treatises from single, named authors were being added to the documentary collections which had previously been produced by Henry's advisers and supporters in committee, and the king was in possession of books by Richard Sampson and Stephen Gardiner, both arguing against papal primacy. Pole later sent Gardiner's work, *De vera obedientia* ('On true obedience') to Gasparo Contarini.[37] In December 1535, Pole told another of his English friends, Edmund Harvel, who informed Starkey, that he wanted the king himself to be the first to read the completed tract, which he intended to finish by January 1536.[38] In the event, having read Gardiner's *De vera obedientia*, Contarini gave Pole help and advice in writing the text that has become known to history as *De unitate* ('On unity'). Contarini thought that Gardiner had written artfully, but that his work lacked substance.[39] In February 1536, Priuli took Contarini the first section of *De unitate*, having previously provided him with the second part, the purpose of this being for Contarini to prune it as necessary, since Pole admitted, truthfully, that he tended to be too verbose.[40] He did however offer an excuse for writing at such great length. In a letter to Priuli, written around the end of February, he said that he was writing for the English public, as well as the king, and therefore

---

[36]  BAV Vat. lat. 5967, fol. 514; *ERP* 1 no. 21; *CRP* 1 no. 80; *LP* IX no. 917.
[37]  *ERP* 1 no. 22; *LP* X no. 7; *CRP* 1 no. 85 (1 January 1538).
[38]  *LP* IX nos 927, 1029; *LP* X no. 124.
[39]  *ERP* I no. 24; *LP* X no. 276; *CRP* 1 no. 88 (1 January 1536).
[40]  *LP* X 124, 479.

had to explain the issues, and his views on them, clearly and fully.[41] Pole took the final section back to Padua from Venice, in the company of Cosmo Gheri. He planned to spend Easter 1536 there with Priuli, and the text was completed by the end of March.[42] In the meantime, Contarini continued his editorial work, urging Pole to add a section which would explicitly affirm papal authority.[43]

The full letter or pamphlet, which was later entitled (not by Pole) *Reginaldi Poli ad Henricum octavum regem Britanniae pro ecclesiasticae unitatis defensione* ('For the defence of Church unity'), not *De unitate*, as it came to be known, exists in three manuscripts, one of which was read by Henry VIII, and two near-contemporary printed editions.[44] In it Pole confronted the arguments that were at that time being developed by the king and his advisers, against papal primacy and in favour of royal headship of the English Church. Although this was clearly a question of jurisdiction, affecting secular life as well as the Church as an institution, it had become clear, by the time that Pole put pen to paper in answer to Henry's request, that 'royal supremacy' was also a matter of belief, and hence of ecclesiology and even of theology. This was evident in one of the earlier treatises on the subject, completed in December 1533 by Bishop Cuthbert Tunstall of London: *Articles devised by the whole consent of the King's Council*. The basis for the English case against papal monarchy was Scriptural, and hence a matter of Christian faith. It was not just a matter of politics and legality, as in the case of disputes between other Catholic rulers, for example in France and Spain, and popes.[45] In a series of letters to Pole, written between February and July 1535, his friend and confidant Thomas Starkey set out the main arguments that were being deployed in favour of the royal headship, under God, of the English Church. On 15 February, Starkey outlined the basic thinking that underlay Henry's position. Papal monarchy and primacy was illegal, and had only come about through the connivance of rulers and the 'simplicity' of the

---

[41]   *ERP* I no. 26; *LP* no. 426; *CRP* 1 no. 90.

[42]   *CRP* 1 no. 91 (*ERP* 1 no. 27; *LP* X no. 441), 92 (*ERP* 1 no. 28, *ERP* 1 pp. 442–449; *LP* X no. 619).

[43]   *CRP* 1 no. 92; *PPP*, pp. 34–39, 90; Mayer, *A reluctant author*, pp. 43–47; T.F. Dunn, 'The development of the text of Pole's *De unitate ecclesiastica*', *Papers of the Bibliographical Society of America*, 70 (1976), pp. 455–468.

[44]   The printed version cited here is *Reginaldi Poli ad Henricum octavum Britanniae regem, pro ecclesiasticae unitatis defensione* (Rome: Antonio Blado, 1539), partially collated with BAV Vat. lat. MS 5970, fols 1r–124r by Mayer, 'Nursery of resistance: Reginald Pole and his friends', *CPEC*, II, pp. 50–74. Folio numbers are in accordance with Mayer's version. The abbreviated version of *De unitate*, as sent to King Henry, is BAV MS Vat. lat. 5967 fols 504ff. There is a full translation in Dwyer (see also Appendix 1), which is referred to alongside the folio references, in this case giving wider references to the the topic concerned.

[45]   Bernard, *King's Reformation*, pp. 225–227.

ordinary people.[46] A week later, Starkey set out the Scriptural argument on which the royal case was based. This consisted first of a passage from Matthew's Gospel [18:1–6], in which the disciples asked Jesus who was the greatest in the kingdom of heaven, and were rebuked when he set a child among them, saying: 'Whoever becomes humble like this little child is the greatest in the kingdom of heaven' [v. 4]. The rest of Starkey's New Testament evidence came from Paul's epistles. Based on Romans 13:1–7, he argued that Christians must be subject to the governing authority, in this case King Henry, while Pauline texts stating the headship of Christ were used to decry papal claims [Ephesians 1:22, 4:15, 5:23; Colossians 1:18, 2:10b]. The lack of any mention of a 'pope' in the Acts of the Apostles was also noted.[47] In this and subsequent letters, sent to Pole in June and July 1535, Starkey also deployed historical arguments in support of the royal supremacy and against papal claims. In this context he made much use, as did other writers on Henry's behalf, of the work of Marsilius of Padua, whose most famous tract, *Defensor Pacis* ('Defender of peace') denounced papal claims to primacy in the Catholic Church, in favour of those of the Holy Roman Emperor.[48] Marsilius was also deployed against the pope by the writer whose work was Pole's main target of attack in *De unitate*. This was Richard Sampson (d. 1554), a Cambridge lawyer who studied in Italy in the early years of Henry VIII's reign, and accumulated an impressive collection of ecclesiastical benefices in plurality, including the deanship of St Paul's in London.[49] In his 'Oration' justifyng the royal supremacy, which was published in 1534/5, Sampson also made much use of the arguments of Marsilius against papal monarchy, as it had developed from the end of the twelfth century.[50] Sampson argued mainly on the basis of Church history, rather than Scripture or theology, because he saw man-made laws and human behaviour, rather than divinity, as the basis of the powers claimed by the popes of his own day. He noted that Marsilius argued for the historic equality of all the apostles, without Peter being uniquely singled out, and, like Tunstall and others, made use of Romans 13 as an argument for the subservience of Christians to their rulers.[51] Other themes in Sampson's 'Oration', which Pole would counteract in *De unitate*, and also in later writings and speech, were the ideas of the early ecumenical councils on parity between the historic patriarchs of west and east, and the story of a British king Lucius, who supposedly asked Pope Eleutherius (c. 175–c. 189) to send missionaries to

---

[46]     *CRP* 1 no. 73.

[47]     *CRP* 1 no. 74.

[48]     Marsilius of Padua, *Defensor pacis*, ed. C.W. Previté-Orton (Cambridge: Cambridge University Press, 1928).

[49]     Andrew A. Chibi, 'Sampson, Richard', *ODNB*.

[50]     Richard Sampson, *Oratio quae docet hortatur admonet omnes potissimum Anglos regiae dignitati cum primis ut obedient* (London: Thomas Berthelet, 1535).

[51]     Marsilius, *Defensor pacis*, p. 279.

his kingdom, long before the arrival of St Augustine of Canterbury at the end of the sixth century.[52]

In *De unitate*, Pole declared that its purpose was to repay the king for the support that he had given him over the years, and was still giving him, in his academic studies. Thus it had a political aim as well as the duty of proclaiming and honouring Christ's name. Claiming that he had now developed, with royal support, considerable skill in deploying political arguments, he goes on the offensive from the start (fols IIIv, VIIr: Dwyer pp. 2–3, 7–8). He declares that Henry is not interested in hearing about the proper basis of the power of popes, and attacks him for usurping to himself the supreme headship of the English Church. Pole now states clearly that he cannot accept this, and therefore finds himself forced to resort to treason and, worse still, ingratitude. Nevertheless, from the very start (fol. I r-v: Dwyer pp. 1–3), he seeks to act with prudence, and much of the following text is devoted to the question of how that might be achieved in practice. European political writing of the late fifteenth and sixteenth centuries was much preoccupied with the use of dissimulation in government, and here Pole asserts that the highest political skill involved the unmasking of such deception.[53] The main, explicit aim of *De unitate* was to bring Henry back within the fold of the Catholic Church, but, as so often in his major writings, Pole includes long, and often emotional, digressions. For example, in order to place the question of his own education in its historical and personal context, Pole creates a word-picture of Henry at the beginning of his reign, when Pole himself was a child at Sheen and then a young student at Oxford [Appendix 1F(i)]. However, the scene quickly shifts from Henry's early, golden, years as king, in 1509–13, to the sombre streets of London in 1535, after the execution of Sir Thomas More. Henry's endless round of parties, artistic performances and chivalrous games, with Catherine as mistress of the revels, is thus transformed into sullen protest at the execution of More, which had shocked Europe in 1535 [Appendix 1G]. Here Pole adopts a role that he would be fond of for the rest of his life, as a stern father confessor. Henry's required course of action was straightforward and urgent: he must repent, do penance for this and other sins and crimes, and then

---

[52]  Felicity Heal, 'What can King Lucius do for you? The Reformation and the early British Church', *English Historical Review*, 120 (2005), pp. 593–614; Andrew A. Chibi, 'Richard Sampson, his "Oratio", and Henry VIII's royal supremacy', *Journal of Church and State*, 39 (2007), pp. 543–560.

[53]  On Pole's early repudiation of Machiavelli's perceived cynicism, see Mayer, 'Nursery of resistance: Reginald Pole and his friends', in Mayer, *CPEC*, II; Sydney Anglo, *Machiavelli – the first century: studies in enthusiasm, hostility and irrelevance* (Oxford: Oxford University Press, 2005), pp. 119–121; Alessandra Petrina, 'Reginald Pole and the reception of the *Principe* in Henrician England', in *Machiavellian encounters in Tudor and Stuart England: literary and political influences from the Reformation to the Restoration*, ed. Alessandro Arienzo and Alessandra Petrina (Farnham: Ashgate, 2013), pp. 13–27.

be received once more into the bosom of Mother Church. Pole recalls to Henry his pious parents, Henry VII and Elizabeth of York, and their respect for papal authority, though this does not prevent him from stressing the importance of other bishops also, as pastors and leaders.[54]

Having seen the case for monarchical control of the Church, as set out in the recent books by Sampson and Gardiner, Pole made the former his main target. He tackled the crucial case in dispute, that of the Emperor Constantine, who had presided over the first Council of Nicaea (325 AD), which had encapsulated orthodox Christian doctrine in the *symbolum*, or 'Nicene Creed'. He told Henry that Constantine had only entered the council in order to make the bishops run things properly and end their sometimes violent disputes, not to supervise, let alone control, their debates and decisions on doctrine (fol. XIXr: Dwyer pp. 45–49). As for the primacy of Peter, which was the basis of papal claims, Pole thought this to be the fundamental issue, though, again, he did not forget to stress the importance of the other bishops. Thus although Petrine authority was important, indeed essential, it was not unique, even in terms of Jesus's commission to Peter, as recorded in Matthew's Gospel [18:16]. Peter did stand out, and not every Christian had the same authority as he did, but the office of bishop, which had value even despite the failings of its individual holders, was essential, too, for the validity and continuity of the Church (fols XLVIIIv, XXr: Dwyer pp. 33–34, 93–105). Thus, although he insisted on Peter's position and powers, Pole was willing to concede that other apostles might have had similar power and authority, if not the same specific role. He pointed to the example of Moses and the 70 elders with whom he worked (Exodus 18:24–26), drawing the conclusion that the pope's power was not diminished by being shared. If, however, a pope did not feed Christ's sheep, the Church had the ability to remedy the situation, though avoiding schism (sig. Cir: Dwyer pp. 79–80).

The model of the Church that Pole presents to Henry in this text is thus hierarchical, and headed by the pope, whom even the Greek Orthodox had been willing to accept at the Council of Florence in 1439, but it was not monarchical, in either the papal or the secular manner (fol. XXXVIIIr: Dwyer p. 246). Clerical authority rested on prophetic charisma, which had the same role in Church matters as prudence did in secular government. Throughout his lengthy, not to say long-winded, tract, Pole frequently, and naturally, resorted to Biblical examples to support his argument. He ranged widely over Old and New Testaments, as he argued with his former master, King Henry, not only finding support for his own high notion of priestly authority but also stressing the faults and follies of Henry's Biblical predecessors, and the punishment and misfortune which befell them as a result, by the hand of God, his priests and his prophets. In the first 'book' of *De unitate*, Pole cited the example of the

---

[54]  *CPEC*, II, pp. 56–57.

Children of Israel, who would not obey the Babylonian king Nebuchadnezzar [Jeremiah 37–39]. The Biblical examples quoted were clearly intended to warn Henry that, if he mistreated the priesthood, as he would do if he severed the English Church from Rome, he would bring disaster on himself and his people. The prophet Samuel, described here as a priest, anointed Saul, but also David, who rebelled against him, and both had difficult reigns, because they at times rejected the Lord, His priests and His prophets [1 Samuel 10:1, 16:1–13, 19]. When King Uzziah usurped the priestly office by seizing a thurible to make an incense offering, he was struck by leprosy, which remained with him for the rest of his life [2 Chronicles 26]. Henry's spoliation of the English clergy was compared by Pole to Saul's slaying of the priests of Nob, while he was pursuing David [1 Samuel 22:11–19], while the earth swallowed up Dathan and Abiram, when they rebelled in the desert against Moses and Aaron [Numbers 16].[55] He quoted, apparently with some relish, the Psalmist's warning that the people of Israel, even if they thought themselves to be 'like gods', would nonetheless 'fall like any prince' [Psalm 82:6 (Vulgate 81)], and Jesus's instruction to the Jewish leaders to 'Give therefore to the emperor the things that are the emperor's, and to God the things that are God's' [Matthew 22:21].[56] He could not, of course, avoid the texts, in the epistles of Paul and Peter, which appeared to instruct Christians to obey their rulers in all things [Romans 13:1–7; 1 Peter 2:13–17], but he argued that these apostles could not have meant that people should subordinate themselves in everything, since all was in any case in the hands of God.[57]

With the fervour that often gripped him when he adopted a prophetic role, he told Henry of his own 'prophecies', which were firmly set in the Europe of the 1530s. Claiming that the Jewish prophets were speaking through him, he declared that Charles V should invade England (XLIXr: Dwyer pp. 267–268), giving the English king's overweening pride as the justification for this. By assuming supremacy over the English Church, Henry had not shown the humility which was proper to its true head, Christ, who was represented on earth by his vicar, the pope. In the Church, humility, not ambition, should have first place, since the House of God was to be ruled by charity, and imbued with God's Holy Spirit. In this situation, which Pole referred explicitly to the model of the early Church, inferiors should never hesitate to criticise their superiors (fol. LXXr: Dwyer p. 182) The Church could only know God's will through the inspiration of the Holy Spirit (fol. LIIv: Dwyer p. 82), and it was constituted by its human members and not by buildings.

---

[55] Pole, *De unitate*, bk 1, fols IX sig. Bii, XXV sig. Ei, XXVI, XXVII sig. Eii: Dwyer pp. 63–68.

[56] Pole, *De unitate*, fol. XII, sig. Biv: Dwyer p. 30.

[57] Pole, *De unitate*, fols XIIIXVI, sigs Biv, Ci–iii: Dwyer pp. 23, 31–32.

Yet this high spiritual discourse contained a very personal and secular thrust. Pole, a descendant of English and very probably of Welsh princes, whose mother was a countess, reminded Henry that he, too, was a member of the English nobility, as well as being king, and was not a 'Byzantine' kind of emperor, as he was claiming to be (fols IIIv, CXXr: Dwyer pp. 45–49) [Appendix 1E]. As he would frequently do in his later years, Pole showed a deep preoccupation and sensitivity concerning his own place, which he saw as exalted, in English secular society, as well as commenting sharply on current political circumstances in England. Thus he tried to exonerate his uncle, the earl of Warwick, who had been executed for supposed treason in 1499 [Appendix 1F(ii)], and told the king that he would never be able to repudiate his daughter Mary as heir to the throne. To disrupt the succession in this way would certainly lead to sedition, unless he removed all potential candidates for the crown by eliminating the entire English nobility (fol. LXXXIr-v: Dwyer pp. 196–198, 203). No doubt with his knowledge and experience of Italy in mind, Pole warned Henry that, while it was proper for a kingdom to have a single ruler, he should not act in an absolutist manner, as he was now doing. Provocatively, Pole compared his king, as he now was, in conflict with Rome, to the Ottoman sultan, the 'Grand Turk', when an English king should in fact rule by consent, from the nobility, of course (fol. Civ: Dwyer pp. 200–201). A king had just two fundamental duties, to administer justice and defend his subjects against attack. On the other hand, and here the influence of Italy surely appears, alongside that of the events of fifteenth-century English history, Pole argued that the people could change their ruler (fols XIIr, XXIIr: Dwyer pp. 202–204). Daringly, in the sixteenth-century context and when addressing a king whose father had won the throne in battle, Pole asserted that the *people* had the choice over who ruled them. He makes no mention of parliament, but instead seeks Biblical precedents as a basis for his views. The Jews had managed for many years without kings, and when God allowed them to have Saul, He did so as a punishment [1 Samuel 8:10–22] (fols XXIIIv, XXXVv: Dwyer pp. 51–52). What is more, magistrates could resist the monarch's absolute power (*imperium*). Henry had to listen to his councillors, even though he had the ultimate authority, and, in the painful recent cases, Fisher and More should have been the king's respected friends, as they were Pole's, and not executed as traitors (fol. XXXr: Dwyer pp. 204–220). Instead, Henry was now at the mercy of time-servers such as Richard Sampson (fols CXVIIr–CXIXr: Dwyer pp. 20, 25, 39).[58]

The first two books of *De unitate* were set out in the form of a verbal duel between Pole and Sampson, as the king's advocate and champion. As so often, Pole saw himself as David, overcoming Sampson's Goliath [1 Samuel 17] (fol. Xr-v: Dwyer pp. 26–27), and wanted to replace his debating opponent as

---

58    *CPEC*, II, pp. 58–60.

Henry's main councillor, who would give him sound advice, in succession to Fisher and More. In this context, he offered an account of his time in Paris, on the business of the divorce, in which he affirmed, as he would do repeatedly from then on, that he had always had scruples about Henry's case. With some subtlety, Pole, who saw Henry's current behaviour, and its consequences, as a form of theatrical tragedy, attacked Sampson for the poor quality of his rhetoric (fol. XXXIIIr: Dwyer pp. 81–82), and asserted that Peter's supremacy over the rest of the apostles and the Church was in fact a metaphor for the mystical body of Christ, and not the material basis of the government of the Church (fol. XLVIIIv: Dwyer pp. 118–122). For defending the old way, More had died in London even more tragically than Socrates had done centuries before in Athens (fol. XCIIIIr: Dwyer pp. 231–232). In this account, More is represented as a Christ-like figure (fols XCr, XCIIv: Dwyer pp. 217–220), who sacrificed himself for his king. Both he and Fisher had been better able than Henry to interpret Scripture in relation to contemporary history, and Pole vividly describes the horror of their deaths (fols LXXXIXr, LXXIIv–LXIIIr: Dwyer pp. 37–39, 204–208). *De unitate* culminates in a spiritual interpretation of events. Henry is threatened with the destruction of himself and his realm if he does not change course in relation to the Church (fol. LXXIXv: Dwyer pp. 198–200). All will be subsumed in the mystery of Christ's passion, while Fisher and More, along with the martyred Carthusian monks of London, who had also been cruelly executed as traitors, were written into the blood-stained book of the martyrs (fols XCVv–XCVIr, CIIr, CIIIr, Cv-r: Dwyer pp. 204–208).[59] On a political note, Charles V's recent military victory at Tunis, in April 1535, had freed him to deal with Henry, and at this point *De unitate* turns into an emotional appeal to the Emperor to act on behalf of the Catholic Church, so that England may return to the fold (fols Cxv, CXIr–CXIIIIr, CXVIv: Dwyer pp. 271–278). In a manner that would subsequently threaten both Pole himself and his family, he went on to assert that there was a fifth column of Catholic supporters in England, who could rise against their king, if he did not change his ways, and there was also the suggestion of an economic blockade. At the culmination of this long and sometimes rambling treatise, Pole asserted that a return to true Christian faith was the only solution for Henry. Only thus could he enter into the divine mysteries, understand his true situation, and reform his conduct (fols CXXVIIr–CXXVIIIr: Dwyer pp. 295–326).[60]

Pole's *De unitate* reached England, by the hand of his trusty friend and messenger, Michael Throckmorton, at a time of increased political tension

---

[59]   On Henry's violence towards the English Carthusians, see Bernard, *King's Reformation*, pp. 160–167 and Anne Dillon, *Michelangelo and the English martyrs* (Farnham: Ashgate, 2013), pp. 19–38.

[60]   *CPEC*, II, pp. 61–64; *PPP*, pp. 13–14, 30 and n. 81.

there.[61] On 7 January, Catherine of Aragon died at Kimbolton, thus leaving Anne Boleyn as undisputed queen, at least in England itself, and her daughter Elizabeth as heir to the throne in place of Mary. In May, however, Anne was arrested on charges of adultery and incest, for which she was beheaded, and all these circumstances suggested to some that there might be an improvement in relations between England and Charles V. The emperor seems to have thought, at this time, that there was indeed a good chance of bringing Henry and his kingdom back into the community of Catholic nations, with a view to the holding of a general council to reform the Church.[62] Paul III, on the other hand, seems quickly to have put the execution of Fisher out of his mind, calling on Henry, by means of a letter to Gregorio Casale, to take the opportunity for reconciliation that God had given him in the death of Anne Boleyn. This interpretation of divine agency may seem somewhat strange, since Henry had had his second wife executed, but Paul nevertheless argued that the English king was now in a fine position to achieve freedom from dependency on either Francis I or Charles V, as long as he submitted once again to the pope. Even in this conciliatory mode, however, Paul still characterised Henry as the Biblical 'prodigal son' (Luke 15:11–32).[63] The pope wrote to Casale between Anne's arrest and her execution, and the seriousness of his intent was demonstrated by the fact that, a week or so later, Cardinal Lorenzo Campeggio was preparing for yet another journey to England, with a view to regaining the bishopric of Salisbury, which had been taken from him by parliament, becoming cardinal protector of England once again, and negotiating Henry's return to the Roman fold.[64] As early as January 1536, having heard of Catherine's death, Chapuys had reported that Thomas Cromwell was saying that a papal legate might indeed return to England, given the new circumstances.[65] Just as Pole's diatribe was being received in London, it now seemed that Paul III might be willing to overlook, if only temporarily, some of Henry's recent church reforms, in return for renewed submission. In this climate, issues of fundamental principle might be treated as minor technical matters, at least in the mind of the Curia. Nevertheless, before anything concrete could happen to improve Anglo-papal relations, in June 1536 Paul at last summoned the long-awaited general council, to assemble at Mantua in the following year. In truth, Henry now wished any such gathering to fail, and a renewal of hostilities between Francis and Charles, in the summer of 1536, further reduced the pressure on the English king to make peace with the pope. Instead, negotiations commenced between Henry's agents

---

[61]  [M.] Anne Overell, 'Cardinal Pole's special agent: Michael Throckmorton, c.1503–1558', *History*, 94 (2009), pp. 265–278, at p. 270.

[62]  *LP* X nos 888, 926, 1161, 1227.

[63]  *LP* X no. 977 (27 May 1536).

[64]  *LP* X no. 1077.

[65]  *LP* X no. 141.

and Lutheran princes, and the dissolution of English monasteries began, by act of parliament.[66] In these circumstances, it was unlikely that Pole's *De unitate* would be well received in England.

On 13 or 14 July 1536, Cuthbert Tunstall wrote a long letter to Pole, from London, in which he described a 'reading' of the tract, which was held there to be entirely Pole's work, despite the editorial intervention in it of others, such as Gasparo Contarini.[67] *De unitate* was condemned in its entirety, for creating plagues but offering no remedy for them, and for endangering both England and Pole himself. Tunstall did not mince his words: Pole should simply burn the whole thing. Nonetheless, the bishop did take the trouble to refute the arguments of *De unitate* in some detail. On the subject of papal supremacy, he observed that no fewer than eight of the first general ecumenical councils had admitted no overall papal authority, such as was subsequently claimed by the bishops of Rome. The decrees of Nicaea and the apostolic canons, which still formed the basis of canon law in the sixteenth century, took the same view. Tunstall argued that all this canonical legislation required spiritual matters, of every kind, to be reserved to the diocese in which each case originated, this having been the practice of the early Church. On this point, he urged Pole to study the 'Catholic concordance' (*De concordantia catholica*) of the pro-Imperial bishop, Nicholas of Cusa (1401–64). Papal monarchy was certainly not ordained by Christ. Emperors, not popes, traditionally called general councils, and Peter's pre-eminence among the apostles derived not from divine commission but from Rome's role as the capital of a mighty empire. Like his opponent sliding easily from theological and historical argument to contemporary and personal matters, Tunstall concluded by bluntly warning Pole that, if he did not take *De unitate* out of circulation, his family and friends would be threatened.

Also, in an undated letter from about that time, another former Paduan student, and much closer friend, Thomas Starkey, wrote in reaction to reading Pole's tract.[68] He accused its author of impudence and lack of gratitude to his king. England had not abandoned Catholicism by removing papal authority, but simply rejected the false claims of the pope. Scripture was more important than tradition, as a guide for running the Church. As St Paul had written, it should be ruled only by faith and charity, which could exist in any system of government. The proper guides were the decrees and canons of the councils, which had Imperial rather than papal authority behind them, and Christian princes, such as Henry, were wholly entitled to make Christian policy and enforce it. After this, on 4 September, Tunstall wrote again to Pole, emphasising

---

[66]  Scarisbrick, *Henry VIII*, pp. 335–337.
[67]  Burnet, *History*, 6, pp. 177–184; *LP* XI no. 72 (1–2); *CRP* 1 no. 101.
[68]  BL Cotton Cleopatra E.VI, fols 379r–383v; *LP* XI no. 402; *CRP* 1 no. 115.

his earlier arguments against Pole's written defence, which is now lost.[69] As Paul wrote (Ephesians 5:23–24), Christ was the true head of the Church, and no bishop, including the pope, was superior to any other. Once again, the bishop of Durham appealed to the experience of the early Church, in which the patriarchal sees had equal status, as had the apostles before them. The later months of 1536 would bring this intellectual debate into English public life, when some of Henry's subjects resorted to open rebellion.

The most significant military and political threat to King Henry and his government began on Sunday 1 October 1536, when there were protests at Louth in Lincolnshire, after evensong in the parish church. The immediate pretext was the scheduled visit to the town, on the following day, of two royal commissioners and the diocesan chancellor, but the underlying motive was rejection of the religious policies that were currently being pursued or proposed by Henry. By then, the pope's name had been removed, by order of the government, from missals and other service books, the dissolution of the smaller religious houses had begun, and there were rumours that precious liturgical objects were to be confiscated from churches, and even that parishes were to be merged, with the closure of many parish churches and chapels of ease. When the officials duly arrived in Louth the next day, there was a confrontation, which quickly developed into a more general uprising in that part of north Lincolnshire, and then in Yorkshire and other areas of northern England. No doubt there were other motives for the rebellions as well, but everything was framed in religious terms, and those around Henry who were perceived as religious reformers, including Thomas Cromwell, Thomas Cranmer and Nicholas Ridley, were targeted for removal. The king and his council were severely frightened, and although the rebellion was eventually suppressed with violence, the entire episode, known then and since as the 'Pilgrimage of Grace', created a sensation throughout Europe, and elicited from Pope Paul III a response that would drastically affect Reginald Pole, his friends, and his family.[70]

In the autumn of 1536, while the fate of the English 'pilgrims' was being sealed by the cynicism and violence of Henry VIII and the duke of Norfolk, Pole set out for Rome from northern Italy, with the intention of travelling there with his friends, Gianmatteo Giberti and Gianpietro Carafa. Paul III had formally summoned Pole to Rome on 19 July, but he took some time to set out. On 10 October, he was at Siena in Tuscany, writing to Gasparo Contarini in Rome, to

---

[69]    TNA SP1/106, fol. 168 r–v; *LP* XI no. 401, *CRP* 1 no. 118.

[70]    R.W. Hoyle, *The Pilgrimage of Grace and the politics of the 1530s* (Oxford: Oxford University Press, 2001); Geoffrey Moorhouse, *The Pilgrimage of Grace: the rebellion that shook Henry VIII's reign* (London: Weidenfeld & Nicolson, 2002); Ethan Shagan, *Popular politics and the English Reformation* (Cambridge: Cambridge University Press, 2003), pp. 89–128; Bernard, *King's Reformation*, pp. 293–404; Edwards, *Mary I*, pp. 53–56.

ask for a commendation to the pope.[71] Although he had started his journey with Giberti and Carafa, he had abandoned them mid-way, ignoring their united and heartfelt entreaties to him to stay with them. Despite this typical hesitancy, when faced with major decisions or moves, Pole did tell Contarini that he felt very much threatened by the machinations of Henry VIII and Thomas Cromwell. He had recently received two letters from England, one from his brother Henry, Baron Montagu, and the other from his mother, the countess of Salisbury. Henry Pole, writing from Bisham on 13 September, had expressed great anger at his brother's tract on the divorce and Church unity, which he claimed not to have known about until he received a letter from its author, dated 15 July and now lost, that referred to it. He had mentioned his concerns at Reginald's writing and views to Cromwell, who had told him to talk to the king about the matter. Henry had recited much of the tract to him, and he had been appalled, grieving as though he had lost his 'mother, wife and children'. Montagu accused Reginald of behaving unnaturally, and not as a subject and relative, towards the king, who had set the Pole family up again, after the troubles of the previous reign. Now, Reginald was placing his own will above the interests of his country, yet the king still wanted to show mercy towards him. If, however, Reginald went to reside with the pope in Rome, he would thereby sever all ties with his closest blood relations. Such 'superstitious' behaviour would 'offend God, lose the benefits of so noble a prince, your native country and [your] whole family'.[72] Margaret, countess of Salisbury, also wrote to her son Reginald, saying that she had received a 'terrible' message from the king, via Henry Pole, about the 'error' of *De unitate*. She said that she had always been well treated by King Henry, and expected her family to recognise this and behave accordingly. Now, however, the king's anger had upset her even more than her husband's death and the loss of any of her children. She bluntly told Reginald that if he persisted in his current direction he would be her undoing. He claimed to have made a promise to serve God first, but that should involve serving his prince as well. The king had been responsible for his upbringing and education, for which he should be grateful. As well as predicting what proved to be her own fate, she stated that, if Reginald did not fully serve both God and king, she even wished that the Lord would take him to Himself.[73]

When Pole eventually arrived in the Eternal City, Paul III quickly co-opted him to the commission that he had set up to propose reforms of the Church, in preparation for the general council. On 22 December, Pole was created a cardinal deacon, effectively 'Cardinal of England', in succession to Wolsey and Fisher. He was initially given Fisher's Roman parish of SS Nereus and Achilleus, but was

---

71   *ERP* I no. 45; *LP* XI no. 654; *CRP* 1 no. 122.
72   TNA SP1/106 fol. 168r–v; *LP* XI no. 451; *CRP* 1 no. 120.
73   TNA SP1/105 fols 66–67; *LP* XI no. 93; *CRP* 1 no. 121.

moved to SS Vitus and Modestus, on 31 May 1537, and finally to St Mary in Cosmedin, on 10 December 1540.[74] Pole's surviving correspondence contains the congratulations of many in Italy on his elevation, whatever may have been thought of it in England. Between 29 December 1536 and 7 January 1537, he received laudatory letters from Lazzaro Bonamico and Pietro Bembo, who had belonged to his Paduan circle, Benedetto Lampradio in Mantua, Cardinal Giulio Ascanio Sforza in Bologna, and Georges Selves and Doge Andrea Gritti in Venice.[75] It quickly became clear that Paul intended the new Cardinal Pole to take an active part in English affairs and this was alluded to in a congratulatory letter from Lucello Maggi, who, as well as praising Pole for his holiness, piety and learning, expressed admiration for his stout resistance to the religious policies of Henry VIII, and expected the English king to submit to the new cardinal's assertion of the truth and authority of Christ's Church.[76]

With hindsight, it is clear that Pole's appointment to the college of cardinals came too late to help the 'pilgrims' in the north of England. At the time, however, Pole, ignoring his mother and brother, as Jesus had told his original disciples to do to their close relatives (Matthew 10:29), was anxious to use his new position in order to restore his king to the Catholic fold. By the beginning of 1537, he had further developed the arguments contained in *De unitate* into a proposal for the form that a Catholic mission to England could and should take, with himself as a legate with full powers to act (*a latere*).[77] Pole was anxious to repay the pope for the honour that he had done him by making him a cardinal. The valiant efforts of the Pilgrims of Grace should be rewarded, and he was the man to do it. He should be given the widest powers, and if circumstances changed, Paul should adapt his instructions. Given the fraught situation in England itself, and the reluctance of Francis I and Charles V to intervene, he advocated subterfuge, to conceal the true purpose of the legation. Friendly ambassadors in London were to be told that it was intended to help secure peace in Europe, by reconciling the French king and the emperor and thus preparing for the forthcoming general council of the Church, with the further aim of uniting Western Christendom against the threat of the Ottoman Turks. On no account was the possible removal of Henry VIII to be mentioned, though in fact this might be necessary. Initially, the legate to England was to work for the return of that kingdom to the Roman obedience, for which purpose it would be necessary to reconcile Henry to the Church as a penitent.

---

[74] *ERP* I no. 39; *LP* XI no. 122; *CRP* 1 no. 107; Mayer, 'Pole, Reginald', *ODNB*.

[75] *ERP* 2 nos 8, 5, 10, 3; *CRP* 1 nos 124, 127, 125, 126; *ERP* 2 no. 7; *LP* XII (i) no. 14; *CRP* 1 no. 130; *ERP* 2 no. 1; *LP* XII (i) no. 24; *CRP* 1 no. 131.

[76] *CRP* 1 no. 128 (undated, but late 1536 or early 1537, see Mayer).

[77] *ERP* 2 pp. cclxxiv–ccxxix; *LP* XII (i) no. 368; *CRP* 1 no. 150.

Pole imagines in detail what the reconciliation, or 'reduction', of England would look like, with an increase in the people's devotion, and the likelihood that a parliament would be called. In such circumstances, Pole wanted the pope to be willing to give him further advice and rulings, on matters such as how to approach the prospect of a general council, and how to deal with 'Lutherans', by which he presumably meant the likes of Bishops Cranmer, Ridley and Latimer, as well as Thomas Cromwell. He also wanted detailed instructions on how to reconcile clergy, and legitimate the activities of the English Church during the time of schism, together with particulars of which matters would be reserved for decision in Rome. As for the 'Pilgrims', he proposed that they should be sent a papal representative, that is himself, who knew Paul III's mind, and who would help them and their cause with action as well as words. This was more than a hint that military intervention, by Catholic powers and with papal approval, was being contemplated. Such a legate would have to have financial resources, in order to assist the opponents of Henry's religious policies, and Pole named the Fuggers and Welzers as bankers who might supply such funds. Although there was not yet a full awareness in Rome that the rebel cause was already, in effect, lost by the beginning of 1537, Pole knew his old friend and master well enough to be certain that Henry's apparent concessions to the rebels, and declared willingness to negotiate with them, were likely to prove both cynical and false. The pope's money would thus be available to the 'Pilgrims' for further resistance, once they saw their king for what he was.

Pole was duly appointed as legate to England in a secret consistory, on 7 February 1537, and a week later the pope wrote to him with the necessary instructions, naming him, a famous Englishman, as his 'angel of peace', who would restore the faithful English to their traditional faith, and prepare the ground for a general council of the Church, and united Christian action against the Turks.[78] Pole acted almost immediately, writing two letters on 16 February, one to Thomas Cromwell and the other to Henry's council. Having fought in Italy, in the service of Louis XII of France, at the beginning of the century, Cromwell presented himself as an expert 'italianate', as well as the king's chief minister.[79] On this occasion, Pole's communication with him was purportedly a response to the secretary's letter to him, dated 20 January, and reflected the personal bitterness that had developed between them.[80] The new legate accused Cromwell of attacking him in a manner that was both violent and lacking in substance. He declared that he would not have replied to his letter if Cromwell had not tried to suborn his servant and messenger, Michael Throckmorton, into

---

[78]   *CT* 4 no. 46; *CRP* 1 no. 151 (14 February 1537).

[79]   Howard Lethead, 'Cromwell, Thomas', in *ODNB*; Susan Brigden, *Sir Thomas Wyatt: The heart's forest* (London: Faber & Faber, 2012), pp. 120–121, 211–212.

[80]   TNA SP1/240 fols 266r–267v; *LP* Addenda I (ii) no. 1195; *CRP* 1 no. 154.

speaking on the secretary's behalf. Returning to *De unitate*, Pole asserted that his text was absolutely clear and could not, as Cromwell had apparently suggested, be interpreted according to the whim of the reader. He would not publish it, as Cromwell suggested, but was happy for his adversary to do so, though he saw no possibility of reconciliation between them, if they continued to communicate only in writing. Pole also referred to a letter that he had received from Henry's council, signed by Cromwell, which intriguingly stated that if the cardinal came to Flanders as a private individual, the king would send a team of learned men to negotiate a religious settlement with him. Pole thought that such a manoeuvre was pointless, but declared that he was still willing to discuss these matters with Cromwell in person, since both men claimed to be defending the king's honour.

In his letter of the same date to Henry's council, Pole undertook to explain further his tract *De unitate* and his acceptance of the cardinalate, both of which had, much to his regret, greatly offended the king and his advisers.[81] He saw it as his duty to justify himself fully to Henry, who had supported him since childhood, but also raised the question of his own conscience which, in the difficult circumstances of the 1530s, was becoming separated, in his case and that of others, such as Thomas More, from the traditionally overriding duty of loyalty and obedience to one's sovereign. He could have set out to please the king, but instead felt it necessary to warn him of the dangers into which his course of action, over his first wife Catherine and the Church, was leading him. He solemnly declared that he had wished the contents of *De unitate* to be as unique and secret to Henry as any dealing between confessor and penitent, with the former trying to make the latter fully aware of his offences. Since completing the tract, he had spent months in Rome, being daily in the pope's presence, without acceding to Paul's repeated requests to let him see it. As he would on so many subsequent occasions, Pole went back over his own career in the royal service, as a student and ambassador, appealing personally to the duke of Norfolk to confirm that, back in 1530, he had often been asked about the replacement of Wolsey as archbishop of York, and might have been appointed to that post himself. Whatever he may have thought at the time, Pole now affirmed that he could not have accepted nomination to York without dishonouring the king, since he by then disagreed with Henry's religious policies and his desire to divorce Catherine. The account which follows here of the outcome of Pole's dilemma over York has, since soon after his death in 1558, become part of the accepted account of his life. He tells Norfolk, and the rest of the Council, that when he went to see the king, at Henry's request, perhaps towards the end of 1530, he had it in his mind, as a result of the persuasion of his family and friends, and particularly of his brother Henry, to accept the archbishopric.

---

[81]    TNA SP 1/116, fols 54r–61v; *ERP* 1 pp. 179–187; *LP* XII (i) no. 444; *CRP* 1 no. 155 (with further textual details).

The king had, most unusually, come himself to welcome him at the door of the chamber, but, at that moment, Pole suddenly changed his mind and found the idea of York abhorrent, something which he put down, by 1537, to the action of God and his own conscience. Henry was greatly displeased, but Pole did not regret his decision [Appendix 2A]. As for his move to Rome, and his becoming a cardinal, Pole asserted, not a little disingenuously, that his actions should in no way be seen as injurious to the king. Pope Paul might be the king's enemy, but that did not mean that he or the other cardinals were his enemies too:

> In this my lords I may say whatsoever other popes have been I will not affirm, but touching the pope that made me cardinal, whose deeds I see daily and other hear his sayings both of the king and the realm, that howsoever he hath been sore irritated as you know best yourself, yet surely I could not perceive that ever the pope did show other mind toward the king than the most tender and indulgent father would against his only son that had offended, and ever is ready to show like affect, and in this I that am daily present, and see how the matter go, and of our country, am better to be believed than any other.[82]

Pole then went on to the question of what was then expected to be an imminent general council, for the purposes of which, he told Henry's councillors, he had first been summoned to Rome. He took a robust line on the question of England's participation in such an assembly:

> In my opinion there can come no greater dishonor to no Christian nation than being denounced [in] a council general of the Christian flock, if there should be any nation that either should be excluded from thence by other or else that would utterly exclude themselves, which I cannot well tell whether [it] were more shame. And surely such a shame that if there remain any sparkle in our nation of this ancient honor, they [the English] least of all other should abide the same, for this they have been wont to appear in general councils with as great honor as in any other. And I remember to read that at the council of Konstanz when the English nation should not have been called as a nation of themselves unto the council, that there was nothing that they took more grievous ... [and] that they brought to pass to be counted for an especial nation and principally to be called.[83]

Pole alludes here to a clash at the opening of the Council of Constance, which was called to that Swiss town in 1414, with the aim of ending the 'great schism' of the Western papacy (1378–1415). England, representing the British Isles, and Castile, on behalf of all the Iberian kingdoms, fought for inclusion as separate

---

[82]  TNA SP 1/116 fol. 59r–v, transcribed in *CRP* 1 no. 155.
[83]  TNA SP 1/116 fols 59v–60r; *CRP* 1 no. 155 (with further textual details).

'nations', which both in the event achieved.[84] It may seem ironical that Pole, in defending the unity of the Church of his own day, under the pope, should have alluded to one of the less glorious episodes in the history of the bishopric of Rome when, between 1409 and 1414, three men claimed to be pope at the same time. In any case, thinking of 1537 and not of the fifteenth century, Pole affirmed that he had only accepted the offer of a cardinal's hat in order to further the interests of England. If this were not so, he roundly declared, 'let me never be admitted to heaven'.[85] However, in accordance with his instructions from Paul III, he set up a smokescreen of plausible reasons for his legation, which did not, of course, include helping the English rebels and overthrowing King Henry. The pope, he said, was worried about three important matters, these being warfare between Christian princes, the increase of heresy in western and central Europe, and the threat of the Ottoman Turks. It was for all these reasons that Pope Paul had named him *legatum ultramontanum a latere*, in order to work for peace between rulers north of the Alps, to eliminate heresy, and to resist the encroachments of the Turks. He did, nonetheless, allude, in a highly diplomatic and euphemistic way, to his own special concern for his native land, hoping that he would not prove to be, as Jesus had suggested, a prophet without honour in his own country and among his own people (Matthew 13:57; Mark 6:4; John 4:44).

In accordance with the apparent urgency of his communications with England in February, Pole left Rome two days later, on 18 February 1537. On 15 February, Paul III had written to the archbishop of Liège, Erard de la Marck, who would later play an important part in Pole's legation, to inform him of his appointment, which had been made 'in order to assist the faith and piety of the people of England, and to keep them in the true religion'.[86] Pole had been given Church funds for his mission, but if he asked for any more, La Marck was to supply them. The legate himself, while at Bologna on 27 February, wrote to another crucial person in the enterprise, the papal nuncio in Paris, Rodolfo Pio da Carpi. Pio had been active for some time in the papal cause against Henry, threatening him with renewed papal censure, including excommunication, if he did not accept the demands of the Pilgrims of Grace, and restore the Catholic order of the English Church.[87] Back in mid-January, Pio had urged the pope to send Pole at least as far as the French frontier, since the legate had the capacity to 'again inflame these good people [presumably the English traditionalists] better than any other, and use the censures, like arms of your Holiness, on their behalf'.[88] Now en route for France, Pole wrote to Pio, not only as a vital papal

---

[84]   *ODCC*, pp. 403–404 for a brief general description of this council and its significance.
[85]   TNA SP 1/116 fol. 60r; *CRP* 1 no. 155.
[86]   *CRP* 1 no. 153 (with further textual details).
[87]   *LP* XII (i) no. 34.
[88]   *LP* XII (i) no. 165.

agent and supporter of his English mission, but as a friend and fellow enthusiast for Catholic reform. Both were more concerned with 'sincerity of spirit' than the 'superficial duties of the court', but now Pole was writing to say that, before he left Rome, his messenger, Michael Throckmorton, had delivered to him letters from Henry and his council. He had written replies before leaving, and now sent them on to Pio, so that he could forward them to their destination, through either the English ambassadors in Paris or the French ambassadors in London. He also attached copies of these letters for Pio to distribute in England, since there was no guarantee that the English authorities would let their contents be known to the public. Pole concluded this dispatch by expressing his complete confidence in the nuncio, and the hope that he had already informed Francis I of his own legation.[89]

Pole's correspondence chronicles his course out of Italy. He was in Piacenza on 4 March and at Asti four days later, at Chieri on the 9th, and eventually in Lyon on 23/4 March.[90] A letter that he wrote from Lyon to his old friend Gasparo Contarini suggests that his progress may in part have been slowed by financial difficulties, somewhat reminiscent of his student days in Italy. He had underestimated the costs, and now needed urgent financial help from the pope, having spent the 500 gold ducats that he had brought with him. He was too embarrassed to ask Paul directly, because of his generosity in the past, and therefore wanted Contarini to intercede for him. He had also asked another old friend, Alvise Priuli, to write to the pope on his behalf.[91] On 31 March, he duly received a letter from Pope Paul, who now recognised the likely need for military force to be used against Henry VIII, and starkly expressed the view that it was better for the king's supporters to die than that he should lead them to hell by means of heresy and schism. He left the choice of action to Pole, prayed that those who might properly use weapons should do so in protection of the Christian faithful, and authorised the issue of a crusading indulgence or jubilee (a special indulgence for visiting Rome) to all who fought for the cause.[92] At this time, Charles V's ambassadors in Rome had a clear understanding that Pole had been made a cardinal specifically to bring about the 'reduction' of England to the Roman obedience, and reported to their master that Paul III had sent him north with a bill of exchange for 10,000 ducats, to be spent on hiring arquebusiers and for any other military necessity related to England.[93]

---

[89]   *CRP* 1 no. 161 (with further textual details).

[90]   *CRP* 1 nos 164 (*ERP* 2 no. 15b; *CSP Ven*, V, no. 140; *LP* XII (i) no. 255), 165 (Parks, 'Parma letters', p. 300), 166 (reference only), 167 (Parks, 'Parma letters', p. 300), 168 (*ERP* 2 no. 15b; *CSP Ven*, V, no. 141; *LP* XII (i) no. 721).

[91]   *CRP* 1 no. 168.

[92]   BL Add. 2096; *LP* XII (i) no. 779; *CRP* 1 no. 169.

[93]   *CSP Span* V (ii) nos 128, 134.

On his long journey from Rome to Paris, Pole had had the company of his old friend Gianmatteo Giberti, bishop of Verona, who had connections with England, but the day after their arrival in the French capital, on 10 April, they split forces, with Giberti going on to Amiens, where he stayed for more than 10 days. Meanwhile Pole himself wrote a letter to Francis I, dated 10 April, in which he said that he had been well received on his journey through France.[94] He had come there to do good to his homeland, and had debated over whether to travel through Francis's kingdom or Imperial Germany, before deciding that the French route, though longer, would be more enjoyable. He acknowledged receipt, that morning, of his credentials to the French court, which had been brought to him by Monsieur de Matignon, who had also, however, told him that he would have to leave at once, because Henry VIII had asked his brother monarch not to receive him, just as he had forbidden Giberti to carry out papal instructions in Amiens. In this letter Pole acknowledged, nonetheless, that Francis was in fact supportive of him and his mission, but announced that he would be leaving shortly for Cambrai, to save the king embarrassment.

Henry had a resident ambassador in Paris, this being Stephen Gardiner, bishop of Winchester. It might have been expected that he would take the main responsibility for obstructing Pole's mission, but his conduct during the legate's brief stay in France was hesitant, not to say contradictory to his king's intentions, which were that Pole should be arrested as a traitor. Not only this, but Gardiner also failed to communicate properly with his newly-appointed opposite number in Brussels, John Hutton.[95] Far from working to thwart Pole's plans, the bishop of Winchester did a deal with Francis I, whereby the legate was expelled from France, rather than being arrested and handed over to the English, at Calais.[96] Also involved in this setback for Henry's diplomacy was one of the gentlemen of his privy chamber, Sir Francis Bryan, who earlier in the year had been dispatched to join Gardiner.[97] He was in Paris when Pole arrived, as was another of Henry's gentlemen, the distinguished poet Sir Thomas Wyatt, who was on his way to Spain as a special envoy to Charles V. According to Wyatt, Pole was naturally, and despite his diplomatic exterior, furious at his rebuff from the French king. He deeply resented being called a traitor, and recognised that his life was threatened.[98] Bryan had been sent to France with a special mission from Henry, and Pole was sure that it was to persuade Francis to have the legate arrested and delivered to

---

[94]   *CRP* 1 no. 171 (with further textual details).

[95]   *LP* XII (i) nos 865, 817.

[96]   *LP* XIII (ii) nos 830, 804; *CPEC*, VII, p. 312.

[97]   Susan Brigden, '"The shadow that you know": Sir Thomas Wyatt and Sir Francis Bryan at court and in embassy', *Hisorical Journal*, 39 (1996), pp. 1–31, at p. 8.

[98]   ASV SS, Principi, 12, fols 27v–29, cited in C. Höllger, 'Reginald Pole and the legations of 1537 and 1539: diplomatic and political responses to the break with Rome', University of Oxford D.Phil. thesis, 1989, p. 40.

his English master. This was not only a mortal threat to Pole, but would be an outrage to the international diplomatic customs of the day.[99] On 15 April 1537, Pio da Carpi reported from Paris to Pope Paul the arrival of Wyatt and Bryan, and clearly understood that their plan was to apprehend Pole, and take him to English territory in Calais, whether dead or alive. In addition, the king had sent to France one of the gentlemen of his privy chamber, with orders to keep Pole under surveillance, in order that he might be kidnapped. By 21 April, Henry's scheme was widely known in the French court, but Stephen Gardiner was not the only servant of the English king who was guilty of vacillation at this time.[100] It appears that both he and Bryan were secretly sympathetic to Pole and the Catholic cause. As noted earlier, Henry and Cromwell had initially offered Pole a conference in Flanders, and, according to Sir John Hussey, who had negotiated with the Lincolnshire 'Pilgrims' in the early stages of the 1536 rebellion, and had until recently had charge over Henry's daughter Mary, reported that Henry was dithering over whether or not to deprive the legate of his English benefices.[101] Up to this time, Pole was still in touch with some of his existing contacts in Henry's court, including Sir Thomas Wriothesley, Bishops Cuthbert Tunstall and John Stokesley, and also, probably, Archbishop Cranmer.[102]

Pole's arrival in Paris, followed by his move into Imperial territory, in mid-April 1537, clearly showed the English that his intentions were not peaceful, and he might indeed, as a consequence, have suffered a much more severe fate than exile from France.[103] Before he reached the comparative safety of Cambrai, he was already aware that Francis Bryan and Peter Mewtas had been sent by Henry and Cromwell to kill him.[104] Back in England, his family also knew of the threat. Wyatt's role in Paris, in mid-April 1537, was ambiguous. Although he and Pole never met, they secretly exchanged messages through servants. Wyatt sent John Mason to see him at Saint-Denis and, according to Edmund Bonner, who also represented Henry in Paris at this time, Pole attempted to send Wyatt a gift of wine, though he refused to accept it.[105] The wine was brought to Pole by one of his own servants, Michael Throckmorton, whom Thomas Cromwell wrongly thought to have turned into a double agent.[106] There is no doubt that Pole's fears were well-founded. Henry himself is recorded as having stated, on 25

---

[99] BL Add. 25114, fol. 255; *LP* XII (i) nos 865, 988.

[100] *LP* XII (i) nos 949, 953.

[101] *LP* XII (i) no. 475.

[102] *LP* XII (i) no. 475; MacCulloch, *Thomas Cranmer*, p. 47.

[103] *CRP* 1 no. 177 (7 May 1537: Parks, 'Parma letters', p. 300).

[104] *LP* XIII (ii) nos 795, 797.

[105] TNA SP1/137, fol. 203; *LP* XIII (ii) no. 65.

[106] On Michael Throckmorton, see Overell, 'Cardinal Pole's special agent', pp. 265–278, and 'An English friendship and Italian reform: Edward Morrison and Michael Throckmorton, 1532–1538', *Journal of Ecclesiastical History*, 57 (2006), pp. 478–498.

April 1537, that: 'We will that you, Sir Francis Bryan, shall secretly appoint such fellows for the enterprise of his apprehension'. The Cardinal was to be 'trussed up and conveyed to Calais', in order to be repatriated for trial, and probably death.[107]

On 27 April, Pole wrote from Cambrai to Cardinal Archbishop Erard de la Marck, of Liège, once again having travelled slowly, this time in order to reach Charles V's lands.[108] He entered the diocese of Cambrai, on 16 April, and was received in the wood at Héraumont by the bishop, Robert de Croy, and other dignitaries. On the Imperial side of the border, he was welcomed for his overt and published purpose, which was to bring about peace between France and the Empire. Even so, he had had a hard time gaining admission to Habsburg territory, and it is uncertain what would have happened if he had not eventually gained success by writing to Archbishop Erard, who was chief councillor to the regent of the Netherlands, Charles's sister Mary, widow of the king of Hungary. Pole told Erard that, on the previous day, 26 April, he had sent an unnamed member of his inner circle, together with one of the bishop of Cambrai's men, to Brussels with a message to the regent. But these envoys had been stopped by the governor of Valenciennes, who refused to allow Pole's man to go further until he had checked with Mary and her government. Pole believed that the governor was acting on the regent's orders, since his own brother, the bishop of Cambrai, had assured him of the legate's good character. Now Pole asked the cardinal of Liège to give assistance. He said that his legation had been arranged in full consultation with the Imperial ambassadors in Rome, the count of Cifuentes and Dr Pedro Oriz, who had insisted that he travel to Flanders through France, though Pole himself had not wanted this. The original plan, agreed with the pope, had been for everything to be prepared in Brussels to receive him and his companion, Bishop Giberti, who would deal with the Habsburgs while he occupied himself with England. In France, Giberti had had an interview with Francis, and Pole had at least been allowed to leave the kingdom alive, but he had expected a much better reception in Imperial territory and asked urgently for Erard's help.

Before he left France, Pole's life had indeed been threatened, at least at the level of intention, by several of King Henry's agents, although the English diplomats then stationed in Paris were apparently more sympathetic to him. One source of danger was the special envoy from King Henry and Thomas Cromwell, Sir Francis Bryan. He had been at court in England since 1514, and had once been a strong supporter of Anne Boleyn. Both he and his fellow envoy Sir Thomas Wyatt had been under suspicion at the time of Anne's trial in 1536, being confined for a while in the Tower of London, and although Bryan was

---

[107]    BL Add. 25114, fol. 263 = *LP* XII (i) no. 1032. For the threats to Pole in 1537, see also Brigden, *Thomas Wyatt*, pp. 328–332.
[108]    *ERP* 2 no. 18; *CSP Ven*, V, no. 143; *LP* XII (i) no. 1052; *CRP* 1 no. 173.

rehabilitated before her execution, his loyalty had subsequently been tested by the king when he was placed in the vanguard of the royal army against the Pilgrims of Grace.[109] In 1536, he was also regarded as sympathetic to Princess, or 'the Lady' Mary, at the time of her submission to her father, and there was some surprise when he and Wyatt were entrusted with delicate diplomatic missions to France and the Empire.[110] In the event, while Wyatt's job, until he left for Spain, was to keep an eye on Stephen Gardiner, Bryan's task was to prevent Pole from being seen by Francis I. Not only this, he was 'by some means' to have the legate 'trussed up and conveyed to Calais'.[111] In addition, Cromwell sent to Paris, from Calais, his agent Peter Mewtas, and announced openly at the English court that the two had been sent 'to kyll hym [Pole] with a hangoone [hand-gun] or oth[erwise as] they should see best'.[112] The plan was evidently unsuccessful, but it could be said that Pole escaped to Cambrai, rather than going there in the normal way. His struggle to be accepted by the Habsburgs, and perhaps even obtain help against Henry, is more or less decipherable from his own surviving correspondence over the late spring and summer of 1537.

On 28 April, Pole wrote from Cambrai to the nuncio Pio del Carpi, saying that he had been forced out of France and regretted not having had a chance to talk to him in person.[113] Giberti had been able to speak to Pio, and he himself had received advice from him, through his servant Francesco, but that had only made him want even more to see his old friend. Giving an account of his travels so far, Pole said that he had been very well received on his journey through France, and that he acknowledged that the French king had had no choice but to expel him from his kingdom. Before he left Rome, Francis's ambassador there, Hémart de Denonville, had assured him, and Pope Paul, that he would be most welcome in France, but the French king's alliance with Henry had prevented Pole from entering the royal palace. As a result, the legate of the vicar of Christ had been placed in danger from the enemy, and Pole was not going to understate the indignity of this, or the importance of his own mission, which he compared to that of the apostles in the New Testament. Surely he could have done nothing better than seek peace and a general council, and the English should have seen that he was acting in their interest too. If Henry and his kingdom responded positively to his mission, there would be no more need for sedition in England, and the country would be restored to its traditional position as a loyal Catholic power. Using the Pauline imagery of the human body (1 Corinthians 12:12–26), which was so beloved of the political theorists of the period, Pole identified the

---

[109]  *LP* X no. 908; Brigden, 'The shadow', pp. 3–4.
[110]  *LP* XI nos 1079, 1103, 1196; Brigden, 'The shadow', pp. 4–5, 8.
[111]  BL Add. MS 25114 fol. 263; *LP* XII (i) no. 1032.
[112]  SP 1/138 fols 199v-200; *LP* XII (i) no. 797.
[113]  *ERP* 2 no. 17; *CSP Ven*, V, no. 143; *LP* XII (i) no. 988; *CRP* 1 no. 174.

problems of England as originating in the head, that is the king. As in *De unitate* [Appendix 1B], he described his native land, under Henry's rule, as a medical patient who was suffering from a disease for which the two possible remedies were surgery and an improved diet. Pole had adopted the gentler, dietary method. Thus he had intended to ask Francis to intercede for him with Henry, and saw the Pilgrimage of Grace, which had initially threatened a return to the old 'surgical' remedy of civil war, as an ideal occasion for the French king to take action. England was now peaceful again, but would not remain so if Henry continued on his current path. Both his own companion, Giberti, and Francis had had good relations with the English king in the past, and Giberti would have conducted any negotiations for reconciliation, as Pole himself was now regarded by Henry as a traitor. The legate wanted to be able to justify his conduct to the world, but in the meantime offered Pio his analysis of the English political scene. He blamed Henry's councillors for leading him astray, arguing that his beloved king would otherwise never have treated Fisher and More as he did. For Pole, these councillors were the real traitors, behaving like thieves in their treatment of him as legate. The tone throughout this letter is one of moral indignation, together with a firm resolve to continue the mission.

Four days later, Pole wrote to Cromwell himself, with the intention of clarifying, once and for all, his attitude to Henry. Referring, no doubt, to the efforts of Bryan and Mewtas in Paris, he asserted that no Christian ruler had ever treated a papal legate in such a manner before. Pole had not previously realised that his king was prepared to flout divine and natural law, in order to capture him. Not for the last time, Pole presented himself as a victim of unjust persecution, saying that, when he learned of Henry's plans for his capture or murder, he had told his household that he now saw himself, for the first time, as a true cardinal of the Church. Even under pre-Christian natural law (*ius gentium*), what Henry was planning would have been an outrage, and in the circumstances he would have been perfectly within his rights to sever all communication with the king, and even to seek revenge on him. Giberti had tried to talk to both Gardiner and Bryan, but had not managed to do so. Nevertheless, he would be able, if he were to be allowed into England, to give Cromwell and his master a full account of all Pole's doings since his return to Italy. He would be able to demonstrate that Pole was a loyal English subject. For one thing, Pole claimed to have helped Henry's interests forward in Rome, at the beginning of the Pilgrimage of Grace, by preventing the sending of papal censures, as well as keeping his *De unitate* from the pope's eyes.[114]

While in Cambrai, Pole also kept Rome informed of his progress, or lack of it. On 7 May he wrote a letter to Paul III's secretary, Ambrosio Ricalcato, in which, as well as reporting his frustrations in Paris, he said that he had sent

---

[114]    Strype, 1, pt 2, pp. 326–332; *LP* XII (i) no. 1123; *CRP* 1 no. 176.

a messenger to Brussels, with a letter under plain cover to a Spanish courtier there, the marquis of Aguilar.[115] Mary of Hungary was upset by the delay in admitting Pole to Habsburg territory, the initiative for the hold-up having come from her brother Charles in Spain. Pole was trying to make further moves by means of letters to an archdeacon in Cambrai diocese and to Archbishop Erard, both containing copies of his instructions from the pope. Pole alluded to the fact that Paul was now expressing a wish that he should abandon the legation, but he said that he had no intention of giving up, and asked for more funds to continue his mission. To abandon it now would be to send a message to Henry that he was under no threat, but Pole was worried that the Imperial ambassadors, the count of Cifuentes and Dr Pedro Ortiz, were now acting against him in the Roman Curia. The instruction to the archdeacon, Jérôme Joseph, referred to above and also dated 7 May, was for him to go to Brussels to see Mary of Hungary, the cardinal of Liège, and other councillors, to persuade them to allow him into their territory. Pole understood, from Imperial servants who had obstructed his entry, that Mary was acting on orders from her brother, who was anxious not to jeopardise his relations with Henry, and for that purpose had even urged Francis to hand Pole over to English agents. In these circumstances, it is hardly surprising that Pole stressed to the archdeacon the divine sanction for his mission. He wished Henry and England no harm, but had his sacred duty to perform. He was indignant at the emperor's attitude, since his agents in Rome had worked hard to have him made a cardinal. Around the turn of the year 1537, both he and the pope had thought that the circumstances in England made such a preferment inopportune, but while the relevant consistory was actually meeting, the count of Cifuentes had taken the extraordinary and irregular step of entering the session with a communication from his ambassadorial colleague in London, Eustace Chapuys, to the effect that all the good people in England wanted Pole to be made a cardinal and a legate. As a result, the pope changed his mind and the election took place. It is clear from this letter that Pole was now thoroughly disillusioned with Charles, who was being even more obstructive than Francis had been, and the legate was putting his hopes in the forthcoming general council.[116]

By 29 May, Pole had at last reached Liège, having left Cambrai on the 20th, escorted by various local dignitaries, but also monitored by a spy working for John Hutton, the English ambassador in Brussels. According to his report to De la Marck in Brussels, Pole was welcomed into Liège on 27 May, Trinity Sunday, or perhaps a few days later, by the archbishop's secretary, but the move, though it possibly made him safer, brought him no nearer to a reception in Brussels itself.[117]

---

[115]  Parks, 'Parma letters', p. 300; *CRP* 1 no. 177.
[116]  *CRP* 1 no. 178 (with further textual details).
[117]  *ERP* 2 no. 18; *CSP Ven*, V, no. 145; *CRP* 1 no. 184.

The legate remained in one of Archbishop Erard's houses in Liège until the latter part of August, still engaging in correspondence with England and Rome. On 29 May, he wrote to Thomas Cromwell, protesting at English obstruction of his attempts to communicate with London.[118] During June 1537, Pole, ever more frustrated by his inability to act effectively, kept in touch with Rome, by means of letters to Paul III, his secretary Ambrogio Ricalcato, and Cardinal Gasparo Contarini.[119] On 30 June, Contarini replied to him from there, expressing the pope's regret at his problems in the Low Countries and offering to send him more funds. Yet, although there had been much discussion in Rome of the English situation, Contarini felt that Pole's legation might soon be downgraded in importance because Paul III was raising money for a large army to oppose the Turks.[120] Another letter to Pole, sent at about that time by Ricalcato, alluded to the earl of Kildare, a young Irish peer who was on the Continent and opposed Henry's religious policies, but never achieved anything against them. The earl was to be placed under papal protection.[121] Also on 30 June, the college of cardinals wrote to thank Pole for his efforts, and in a separate letter the pope finally recalled him to Rome. He had done his best, but the mission seemed hopeless, in the prevailing circumstances.[122]

Once again, Pole moved slowly in response to the pope's instruction, and before his eventual departure, he received an intriguing letter from John Helyar, who was chaplain to Pole's mother Margaret, as well as rector of Warblington in Hampshire, and was then in Leuven/Louvain.[123] Welcoming Pole's presence in the Netherlands, Helyar gave a gloomy account of the state of the English Church, after the defeat of the Pilgrimage of Grace. The 'hireling shepherds' of Henry's Church, like those whom Jesus had criticised for heir disloyalty (John 10:12–13), had poisoned the faithful sheep, and Henry's army, which had killed rebels, had not acted according to God's will. Most people in England knew that Pole had become a cardinal and a legate. Many nobles and clergy greatly admired him, and if he could reach England he would have plenty of support among the people. In the meantime, the whole of Christendom should pray for England, and its prayers would be as effective as those of the Christians in the

---

[118]    TNA SP1/120 fol. 231r–v; *LP* XII (i) no. 1302; *CRP* 1 no. 185.

[119]    *CRP* 1 nos 186 (*ERP* 2 no. 21; *CSP Ven*, V, no. 149; *LP* XII (ii) no. 71), 187 (*ERP* 2 no. 24: *CSP Ven*, V, no. 150; *LP* XII (ii) no. 73), 188 (further textual details), 189 (*ERP* 2 no. 25; *LP* XII (ii) no. 169).

[120]    *ERP* 2 no. 26; *LP* XII (ii) no. 176; *CRP* 1 no. 190.

[121]    BAV Vat. lat. 5967, fol. 313r; *CRP* 1 no. 191.

[122]    *CRP* 1 nos 192 (*ERP* 2 no. 23; *LP* XII (ii) no. 175), 193 (*ERP* 2, p. cclxxiii; *LP* XII (ii) no. 174).

[123]    *ERP* 2 no. 29 (inaccurate); *LP* XII (ii) no. 310 (2); *CRP* 1 no. 195a. The writer of this letter was identified in Herbert Thurston, 'The first Englishman to make the Spiritual Exercises', *The Month*, 142 (1923), pp. 336–347, at pp. 346–347.

Acts of the Apostles (12:5–11) who prayed successfully for the apostle Peter to be released from Herod's prison by an angel. After giving a scathing account of Henry and his religious advisers, Helyar wrote that he was sure Pole could refute the heretics, and recommended that he should have a book produced on the subject, which could be placed in the hands of the faithful English population. Pole would never write such a treatise.

During July 1537, the legate slowly began to prepare for his departure from Liège, where he felt relatively safe, and for his return to Rome. According to a letter that he wrote to Contarini, on 21 July, he still deeply mistrusted the emperor and his agents. He had been told of a safe-conduct from Charles's brother Ferdinand, king of the Romans, to pass through Germany, but was unwilling to trust even that, relying only on God.[124] In the last week of July, Pole wrote to the pope, with an undertaking to return to Italy with the minimum of delay, but in August he was still in Liège, telling Contarini, on the 10th, that he was not going to leave until his friend Bishop Giberti returned from a trip to Italy.[125] On 21 August, arrangements for the legate's journey were still in the hands of Giberti and Erard de la Marck, but on the following day, after a delay of about six weeks, he finally left Liège, taking several more weeks to reach Rome.[126] After all this time, Henry's ambassador in Brussels, John Hutton, was surprised, given Pole's reputation for dithering, to learn after the event of his departure to Italy. The delay resulted in part from the efforts of the exiled Observant Franciscan, William Peto, to cover Pole's tracks.[127] The English cardinal's first legation to his homeland was temporarily in abeyance, but it would not be long before he was again active on the European scene.

In 1538, there was yet another realignment of European politics. After years of conflict with Charles V, Francis I decided to be more conciliatory. He did so apparently under the influence of the Constable of France, Anne de Montmorency, who now took such a major role in the conduct of foreign policy that diplomats normally communicated with him directly, as well as with the king. Once again, control of the duchy of Milan was the main bone of contention between France and the Habsburgs. Montmorency wanted a peaceful solution, but one negotiated from a position of strength, and to that end he planned to consolidate French control over the neighbouring Italian borderlands of Piedmont and Savoy, giving each its own French-style high court (*parlement*) and treasury (*chambre des comptes*), while fortifying the Piedmontese capital, Turin. On the northern frontier, between France

---

[124] *ERP* 2 no. 28; *CSP Ven*, V, no. 153; *LP* XII (ii) no. 310; *CRP* 1 no. 196.

[125] *CRP* 1 nos 198 (further textual details), 199 (*ERP* 2 no. 31; *CSP Ven*, V, no. 655; *LP* XII (ii) no. 499).

[126] *CRP* 1 nos 200 (12 August 1537; *ERP* 2 no. 32; *LP* XII (ii) no. 510), 204 (21 August 1537; *ERP* 2 no. 36; *CSP Ven*, V, no. 156; *LP* XII (ii) no. 559).

[127] Mayer, *CRP* 1, pp. 177–178.

and Flanders, attention was paid to the fortifications of towns in Picardy and Champagne, to protect against any violation of the current truce by Charles V's forces.[128] In December 1537, anxious to keep European peace, in order to allow for the long-delayed general council of the Church and a crusade against the Turks, in December 1537 Paul III had sent new legates to Francis in Paris and Charles in Spain: thus the former nuncio, Rodolfo Pio, returned to Paris, while Pole was to go to the Emperor in Spain. These developments worried Henry VIII very much, as he continued to see peace between France and the Empire as a threat to English influence, and, given Pole's activity in the previous year, even to his own continuing rule. Therefore in January 1538 he sent Sir Francis Bryan back to Paris, partly to inquire after his king's unpaid 'pension' from Francis I and partly to find out what was going on politically.[129] On 14 February, the French ambassador in London, Louis du Perrau, Sieur de Castillon, reported to Montmorency that Henry was still hoping to provide the balance between the two major powers.[130] Earlier, the English king had agreed that Francis could suspend the payment of the pension, but only on condition that he did not make a separate peace with the emperor. However, when Bryan arrived in Paris, he discovered that the truce between Francis and Charles had indeed been extended without Henry being consulted. Nevertheless, at that time Sir Thomas Wyatt, who was still representing Henry at the Imperial Court in Spain, reported that the fate of Milan remained an issue between Charles and Francis, though the Emperor had suggested that either Henry or Pope Paul III might provide mediation over this issue.[131] In an account of the latest news received from England, and dated 19 February, Charles's secretary, Francisco de los Cobos, and his leading councillor, Nicholas Perrenot de Granvelle of Arras, reported that there was indeed still Imperial interest in English mediation with France. Nevertheless, the peace terms that the French had offered via Bishop Stephen Gardiner, who was still a resident ambassador in Paris, had been rejected, presumably because they did not give satisfaction over Milan. Despite this, another document, undated but apparently written at about this time, confirms that Charles was, at least in principle, supportive of the efforts of Paul's legates, Pio to France and Pole to himself.[132]

Eventually, between 15 May and 20 June 1538, a conference was held on relatively neutral territory, in the duchy of Savoy at Nice, between Charles, Francis and Pope Paul, but the path to this encounter was neither easy nor straightforward. On 8 February, yet another 'Holy League' had been formed

---

128    Knecht, *Renaissance warrior*, p. 385.
129    Brigden, 'The shadow', p. 13.
130    *LP* XIII (i) no. 274.
131    *LP* XIII (i) nos 273, 279; *LP* XIV 33; Brigden, 'The shadow', p. 13.
132    AGS E 806–59, 63.

between the pope, Ferdinand, king of the Romans, and Venice. Its ostensible intention was to confront the Turks, this being a major issue for the Venetians, but Francis took the alliance to be directed at him and protested to Pio. He was also worried and offended that Paul III was apparently planning to marry his own grandson, Guidantonio Sforza, to Ferdinand's daughter, which he saw as a move to compromise the pope's neutrality in favour of the Habsburgs. Charles, on the other hand, insisted on meeting Paul at Nice, and Francis eventually agreed, reluctantly, to go there.[133] Pole himself left Rome for Nice, unusually with Pope Paul in person, on 4 April, but before that, on 21 March, he wrote to Camillo Orsini, who had been appointed as a papal envoy to Francis, with the mission of persuading him to attend the conference.[134] In his most exalted and lyrical mode of letter-writing, Pole compared Orsini, in his efforts to bring Francis I on side, to St Paul writing to the church at Corinth, about the spirit and the flesh, spiritual childhood and spiritual maturity (1 Corinthians 3:1–3). Pole evidently believed that Orsini was showing this kind of spiritual depth.

When Pole and the pope finally reached Nice, after nearly two months' travel, they had to lodge, not in the citadel, which the duke of Savoy refused to make available, but with the Observant Franciscans of Cimiez. The heat was excessive and the water and wine were bad. Diplomats naturally complained, including Wyatt, who later wrote that he had 'trotted continually up and down that hell, through heat and stink'.[135] There is no trace of Pole's presence during the interviews that were held between Francis, the pope and Charles, but Pole's later biographer, Ludovico Beccadelli, who was at Nice in Cardinal Contarini's entourage, said that the emperor did ask about the legate, and had a conversation with him at nearby Villefranche-sur-mer (Villafranca), where he was staying during the conference, off-shore on one of his own galleys.[136] Pope Paul, on the other hand, met Charles four times, and Francis twice. At his first meeting with the pope, on 2 June, the 'Most Christian King' of France promised him total obedience, but refused to meet the emperor in his presence, and also declined to give him and the League any assistance against the Ottomans, unless Milan was restored to him first. A week later, Paul offered a new peace plan, in which the daughter of Ferdinand, king of the Romans, would marry Henry, duke of Orléans, and after an interval of three years the couple would be granted the duchy of Milan, which would be held in trust, in the meantime, by King Ferdinand, who ruled the central European territories of the Habsburg dynasty.

Although this scheme would in effect have made Milan into French territory, the Imperial involvement compelled Francis to reject it. In these circumstances,

---

133    Knecht, *Renaissance warrior*, p. 386.
134    *ERP* 2 no. 57; *LP* XIII (i) no. 570; *CRP* 1 no. 222.
135    Muir, *Life and letters*, p. 181.
136    Beccadelli, *Vita Reginaldi Poli*, pp. 296–297.

the pope had to be satisfied with a further military truce between Francis and Charles, though even this caused dispute, since Francis wanted it to last 20 years, while Charles would only accept a maximum of five. It was eventually agreed that the status quo between the two powers should last for 10 years, something with which Pope Paul claimed to be overjoyed, although it fell far short of his original aims. Even though there was no personal meeting between Francis and Charles, their agents kept talking, and on 1 June, Montmorency finally persuaded his master to meet the emperor, once the pope had left Nice. He was assisted in this by the mediation of Francis's wife Leonor, who was also Charles's sister. She and her ladies came to Nice and she had two meetings with her brother. Meanwhile Pope Paul left on 20 June, having further talks with Charles at Genoa, before proceeding to Rome. Finally, on 14 July, Charles sailed to the southern French town of Aigues Mortes, where he was received by Francis, first on the Imperial galley and then on land. Observers were amazed to see the two old enemies showing such apparent friendship towards each other. They agreed to co-operate in future, in the defence of Christendom, and in bringing 'heretics' back to the Church. Not unreasonably, Montmorency regarded the whole episode as a personal triumph, but the pope had been marginalised.[137]

Meanwhile, once he had parted from Pope Paul, Pole returned to his familiar haunt in Treville, where he seems to have spent the rest of the summer, meeting his Paduan and Venetian friends.[138] From there, he wrote to the pope, on 23 August, praising his role in the quest for peace, though urging him, it might be thought superfluously given the identity of the addressee, to see the 'finger of God' in the renewed friendship between Charles V and Francis I. However, he also took this opportunity to renew his attack on Henry VIII, with his habitual accusation that the English king was a greater danger to Christendom than the Turks.[139] Paul III ordered Pole to leave Treville on 22 September, though he appreciated the English cardinal's desire and need for leisure, and did not expect him to come immediately to Rome. In the event, Pole left Treville on 8 October, and went to stay at Tivoli, in the palace of the Cardinal of Santa Croce, Francisco de Quiñones, but King Henry still pursued him. At about this time, an Englishmen, Harry Phillips, arrived in his household, disguised as a Swiss soldier. Pole's life continued to be under threat throughout this period, and Phillips, who in May 1535 had been responsible for luring the Bible translator William Tyndale out of the Merchant Adventurers' house in Antwerp, to arrest and eventual trial and burning, was an evident source of danger. An Oxford bachelor of Civil Law, Phillips had a chequered subsequent career as a gambler and debtor, as well as being involved in English espionage. He was duly identified by servants

---

[137]    Knecht, *Renaissance warrior*, pp. 386–387.
[138]    *ERP* 2 no. 60; *LP* XIII (ii) no. 36; *CRP* 1 no. 224 (4 August 1538).
[139]    *CRP* 1 no. 225 (further textual details).

of Pole, but his presence in Italy confirmed the need for the caution and secrecy with which the cardinal now conducted his life, especially when away from known sanctuaries.[140] Pole's fears were further confirmed by the arrival of one of Thomas Cromwell's agents, Thomas Theobald, who was apparently trailing Phillips, and reported that when Pole had finally reached Rome, by 28 October, he had been visited by another suspicious agent, James ap Hywel, alias Robert Brancetor, who was also identified and repelled from the cardinal's household.[141] Events in England, however, in the autumn and winter of 1538–9, would make the threat posed by Pole to Henry seem even greater, and also involve his close family in terrible judicial violence.

The smaller English religious houses had been closed down by 1538, and early in that year, the larger monasteries and convents began to be 'voluntarily' surrendered to Henry VIII's commissioners, and their communities dissolved. This process would take until 1540, and it was accompanied by the destruction of images and shrines which had previously been the object of pilgrimages. Particular fury and rancour, on King Henry's part, attached to the famous and much-visited shrine of Archbishop St Thomas Becket, at the east end of Canterbury cathedral. On 29 December 1170, the archbishop had been brutally murdered there by royal agents, and King Henry II had done penance for this desecration, before establishing the shrine in the martyr's memory. Now, in September 1538, another King Henry ordered the destruction of this shrine, as well as a rewriting of Becket's history. The twelfth-century archbishop was now seen, not as a martyr for the rights of the Church, but as a stubborn resister of the 'wholesome laws' that Henry II had established to curb the 'enormities' of the clergy. Henry VIII declared to his subjects that there was nothing in Becket's life that justified his being regarded as a saint. His feast was to be deleted from the liturgical calendar and service books, while his images were ordered to be removed or erased from churches and chapels.[142]

When the news of this action reached Rome, there was shock in the Curia, and Pole's reaction was particularly strong. He immediately began to spread the 'news', the truth of which still cannot be proved, despite much effort, that Becket's bones had not only been exhumed, but had been burned, in the manner prescribed in canon law for those who were deemed to have died as relapsed and unrepentant heretics.[143] The Becket episode, and Pole's response to it, whether or not the bones were indeed burned, could only deepen further the personal rift

---

[140]   *CPEC*, VI, pp. 288–294; *CPEC*, VII, pp. 320–321; David Daniell, *William Tyndale: a biography* (New Haven and London: Yale University Press, [1994] 2001), pp. 361–362.

[141]   *LP* XIII (ii) nos 507, 509 (BL Cotton Nero B VI fols 138r–v, 124v–5r); *CRP* 1 no. 225.

[142]   Hughes and Larkin, *Royal proclamations*, 1, nos 168, 186, pp. 273–275; Bernard, *King's Reformation*, pp. 488–490.

[143]   Mayer, 'Becket's bones burnt! Cardinal Pole and the invention and dissemination of

between cardinal and king. Having, very probably, sat on a papal commission devoted to the punishment of Henry VIII for his recent actions, Pole seems to have been persuaded by the desecration of Becket's shrine to accept appointment to a new legation to England. The plan was that he should shuttle between Charles V and Francis I, with the aim of persuading them to publish in their territories the latest bull excommunicating Henry, which had been issued on 17 December 1538, in reaction to the supposed burning of Becket's bones. The two rulers were also to be urged to mount an economic blockade of England, and the pope, as well as Pole, clearly envisaged military action in addition.[144] However, Paul III weakened his legate's hand from the start, by telling Charles V that Francis I would take no action against England unless the Habsburgs were involved too.[145] As Imperial diplomats and councillors already knew that Francis intended to partition England, in the case of an invasion to end Henry's rule, the legation was doomed from the start. Such a shift in the balance of power, involving a serious threat to maritime communications between the Habsburg territories in Spain and the Netherlands, could clearly not be countenanced in Charles's court at Toledo or by his administration in Brussels.[146]

Meanwhile, King Henry had launched a direct attack on the Pole family, and some of their relatives and supporters. On 29 August 1538, Reginald's younger brother Geoffrey was arrested and imprisoned in the Tower of London, though it was not until 26 October that his interrogation began.[147] Geoffrey talked very freely indeed, and his evidence led to the arrest of others, including his own closest relatives, some of them members of the Courtenay family. On 4 October, Reginald's older brother, Henry, Lord Montagu, was arrested along with Henry Courtenay, marquess of Exeter, and the next day they were joined in the Tower by Sir Edward Neville, younger brother of Lord Bergavenny.[148] A week later, Sir William Fitzwilliam, Thomas Wriothesley, earl of Southampton, and Thomas Goodrich, bishop of Ely, arrived at Warblington, Hampshire, to interrogate the 65-year-old Margaret Pole, countess of Salisbury. On 15 November, she was escorted to the earl of Southampton's nearby residence of Cowdray, where she was placed under house arrest.[149] By the end of November, there had been many further interrogations, and in the following month a series of trials began with

---

an atrocity', in *Martyrs and martyrdom in England, c. 1400–1700*, ed. Thomas S. Freeman and Thomas F. Mayer (Woodbridge: The Boydell Press, 2007), pp. 126–143.

[144]   *CRP* 1 nos 235 (*ERP* 2 pp. cclxxix–cclxxx; *LP* XIII (ii) no. 1110), 248 (further textual details).

[145]   *CSP Span* VI (i) nos 33, 34; Höllger, 'Pole's legation', p. 1145.

[146]   *CSP Span* VI (i) no. 35; *PPP*, pp. 91–92.

[147]   TNA SP1/139 fol. 131r–v: letter from Margaret Pole to Henry, Lord Montagu; Pierce, *Margaret Pole*, p. 115.

[148]   *LP* XIII (ii) nos 232, 752, 753, 784.

[149]   *LP* XIII (ii) nos 818, 855.

Lord Montagu and the marquess of Exeter on the 2nd and 3rd. The day after that, the trials began of Sir Edward Neville, Sir Geoffrey Pole, George Croftes, chancellor of Chichester diocese, Lady Margaret Pole's chaplain John Collins, and Hugh Holland, who was a yeoman and servant of the Pole family. Both Montagu and Exeter pleaded not guilty to charges of treasonable conspiracy in favour of Reginald and the Church of Rome, but they were nevertheless convicted unanimously by their peers. On 9 December, the two men, with Neville, were beheaded on Tower Hill, while Croftes, Collins and Holland were hanged, drawn and quartered at Tyburn. In total, over 20 were examined, and 13 arrested, of whom seven were executed and four pardoned, while one vanished in or from the Tower, and the fate of the last, Thomas Standish, clerk, is not known. Those pardoned by the king were Gertrude, marchioness of Exeter, Lord Delaware, and the chief informer, Sir Geoffrey Pole, while Edward Courtenay, son of the marquess and marchioness of Exeter, would remain in the Tower until he was pardoned as one of the first acts of Queen Mary I, in 1553.[150] Margaret Pole's biographer, Hazel Pierce, expresses the view that Henry had reason to believe, given recent events in England and on the Continent, that there was a genuine conspiracy against him, involving members of the aristocracy, and others, including clergy, who opposed his religious reforms.[151] Thomas Mayer takes a similar view, at least to the extent that there were undoubtedly a large number of prominent English people who wanted to see policy change in England, and in some cases may even have wanted the king overthrown, and replaced by his daughter Mary.[152] However, even if Henry's actions against the 'conspirators' might have seemed justified in terms of *realpolitik*, the legal processes employed were notably arbitrary and violent. They were hardly likely to diminish the ardour of Cardinal Reginald, even though his mother was, for the moment, spared the executioner's sword.

On or about Christmas Day 1538, Pole was appointed once more as legate to England, receiving his written instructions from the pope either then or at the beginning of January 1539.[153] Given the way in which Pole had been threatened in the previous two years, it is unsurprising that his initial mission to the emperor at Toledo was conducted with a high degree of secrecy. He travelled by land, in a poor state of health and naturally depressed by what had happened to his family. Just as he was setting out, he heard of the execution of his brother Henry, and in the circumstances he naturally resorted to his now frequent comparison between the evils of Henry and those of the Turks, to the moral advantage of the

---

[150] Pierce, *Margaret Pole*, pp. 115–116.
[151] Pierce, *Margaret Pole*, pp. 116–140.
[152] *CPEC*, VI, pp. 301–306.
[153] *ERP* 2 no. 51; *CSP Ven*, V, no. 194; *LP* XI no. 93; *LP* XIII (ii) no. 1110.

latter.[154] Pole reached Carpentras on 21 January, and Avignon the following day, planning to leave for Nîmes on the 23rd.[155] On 28 January, Cardinal Alessandro Farnese sent him his credentials, to Francis and Charles respectively.[156] While on his journey, the legate was in correspondence with Charles V, who commiserated with him over what had happened to his family, thus suggesting, falsely as things turned out, that the emperor would view his mission favourably.[157] Pole travelled round the Mediterranean coast from Provence to Barcelona, whence he took a post-chaise (in Italian *staffetta*) to Toledo, arriving there on 11 February. He cooled his heels, and no doubt recovered from the uncomfortable journey, while the papal nuncio, Giovanni Poggio, tried to delve into Imperial thinking. On 13 February, Charles received Pole in audience for about an hour, but the discussion was inconclusive, and the emperor concluded by saying that he should pursue matters further with his chief secretary, Francisco de los Cobos, and with Nicholas Granvelle. According to the Venetian ambassador in Toledo, Alvise Mocenigo, Charles accused the pope and Pole of having changed their position since the Nice conference of the previous year. Back then, the Turks had been the greatest threat to Christendom, but now, apparently, it was Henry VIII. Charles also saw a contradiction between the two policies that Rome was urging him to adopt towards England. A trade blockade was not compatible with full military action, and the clerics should make up their minds what they wanted.[158] In his own report to Pope Paul on his dealings with Pole, written personally on 17 March, after the legate's departure, Charles said that they had spoken at length about the main matter of his mission, but that he had made it crystal clear that he was primarily concerned with military action against the Turks, not England.[159] The Emperor was generally sympathetic to the papal cause, but did not want to upset either Francis or Henry. Los Cobos and Granvelle had told Pole that the papal censures on the English king were excessively severe, even though he had heard from the nuncio, Poggi, that they had previously been in favour of the publication of the censures and of an economic blockade of England.[160] If this is so, it appears that Pole, in his personal distress about his family and fury against Henry, had in fact set back papal interests, and probably his own as well.

Pole's 1539 'peace' legation seems initially to have caught English diplomacy on the hop. He was already en route at Bologna when, on 5 February, Henry's agent in Rome, Guido da Fano, reported the news in full to London. However,

---

[154]    *CSP Span* VI (i) 237; *ERP* 2 no. 63; *LP* XIV (i) no. 46; *CRP* 1 no. 237.

[155]    TNA PRO 31/9/65, p. 232; *LP* XIV (i) no. 126; *CRP* 1 no. 239.

[156]    *CRP* 1 no. 240 (further textual details).

[157]    BAV Vat. lat. 6754, fol 1ar; *CSP Ven*, V, no. 1999; *CRP* 1 no. 241.

[158]    Gustav Turba, ed., *Venetianischen Depeschen vom Kaiserhofe (Dispacci di Germania)*, erste Abteilung, 3 vols (Vienna: Tempsky, 1889–1901), i, no. 69, cited in *PPP*, p. 93.

[159]    AGS E 868–18.

[160]    *PPP*, p. 204.

Sir Thomas Wyatt, who was still resident ambassador at Charles's court, duly heard about the mission soon afterwards, and sent to London for instructions. It was clearly understood that Pole's new legation posed a direct threat to Henry and his regime. England was to be 'reduced' to Catholic obedience, by military means if necessary, and Pope Paul was prepared to suspend hostilities against the Turks in order to concentrate on this enterprise.[161] At the end of January, Wyatt demanded the removal of Pole's diplomatic immunity, even though he was a legate, on the grounds that his 'treachery' against his king should override that privilege. The request was refused by Charles, but this did not mean that he agreed with the papal line on England. Pole and Poggio wanted the papal bull of excommunication of Henry to be read publicly, with the ceremonies of anathema, in Toledo cathedral, but this too was refused. Efforts seem to have been made to keep Wyatt and Pole away from each other and this led to further misinformation. Wyatt apparently believed at first, falsely, that Pole had already done a deal with the emperor for 7,000–8,000 German troops to be sent to Flanders to take part in an invasion of England.[162] There is no doubt that Pole was in physical danger, as long as he remained in Toledo, since Wyatt, having failed to do away with him in Paris in 1537, and having seen other efforts fail in Italy in 1538, still wanted to kill him or have him killed. While in Spain, Pole learned this and the threat continued after he left the Imperial court. Wyatt even pledged his own wealth as blood-money to secure Pole's death, probably not while he was in Spain but when he returned to Italy.[163] Charles and his courtiers were aware of the risks, however, and, on 23/24 February, just over a week after his interviews with the Emperor, Los Cobos and Granvelle, Pole was able to leave safely and return to Barcelona, in more comfortable transport on the recommendation of Poggio, though he had evidently wanted to get away fast in a *staffetta*.[164] It is clear from the legate's dealings with Charles in Toledo that, no doubt because of his experience in Paris in 1537, he was determined not return there and meet Francis I in person, although this was what both emperor and pope wanted. While on his way out of Spain, he wrote from Girona, on 16 March, to the constable Montmorency, telling him that he was awaiting further orders from Pope Paul. In a second letter, written on the same day, Pole told King Francis that he wanted, as Charles V had requested, to know whether the French would be willing to blockade or even invade England, but said that he would not come to France in person, until he had received new instructions from Rome. In a third letter, he instructed his servant Vincenzo Parpaglia to take this correspondence to Montmorency and Francis, but also to make contact

[161]   *ERP* 2 pp. cclxxix–cclxxx; *CRP* 1 no. 235.
[162]   Muir, *Life and letters*, pp. 89, 91.
[163]   Brigden, *Thomas Wyatt*, pp. 427–435.
[164]   *CRP* 1 no. 242 (further textual details).

with the French king's sister, Margaret, queen of Navarre, who was known for her reforming attitudes in religion, and might perhaps mediate.[165] By the end of March 1539, Pole was back in papal territory at Carpentras, where he stayed with his old friend Jacopo Sadoleto until about 23 September.

While there, he remained in touch with developments concerning England, and put his thoughts on paper. On 17 May, the nuncio in Spain, Giovanni Poggio, wrote to him from Toledo, saying that the emperor still wanted him to go to France, and tell Francis what he had said in the Imperial court.[166] Thereafter, pressure continued to mount on Pole to go to England. On 12 June, he mentioned in a letter to Durante Duranti that the pope had ordered him to go to Henry's court, but he obstinately insisted that he would not do so unless and until Charles agreed to undertake military action against England. However, the next day he wrote to Contarini, giving a different impression, that Pope Paul was in fact leaving it to him to decide how to proceed. This change of tactic was no doubt connected with the fact that the pope had by then decided to replace Pole as his legate to Charles, sending instead his own nephew, Cardinal Alessandro Farnese, whom he may have thought a more congenial representative of the Holy See, given Pole's natural emotional commitment to English affairs.[167]

By the end of December, Pole was back in Rome, with his legation at an end but still under potential or actual threat from Henry's spies and assassins, and once again, he tried to justify himself in writing. In March and April 1539, he was provoked into developing the ideas in *De unitate* by the receipt of a polemical work by Richard Morison, *Invectiva in proditionis crimen* ('Invective against the crime of treason'), which had been published in London by the printer Thomas Berthelet, in February of that year. Pole was particularly stung by this work, because he had previously had close and friendly connections with Morison, who had been in Padua and Venice between 1532 and 1536, though even then he was a supporter of the cause of reform, as exemplified by Cranmer and Latimer. In 1534, Morison registered as a law student in the University of Padua, but his studies widened to include theology and philosophy. On his own admission, he was economically, as well as emotionally, dependent on Pole, as the cardinal himself would point out, in no uncertain terms, when he replied to his former protégé's 1539 work, which was evidently a pro-government response to Pole's current legation.[168] In a partial draft, entitled *Reg. Card. Poli. Ad Rich. M. accusatus. Apol.* ('Apology by Reginald, Cardinal Pole to the accused Richard

---

[165]    *CRP* 1 nos 246 (*ERP* 2 pp. 232–236; *LP* XIV (i) no. 536), 247 and 248 (further textual details).

[166]    *CRP* 1 no. 268 (further textual details).

[167]    *CRP* 1 nos 274 (*ERP* 2 no. 78; *LP* XIV (i) no. 1110), 275 (*ERP* 2 pp. ccxciii–ccxciv; *LP* XIV (i) no. 1143).

[168]    Overell, *Italian reform*, pp. 23–24; Woolfson, *Padua and the Tudors*, pp. 33–35; *LP* IX nos 101–103; *LP* X no. 320.

Morison'), which survives in the Vatican library, Pole took a highly personal line.[169] He said that he had never expected to be so hurt by one who owed him so much. In Italy, Morison had been his *germanus frater* ('true brother', literally with the same parents), but now he was turning violently against him. Pole's only ironical consolation was the affliction this caused him, because it was good for his soul, but he could not bear to condemn the younger man. In one of his habitual Biblical analogies, he said that he felt like Balaam, the pagan prophet who was asked by Balak, king of Moab, to curse the people of Israel, and on God's orders refused to do so (Numbers 22:1–14).[170]

Pole also accused Morison of having changed his tune in order to curry favour with King Henry. He was now using the same arguments as Bishop Sampson (and therefore was not even original), but the cardinal more or less admitted the truth of the charges laid against him by saying that, if Henry acted like the tyrant Nero, he could only expect there to be conspiracies against him. In a second, incomplete draft, in the same Vatican manuscript, Pole confronted Morison's argument, in his 'Invective', that Henry would always be safe because he had divine protection, like the Jewish kings David and Saul, and the three young Jewish men, Shadrach, Meshach and Abednego, in the Babylonian King Nebuchadnezzar's fiery furnace (Daniel 3:8–26).[171] Morison argued that Henry's rebellious subjects were ungrateful, and that treason was evil. Pole agreed with the latter point, but downplayed the Courtenay 'conspiracy' and defended his own brother Henry, as well as Sir Edward Neville. Morison had told the story as a tragedy, in which the king had been betrayed by ungrateful subjects, but Pole referred back to those who had, in his view, been martyred by Henry himself – John Fisher, Thomas More and the London Carthusian monks. Pole's own relatives were noble and innocent. The same Vatican manuscript contains a version of what has become known as Pole's 'Apology to Charles V', which like many of his major texts seems never to have reached its intended recipient in any form, but is essential for understanding its author's state of mind, after his unsuccessful visit to the Emperor and his ministers at Toledo.[172] It is directed at Charles, not at Richard Morison, and is an explicit and verbally violent attack on King Henry's misdeeds, against which it is the emperor's duty to act, as the leading Christian prince. If its wording represents his authentic thought, it may help to explain why there was no rapport between the two men, in Toledo in February 1539. Once back in Rome, at the end of that year, the cardinal of England was now able to attend to other matters of a religious character.

---

[169] BAV MS Vat. lat. 5970 fols 376r, 377r–79v; *CRP* 1 no. 243.

[170] Later in this text, no doubt because of his emotion, Pole referred to Balak incorrectly as Amalek, another enemy of the children of Israel, in the time of Moses and Joshua (Exodus 17:8–17).

[171] BAV MSS Vat. lat. 5970 fols 380r–82v, 384 r–v; *CRP* 1 no. 244.

[172] BAV MS Vat. lat. 5970 fols 303r–12v; *CRP* 1 no. 245; *PPP*, pp. 95–99.

# Chapter 4

# Reform

Once he became a cardinal, Reginald Pole quickly began to express his developing ideas in how to reform the abuses in the Church that had been identified by Luther and were being exploited by King Henry VIII. Ever since the beginning of Christianity, following the 'way' set out by Jesus of Nazareth, to bring about the Kingdom of God on earth, had required a conversion, or turn-round (*metanoia*), in one's life: by God's grace, the individual Christian might then live better. For the first thousand years of the Church's history, this conversion, or reformation, was seen very largely as a personal matter, but from then onwards, in the Western Church but much less so elsewhere, it began to be suggested that the institution itself also needed 'reformation'. In the first Christian millennial year, which caused both excitement and fear among Europe's population, Pope Sylvester II (reigned 999–1003) made mighty claims for his own religious and political authority as pope. Then, as the eleventh century went on, the pretensions of popes to exercise direct control over the Church became focused on a conflict with the Holy Roman emperors, who had at least theoretical authority over much of central Europe, concerning the appointment, or 'investing', of senior clergy, such as bishops and abbots. Out of this lengthy dispute arose the idea that the very institutions of the Church, as well as its individual members, were in need of conversion and reformation. Between the year 1000 and the election of Hildebrand as Pope Gregory VII (reigned 1073–85), the main impulse, in the minds of successive popes and their advisers, including prominent advisers from the Cluniac branch of the Benedictine order, was to return to the ancient, or 'primitive' ways of the Church. The main weapon for achieving this was canon law, which consisted of the decrees of earlier Church councils and the written rulings of popes in specific cases. In fact, the very idea that the Church as a whole needed radical reform, in the literal sense of a return to its roots in the first century, arose out of increasing study of canon law in the eleventh century, especially in Germany and Italy, where the 'investiture contest' was being fought out. These developments only affected the West, and many of the documents used were forgeries, but this did not shake the growing belief, among popes and their allies, that the early Church, which had followed Jesus's teaching, and the practices of the apostles, had been much more authentic and holier than what they were experiencing in their own day. Thus the popes and the monks of

Cluny, in eastern France, became the first 'reformers', and were prepared to use propaganda, and at times even violence, to achieve their goals.[1]

It fell to Gregory VII to start putting these pretensions into practice. From his time onwards, canon law became normative at the heart of Christian life, and the notions of 'reform' and 'reformation', which in many European languages have only a single word to refer to them, became identified with the assertion, and if necessary the re-establishment, of ancient values and standards, according to the historic canons. These were ever more intensively studied and brought together in collections, for everyday use by senior clergy and lawyers. Efforts to achieve reform, on these lines, initially meant legislating for the habits and behaviour (*mores*) of Christians, whether institutionally or individually, but by the fourteenth and fifteenth centuries the focus had widened to include Christian belief itself. The popes and the councils had been joined, in the first half of the thirteenth century, by institutions that were specifically designed to identify, punish and remove what was deemed to be false belief.[2] The Fourth Lateran Council (1215), summoned by Pope Innocent III (reigned 1198–1216), had re-emphasised the duty of all diocesan bishops to ensure the orthodoxy of their flocks, and from the 1230s onwards, in parts of Europe where heresy was believed to be particularly widespread and threatening, full-time inquisitors began work. The late Middle Ages saw further crises and alarms in the Western Church. Between 1378 and 1415, the authority of the papacy was severely questioned when, in the 'great schism', rivals set themselves up as popes in Rome and Avignon, and in Pisa as well from 1409, and each touted for support among European states. A single Roman papacy was restored by the Council of Constance (1414–18), which was convened by the Emperor Sigismund, and after that there was a growing belief, in some ecclesiastical and academic circles, that councils, rather than popes, should take the lead in the government of the Church. The restored Roman papacy fought back against conciliar ideas, however, and by the early sixteenth century, it had come to be generally assumed that reform of the Church, which was necessary from time to time, should happen on the initiative of the papacy, and not that of secular rulers, with the authority to call councils being wholly invested in the pope. It was precisely this power that Pope Paul III was intending to exercise when, at the end of 1536, he set up a committee of cardinals, including Reginald Pole, to set out a new programme for the reform of the Catholic Church.

In spiritual terms, Paul was elected pope in a climate of high emotion, discontent and expectation. The restoration of the Roman papacy, after the council of Constance, had by no means quelled complaints, in Italy and

---

[1]    John W. O'Malley, *Trent and all that: renaming Catholicism in the early modern era* (Cambridge, MA and London: Harvard University Press, 2000), pp. 16–17.

[2]    John Edwards, *Inquisition* (Stroud: The History Press, [1999] 2009), pp. 31–47.

elsewhere in Europe, about the corruption of the popes and their Curia, and of the institutional Church in general. In the decades around the year 1500, such protest commonly took the form of prophecy, in the Biblical sense of interpreting current events with an eye to the future, and in particular to the dire predictions of the Old Testament Book of Daniel and the New Testament Apocalypse, or Book of Revelation. Notable among such prophetic preachers in Italy in this period was the Dominican friar Girolamo Savonarola, who arrived in Florence in the spring of 1490, in large part at the instigation of the ruler of that city and republic, Lorenzo de' Medici. Based thereafter in the friary of San Marco, Savonarola preached the imminent coming of the end of the world, as predicted in Scripture. If it did not repent and convert, what he regarded as the corrupt and degenerate Florentine society would be destroyed. While many others preached this message, in Italy as elsewhere, and would continue to do so up to the 1530s, Savonarola was exceptional in securing political power in Florence, after the exile of Lorenzo's son and successor, Piero de' Medici, and the brief occupation of the city by King Charles VIII of France, at the end of 1494. An active proponent of the reforming Observant movement in the Dominican order, Fra Girolamo had become the prior of a separate Tuscan Congregation. He sought, on the model of the early Church, to establish in Florence a new Christian society, which would exalt the Bible, traditional scriptural morality, and apostolic simplicity of life. In pursuit of these aims, he tried to drive out of Florence what he regarded as 'pagan' influences, in the often voluptuous form of Renaissance art and architecture, but his regular preaching perhaps inevitably polarised his listeners, and quickly brought him into conflict with Pope Alexander VI, who represented very different values. In July 1495, Alexander summoned him to Rome to justify himself, but he pleaded that his responsibilities did not permit him to leave Florence. In response, the Borja pope began moves to lessen Savonarola's power and independence in the Dominican order by merging his Congregation with a larger body based in Rome. Eventually, on 13 May 1497, the friar was excommunicated by the archbishop of Florence, but declared that God had told him the measure was invalid. He continued to preach, announcing 'revelations' which he claimed to be supplementary to those in the Book of Revelation. He always firmly believed that he was a wholly orthodox Christian, and in 1497 published a doctrinal summary, entitled 'The triumph of the Cross' (*Triumphus Crucis*). Despite this, and the efforts of various intermediaries, the conflict between Savonarola and Pope Alexander grew still more fierce in 1498, and culminated in the friar's decision that the Valencian was a false pope. He sent letters announcing this to various Christian rulers, asking them to summon a general council of the Church. In the immediate future, however, this action brought about the friar's demise. His enemies in Florence, who disagreed with him politically or envied his religious charisma, persuaded the Florentine government to arrest him on charges of subversion and heresy, and on 23 May 1498 he was hanged and then burned for these offences.[3] Even so, his influence remained strong, well into the sixteenth century.

The election of Giulio de' Medici as Pope Clement VII, in November 1523, led to great rejoicing in Rome as it was believed, rightly, that Renaissance glories and festivity would return, after the brief reign of the severe Dutchman, Hadrian VI. Two men who would later be in Pole's circle, Pietro Bembo and Michelangelo, both hoped for an end to austerity under Clement. Michelangelo told his quarryman that there would be a lot of new artistic creation, and he proved to be right.[4] All the old ways of the papacy returned, leading eventually to the Sack of 1527, which provoked a new outpouring of moral rage against the ways of the Holy See. This appeared in various ways, including literary creation. The Spanish priest Francisco Delicado's semi-dramatised and moralistic satire on the Rome of Leo X and Clement VII, *Retrato de la Lozana andaluza*, describes the cardinals of the 1520s as behaving like Mamalukes, the Muslim rulers of Egypt under Ottoman Turkish hegemony, and is full of foreboding when it describes the years up to 1527. The book lives in the prophetic climate of Joachim and Savonarola, and describes the horrors of the Sack as justified as well as terrible.[5] On a semi-official level, Charles V's Erasmian Latin secretary, Alfonso de Valdés, used a fierce critique of the greed and violence of the papacy to absolve the emperor of any responsibility for the Sack, and in a sense to justify it.[6]

One guide to Pole's views, in the late 1520s and 1530s, on the burning issue of Church reform is the part that he was given by his former protégé Thomas Starkey, in his 'Dialogue of Pole and Lupset'. In it, Starkey puts into his old friend's mouth words that suggest a considerable concordance between his views on the Church and those prevailing at Henry VIII's court. 'Pole' and 'Lupset' (Thomas Lupset, another of Pole's friends) debate the subject of Scripture in the vernacular, with the former expressing the view that ordinary English people ought to have it, and that they should also have church services in English. 'Lupset' protests that these ideas are Lutheran, but 'Pole' does not budge.[7] 'Pole' adds that preaching, too, should be a major weapon in achieving reform, following Christ's 'exampul of lyfe and exhortacyon'. Once Christ's Law

---

[3]   Lauro Martines, *Scourge and fire: Savonarola and Renaissance Italy* (London: Jonathan Cape, 2006), *passim*.

[4]   Gouwens, 'Clement and calamity', p. 3.

[5]   Francisco Delicado, *Retrato de la Lozana andaluza*, ed. Claude Allaigre, 3rd edn (Madrid: Cátedra, 2000), pp. 213, 242, 503.

[6]   Alfonso de Valdés, *Diálogo en que particularmente se tratan las cosas acaecidas en Roma el año de MDXXVII*, in Alfonso de Valdés, *Obra completa*, ed. Ángel Alcalá (Madrid: Fundación José Antonio de Castro, 1996), p. 303.

[7]   Starkey, *Dialogue*, pp. 108–109.

(the Bible) and the liturgy were in English, the works of Erasmus should be circulated. Later in the dialogue, 'Pole' adds:

> Then I thynk schortly yo schuld see more frute of the gospel than we have, you
> schold see wyhtin few yerys men wyth love dow such thyng as now they can not
> be brought to be [by] no mannys law.[8]

It is impossible to ascertain whether these really were Pole's views at this time, but, if they were, they would certainly have fitted in well with his willingness to work to help secure King Henry's divorce from Catherine.

As far as Pole's personal religion was concerned, his faithful servant Alvise Priuli offers a vivid picture of life in his household, while he was in Liège during his first legation, in 1537. The schedule was quasi-monastic, with the daily worship beginning an hour and a half before breakfast, in a domestic oratory. Then and later in the day, the hours, presumably in Latin, were said 'in the Theatine manner, without chant' ('*more theatinico senza canto*'), this being a reference to the religious order of which Gianpietro Carafa was joint founder. Mass was celebrated by Gian Matteo Giberti, Pole not being a priest, and this was followed by the reading of a chapter of Eusebius's *De demonstratione evangelica* ('On demonstrating the Gospel'), probably in the Latin version of the Greek original that the Bishop Giberti had then recently commissioned, and dedicated to Pope Paul III. At breakfast, writings by Bernard of Clairvaux would be read and discussed, and there would then be a period of community conversation, lasting from one to two hours. In the evening, there would be vespers and compline, and Pole himself would read from Paul, starting with the first letter to Timothy. In this frame of mind, Pole prepared for more active involvement in efforts to reform the Church.[9]

It was on 7 January 1538 that Pole was appointed to Paul III's commission with the task of preparing for a general council. Also included were Carafa and Contarini, and at this time Pole tried to co-ordinate with the latter his ideas on reform, after the unofficial publication, in May of that year, of the report of the 1537 reform commission, *Consilium de emendanda ecclesia* ('Advice on reforming the Church'). If it had been implemented, it would have undermined the finances of the papacy by using the Curia's own methods against it.[10] Pole's inclusion in Paul III's commission for reform indicated his newly-acquired status in Rome, which he achieved partly as a result of the support of Contarini,

---

[8]  Starkey, *Dialogue*, pp. 137–141, at p. 141.

[9]  *ERP* 2 pp. liv–cvii; *PPP*, pp. 69–70.

[10]  An English translation of the text of the *Consilium* is in Elizabeth G. Gleason, *Reform thought in sixteenth-century Italy* (Chico, CA: Scholars Press, 1981) [= American Academy of Religion, Texts and Translations Series, ed. James A. Massey, 4], pp. 81–100 (see also n. 47).

who had himself become a cardinal in May 1535, and personally presented the report to the pope in March 1537. Partly written by Pole, although it affirmed the validity of papal authority, it did not hold back from blistering criticism of some individual popes.

> And your Holiness, taught by the Spirit of God, who, as Augustine says, speaks in hearts without the din of words, had rightly acknowledged that the origins of these evils [in the Church] was due to the fact that some popes, your predecessors, in the words of the apostle Paul, "having itching ears heaped up to themselves teachers according to their own lusts" [II Timothy 4:3], not that they might learn from them what they should do, but that they might find through the application and cleverness of these teachers a justification for what it pleased them to do. Then it came about, besides the fact that flattery follows all dominion as the shadow follows the body, and that truth's access to the ears of princes has always been most difficult, that teachers at once appeared who taught that the pope is the lord of all benefices and that therefore, since a lord may sell by right what is his own, it necessarily follows that the pope cannot be guilty of simony. Thus the will of the pope, of whatever kind it may be, is the rule governing his activities and deeds, whence it may be shown without doubt that whatever is pleasing is also permitted.[11]

In contrast to some of his predecessors, Paul III was praised by the commission for his reforming zeal, without reference to his zealous pursuit of Farnese family interests. However, their report provided a detailed catalogue of failings in the Church, including various kinds of misconduct by clergy, including the abuse of benefices and other Church offices by non-residence, pluralism and other means, the degeneracy of the religious orders, pagan Greek and Roman influences in ecclesiastical education, and simoniacal trading in benefices. The commission's view of the city of Rome itself corresponded to that of contemporary Spanish commentators, such as Francisco Delicado and Alfonso de Valdés:

> Also in this city harlots walk about like matrons or ride on mules, attended in broad daylight by noble members of the cardinals' households and by clerics. In no city do we see this corruption except in this model for all cities. Indeed, they even dwell in fine houses. This foul abuse must also be corrected.[12]

Evidently the initially sobering effect of the 1527 Sack had quickly worn off.

---

[11]    English version of the *Consilium* in John C. Olin, *The Catholic Reformation: Savonarola to to Ignatius Loyola* (New York: Fordham University Press, 1992), pp. 186–187.

[12]    Olin, *Catholic Reformation*, p. 196.

The commission did recommend remedies for the problems it had identified, and in the case of the religious orders, then under such pressure in Pole's native land, its report stated:

> Another abuse ... must be corrected with regard to the religious orders, for many have become so deformed that they are a great scandal to the laity and do grave harm by their example. We think that all conventual [unreformed] orders ought to be done away with, not however that injury be done to anyone [already in them], but by prohibiting the admission of novices. Thus they might be quickly abolished without wronging anyone, and good religious could be substituted for them. In fact, we now think that it would be best if all boys who have not been professed were removed from their monasteries.[13]

In this document, Pole and his colleagues constantly stressed the prime importance of pastoral concerns in the life of the Church, and its desperate need of further spiritual renewal. The organisations within the Church emanated directly from Christ Himself, and the Holy Spirit dwelt in them. Thus the Body of Christ, the Church, needed to be cleansed, so that it became as beautiful as a dove and achieved peace within itself.[14]

Yet the waiting for reform continued, as the promised council failed to materialise, and Pole's English legation lapsed as well. On 13 August 1541, he was appointed as papal legate to the Patrimony of Peter, with full powers to govern it, dealing with civil, criminal, matrimonial and ecclesiastical property matters. Indicating the unstable character of central Italy at the time, he was also empowered to punish and remove papal officials, annul pacts and truces made against the interests of the Holy See, and punish murderers and those who breached the peace. The emphasis throughout the relevant bull is on restoring and keeping the peace.[15] Having spent much of the summer in Capranica and Bagnoregio, the new legate took up residence in Viterbo in September 1541.[16] He was formally received into his territory by four nobles at Ronciglione, and when he reached the boundary of Viterbo itself, he was met by the town's *gonfaloniere* (municipal standard-bearer) and a hundred young men in uniform. More ceremonies took place in the town, at the gate of the Dominican convent of Santa Maria de Gradi, where 15 noble citizens and a large crowd awaited him, and at the San Sisto gate, where he was welcomed by the mass of the citizens.

---

[13]    Olin, *Catholic Reformation*, p. 193. For a discussion of Cardinal Thomas Wolsey and King Henry VIII's similar concerns for the reform of the religious orders, in the 1520s and 1530s, see G.W. Bernard, 'The dissolution of the monasteries [in England]', *History*, 95 (2011), pp. 390–409.

[14]    Bruce Gordon, 'Italy', in *The Reformation world*, ed. Andrew Pettegree (London: Routledge, 2000), pp. 277–295, at pp. 281–283.

[15]    *CRP* 1 no. 335 (further textual details).

[16]    *ERP* 4 no. 15 *CSP Ven*, V, no. 209; *LP* XVI appendix no. 6; *CRP* 1 no. 336.

He was then escorted to the Rocca, since his predecessor, Cardinal Francesco Corner, still occupied the legate's official residence, the Palazzo San Sisto, and would do so for another two years. Despite the monastic nature of his domestic life, Pole entered fully into the political and administrative matters involved in governing the Patrimony of Peter, although much of the business was done by a deputy, and he generally worked only in the mornings. As legate, he issued proclamations (*bandi*), forbidding blasphemy in strong terms, and enforcing religious holidays on which there was to be no work done, and no trading or banned games. He tried to end faction conflict, and, perhaps in reaction to the goings-on back in Rome, to restrict prostitution.[17] Such experience, even if much of the actual work was delegated, would stand him in good stead when he eventually reached England.

During this period, it is clear that Pole still gave priority to his spiritual life. The significance of the ideas and activities of his household, which has sometimes been named the 'Viterban church' (*ecclesia viterbiensis*), attracted much attention at the time and remains a controversial topic. In his last years, when he was legate and archbishop in England, Pole found that his doings in the 1540s were being raked over by the Roman Inquisition, at the instigation of his former friend and collaborator Gianpietro Carafa, who from 1555 was Pope Paul IV. The issue was Italy's flirtation with ideas of Church reform that went far beyond the programme of the reform commission of Paul III, in the late 1530s, and led some of Pole's circle, notably Bernardino Ochino and Piero Martire Vermigli, to join the Reformation north of the Alps. Until recently, most historical study of Pole's religious life in these years, and that of his friends and associates, has been expressed in the terms of an Italian historiography that reflects the country's experience in the nineteenth and twentieth centuries, with the loss of territorial authority by the papacy and the establishment of a secular Italian republic, covering the whole of the peninsula. Perhaps paradoxically, the traditional ecclesiastical division between 'clergy' and 'laity' has thus been transferred to the historical profession. When added to a view with hindsight of the division between 'Catholic' and 'Protestant' that coagulated after 1560, this development has often resulted in a distorted vision of the fluid situation in which Pole and his satellites lived in the 1540s. Reformers within the Catholic fold have come to be known, on some contemporary basis, as believing in and practising '*evangelismo*', in the broad sense of a Gospel faith, which retained the institutional and sacramental framework of the Church, while emphasising a deep and intense personal spiritual life. Even at the time, and not only by later historians, such Christians, including Pole, were seen as *spirituali*. One of the most prominent lay scholars of Italian *evangelismo*, Paolo Simoncelli, saw the

---

[17]   The records of the city council on this matters are summarised, with references, in *PPP*, p. 115.

*spirituali* as virtually a political movement, with a moderate wing, in which Pole's mentor Contarini was prominent, and a more radical tendency, which included Ochino and Marcantonio Flaminio.[18] According to this account, the two groups moved apart from each other after 1541, when they both began to suffer increasing pressure from their more traditionalist opponents, including Carafa, who are known to some modern historians as *'intransigenti'*.[19] A detailed look at some of the major figures in Pole's Viterbo circle may help to reach behind the 'party' labels imposed by later historians.

Ever since his early days as a student at Padua, in the 1520s, Pole had received the friendship and influence of Pietro Bembo (1470–1547), who had been one of Pope Julius II's two secretaries of briefs, and between 1505 and 1511 was associated with the court of Francesco Maria della Rovere at Urbino. He had continued to be prominent at the courts of Julius's successors and took a particular interest in music and literature. His re-creation of Ciceronian rhetorical strategies was rendered musically by the noted lutenist and composer Francesco Canova da Milano, and he was particularly noted for his revival of Petrarchan style, which became one of the main genres of Italian literature in the late Renaissance. Having been made a cardinal by Paul III in 1539, he was also associated with *evangelismo*.[20] Equally prominent was Giovanni Matteo Giberti, who also came to know Pole during his first period in Italy. Having earlier been a protégé of Pope Julius II, he became datary under Clement VII, and a close adviser to that pope. In 1528 he became bishop of Verona, and initiated a programme of reform in his new diocese that anticipated much of the later activity, in this direction, of enthusiasts including Pole himself, as well as the Tridentine fathers. Giberti resided personally in his diocese for much of the time, something that was unusual in the period, though not unique to him. Further, his understanding of the Christian faith also had implication for religious art. He ordered the customary spouting blood to be removed from portrayals of Christ's Passion, on the grounds that it was unseemly to show Him in His agony on the Cross, at the very moment when he was in reality triumphing over sin and death. In this respect, he appeared to be moving away from the late medieval stress on Christ's physical suffering, and back to the earlier emphasis, in East and West, on his kingly triumph. Judging by what he did in his own diocese, Giberti, like many of his Italian contemporaries, combined a strong Christocentric faith,

---

[18]   Paolo Simoncelli, *Evangelismo italiano del cinquecento: Questione religiose e nicodemismo politico* (Rome: Edizioni di Storia e Letteratura, 1979), pp. 84–100.

[19]   *PPP*, pp. 303–304.

[20]   Cecil H. Clough, 'Clement VII and Francesco Maria della Rovere, duke of Urbino', in Gouwens and Reiss, *Clement VII*, pp. 75–108, at p. 80; Victor Anand Coelho, 'Papal tastes and musical genres: Francesco da Milano "Il Divino" (1497–1543) and the Clementine aesthetic', in Gouwens and Reiss, *Clement VII*, pp. 277–292, at pp. 285–286; Abigail Brundin, *Vittoria Colonna and the spiritual practice of the Italian Reformation* (Aldershot: Ashgate, 2008), pp. 2–3, 7, 10–11.

which bore more than a passing resemblance to that of Protestant reformers, with the humanistic culture and imagery of the Renaissance.

The latter could lead the bishop of Verona, and others, to what seemed, to some contemporaries and to later commentators, to be 'paganising' excesses. A notable example centred on a pillar altar, made by Johann Goritz in the church of Sant' Agostino in Rome. Its sculpted figures, by Andrea Sansovino, represented the Virgin and Child, with Mary's mother, St Anne, and above them was a fresco of the prophet Isaiah, by Raphael. In the first decades of the sixteenth century, on the feast of St Anne each year, poets would read from an anthology which they had composed for the occasion, called a 'Coryciana', after Goritz. Giberti was associated with this group, which in 1524 produced a collection that contained an unusually strong series of pagan Classical references, applied to Jesus and His family. The poets used Greek and Roman metres, referred to the saints as 'gods' or 'deities', and called the Virgin Mary the 'Mother of the Thunderer (Jupiter)' and 'Queen of Olympus', the mountain of the Greek and Roman pantheon. Such activity did not go uncriticised, for example being attacked by Francesco Berni, who, in a work composed in 1525, said of the poets of the 'Coryciana' circle, in which Giberti was included, 'They call Our Lord Jesus Christ now Jupiter, now Neptune, now the Thunderer, now the Father of the Gods'.[21] Such criticism of the paganising tendency of Christianity in the Renaissance, especially in Italy, had earlier been forcefully made by the Dutch humanist Erasmus, in his tract *Ciceronianus*.[22]

Nevertheless, when it came to the identification of religious abuses, Giberti, at least, adopted an approach that Erasmus would have approved of, the two, indeed, having been correspondents, for example concerning the Italian's edition of the works of St John Chrysostom.[23] In 1533, while governing an area of papal territory that included the 'Holy House' of Loreto, Giberti wrote to Giovan' Battista Mentebuona, adopting a sceptical, Erasmian approach, while at the same time having it restored by Andrea Sansovino, who had carved the figures on the Goritz altar in Sant' Agostino in Rome. When Erasmus fell out of favour with traditionalists in the 1530s, Giberti continued to defend him against, for example, Alberto Pio da Carpi, Girolamo Aleandro, and the Spanish humanist Juan Ginés de Sepúlveda. Giberti seems to have shared the view of Gasparo Contarini that money should not be spent on elaborate church ornaments while the poor needed food and shelter.[24] Giberti wrote ordinances and guidelines for his diocese of Verona, in which he tried to reach every level of society, including

---

[21]    [Janus Corycius] *Coricianus*, ed. J. Ijsewijn (Rome: Herder, 1997), p. 240, and poems nos 56, 127, 143, 171, 276, 279.

[22]    *Collected works of Erasmus*, 28, 437.

[23]    *OEE*, 8, 470; 9, 30, 328.

[24]    Alexander Nagel, 'Experiments in art and reform in Italy in the early sixteenth century', in Gouwens and Reiss, *Clement VII*, pp. 385–409, at pp. 395–403.

special care for the poor. He personally supervised the implementation of his programme, and also paid particular attention to preaching:

> We ask all [members of] religious [orders], after they have received permission from us to preach in the city and our diocese, by the compassion of our Lord Jesus Christ to preach and proclaim His Gospel sincerely to the people and to follow in His footsteps when He taught the Apostles ... Let them put their reliance in the interpretations of the holy doctors of the Church of old, as has also been decreed in the [Fifth] Lateran council under pain of excommunication. Let them avoid in those holy sermons citations of profane laws [which are] not at all necessary, the superfluous appeal to the authority of poets, the advancing of subtle themes very often worthless. Let them be ever mindful that he who teaches and instructs uneducated minds ought to be able to adapt himself to the intelligence of those in his audience. Let them instruct the people to observe the precepts of God so that they may firmly keep the faith and obey the commands of God and the Church. Nor let them deviate from the decrees and ordinances of the same Church.[25]

Evidently Giberti had repented at least somewhat of the excesses of the 'Coryciana'.

One of the more intriguing initiatives of Giberti, in his diocese, was to introduce the practice, which would later be advocated by Pole in Mary I's England and at the Council of Trent, of having the reserved sacrament of the Body of Christ placed, not in a pyx suspended above the altar but in a tabernacle fixed to it. The history of this practice in Italy is interesting in that it seems to have begun in Florence in 1497, when Savonarola was the dominant force there, and to have spread to Siena in 1506.[26] The intention seems to have been to bring Christ in His real presence back to the centre of devotions at the altar, in place of painting and sculpture, and such would be the emphasis in the religion of the Viterbo 'church' and of Pole's own approach when he returned with authority to England. Despite this echo of Savonarolan practice, Giberti, no doubt enforcing his own guidelines, did not allow extreme prophetic preaching in his diocese of Verona. In 1535, a Joachimite Augustinian friar of the old school, Fra Girolamo of Verona, came to his home town with the apocalyptic message that had been so popular with many between 1490 and the 1520s, but Giberti had him expelled.[27] If the Church was to be reformed, something that the bishop of Verona desired as much as any firebrand friar, it was to be done through official channels, such as Paul III's reform commission and the expected general council, and not by rabble-rousing in public squares.

---

[25]  Olin, *Catholic Reformation*, p. 146.

[26]  Nagel, 'Experiments in art and reform', pp. 404–405.

[27]  Ottavia Niccoli, *Prophecy and people in Renaissance Italy*, trans. Lydia C. Cochrane (Princeton: Princeton University Press, 1990), pp. 108–111.

In many aspects, one of the most influential members of Pole's own circle at Viterbo, in the 1540s, was Vittoria Colonna. Later in his life, Pole was accused by the Roman Inquisition of 'seducing' Colonna, and others in his Viterbo circle, away from the Catholic faith. Although she only became close to Pole in the 1540s, she had known his friend and confidant Alvise Priuli well since 1536.[28] Vittoria was born in 1490/2, at the Colonna family seat in Marino, near Rome, and was the second child of Fabrizio Colonna (d. 1520) and Aguere da Montefeltre (1470–1506). As a small girl, in 1495, she was promised in marriage to the Neapolitan Francesco Ferrante d'Avalos, marquis of Pescara, and eventually, in December 1509, the couple were duly married on the island of Ischia, as a means of cementing the alliance between the Colonna and the Aragonese Trastamarans. Thereafter, Vittoria lived on that island with her aunt, Costanza d'Avalos, and her first known poetry dates from 1512. In 1525, her life was drastically changed by the death of her husband, from wounds sustained in the Imperial service at the battle of Pavia. Her association with Catholic reform began in earnest while she was in Naples, and then, in Rome, between 1536 and 1539, there meeting Michelangelo Buonarroti, who had been influenced by Savonarola earlier in his life, and retained a desire for renewal in the Church. At that time, Vittoria lived in the convent of San Silvestro, on the Quirinale, where she pursued her writing of 'poetry of faith', which had begun after her husband's death. However, during the 1530s she was mainly based in Naples, where she became associated with the Spanish reformer, Juan de Valdés.[29]

Born in Cuenca, in Spain, in c. 1509, Juan was a brother of Charles V's Latin secretary, Alfonso de Valdés, and studied briefly at the university of Alcalá de Henares, where theology was the main subject. Before that, in 1523–4, Juan had become involved with a controversial group of Christians, at the marquis of Villena's castle of Escalona, who sought inner renewal by direct connection with God, and enlightenment which led to their becoming known as *alumbrados* ('illuminated' or 'enlightened ones'). Their relative lack of interest in the hierarchical and sacramental frameworks of the Church brought them within the purview of the Spanish Inquisition, and from this time onwards, Juan became committed to reform, first in Spain and then in Italy, where he fled to avoid inquisitorial arrest, a fate that befell two of the leaders of the Escalona group, Pedro Ruiz de Alcaraz and Isabel de la Cruz. Valdés's first major work, *Diálogo de doctrina cristiana* ('Dialogue on Christian doctrine'), was dedicated to the marquis of Villena. This was printed in Alcalá de Henares by Miguel de Eguía. Remarkably, this book, displaying the influence of the *alumbrados* of Escalona, was produced when Juan was a second-year undergraduate. In it, he stressed the priority of faith over works, as a means of securing salvation. Indeed,

---

[28]  *PPP*, pp. 103–104.
[29]  Brundin, *Vittoria Colonna*, pp. 102–105.

he denied any salvific value at all to human reason and intellect, trusting instead in the power of the Holy Spirit, the third Person of the Trinity. In a manner similar to Luther, but apparently without any direct influence from him, Valdés recognised just three sacraments as having a New Testament basis, baptism, the Eucharist and confession. He also anticipated Luther by publishing a reformed catechism. Having been investigated by the Inquisition in 1529, and threatened with a further intervention by its Toledo tribunal, Juan fled to Rome and then to Naples, where he arrived in 1535, and remained until his death in 1541. He was appointed overseer of the castles in Naples, by the viceroy, Pedro de Toledo, and, in the relatively open climate of the 1530s, even became a papal steward under Clement VII. His works, many of which were not published in print until after his death, included a 'Christian alphabet' (*Alfabeto cristiano*, 1545), a catechism for children (1540), and commentaries on the Psalms, St Mark's Gospel, and Romans and I Corinthians.

The main emphasis of Valdés's theology was on inner revelation by God and the direct activity of the Holy Spirit, and his suspicion of external religious ceremony made him suspect also to reformers, whether or not they remained obedient to Rome. His impact was far greater in Italy than in his native land, and his Neapolitan circle had a direct influence on Pole in Viterbo, and not only through Vittoria Colonna, who moved to the town in 1541, after Juan de Valdés's death, residing in the convent of Santa Catarina.[30]

In the years 1541 and 1542, when Pole was beginning his term as legate in Viterbo, his little group of spiritual associates began to be convulsed by tensions and divisions among the various tendencies within the Italian Church. Paul III's reform commission had had little or no result, and the promised general council had not met, but this did not mean that the hope of bringing at least the Lutherans, if not Henry VIII or the Swiss reformers, back into the fold had been entirely abandoned in Rome. During the Diet of Augsburg in 1530, Alfonso de Valdés and Philipp Melanchthon had reached a draft agreement for reunion between Catholics and Lutherans, and although this had been vetoed by the Curia and by Luther, it still seemed, 10 years later, that talks might be revived.[31] Nevertheless, when the matter was taken up again by Paul III in 1541, his main motive seems to have been to prevent Charles V making too many concessions to the Protestants at the forthcoming Diet of Regensburg. Initially, Pole was considered as a possible legate to the Emperor and Diet, but in the event the mission was led by Gasparo Contarini, who was acting at the time as protector of the Cassinese Benedictine congregation in Venice. Having initially been

---

[30]   José C. Nieto, *El Renacimiento y la otra España: Visión cultural socioespiritual* (Geneva: Librairie Droz, 1997), pp. 104–108; Gordon, 'Italy', pp. 286–288.

[31]   The Augsburg talks are described by Valdés in letters to Cardinal Benedetto Accolti, and a report on the Diet, dated September 1530, in Valdés, *Obra completa*, pp. 208–240.

appointed to participate in a colloquy at Hagenau, Contarini left Rome in late June 1541, and duly took part in the far more significant meeting at Regensburg, which involved the Strasbourg reformer Martin Bucer as well as the German Lutherans.[32] Roman participation in the Regensburg colloquy resulted from considerable pressure placed on the pope by Charles V, to come to an agreement with the Protestants, and thus end destructive conflict in Germany. However, Paul III's instructions to Contarini hardly indicated an enthusiastic response to the Imperial call. No power was delegated to the Venetian cardinal to agree formally to anything, on the spurious grounds that the views of Melanchthon and Bucer on crucial theological questions were unknown in Rome. Instead, the instructions included a blistering attack on 'heretics', which evidently referred to Contarini's interlocutors at Regensburg. The Protestants would be received back into the Church only if they fully submitted to Catholic teaching, meaning that no negotiation of any kind was envisaged. Any disputed points were to be submitted to the pope for decision. Even so, Paul expressed the hope that he would not have to resort to harsh measures. All this put Contarini, and others in the Roman team, including Tommaso Badia, who was one of his and Pole's circle, as well as the nuncio in Germany, Giovanni Poggio, in a difficult position. Those who became known to history as the *spirituali* had views on salvation that chimed in with those of Bucer and the Lutherans, but their hands appeared to have been tied in advance by the pope, and one of the more radical members of the 'Viterbo church', Marcantonio Flaminio, refused to go to Germany at all.[33]

Despite all these difficulties, Contarini did manage to achieve agreement with the Protestants on the question of the justification of sinners to salvation, which was dividing the formerly united Catholic Church.[34] On 2 May, the Catholics agreed a formulation on this subject with the Protestants. The fifth article of agreement stated that such justification was achieved 'by that faith which is effective through charity'. This was Christ's justice, imputed by faith to the sinner, and this inherent justice led the sinner to do good works, although these did not contribute to his or her salvation. The inclusion in it of both faith and works led to this doctrine being described as 'double justification', though such a designation is misleading, since it is clear that the Regensburg agreement

---

[32]   *CRP* 1 307 (further textual details), 315 (*ERP* 3 no. 6; *LP* XVI no. 536), 316 (*ERP* 3 no. 7; *LP* XVI no. 624), 317 (*ERP* 3 no. 9; *LP* XVI no. 643), 318 (*ERP* no. 8; *CSP Ven*, V, no. 247; *LP* XVI no. 715); Gleason, *Reform thought*, p. 203; *PPP*, p. 106.

[33]   *PPP*, p. 106.

[34]   For an account of the 1541 Regensburg colloquy, see Basil Hall, 'The colloquies between Catholics and Protestants, 1539–1541', in *Studies in Church History*, 7, ed. G.J. Cuming and D. Baker (1971), pp. 235–266. A full discusion of the theological issues concerning Contarini and the doctrine of justification may be found in Alister E. McGrath, *Iustitia Dei. A history of the Christian doctrine of justification. From 1500 to the present day* (Cambridge: Cambridge University Press, [1986] 1993), pp. 56–63.

put faith in the first, indeed the only, place. Nevertheless, it was agreed that preachers should continue to urge repentance and good works on their listeners. Contarini recorded this result in an *Epistola de justificatione* ('Letter on justification').[35] In this work, he sought to show that what had been agreed at Regensburg was in accordance with Catholic teaching. He himself believed that faith was essential to salvation, and that good works were not, being instead the result and proof of justification that came entirely from God's gratuitous mercy. However, Contarini, like Pole, was not trained as a systematic theologian, and his views proved to be vulnerable to attack in Rome.[36] Contarini distributed the *Epistola* to those whom he thought would be sympathetic to what had been achieved at Regensburg, including Bembo and Pole, but the latter's reaction would raise questions concerning his character, when faced with conflict. A month after the Regensburg meeting, Pole told Contarini that he was leaving Rome, just at the moment when his mentor needed all the friends he could find to gain acceptance there of his agreement with the Protestants. Pole seems to have been pessimistic about the likelihood of such an acceptance, and to have assumed that Contarini thought the same, saying that he himself was planning to spend the summer in his diocese of Belluno. On this basis, Pole told Contarini that his faithful retainer Alvise Priuli would handle matters in Rome.[37] Pole left the 'Eternal City' on 12 May 1541, and thus began to acquire the reputation that he would later have for absenting himself in times of personal and more general crisis [Appendix 1A]. Perhaps the agreement with the Protestants would have been rejected even if Pole had spoken for it, but in fact there seems to have been a cooling in his relations with Contarini, which would last until the latter died in the following year.[38]

Initially, Contarini does not seem to have been too perturbed by Pole's departure from Rome. He quickly named the latter's mentor, Pietro Bembo, now a cardinal, to represent him at the Curia, and worked to gain the support of Cardinal Ercole Gonzaga for the Regensburg agreement. Contarini in fact saw four or five cardinals as likely allies, thus rendering Pole's presence less vital. Pole's first reaction to the compromise came in a letter to Contarini, dated 17 May, in which he said that he had read the agreed formula on the previous day. However, he offered no excuse for not being in Rome when it arrived, instead repeating that Priuli would handle the matter on his behalf. His own inclination was to publish the Regensburg agreement as widely as possible, but he said that

---

[35]   Published in Massimo Firpo and Dario Marcatto, eds, *Il processo inquisitoriale del Cardinale Giovanni Morone*, 6 vols (Rome: Istituto storico italiano per l'eta moderna e contemporanea, 1981–9), 2, pp. 1039–1056.

[36]   Elizabeth G. Gleason, *Gasparo Contarini: Venice, Rome and reform* (Berkeley and Los Angeles: University of California Press, 1993), pp. 228–235.

[37]   *ERP* 3 no. 11; *CSP Ven*, V, no. 249; *LP* XVI no. 773; *CRP* 1 no. 321.

[38]   *PPP*, pp. 107–108; Gleason, *Gasparo Contarini*, p. 249.

he would keep quiet about it, as Contarini had requested.[39] In July, Pole wrote again to Contarini, as he was wont to do, in response to a further request for him to give his assessment of the Venetian cardinal's treatise on justification. Pole gave his customary uncompromising response to Contarini's work, saying that, like all his friend's writings, it started strongly, provided many strong arguments for belief in justification by faith, was courteous to opponents, and came to a logical conclusion. Nevertheless, *De Iustificatione* left Pole unsatisfied, as it did not fully explore the arguments in favour of the author's position, and he wished that Contarini had been faced with a more formidable opponent, who would have drawn him out more. Pole did however conclude that Contarini had, in this treatise, demonstrated that many Catholic traditionalists, who opposed any accommodation of 'Protestant' views, were simply not interpreting Scripture correctly. By this time, Pole was annoyed that Contarini objected to his absence from Rome at such a crucial time. He said that he had thought he was no longer needed there, in order to gain support for the Regensburg compromise, and asserted that his absence was required by 'time, place, duty and piety'. He had not, he claimed, simply left in order to avoid an expected storm.[40] Nevertheless, this and other important episodes in his life do appear to indicate that Pole would, as he himself suggested in *De unitate* [Appendix 1A], avoid a controversy wherever possible, especially if it might involve personal confrontation, and in the case of the Regensburg formula, Bembo, at least, had no hesitation in blaming him for its rejection by Rome.[41]

The months after this failure would be bad for religious diversity in Catholic Italy. On 21 July 1541, the Roman Inquisition was re-established as a distinct institution, under the leadership of one of Pole's former collaborators in reform, Cardinal Gianpietro Carafa of Naples, as the 'Congregation of the Holy Office'. Although it theoretically had jurisdiction over all who were subject to the authority of the Roman See, in practice it devoted itself to seeking out heretics in the Italian peninsula. Then, in August, Contarini died, removing one of the most open-minded leaders of the Italian Church, and this loss, to Pole and others, together with the new threat of the Inquisition, caused a crisis among reformers, at Viterbo and elsewhere.[42] Dermot Fenlon's verdict on the situation of reform, in 1541–2, is just:

> What kept [Contarini] secure in the faith to which he adhered was his confidence that, beyond theology and the resources of human ingenuity, there lay the

---

[39]  *ERP* 3 no. 12; *LP* XVI no. 837; *CRP* 1 no. 322.

[40]  *ERP* 3 no. 13; *LP* XVI no. 1007; *CRP* 1 328; *PPP*, pp. 108–110; Simoncelli, *Evangelismo italiano*, p. 105.

[41]  Gleason, *Gasparo Contarini*, p. 251.

[42]  Gordon, 'Italy', p. 286.

indefectible authority of the Church. Some might assert the doctrine of salvation by works alone, others presumptuously abandon the Church. Pole and he must submit to the Church's doctrine. Let them steer securely through Scylla and Charybdis, "not abandoning the doctrine of the Church, but believing in it more than in our wits".[43]

In 1543, an anonymous devotional tract, in Italian, was published in Venice, and entitled *Trattato del beneficio di Gesù Cristo crocifisso verso i Cristiani* ('Treatise on the benefit of Jesus Christ crucified for Christians').[44] The work achieved immediate popularity and Pier Paolo Vergerio, who was associated with Pole and later left the Catholic fold, claimed that 40,000 copies were printed. The work was well received by Cardinal Giovanni Morone, bishop of Modena, who was at the time facing the problem of unorthodox preaching in his diocese and would later receive the life-threatening attentions of the Roman Inquisition. Morone promoted the *Beneficio di Cristo* in his diocese and Cardinal Gregorio Cortese, who was in Modena to investigate suspected heresy, declared that reading it was the best possible preparation for starting every day. It was also taken up by Pole and his circle at Viterbo, but one of his traditionalist friends, Marcello Cervini, the future Pope Marcellus, when he examined it in the following year, as an inquisitor, found its contents to be somewhat mixed. He felt that the Catholic view on the vexed question of justification was inadequately expounded, but he did not think that the work should be banned. Nevertheless, those who read it should be warned that they should take care not to be influenced by some of its dubious and confusing aspects.[45] The *Beneficio* was, however, placed on the 1549 index of forbidden books of the Venetian Inquisition, and it was publicly burnt in Naples. Probably as a result, the text disappeared from knowledge until, in 1843, a copy was found in the library of St John's College, Cambridge.[46]

In recent decades, there has been much discussion of the authorship of the *Beneficio*, and the current consensus is that the original author was a Benedictine monk from a Sicilian house near Mount Etna, Benedetto da Mantova, who was associated with the Neapolitan circle of Juan de Valdés. The text was however rewritten, apparently with intervention from Pole and others, by Marcantonio

---

[43]    Dermot Fenlon, *Heresy and obedience in Tridentine Italy: Cardinal Pole and the Counter-reformation* (Cambridge: Cambridge University Press, 1972), p. 65.

[44]    Benedetto da Mantova, *Il Beneficio di Cristo*, ed. Salvatore Caponetto (Florence: Sanzoni, 1972); Gleason, *Reform thought*, pp. 103–161.

[45]    William V. Hudon, *Marcello Cervini and ecclesiastical government in Tridentine Italy* (DeKalb: Northern Illinois University Press, 1992), p. 119.

[46]    Gordon, 'Italy', p. 289.

Flaminio, who was one of the more radical members of the Viterbo circle.[47] The book is a spiritual guide, laying out the road to Christian salvation. Its central theme is the remission of sins, as a gift received by the believer as a result of Christ's Passion and death on the Cross. It has no place for works, in the process of achieving salvation. The imitation of Christ is, however, essential to this. Scholars have posited many influences on the *Beneficio*, including traditional Benedictine spirituality, Juan de Valdés, and the Greek Fathers, as well as reformers – Luther, Melanchthon and Calvin – who are indeed quoted at some length, including extracts from Calvin's *Institutes of the Christian religion*. Another important influence on the *Beneficio* was the Cassinese Benedictine congregation of Santa Giusta, in Padua, with which Pole was closely connected.[48] The first four chapters focus on justification by faith alone and, avoiding the compromises of the Regensburg formula, see works only as the fruit of faith. The fifth chapter is a meditation on the need for Christians to suffer humiliation and persecution from non-Christians, on the model of their Saviour, and to rejoice in such suffering. Christians are also to follow their Lord's example in prayer, frequent communion, constant recollection of their baptism, and awareness of the reality of predestination. Above all, the Eucharist, or Mass, gives assurance of salvation and is the seal of redemption. Thus the *Beneficio* is a concise, comprehensive and passionate, expression of the main ideas of the Italian 'evangelical' reformers, and of the Reginald Pole of the 1540s, also reflecting the continuation and revival of the medieval tradition of imitating Christ that was then being undertaken by Ignatius of Loyola.[49]

Meanwhile, Bishop Giovanni Morone's troubles in his diocese of Modena had caused disturbance among Italian Catholic reformers, including Pole's Viterbo circle, and attracted the attention of traditionalists, and the revived Roman Inquisition. In mid-1542, conflict had developed between Morone and the Modena Academy, some members of which were accused of 'Lutheranism'. In reality, the academy was predominantly a standard-bearer for anti-scholastic humanism, though some of those who preached in the city at that time did show a strong tendency towards the views of Paul and Augustine on salvation, if not those of Luther himself. The resulting disturbance caused the city's governor, Battistino Strozzi, to ask the duke to restore order. At the time, Morone was away from his diocese, but he returned in May, and his *spirituali* friends rallied

---

[47]    Philip McNair, 'Benedetto da Mantova, Marcantonio Flaminio, and the *Beneficio di Cristo*: a developing twentieth-century debate reviewed', *Modern Language Review*, 82 (1987), pp. 614–624; Mayer, *PPP*, pp. 119–201.

[48]    Barry Collett, *Italian Benedictine scholars and the Reformation: the Congregation of Santa Giustina of Padua* (Oxford: Oxford University Press, 1985), pp. 184, 185.

[49]    Gordon, 'Italy', p. 91; Euan Cameron, 'Italy', in *The early Reformation Europe*, ed. Andrew Pettegree (Cambridge: Cambridge University Press, 1992), pp. 188–214, at pp. 199–200; Brundin, *Vittoria Colonna*, pp. 49–56; Overell, *Italian reform*, pp. 29–31.

to his support, among them Gregorio Cortese and Jacopo Sadoleto, both of whom came from Modena. Cortese had in fact been in the city since the previous December, having been sent by the pope to investigate the situation. In particular, Gasparo Contarini produced what proved to be one of his last works, a catechism that aimed to address the Modenese Academy's concerns while remaining within the confines of Catholic orthodoxy. With the active support of Cortese, Bishop Morone circulated the catechism widely, and urged the Academicians to indicate their agreement with it by means of their signatures, along with those of the diocesan bishop himself, and the city's magistrates. This was done in June 1542. Pole, on the other hand, seems to have tended to the Academy's side, and disagreed with Contarini's approach to the issue of heresy in Modena. The complexity of the situation at the top of the Roman Church, suggesting that a simplistic distinction between 'reformers' and 'traditionalists' in the 1540s is inadequate, is indicated by the appointment of Morone as a cardinal, in the midst of the crisis, on 12 June 1542. A further illustration of the point was the inclusion of another *spirituale*, and friend of Pole, Tommaso Badia, to the newly-constituted council of the Inquisition, with Gianpietro Carafa and Juan Álvarez de Toledo, who by this time appeared as zealous defenders of tradition. In Modena, meanwhile, the Academicians went underground, becoming secret reformers, their organisation not being dissolved until the 1560s.[50]

The events in Modena in part precipitated the break-up of the *spirituali*, in so far as they had ever been a coherent movement. Not only did Contarini die, on 24 August 1542, but, at about the same time, two prominent reformers, Piero Martire Vermigli, who was an Augustinian canon of the basilica of St John Lateran in Rome, and Bernardino Ochino, an Observant Franciscan who had become the general of the recently-established Capuchin order, left Italy to join the reformers north of the Alps. Both had been in the Valdesian circle in Naples, and had later attached themselves to the Viterbo group. Vermigli apparently left Lucca on 12 August, and on the 24th wrote a now lost letter to Pole, giving him the news. The letter's dispatch had been delayed until Vermigli was safely outside Italy.[51] Ochino's departure seems to have been precipitated by a summons to Rome, in July 1542, which he no doubt suspected to be connected with accusations of heresy, since the bull proclaiming the re-organisation of the Roman Inquisition was published on 21 July. The Franciscan dithered over whether or not to obey, and involved, to varying degrees, Contarini, Ercole

---

[50]  Massimo Firpo, *Inquisizione romana e Contrariforma: Studi sul Cardinal Giovanni Morone e il suo processo d'eresia* (Bologna: Il Mulino, 1992), pp. 29–118; Mayer, *PPP*, pp. 125–127; Gordon, 'Italy', pp. 290–291. On the devotional life of Pole and his circle at this time, see Anne Overell, 'Pole's piety? The devotional reading of Reginald Pole and his friends', *Journal of Ecclesiastical History*, 63 (2012), pp. 458–474.

[51]  Philip McNair, *Peter Martyr in Italy: an anatomy of apostasy* (Oxford: Clarendon Press, 1967), pp. 270–272, 279–282.

Gonzaga, Pole, Giberti and Vittoria Colonna. The implication of the *spirituali* in the case was inevitable since Ochino was staying in Verona with Giberti when the summons arrived. On 19 August, the Capuchin general consulted the dying Contarini, who rallied in response, and intimated that he did not want him to depart. Cardinal Ercole Gonzaga later claimed that he had seen Ochino on the road near Mantua, dressed not in his Capuchin habit but as a soldier, yet he had not thought to inform anyone of this at the time. On 22 August, Ochino told Pole and Colonna that he was indeed going to leave Italy, and the Roman Church, and Giberti was also told, though he omitted to report this news to the Curia.[52]

Meanwhile, on 21 November 1542, Paul III finally called a general council, which was to assemble at Trent, in northern Italy, close to the border of the Holy Roman Empire. At the same time, legates began to be named, to preside over the assembly, if the pope himself did not attend. To the surprise of many, one of them was Reginald Pole, who had attended a consistory, back in October 1542, at which the matter had been discussed, and Alvise Priuli, at least, had supposed that Badia, Morone and Pierpaolo Parisi would be chosen. Morone was known to be very keen that the council should be held in Trent, in the hope that there would be a large German attendance, but Pole had left the consistory without showing any special interest in the assignment.[53] Once they reached Trent, Pole lodged in the 'Rocca', probably the Castello del Buonconsiglio. During his brief stay (he left for Treville before 20 February 1543), Pole met the Imperial ambassadors, including Nicholas Perrenot de Granvelle, whose son Antoine, possibly also in attendance, would play an important part in his subsequent life. The council did not materialise, though on 3 May Cardinal Alessandro Farnese summoned Pole to Bologna, to discuss its future. By this time, Pole and Morone were forming a friendship that would be strongly reflected in their later correspondence, particularly during the reign of Mary I of England. While Morone remained in Trent, on 10 May Pole attended a consistory at Bologna, in which the question of withdrawing the remaining legates, Morone and Parisi, was debated. In the event, nothing more would happen at Trent until 1545, while Pole and his friends tried to piece together their shattered group and preserve the reforming ideas that they had previously developed.[54] In their correspondence towards the end of May 1543, Pole and Morone shared views of the Church, and of Christian discipleship, that strongly resembled those expressed in the *Beneficio di Cristo*. Yet, during the rest of 1543, Pope Paul III

---

[52]  Gigliola Fragnito, 'Gli "spirituali" e la fuga de Bernardino Ochino', *Rivista Storica Italiana*, 74 (1972), pp. 777–811, at pp. 780–783, 791, 805–807; Overell, *Italian reform*, pp. 33–35.

[53]  Parks, 'Parma letters', p. 302; *CRP* 1 no. 391; *PPP*, p. 134.

[54]  *PPP*, pp. 135–138.

continued to employ Pole as a consultant, particularly on matters related to the Empire, since he feared that Charles V would come to some kind of settlement with the German reformers without consulting Rome. At the beginning of June, the news reached the Curia that such an agreement had indeed made, at Speyer, and Pole probably helped to draft the highly critical response that Paul III dispatched to Charles.[55] This document circulated widely in Europe, mostly via unofficial channels, but the peace made between France and the Habsburgs, at Crépy on 18 September, severely reduced its impact.[56]

Finally, in November 1544, Paul III felt able to begin organising the resumption, in effect the opening, of the Council of Trent. The bull *Laetare Hierusalem* ('Rejoice Jerusalem'), convoking it, began to be drafted, and was issued on 12 January 1545. On 22 February, three papal legates were named, these being two future popes, Innocenzo del Monte (Julius III) and Marcello Cervini (Marcellus II), and Reginald Pole, who very nearly became pope.[57] Pole travelled to Trent two months later than the other legates, on security grounds and his correspondence, between May and July 1545, indicates that the threat to his life was still genuine.[58] On 19 July, Pole wrote from Trent to thank Pierluigi Farnese, duke of Castro, who was then at Piacenza, for warning him of a planned ambush, and making arrangements for his security. A few days earlier, Farnese had written to inform the legates of the planned ambush and capture of Pole by from three to five English agents, who had been recruited by Henry VIII's then representative in Venice, Edmund Harvel. Pole took this threat seriously enough to contemplate changing his lodgings, if not temporarily leaving Trent altogether.[59]

In March or April 1545, Pole had drafted, for the initial perusal of Paul III and the other legates, a treatise, *De Concilio*, on the forthcoming council, its ideals and purpose.[60] It is not clear whether Cervini and del Monte actually read *De Concilio*, which mainly consisted of 70 questions and answers, but they undoubtedly knew of its contents, since they appeared in Pole's sermon for the opening of the council, which was read by its secretary, Angelo Massarelli, on 7 January 1546. The text, in both its treatise and its sermon form, was explicitly based on Scripture, this being the only proper approach, in Pole's view, whether or not it was intended to appeal also to Protestants, as has been suggested. Pole begins by asserting the hierarchical nature of the Church, and accepts the

---

[55]   *CT*, 4, pp. 374–379; *CRP* 1 no. 414.

[56]   *PPP*, pp. 141–143.

[57]   *CT*, 4, pp. 391–392.

[58]   Parks, 'Parma letters', p. 304 (Pole to Cardinal Guido Ascanio Sforza, Trent, 4 May 1545); *CRP* 1 no. 430.

[59]   Parks, 'Parma letters', pp. 304–306; *CRP* 1 nos 439, 440; *LP* XX (i) no. 650 (2).

[60]   Pole, *De Concilio liber Reginaldi Poli cardinalis* (Rome: Paolo Manuzio Aldi, 1562), a posthumous publication; Mayer, 'Reluctant author', pp. 26–27, 83–84.

monarchical status of the papacy, but he does not conclude from this that the pope therefore rules the Church. He evades the question of papal infallibility, which would not in any case be formally defined for several centuries, stating instead that the council, as a body, including the pope, depended on the Holy Spirit, and should not concern itself with human concerns and powers. The model for Trent was not to be found, as some contemporaries had suggested, in the Old Testament, but in the first-century Council of Jerusalem [Acts 15:1–35], which followed the gift to the Church of the Holy Spirit at Pentecost, and was primarily concerned with the basis on which Gentiles (non-Jews) might be admitted to the Christian community.

Given his leadership at this first Church council, Pole naturally proceeded directly to the question of Peter's primacy, which has traditionally been seen as the scriptural basis of papal supremacy. Here, Peter is identified with the faith that Christ guaranteed would never fail, and that depends completely on the infusion of the Holy Spirit. Jerusalem was the model for Trent because it was the first council to expound and confirm the Christian faith, and order its implementation with charity. Moving on to the question of pastors, or the clergy, Pole states that their authority is based on that of the prophets, particularly as it was expounded by Ezekiel. Christian pastors should be both merciful and judgmental, as required in each case, since they possessed both human and divine powers that they derived from Christ Himself. In this context, Christ requires a vicar, or deputy and representative, but even though He willed his power to Peter, the first pope, the true ruler of the Church was still the Holy Spirit, and not any man. Under this authority, the pope is father, tutor or guardian, and shepherd to Christians. Peter did not preside alone at the council of Jerusalem, since James and Paul had leading roles as well, so that the legates at Trent should propagate the faith of all the apostles, and not just Peter's. Faith should always have priority over all human considerations. Nevertheless, dependence on faith alone for salvation should not lead, as it did in the case of some contemporary preachers, Catholic as well as Protestant, to disparagement of works of goodness and charity. Echoing Contarini's Regensburg formula, Pole stresses that works of mercy are the necessary fruits of faith, as part of a pact or treaty (*foedus*) between God and His Church.

Pole continues by reiterating another of his favourite themes, at least since the execution of Thomas More, John Fisher, the London Carthusians and some members of his own family, that the Church is built on the blood of the martyrs, and the miracles, that attested to Peter's faith, and were again particularly shown in the conversion of the Emperor Constantine to Christianity [Appendix 1G]. The prophets foresaw afflictions for the popes, as well as honours, and one of these, he asserts controversially, is Christian emperors. Nevertheless, and no doubt with Charles V in mind, Pole argues, further on in the treatise, that emperors did have a role in councils, and should support their work, not least by keeping the peace. Princes are shepherds alongside the clergy, even though they are in need of priestly blessing, and are duty bound to imitate Christ and pray constantly for their people. The future of the council, and of the Church in general, depends on the honest and full confession of sins, led by the pope himself.[61]

The bulk of the content of *De Concilio*, was included in Pole's opening sermon to the council, which was read on behalf of the legates by its secretary, Angelo Massarelli, on 7 January 1546.[62] It set out the council's three main tasks, which were to extirpate heresy, to reform ecclesiastical discipline and morals, and to restore the peace of the Church. Pole also took part in the earlier debates, taking a typically spiritual and idealistic approach. Complete trust must be placed in Christ, and if any progress was to be made, the leaders of the Church, who had brought it to its parlous situation, should take responsibility for their actions. Each member of the council could only produce reform in proportion to his acknowledgment of his personal unworthiness and sin. Failure to stamp out heresy was equivalent to sowing its seeds, and clerical abuses, such as granting bishoprics to laymen, had to be tackled first. Significantly, in view of what would happen in England in Mary's reign, Pole also asserted that to alienate church goods to lay people was directly to rob the poor. Those who received such property would be punished by God, as the sinful cities of Sodom and Gomorrah had been [Genesis 13, 18]. Pole continued to invoke the prophetic voice of Ezekiel, in his demands for the urgent reform of the Church. He evidently regarded the bishops as the crucial participants in the council, and frequently addressed them as the main instruments of reform. They had brought the Church to its current parlous state, and now it was their responsibility to put things right. As 1546 went on, Pole seems however, to have become increasingly disillusioned. He objected to the reaffirmation, without investigation or debate, of the traditional canon of Scripture, although he accepted that individual consciences, including his, could be overruled by the decision of the majority. It was, however, to be the fundamental question of God's justification of the sinner that would bring him to a personal crisis.[63]

On 21 May, Pole missed the council session on preaching, pleading bad health, and a week later his fellow legate, Marcello Cervini, noted that he was suffering from a deep-rooted and severe pain in his left arm.[64] On 14 June, he was well enough to intervene in the drafting of the decree on original sin and just a week later, he spoke in the initial debate on justification, saying that deep prayer was needed for its adequate consideration, as well as a serious and discriminating

[61]  *PPP*, pp. 145–47.
[62]  *CT*, 4, pp. 548–53 (7 January 1546).
[63]  *CT*, 4, p. 578; *PPP*, pp. 150–151.
[64]  *CT*, 10, p. 505.

reading of Protestant writings on this subject, which was so vital to them.[65] This was to be Pole's last utterance at Trent. A few days later, news reached Rome that he had been granted licence to leave the city, and he went to Treville on 21 June, apparently intending to recuperate there for the rest of the summer.[66] Angelo Massarelli stated at the time that Pole had in fact been ill for more than a month, and Dermot Fenlon has suggested that he may have suffered from a psychosomatic illness, or even a nervous breakdown, precipitated, no doubt, by the way in which the justification debate was going.[67] By the later 1550s, when Pole's circle was under heavy pressure from the Inquisition, it was suggested that he had in fact left Trent in order to avoid having either to oppose or accept the council's views on justification, but, whatever the truth, he was not allowed to remain silent on the subject, even though he was not present at the council.[68]

The cardinal of England's reluctance to pronounce on the council's decree and canons on justification, which rejected the Regensburg compromise, was initially based on the need for caution in considering the subject, which had not been broached in such a way during the entire 1,500 years of the Church's history. Whether or not as a result of Pole's intervention, a further consideration of the subject of justification was postponed until September 1546, when more bishops had arrived at the council, and the formal decree was eventually made on 13 January 1547. Before the debate resumed, Pole had been forced to comment on the draft decree and canons, which he did by 9 October.[69] He produced two texts, one being a critical discussion of the general issues, and the other a commentary on the council's document, point by point.[70] In these texts, Pole tried to adhere to his belief in justification by faith alone, which he had held for some years, along with many of his friends in Viterbo and elsewhere. He based his comments, at least some of which reached Trent during October, on Scripture, and on the experience of Christian believers, and the main thrust of what he wrote was aimed at preventing a definitive rejection, such as eventually happened, of all Protestant teaching on the subject. While his views were becoming known, on 17 November 1546, Pole was back in Rome, and was soon to hear of momentous developments in his native country.[71]

---

[65]　*CT*, 1, pp. 75–76; 5, p. 220; *CT*, 1, pp. 82–83; *CT*, 5, p. 257.

[66]　*CT*, 10, p. 545; *ERP* 4 no. 13; *LP* XXI (i) no. 1164; *CRP* 1 no. 474.

[67]　*CT*, 1, pp. 442, 557; Fenlon, *Heresy and obedience*, p. 135.

[68]　*PPP*, pp. 152–154.

[69]　*ERP* 4 no. 64; *LP* XXI (ii) no. 119; *CRP* 1 no. 496; Fenlon, *Heresy and obedience*, p. 172.

[70]　*CT*, 12, pp. 671–676.

[71]　*PPP*, pp. 157–160.

# Chapter 5
# Homecoming?

In January 1547, King Henry VIII, Reginald Pole's nemesis, was declining. By the 27th of the month he had lost the power of speech, and could only squeeze the hand of Archbishop Thomas Cranmer, who had been summoned from Croydon to administer the last rites to him. The king died in the early hours of 28 January, but news of his death was kept secret for three days, while his councillors manoeuvred to control the new boy king, Jane Seymour's son, Edward VI.[1] At the end of Henry's reign of nearly 38 years, opinions differed, both in England itself and on the Continent, about what would happen next. The Roman Curia and Catholic princes remained convinced that Edward was illegitimate, like his older sister Elizabeth, and that Mary should become queen. As far as religion was concerned, the situation seemed more ambiguous. Although he had caused schism between his kingdom and Rome, Henry had died in the belief that he was a Catholic Christian, and Cranmer appears to have been willing to go along with this notion at the time. With hindsight, it has seemed absolutely clear that the Church in England under Edward was to veer sharply in a reformed direction, making links with the cities and territories of the Continental Reformation, rather than Rome, but things were not necessarily seen in that way at the time. With conservative bishops still at the head of many English dioceses, it did not seem far-fetched to suppose that, given the right steer by Edward's council, the Henrician schism might be ended, and at least some of these prelates might attend the Council of Trent, when it eventually resumed.[2]

In Rome, Pope Paul III quickly realised that the English king's death threatened the political, and perhaps also the religious, stability of Europe. Once the accession of Edward had been confirmed, he responded by naming three new diplomatic legates, who were to be directed respectively to England, the emperor and France.[3] In these circumstances, the cardinal of England naturally became prominent in Roman political counsels. At some point between 18 and 25 February, Pole wrote to Pope Paul, saying that Henry's death offered an opportunity to restore England to the Church, thus giving it and the pope everlasting glory. He applauded Paul's intention to send the legates, but correctly

[1]   Scarisbrick, *Henry VIII*, pp. 495–496; MacCulloch, *Thomas Cranmer*, p. 360.

[2]   Chris Skidmore, *Edward VI: The lost king of England* (London: Weidenfeld & Nicolson, 2007), p. 68.

[3]   *CT*, 10, p. 821; Mayer, *PPP*, p. 163.

observed that any Catholic intervention in England would be impossible without the consent and support of Charles V. Also, someone with deep experience of the country should be sent to England, and that person would have to be welcome there as a *persona grata*. Given that he himself was unlikely to fulfil this last criterion, Pole recommended the archbishop of Trent, Cristoforo Madruzzo.[4] A day later, Pole dispatched a second letter to the pope, in which he affirmed even more strongly that Charles would have to have the leading role in seeking a new settlement, both on the Continent and in England. Thus the choice of a legate to be sent to the Imperial court was a vital and delicate matter.

The appointee would have to work well not only with the emperor himself but also with his leading councillors, since relations between Charles and Pope Paul had been poor since the previous year. In the circumstances, Pole again suggested that Madruzzo might be the right man for the job.[5] It is likely that Pole was worried that Charles would seek to control what happened in England, this concern indicating that the tension between cardinal and emperor, which had developed in the late 1530s, still existed: indeed, it would last for the rest of their respective lives.[6] On 25 February, Paul III duly appointed two legates, but did not name Pole, apparently because Bishop Granvelle of Arras, whose influence over the emperor was great, had objected to his appointment.[7] Mayer ascribes Granvelle's attitude to the fact that Pole had earlier quarrelled, over a pension assigned to the revenues of the archdiocese of Granada, with its archbishop, Cardinal Francisco de Mendoza y Bobadilla.[8] Perhaps a more significant factor, along with the negative outcome of Pole's visit to Toledo in 1539, was that Mendoza had concerns about Pole's theological orthodoxy, particularly in relation to the doctrine of justification. The Cardinal of Granada's judgment of his brother of England would affect the latter's reputation in the Curia for the rest of his days. More immediately, any hope that Pole might have had of being appointed once again as legate to England was dashed, on the very reasonable grounds that he might offend Edward VI's new government.[9] Despite these obstacles, Pole later claimed that he had made an approach to the English Council as soon as he heard that Henry VIII had died, though the episode in question may in fact have occurred in 1548, by which time Edward Seymour, duke of Somerset, was established as lord protector of King Edward.[10] In the event, in January 1547, Paul III named Pole as 'perpetual' governor of Bagnoregio, in the papal states, whither he transferred his residence, although

4    *ERP* 4 no. 20; *CSP Ven*, V, no. 453; *CRP* 2 no. 515.
5    *ERP* 4 no. 21; *CSP Ven*, V, no. 454; *CRP* 2 no. 516.
6    *CT*, 10, p. 821; Mayer, *PPP*, p. 163.
7    *CT*, 10, p. 891.
8    *CT*, 10, pp. 641 n. 2, 821, 827; *CT*, 11, p. 105.
9    *CT*, 11, p. 157.
10   BL Add. 41577, fols 3r–27v; *CSP Ven*, V, no. 575; *CRP* 2 no. 555 (further textual details).

he did not relinquish his legation to Viterbo until 1550.[11] In the late 1540s, he continued to resist the proposed move of the general council from Trent to Bologna, and retained his desire that the Lutherans should somehow be brought to take part in it.[12]

In 1548, Pole renewed to his quest for a return to his native land. Nothing happened immediately, but in October of that year, a Cambridge theologian, John Yonge, wrote to Pole's agent, Michael Throckmorton, suggesting that the lord protector would be prepared to receive correspondence from Pole, as long as he sent it as a private English subject, and not as a cardinal or legate.[13] If true, this would have been a remarkable move on Somerset's part, seeing that Pole was still under attainder as a traitor, as he had been when earlier attempts were made by English agents to assassinate him. Yet this story receives some kind of corroboration from an opinion supposedly expressed by the reforming bishop of Worcester, Hugh Latimer, that Pole could have been a good preacher, had he not been a cardinal, presumably because he believed him to hold a Protestant view of justification.[14] Edward VI's tutor, and secretary to the council, William Thomas, in a dialogue in Italian that was probably written in 1547 and was published in 1552, described Pole as 'virtuous and learned', saying that '[he] secretly professeth to be a Protestant and openly maintaineth the papacy'.[15] In the event, Pole did not seek to go home until the English government directly threatened the Mass, and the rest of the traditional Latin liturgy, with the production, and endorsement by parliament, of the first English Book of Common Prayer, in January 1549. On 15 February, passports were issued for two representatives of Pole, Richard Hilliard and Throckmorton, to travel to the Netherlands, with credentials to Charles V's then confessor, the Spanish Dominican theologian Domingo de Soto, whom Pole had met at Trent, and also to a member of Edward VI's council, John Dudley, earl of Warwick and duke of Northumberland.[16]

Pole's accompanying letter to Dudley, dated 6 April, appears to be a reply to Yonge's letter to him, in the previous year. In it he professed his deep and continuing love for his native England, and introduced Hilliard and Throckmorton as his messengers to Edward's court. He wanted Warwick to use his influence in the council to obtain licence for his return to his homeland, and asserted that his writings, even the *De unitate*, were pacific in intent. Whether or

---

[11]   *ERP* 4, Carte Cerviniane, no. 30; *CRP* 2 no. 511.

[12]   *ERP* 4 pp. 382–402; *CT*, 6, no. 3, pp. 728–738; *CRP* 2 no. 524 (1 February 1548, with further textual details).

[13]   *CSP Dom I*, p. 11; Overell. 'Pole's special agent', p. 274.

[14]   G.E. Corrie, ed., *Sermons by Hugh Latimer, sometime bishop of Worcester, martyr 1555* (Cambridge: Cambridge University Press, 1844), p. 173.

[15]   William Thomas, 'Il pellegrino inglese', BL Cotton Vespasian D.XVIII, cited in Overell, *Italian reform*, pp. 88–89 and n. 44.

[16]   Mayer, *PPP*, p. 169.

not Pole knew that John Dudley's influence was then increasing, at the expense of that of the duke of Somerset, is uncertain, but it is perhaps not surprising that his missive received no positive response.[17] On the same day, Pole wrote to Domingo de Soto, alluding to Charles V's condemnation of the new English Prayer Book, and in particular of the eucharistic rite that replaced the Mass. Pole told Fray Domingo of his hope that the emperor's reaction would stop the English making this change, adding that he had tried to get in touch with those responsible for it, but had been rebuffed. He feared that Hilliard and Throckmorton would not be able to achieve anything, but he still intended to send them, in the hope that Edward's council might be chastened and change course.[18] Having failed with John Dudley, on 6 May Pole wrote, from Civitella San Paolo, to the duke of Somerset and the whole royal council. He told them that he had not wanted to approach them until the English government was established, but now he was willing to let bygones be bygones, overlooking all that the late king had done to him and his family, for the sake of his love for his country. Nevertheless, he had to say that he deeply disapproved of what the council was doing, particularly in relation to religion. He offered papal support and protection against other countries that might otherwise threaten England, but only if the new Prayer Book was not introduced.[19] Pole did not mention having read the new book, but he had evidently learned of its salient changes, in particular the deliberate and explicit denial of any sacrificial content in the offering of the elements in the Eucharist. This was symbolised by the prohibition of the celebrant's elevation of the consecrated bread and wine.[20]

On the same day, Pole issued instructions to Richard Hilliard, for use should he succeed in meeting the English council. He was first to obtain an Imperial safe-conduct at Antwerp, and then letters patent from the lord deputy of Calais, Lord Cobham. He was to follow strictly a pre-arranged route to London, and when he arrived he was to convey, in the strongest terms, his master's deep affection for England. Hilliard was to be aware that Pole saw England in its current state, and the lord protector in particular, as a threat both to itself and to its neighbours, not least because the country now had a boy king. Deploying, as he so often did, his detailed knowledge of English history, Pole pointed to the conflict and instability that had ensued in the previous century, both when Henry VI succeeded his father, Henry V, while still a child, and when Edward IV left the kingdom to his young son Edward V. Coming from one of the last of the Yorkists, who had fought the Lancastrians in the Wars of the Roses, this was

---

[17]   TNA SP 10/6, no. 32; *CSP Dom*, p. 14; *CSP Dom rev*, no. 208; *CRP* 2 no. 538.

[18]   *ERP* 4 no. 24; *CRP* 2 no. 539.

[19]   *ERP* 4 no. 23; *CRP* 2 no. 544 (further textual details).

[20]   *The First and Second Prayer Books of Edward VI* (London: The Prayer Book Society, 1999), p. 223: 'These wordes [of consecration] before rehersed are to be saied, turning still to the Altar, without any elevacion or shewing the sacrament to the people'.

a shrewd barb, given that Edward V and his brother were firmly believed to have been murdered by their uncle, Richard III. Even nearer to the bone was Pole's instruction to Hilliard to allude to the lord protector's own current problems with his brother, Thomas Seymour, who would soon be executed for supposed treason. The instructions indicate that Pole saw England as being isolated, in terms of European politics, and liable to attack by all or any of the Empire, France and Scotland. The main focus of Hilliard's mission was to be on Thomas Cranmer and the other reforming bishops. Pole claimed that many of the ordinary English clergy opposed the introduction of the Prayer Book. Using his particular international experience, he wanted Hilliard to point out to Edward's council that 1549 was a bad time to embark on such reforms. The Council of Trent had been suspended in 1547, Charles V had imposed a restrictive 'Interim' on the German Protestants at Augsburg in 1548, and liturgical disputes in England would destabilise Edward VI's regime. Pole devoutly wished that the English would refer their religious disputes to the pope for decision, but if that was impossible, he proposed a surprising way forward. A disputation should be organised by the king's council, between bishops and theologians, and a majority vote would decide the future course of the English Church. This proposal bears a remarkable resemblance to the process whereby some of the Continental cities had earlier arrived at reformation, a notable case being Nuremberg, where Cranmer had found his wife. Evidently Pole was confident that there would be a Catholic majority. Despite the failure of his friend Contarini's efforts at Regensburg in 1541, and the fact that Trent and Augsburg were hardly inspiring examples of the merits of such disputations, Pole bravely referred to Jesus's promise that 'where two or three are gathered in my name, I am there among them' [Matthew 18:20]. The proposed English colloquy should have a moderator who was acceptable to both sides and, in a fascinating but now little-known move, Pole suggested that he himself would be the best man for the job. His notorious attachment to the Roman Church should not be a cause for concern, since it did not affect his deep love for England. Somerset and his colleagues should therefore put aside past disputes over matters such as the divorce of Catherine and the royal supremacy, and accept his offer of mediation. If they did so, Pole would ensure that all sanctions imposed on England by Catholic powers were lifted for the duration of the conference. In conclusion, Hilliard was to make it clear to the English that Pole saw Henry VIII's death as a great opportunity for reconciliation between England and Rome.[21]

A month later, Somerset replied to Pole, in a letter written in Latin at Greenwich Palace, with which he enclosed a copy of the English Prayer Book, which remains in the Apostolic Library in Rome. The lord protector said that he had indeed hoped that he would receive some 'consolation' from Pole, despite his

---

[21]  *CRP* 2 no. 545 (further textual details).

office as a cardinal, and did recognise his attachment to his native land, Indeed, he said that he had actually wanted to send Hilliard and Throckmorton back with a royal pardon for Pole. However, having read Pole's letters, he had realised that the cardinal preferred the pope to King Edward and himself, 'on the pretext of piety'. The cardinal was now in fact behaving like a foreign potentate, and not the loyal English subject that he claimed to be. On the basis of the arguments that had been developed at Henry VIII's court in the 1530s, Somerset told Pole that Edward's council continued to reject the usurped authority of the papacy. He also rebuffed Pole's comparison between the situation under Edward VI and the difficulties that had earlier been experienced by the sons of Henry V and Edward IV. The 'princes in the Tower', as they were later to become known, had suffered only because of the evil behaviour of Richard, duke of York, while Somerset's own family problems, with his brother and his marriage to Henry VIII's widow Catherine Parr, were not relevant to the general political situation of England. As far as external dangers to the kingdom were concerned, Somerset stated that he expected other rulers soon to convert to 'the Gospel', and he rejected Pole's offer to preside over a debate on the future of the Church in England, on the grounds that the matter had already been settled by Cranmer and the other English bishops. In a brave statement that would soon be proved wrong, when rebellion and disturbances broke out over the summer of 1549, in Cornwall, Devon, the Thames Valley and Norfolk, Edward's lord protector told Pole that there was no dissension in England, as he supposed. The people of England had agreed, he claimed, to the removal of superstition and clerical abuse from their Church. If Pole was really motivated by patriotism, and wanted to retire to his homeland after his long exile, the disputation that he wished for would indeed be organised, in order to convince him of the truth of the reformed faith.[22]

Far from accepting Somerset's rebuff, Pole set to work on a counter-blast, just as disturbances indeed broke out in England [Appendix 2]. As a result, on 12 October, he dispatched to the council, and to the lord protector, who was probably overthrown before he could answer it, a lengthy document in Italian, which survives in several versions, one in the British Library and others in Rome.[23] The text was probably begun before news reached Italy of the West Country Prayer Book rebellion, which broke out in early June. Some of the rebels demanded the recall of Pole to England, and the lifting of his attainder, and these developments seem to have been known in Rome by the end of June.[24] The text, which was typical of Pole's complex and long-winded writing, began as a reply to Somerset's letter to him, which had been sent just before the

---

[22]   TNA SP 10/7, no. 28; *CSP Dom*, p. 17; *CSP Dom rev*, no. 265; *CRP* 2 no. 549.

[23]   BL Add. 41577, fols 3r–27v; BAV Vat. lat. 5968, fols 258r–74v; *CRP* 2 no. 555.

[24]   Jennifer Loach, *Edward VI*, ed. George Bernard and Penry Williams (New Haven and London: Yale University Press, 1999), p. 72.

outbreak of rebellion in the West Country. In it, Pole suggests that Somerset completely misunderstood his offer to return as a loyal subject and to mediate in a religious disputation. In addition he suggested, on the basis of the reports that Hilliard and Throckmorton had given him when they returned from their mission, that the reaction to it in the council had not in fact been the unanimous and implacable rejection that Somerset had suggested in his letter. Tactfully, if inaccurately, Pole suggested that the duke's secretary, in drafting the text, might have significantly distorted the true message, but added that he would answer his missive in any case.

The cardinal of England, probably aware already that Pope Paul III's health was declining, admitted that not having to go home to England at that stage would save him much effort. He added, pointedly, that any royal councillor who expressed himself in the abrupt manner of Somerset's letter would (or should?) suffer ruin. The duke should not mock foreign princes, thus sitting 'in the seat of scoffers' [Ps.1:1], such ruin being the fate of rulers who behaved in such a way. The overwhelming impetus of this text, as in so many of his other writings, is Pole's fierce sense of his own aristocratic honour and dignity. Somerset had accused him, a 'man of honour', of acting maliciously, and this was nothing less than 'the sin of blasphemy against the Holy Spirit', which, according to Jesus Himself, cannot be forgiven [Mark 3:29; Luke 12:10]. Using the language of contemporary Italian warfare, Pole stated that as a result, God had a vendetta against the duke, this being a poignant thing to suggest, given Somerset's political and military circumstances at that time. So angry was Pole, that he accused the lord protector of being a fiercer enemy to him than Henry VIII had ever been. Reference was then made to the issues discussed in *De unitate*, and the refashioning of Pole's autobiography began, in particular his last interview with the late king, and his brother Henry's role in connection with it. It is difficult, reading this text, not to see Reginald as something of a self-regarding snob. He implied Somerset that his secretary had made him, Pole, seem like a mere upstart, who had come from a base condition to some grade of honour, whereas in fact it was Seymour who had done this [Appendix 2B]. This lofty Plantagenet view of society was always a feature of Pole's outlook. He also accused the lord protector of neglecting the political interests of England, and the kingdom's security, then going on to the more specific points in Somerset's letter.

First came the issue of the pardon that Pole was being offered for his supposed treason. He was required simply to sue for this, without presuming to give political advice to Somerset and the council. Pole retorted that, instead, Edward VI himself, now aged 12, should ask him for pardon, for what had happened to the cardinal's family, the details being rehearsed once again. Edward should resolve to satisfy his own debt to his father, and thus help his own soul. If he was still too young to understand the issues involved, Somerset and the council should advise him, or else, as Reginald was convinced, God would avenge the Pole family. The next issue to be raised was Pole's refusal to obey Edward as Supreme Head of the English Church. He still did not believe that any human ruler could have that role and authority, which belonged to God and his Son, who freed us through His Passion. On this point, Pole explicitly supported the views of John Fisher and Thomas More, meaning that he could obey King Edward as his natural lord, but always and only, subject to Divine law. In any case, he no longer regarded himself as an English subject, being still under attainder, as long as the Henrician royal supremacy remained in place.

In an intriguing passage, Pole then turned to his beloved religious matters. He admitted that he saw some attraction in concept of the 'pure', godly religion then being advocated and enforced in England. Nonetheless, he thought that Somerset himself lacked deep understanding in this area, having confirmed what Pole regarded as Henry's bloodthirsty and tyrannical laws. As the duke showed no contrition, he was in a poor position to understand God's law, as opposed to that of secular rulers. Pole did not see any value in talking to King Edward at this stage, because of his young age, but he waspishly expressed the hope that the councillors would not prove to be as childish in great matters as their sovereign. There was heresy in England, some of it going so far as to be anti-Trinitarian, and Pole was not naïve, but simply wanted to help the Church there to deal with it. He now sympathised with Somerset, to the extent that he had had to have his brother Thomas executed, thus sharing with him in family bereavement. The lord protector should not underestimate Charles V's threat to England, if his government did not change its ways and return to the Catholic fold. Somerset's claim that Edward's kingdom was adhering to God's word might be more credible if he made peace with Catholic Europe, and if he dealt with the schism that had placed Bishop Gardiner of Winchester in the Tower of London. Henry VIII had been excommunicated by the pope for offending God, and not just the Church. As would happen later, when he was in correspondence with Mary, Pole particularly objected to Somerset's referring to the late king as 'of most blessed memory'. He concluded by refusing the duke's offer to allow him to return to England, as long as he retained the new Prayer Book, not least because many of King Edward's subjects were rebelling against it. Although there was evidently no meeting of minds between the cardinal and Somerset, it is notable that, in this correspondence, Pole managed to avoid any direct reference to papal primacy.[25] In view of what was about to happen to him in Rome, this omission may seem ironic, and possibly harmful.

On 10 November 1549, Pope Paul III died in Rome, at the age of 82, and it quickly became apparent that the cardinal of England was a strong candidate to succeed him, even though the late pope's nephew, Alessandro Farnese, let it be known, by the 16th of that month, that he regarded Pole as insufficiently

---

[25]   Mayer, *PPP*, pp. 169–174.

'Italian'. By long tradition, the major Catholic powers, notably the Empire, France and Spain, reckoned to have blocks of voting support in the supposedly secret conclave that elected a new pope. In the circumstances of Europe at the end of 1549, this in effect meant that Charles V and the new king of France, Henry II, expected, and were expected, to be the main contenders to decide on the successor to Paul. It was not essential for the entire body of cardinals to be present in conclave for a papal election, and those who did reach Rome were, famously, confined to a section of the Vatican Palace adjoining the Sistine Chapel, once the Mass of the Holy Spirit had been celebrated by the dean of the College of Cardinals, who in this case was Giandomenico de Cupis. The cardinals were not totally isolated, however, as each had in his apartment a staff of about three, known as 'conclavists'. As would become clear during this particular election, there was considerable opportunity for communication with the outside world, during the period of enclosure. Meals were brought in by servants, and the many diplomats accredited to the papal court, including the representatives of the major European powers, seem to have had no difficulty in gaining access to the electors.[26]

The conclave opened on 29 November, a week later than planned, and the first vote took place on 3 December. In it, Pole was the winner, with 21 votes, though he needed at least 28 in order to win outright. In this ballot, Juan Álvarez de Toledo received 13 votes, Francesco Sfrondati and Giandomenico de Cupis gained 12 each, while Gianpietro Carafa had 10. It seemed clear, both to the voters and to the observers outside, that Pole was close to victory, and in that expectation a second ballot was held on the following day. This time, the Englishman increased his vote to 24, still short of the required total, but Alessandro Farnese then proposed an unusual though not unprecedented procedure, that no further votes should be held and, instead, Pole should be declared pope by acclamation, or 'adoration', as curial usage had it. At this stage, it was thought that Pole was only one vote short of the necessary total, but on 5 December Gianpietro Carafa startled the assembly by accusing him of heresy. The charge related to the recent controversy over the doctrine of justification, which had supposedly had been settled by the decrees and canons of the Council of Trent in 1547, even though these had not yet been formally promulgated. Despite this dramatic move, the ballot on 5 December still produced 24 votes for Pole, and such was the head of steam behind him that two more votes were then added to his total, from Alessandro Farnese and Rodolfo Pio da Carpi. This was still insufficient, however, and during the next few ballots Pole's total stagnated. By 11 December, he appears to have thought that his cause was hopeless, and was prepared to make what amounted to a concession speech, even though it

---

[26]   Mayer, 'The war of the two saints: the conclave of Julius III and Cardinal Pole', *CPEC*, IV, *passim*.

was still unclear who would be victorious. The speech was not in fact made, and from then until 22 December, after which the conclave was suspended for the Christmas and Epiphany festivals, there was no further progress. At the session on the 22nd, Carafa himself made a speech admitting defeat. When the conclave resumed, on 13 January 1550, the rumour in the Roman Borgo was that Pole had actually been elected, but this proved to be false. Instead, he was by now writing one of his most important works, a treatise on the papacy, entitled *De summo pontifice*.[27]

The context of the treatise, within the 1549–50 conclave, was Gianpietro Carafa's attempt to gain for himself the vote of Giulio della Rovere. It purported to tell young Giulio how to decide where his vote should go, and contained many of the common themes of Pole's writing. In accordance with his academic training, it was framed in a humanistic rather than a scholastic manner and was entirely based on Scripture, in particular his beloved Old Testament prophets and the writings of Paul. Pole saw the papacy as coming directly from Christ and the Holy Spirit, and firmly asserted that popes sat in the seat of mercy, unlike secular rulers. The pope's chief weapon, excommunication, was intended for healing, not damnation, and the institution of the papacy had grown out of Peter's love for Christ, and Christ's love for His flock. This love was to be the hallmark of the papacy, and each pope had to devote himself to the imitation of Christ, following God's counsel as it had been expressed on the Cross. This involved rejecting the human prudence that was generally regarded as the main virtue of good government. The pope should possess *imbecillitas* (weakness and vulnerability), and divine wisdom, rather than human prudence and common sense. If he acted thus, he would have no desire to expand his earthly power, but rather to defend his flock, as a pope should, by means of the angelic and ecclesiastical hierarchies. Thus he should eschew both human domination and government. In this spirit, Pole used about a tenth of his final text to urge that the main duty of a pope was to establish peace in the Church and the world. Nevertheless, a pope did have a political role, but he should exercise it in the role of senior confessor to rulers, working perpetually to avoid or end conflict between them. If he had to engage himself with secular business, he should always take his cross with him, and even act as if hanging on it, this being a characteristically extreme and dramatic interpretation, by Pole, of the imitation of Christ. Popes and bishops should not harm their flocks by withdrawing totally from the world, and popes, in particular, did have the power to punish rulers or magistrates, although they should make all possible use of clemency first. Within the Church hierarchy, Pole saw the role of the pope as being different only in degree from that of the bishops and, as he had done in previous works, he stressed that the authority of the bishops of Rome derived from all the apostles, and not only

---

[27]   Mayer, 'Reluctant author', pp. 75–80.

from Peter. Yet the true power of a pope was most fully expressed when he was in a general council, as at Trent, with the other leaders of the Church. Perhaps surprisingly, given the failure of the council of Pisa in 1511–12, Pole also stated that it was possible for such a council to depose a false or inadequate pope, and elect another.[28]

The treatise *De summo pontifice* brought its author no nearer to the papal throne, although his supporters still believed him to be *papabile*, despite the accusations of heresy against him. Eventually, on 6 February 1550, Giovanni del Monte, who at the beginning had been an outsider, was elected as Pope Julius III. It has been suggested that Pole's prospects of election were destroyed by the work of the Roman Inquisition, over which Gianpietro Carafa had presided since its re-foundation in 1542, but things were much more complicated than that. The factors involved were the rival interests of France and the Habsburgs, Italian family ambitions, and a feeling that, after the experience of Hadrian VI's short reign, the pope should always be Italian. The additional question of Pole's doctrinal orthodoxy appeared to be put to one side early in Julius's reign, when the new pope placed him on the commission of cardinals which supervised the Inquisition. Although there was undoubtedly inquisitorial concern, in the 1540s and 1550s, about both indigenous Italian reform and the importation of theological ideas from centres of the Reformation abroad, the 'Holy Office', as it became known, was very much the creature of the reigning pope, and this would become evident in Pole's case, once he reached England as papal legate, and then also as archbishop of Canterbury. In the meantime, Julius also placed Pole on a commission to reform the papal Datary, its authority being extended to cover another department of the papal government, the Penitentiary.[29] Although disputes continued in the upper reaches of the Roman Curia, and Pole was sometimes even more critical of Julius than he had been of his predecessor, English circumstances would soon give him new opportunities, including a longed-for return to his native land.

Either towards the end of 1552 or early in 1553, Reginald Pole at last addressed Edward VI in person, on the grounds that he was now approaching adulthood (*adolescentiam ingrediens*), and was therefore able to respond personally to the problems of Church and state. The complex history of the text in question is meticulously described by Mayer, but it is clear that it took the form of a new preface to *De unitate*.[30] Pole told Edward that many people had tried to dissuade him from writing, but that good reports about the king had persuaded him to ignore their advice. He aimed to give Edward knowledge and vision that he could not obtain from his advisers in England,

28 Mayer, 'The war', *CPEC*, IV, pp. 1–2; Mayer, *PPP*, pp. 176–179.
29 Mayer, *PPP*, pp. 187–188.
30 Mayer, 'Reluctant author', pp. 47–51.

and in particular to explain to him the actions by Pole that had so offended his father, Henry VIII. He asked Edward to judge the case dispassionately, on the basis of the facts, which he proceeded to supply, as he saw them. When he claimed royal supremacy over the English Church, Henry had acted with the consent of parliament, and proceeded to punish those who opposed the move. Pole himself had been deterred by this threat of punishment from expressing his opinion, but had eventually done so, in *De unitate*, when thus ordered by the king. As so often, he protested his love for Henry, and his gratitude to him for helping his education. He now wanted to publish *De unitate* in print, after a long delay, in order to make sure that Edward did not make the same mistakes as his father. Once again, he rehearsed his version of his own conduct, in relation to England, in the late 1530s, including the assertion that he had indeed been offered the See of York by Henry. If Edward needed confirmation of the truth of his account, he should consult the elderly duke of Norfolk, Thomas Howard, who, Pole observed somewhat waspishly, he understood to be residing in the Tower of London. Now, in order to avoid present dangers, Edward should read what Pole had written to his father.[31] The sick young king did not respond to this urgent plea.

On 8 June 1553, as Edward's death approached, Pole informed Pope Julius that he would be using the leave that the pope had granted him from curial business to spend the rest of the summer in the northern retreat of Maguzzano, but events in England would drastically change his plans.[32] The death of Edward, on the evening of 6 July, was, like his father's, kept from parliament and the public for several days, in this case until 10 July. The next nine days, culminating in the proclamation in London of Henry's elder daughter Mary as queen, saw just the kind of instability that Pole had warned against. The 'devise for the succession', which Edward had approved in his dying days, and forced upon reluctant councillors and judges, admitted as queen Lady Jane Dudley, née Grey, a descendant of Henry VIII's younger sister Mary. John Dudley, duke of Northumberland, formerly a correspondent of Pole as well as Edward's lord president of the council from October 1549, tried to enforce Jane's succession militarily, but Mary, who fled from Hunsdon in Hertfordshire to East Anglia, rather than obey a summons to London, proved to have too much support, and herself became queen, without a major battle being fought.[33] To the amazement of Europe, a female ruler who not only regarded herself as wholly Catholic, like her father, but also, as it turned out, longed for England's reunion with the Roman See, was on the throne. Rome's reaction was rapid.

---

[31]   *CRP* 2 no. 601 (a compilation from several versions of the text, detailed on pp. 102–103, and in 'Reluctant author', pp. 47–51).

[32]   *ERP* 4 no. 38; *CSP Ven*, V, no. 752; *CRP* 2 no. 613.

[33]   Edwards, *Mary I*, pp. 87–122.

On 2 August 1553, Pope Julius wrote a brief to Pole, which was not actually sent until the 5th, by which time more news had been received from England: it does, however, give a vivid impression of the pope's initial response. He had heard of Edward's death, and of the subsequent disturbances in the kingdom. Seeing an opportunity, he consulted the cardinals, and now particularly sought Pole's advice on how to proceed. He would be happy to send him to England, if he thought that appropriate, and said that it would be good to combine such a mission, as in the late 1530s, with a peace legation to Charles V and Henry II of France.[34] The surviving papal documents concerning Pole at this time have certain unusual features. He was in fact appointed legate to England on two successive days. In this period, papal legates normally received three bulls on appointment, one granting general faculties, or powers (*facultates generales*), one as the commission for the legation (*commissio legationis*), and the other giving the legate authority to deal with heresy. Pole, however, received four bulls on his appointment, none of them dealing specifically with heresy. Nevertheless, as Mayer has noted, 'When combined with his appointment as Julius's proctor, intended to remove any obstacles to acting with maximum dispatch, it is apparent that Pole was virtually equivalent to the pope in every way'.[35]

On 5 August, better informed, Julius sent Pole a new and highly optimistic document from Rome. He was now absolutely certain that Mary was safely on the English throne, and that she was a true Catholic. She would marry and have a male heir, and England would be permanently restored to the Roman obedience. Pole, therefore, was appointed as legate, with full powers to facilitate all this, comfort the queen and restore to the Church those who had been in error.[36] In a second document, with the same date, Julius detailed Pole's legatine powers, in the form of faculties to reconcile all heretics, and others who were penitent after the schism, to remove the canonical penalties that they had received during the break with Rome, and absolve even those whose cases would otherwise have been reserved to the pope. The offences under Roman canon law that were covered included celebrating Mass during the schism, as Henry VIII had required, clerical marriage, as had been permitted under Edward VI, and taking clerical orders not with the Roman ordinal but with the new, reformed version issued by Archbishop Cranmer, and thereafter receiving benefices in the schismatic Church of England. Pole was to ensure that everything was restored to its pristine state (*pristinum statum*). All relevant offenders were to make their confession to a priest and do the required penance, in private if the legate remitted the requirement for a public ceremony. As legate, Pole was also empowered to absolve religious communities and universities, the latter probably

---

[34]   *CRP* 2 no. 618.
[35]   *CRP* 2 pp. 127–128.
[36]   *CRP* 2 no. 619 (further textual details).

referring to a wide range of institutions and corporations, as well as Oxford and
Cambridge, from any contracts that they had made against their true, Catholic,
interests, during the schism. Members of male and female religious orders who
had left their communities without Catholic licence, were pragmatically to
be allowed, subject to legatine absolution and dispensation, to remain in the
benefices they had received during the schism, in the case of males as secular
parish clergy. The legate would also have the power to dispense Christians from
the Lenten prohibition on eating meat and drinking milk, for example in cases
of ill-health. On a sterner note, it was made clear that, while clergy might be
absolved for having married, if they wished to continue to officiate they would
have to repudiate their wives, though any children of the marriage might be
legitimised. The legate was also given the power to unite or dissolve benefices,
in order to respond to current pastoral needs, and Julius's bull also raised what
would prove to be one of the most controversial questions during Pole's years
back in England, the possession by lay people of property that had belonged to
the Church. Such individuals might be absolved for having received these goods
from the Crown, and either deriving income from them or making personal use
of them, but only if they had first offered to return the property concerned to
the Church. In accordance with the reforming ideas in Catholicism at the time,
Pole was also permitted to use the revenues from such restorations to support
university students in their academic work, or for any other charitable activity
that the legate might determine. Clearly all this work was likely to prove to
be far too much for one man, so Julius allowed Pole to delegate some of his
powers to suitable clergy, as long as they had been fully reconciled with the
Roman Church.[37]

In a further bull, also issued on 5 August, Pope Julius gave Pole two
legations, one to England and the other to work for peace between France and
the Habsburgs. Under these *a latere* commissions, the legate's 'familiars', or
household, were to have special rights, and he himself was to have powers to hear
all categories of case in canon law, including appeals to the pope himself. He
was to have full papal powers of ecclesiastical censure, and to appoint registrars
and apostolic prothonotaries to transact church business and, more fancifully,
to uses the papal powers to honour loyal sons of the Church, as *milites aurati*
(lit. 'gilded soldiers', who fought for Rome), counts palatine, and even poets
laureate. Pole was also to work to reincorporate the English universities into the
European Catholic system, where necessary raising individuals to the degrees of
doctor or bachelor of laws, and masters of theology, arts and medicine. He was
also given the power to grant dispensations to noblemen and graduates to hold
benefices in plurality, or offices that were juridically incompatible, for example
where one was ecclesiastical and the other secular. He was also empowered to

---

37    *CRP* 2 no. 620 (further textual details).

dispense secular and religious clergy who had been ordained when below the minimum canonical age, and permit illegitimate clergy to hold benefices. If it was pastorally necessary, he was to allow the minor and major orders to be conferred on the same day. He was to license clergy to be absent from their benefices for up to five years, to pursue their studies, but only on condition that they proceeded to priest's orders immediately thereafter.[38] To emphasise Pole's status, also on 5 August Julius named him as his personal proctor, or deputy.[39] Yet the pope was still not satisfied, and on 6 August he granted Pole yet another bull, whereby he delegated to him papal powers over former and current members of religious communities, and also a faculty to reconsecrate former convent churches, but not if they had been used for schismatical and heretical worship. It was clearly envisaged that there would be a monastic restoration in England.[40]

Also on the 6th, Julius wrote to Pole to tell him to write in turn to congratulate Mary on her accession and call her back to the 'pristine discipline of the [Church] fathers (*ad pristinam patrum disciplinam*)'.[41] On 7 August, Pole wrote to the pope from Maguzzano, expressing his own joy at Mary's success, which he believed to be entirely due to God's providence, and his amazement at this outcome, which was 'such a major manifest victory of the divine goodness against the malice of men, beating down to the ground, in a moment, their long-laid plans, by means of a lady who, against all justice, has suffered such great oppression for so many years'. Pole hoped that she would now restore 'religion and the original obedience of that kingdom to this Holy See'. He sent Julius his views on the current English situation via his friend Vincenzo Parpaglia, abbot of San Saluto.[42] In his instructions to Parpaglia, issued on the same day, Pole said Julius should be told that great things were to be expected of Mary after all that she had suffered from Edward VI and his council (in particular her difficulties in retaining the Mass in her household), but, ominously, he also expressed, at this early stage, some doubts that he had about her. She had made no public objection to the executions of More and Fisher, in 1535, although Pole knew that she had not at all approved of them, but he nonetheless thought that she would cause no trouble, as queen, to the Roman See. He did, however, expect problems with the holders of formerly ecclesiastical property, and instructed the abbot to tell Julius that it was necessary for the guilty parties to submit first to Rome, before the question of their income from that property was dealt with. However, if Mary agreed to receive a papal legate, which she had not yet done, Pole expected that all would be well. If she did not, he suggested to Julius a reversion to the

---

[38]  *CRP* 2 no. 621 (further textual details).
[39]  *CRP* 2 no. 622 (further textual details).
[40]  *CRP* 2 no. 623 (further textual details).
[41]  *CRP* 2 no. 624 (further textual details).
[42]  BAV MS Vat. lat. 6754; fols 42 r–v; Tellechea, *Legación*, no. I, pp. 65–66; *CRP* 2 no. 633.

approach that had been tried with her father, that she might send representatives to meet Pole in Flanders or Picardy, under Habsburg auspices. Such a method had earlier been proposed by Pole to the duke of Somerset. Julius should send messengers to Mary, since it was proper that kings should be approached about such matters, rather than taking the initiative themselves.[43]

Then came a setback. On 10 August, Pole received a letter from Charles V's ambassador in Rome, Francisco de Vargas, conveying what would be his master's approach to Pole's legation until November 1554. The utmost caution should be exercised in Roman approaches to England, since Mary's position on the throne had to be completely safe before anything was done about religion. Here, Charles and his government were evidently influenced by the reports of Simon Renard and his other ambassadors in London, who had not believed in Mary's success until the very last moment. Vargas told Pole that the papacy should still work solely through Charles, when dealing with England, and that he certainly should not go there unless and until he was summoned by Mary and her council. The emperor's support for the English cardinal, in the papal election of 1549–50, was adduced as evidence of his good faith in these new circumstances.[44] On his way to Rome, Abbot Parpaglia crossed with the pope's envoy, who was bearing the bulls of legation, and they returned to Maguzzano together, after which, on 12 August, Pole wrote again to Julius. Having thanked the pope for the confidence that he had placed in him, he reported that he had already dispatched one of his faithful servants, Henry Pyning, to Flanders, to confer with the legate to the Imperial court, Cardinal Girolamo Dandino. Having learnt that Julius had sent Bishop Richard Pate of Worcester to Charles, Pole put Parpaglia once more on the road to Rome, on the same day writing to Cardinal Innocenzo del Monte that he had duly received his bulls of legation, and rejoiced in 'the manifest work of God in these events in England', adding that the reversion of his native land to the Roman obedience, after 'such a great and miraculous beginning' would be of benefit to the whole Church.[45]

On 13 August, Pole wrote what appears to be his first personal letter to Queen Mary, which survives as an Italian translation from Latin. In it he naturally congratulated her on her accession and once again ascribed it to the action of divine providence. Her enemies had been overthrown by the Holy Spirit, and she had even more right than the Blessed Virgin Mary to sing her song *Magnificat* [Luke 1:46–55], including the words 'he has brought down the powerful from their thrones and lifted up the lowly' [v. 52]. This line of thought would recur in future relations between Pole and Mary. She had suffered her parents' divorce, and the cruelty of Anne Boleyn: now, though, Pole was ready to help in any

[43]   Lutz, no. 1; *CRP* no. 634.
[44]   AGS Estado 1320; *CSP Span* X pp. 160–162; *CRP* 2 no. 637.
[45]   Tellechea, *Legación*, p. 18, II and III, pp. 66–68; *CRP* 2 nos 642, 647.

way and was eager to come to England and defend her from there. Returning to another of his regular themes, he did however remind her that she should always be obedient to the Roman See.[46] On 19 August, Parpaglia reported from Rome that Pope Julius approved of Pole's decision to delay his return to England. Intriguingly, the abbot indicated that Julius had gained the impression that Pole in fact, despite his effusiveness in writing to her, suspected that she would not simply submit to Rome on her own authority, but insist that the matter be dealt with in parliament, through the repeal of her father and brother's legislation on ecclesiastical matters.[47] This would prove to be a bone of contention over the next six months or so, as Mary did indeed pursue the parliamentary route. The uncertainty in Rome, over Mary's future actions, was communicated to Spain by Prince Philip's ambassador to the Holy See, Juan Manrique de Lara, who wrote to his master, on 20 August, that he simply did not know how to advise him to proceed in relation to England. Pole and Dandino were hesitating, Philip's father was being obstructive, and news that Mary was beginning to think of a Habsburg husband had evidently not leaked out.[48]

In the meantime, Charles, who had been betrothed for a while to Mary when she was a child, would prove to be the main obstacle in the way of Pole's return to England. On 21 August, the legate wrote to him from Maguzzano, eloquently acknowledging his important role, but firmly insisting that the restoration of papal authority should be Mary's priority. All the English were indebted to the emperor, after God, for her success, but now it was just as necessary for him to act, in order to push her towards the pope. He also provocatively suggested that Charles had been partly responsible for the loss of papal authority in England, presumably because of his support for Catherine against Henry, and in recompense he should now clear the way for Julius III's legates, including himself.[49] At the same time, Pole also gave instructions to his envoy to Charles, Antonio Fiordibello, who was his second choice after Bishop Richard Pate of Worcester. The Italian was to counter Charles's argument that the situation was still too unstable in England for a legate to be sent there. Pole had considered this view, but had concluded that delay would only make things worse. Pole expected the whole matter to be resolved in Mary's first parliament, the summoning of which was already being considered. Pointedly, Fiordibello was to remind Charles that the schism and violence in Germany were a warning of what could happen in England, if firm leadership was lacking. Pole believed that England would have remained Catholic if Henry had not wilfully broken with Rome, and that the people would now quickly return to the fold, if given the opportunity. In any

---

[46]   BAV Vat. lat. 6754, fols 42v–45v; *CSP Ven*, V, no. 766; *CRP* 2 no. 649.
[47]   Lutz no. 6; *CRP* 2 no. 651.
[48]   AGS Estado 879 no. 66.
[49]   AGS Estado 506 no. 152; Lutz no. 71; *CRP* 2 no. 652.

case, under Henry VIII the English Church had retained the sacraments, and Pole expected little difficulty over doctrine, now that Mary had been accepted as queen. Pole had clearly been impressed, also, by the petition of the 1549 Prayer Book rebels in the West Country, who had demanded his recall to England and the lifting of his attainder. In the matter of ecclesiastical property in lay hands, which so exercised him, Pole proposed that a meeting should be held with agents of Mary, as he had proposed years before to Henry. Urgency was added to the reconciliation of England to Rome by the danger that, as long as the kingdom remained in schism, it might be attacked by a foreign power, and also that there were other candidates to the throne, including himself, although Fiordibello was not apparently intended to mention that. Mary would be much more secure on her throne as the Catholic ruler of a Catholic kingdom, and crowned by a papal legate.[50]

Pole was then still in Maguzzano, and on 26 August Abbot Parpaglia reported to him from Rome that the view there was that it would probably take years to sort out matters satisfactorily in England. The problem of church property in lay hands was a major preoccupation, and it was generally thought, in Julius III's curia, that Mary would need to reform her council, which had been assembled initially when she was still at Framlingham and much added to when she reached London. It was felt that most of her close advisers had no particular fervour for the papal cause, but were happy with a Henrician 'Catholic' revival. Thus Pole faced an uncomfortable choice: if he went into England and started reclaiming the lay possessioners' goods for the Church, he would lose his good reputation in the country, and probably ruin his whole enterprise, but if he went gently in the matter of property, he would be going against his own conscience as well as canonical correctness. Parpaglia apologised for confronting his friend with this dilemma.[51] For the rest of 1553, and 11 months of 1554, Pole would be forced to observe and comment on English affairs from abroad.

On the night of 19 September 1553, Henry Pyning dispatched a report from London, in which he vividly described to his master the secret audience that he had just had with Mary after dinner, in the presence of just one lady-in-waiting and Sir Anthony Browne, Mary's Master of the horse. In it Pyning had handed the queen the letters that Pole had written to her on 13 and 27 August. They delighted her and, with the spontaneous effusiveness that she showed when she was emotionally committed, she said that she would give half her kingdom to have Pole with her at that moment. Yet because of her heretical subjects, she had to proceed with caution. She wished that he could be at her coronation, which was planned for the beginning of October, but there was no time to arrange that,

---

[50] *CRP* 2 nos 653 (Lutz p. 15n), 654 (BAV Vat. lat. 6754, fols 48v–49r; *CSP Ven*, V, no. 773), 655 (Lutz no.7(ii); *CSP Ven*, V, no. 772).

[51] Lutz no. 9; *CRP* 2 no. 661.

and she feared that her subjects would tolerate no delay of the ceremony. Pyning also reported that a representative of Julius III, Gianfrancesco Commendone, had told her, during his visit to London, that she would receive a personal papal dispensation to be crowned as a Catholic ruler, although her kingdom was still in schism, but Dandino and Pole had not previously been informed of this. As though they were excited pen-friends, or even more, Pyning urged his cardinal to write to Mary more often.[52]

Her coronation duly took place in Westminster Abbey on 1 October, with full Catholic ritual, and the next day, obviously before he had heard this news, Pole wrote to her from Trent, full of delight and congratulations on her 'miraculous elevation to the royal throne', and answering letters from her, now lost. His main agenda, as before, was reconciliation of England with Rome. Under Henry and Edward, schism had turned to 'manifest heresy', since what they called 'sacraments' were no such thing. Pole accused the English clergy, and particularly the bishops, of dissimulation over the question of Church lands, in that they had allowed their expropriation by the Crown while all the time telling the people that their Church was still 'catholic'. Bluntly, and perhaps surprisingly, he told Mary not to use similar tactics, and perhaps realising that this was not the best approach to them, he then changed to a more uplifting tone, calling her a 'light that should not be hidden under a bushel' (or bucket; Matth. 5:15; Mark 4:21; Luke 11:33), and 'a most virtuous lady', graced by God, who had been through 'such a stormy time', but had coped with 'serenity'. Descending to mundane politics, he told Mary that he thought most of her subjects were grateful for her accession, and her action over religion, and only a minority of them were likely to put up any resistance. Nevertheless, former church goods were still the main problem, and the pope should be the arbiter in this matter.[53]

Pole's next surviving letter related to England, also dated at Trent on 2 October 1553, was addressed to Edward Courtenay, the son of the marquess of Exeter who had been executed on the orders of Henry VIII, alongside Henry Pole, Lord Montagu. Mary had had young Edward released from the Tower of London, where he had spent his youth, and made him earl of Devon. Many regarded him as a likely husband for the queen, as indeed others saw the cardinal himself, who in this letter congratulated Courtenay on his release. Once again adopting a lyrical and religious style, he called the young earl a sprig of true nobility, and the queen, who had released him, a virgin who saves, like the Mother of God herself. Pole noted that, while in prison and very probably under the tutelage of Bishop Gardiner, Courtenay had translated into English a text

---

52  Lutz no. 18; Tellechea, *Legación*, XLII, p. 46; CRP 2 no. 689.
53  BAV MS Vat. lat. 6754 fols 69v–74r; Lutz p. 64 n. 3; *CSP Ven*, V, no. 805; *CRP* 2 no. 719.

of deep significance to the writer of this letter, the *Beneficio di Cristo*.[54] After this, on 8 October, Pole received a personal letter from Mary, which survives in an Italian version in the Vatican Library. In it, the Queen, writing to her 'good cousin and very reverend father in Christ', again stressed her 'obedience and due devotion towards the Bride of Christ and my spiritual mother', the Church of Rome. She grieved that she could not 'by any suitable means demonstrate all the intention of my heart in this matter'. She wanted to proclaim to the world 'my due [and] sincere mind' and now, having been crowned and with her first parliament in session, she was confident that the offending religious laws would be repealed and hoped to obtain a general pardon for herself from the pope.[55]

By 21 October, Pole had travelled north from Trent to Dillingen, near Augsburg, where a Spanish Dominican, Pedro de Soto, who would later hold an academic post in Oxford, was head and joint founder of a new Catholic university, aimed at counteracting the advance of the German Reformation. From there Pole wrote again to the pope, enclosing Mary's letter to him, but asking Julius to give it no publicity at that stage. He himself was now awaiting a safe-conduct from the duke of Württemberg, in order to proceed around Lutheran territory, in the direction of the Netherlands and Charles V. He claimed, perhaps on the basis of a lost communication from Cardinal Dandino, that he would now be received in Brussels as legate to England, but he was still apprehensive about what might be facing him.[56] On the same day he wrote to his previous host, Cardinal Madruzzo of Trent, to tell him that he had just received new reports from England, via his messenger Henry Pyning, and was feeling more hopeful.[57] Perhaps as a result of this news and his safe-conduct, two days later Pole was on his way to Brussels.[58] Pyning reported to the pope that, as she had written herself to Pole, Mary wanted to make an open display of her true faith as soon as possible, and he referred to her earlier successful request for a dispensation to be granted to Bishop Gardiner to crown her. She had sent duplicate letters to Granvelle, in case Pyning was arrested, which he clearly was not.[59]

During his months of waiting, first in northern Italy and then in Germany, Pole increasingly confided in Cardinal Giovanni Morone, to whom he had become close when he was in Viterbo and Morone was bishop of Modena. On 1 December 1553, still from Dillingen, he expressed his frustrations to his

---

54    *CSP Ven*, V, no. 806; *CRP* 2 no. 720; Edward Courtenay, trans., *A treatice most proffitable of the benefite that true christians receiue by the dethe of Jesus Christe* (London, 1548); Overell, *Italian reform*, pp. 61–80.

55    *ERP* 4 pp. 429–430; Lutz p. 64 n. 3; Tellechea, *Legación* no. XI, pp. 78–79; *CSP Ven*, V, no. 807; *CRP* 2 no. 721.

56    Tellechea, *Legación*, no. X, pp. 77–78; *CRP* 2 no. 723.

57    *CSP Ven*, V, no. 809; *CRP* 2 no. 730 (further textual details).

58    Tellechea, *Legación*, no. XII, p. 80; *CRP* 2 no. 729.

59    *CSP Ven*, V, no. 813; *CRP* 2 no. 741 (further textual details).

friend, now in the Curia, suggesting that he was even becoming fed up with Mary herself. He had consulted Pedro de Soto, who thought that pressure should be put on the Emperor to have Pole introduced to England as legate. Pole thought that Mary was being much too timid. Parliament had failed to act, and there was no hope now of the Roman obedience being restored before Christmas. In any case he still would not accept that English religion could only be adjusted by statute. He told Morone that he would have to be back in England himself before parliament met again, in three or four months' time. Mary's own legitimacy as sovereign was completely bound up with the Roman See.[60] At the same time, Pole wrote to the queen herself, in response to the material that Pyning had brought from her. As well as expressing his discontent at the slowness of her proceedings, he adopted, as he had earlier done with Vittoria Colonna, the approach of a somewhat severe spiritual director. Interestingly, he suggested that her inertia was caused by the fact that she was suffering from the same kind of melancholy as had afflicted her back in 1536, just after her mother's death, when she abjectly submitted to her father's demand that she agree that she was illegitimate and that he was rightly Supreme Head of the Church of England. He prayed God to grant that she might find some better counsellors, and professed his disappointment that parliament had achieved so little in the question of religion. He also pointed out, most unhelpfully in English circumstances at the time, that except in the cases of those who had been personally absolved, such as herself and Bishop Gardiner, any Mass celebrated in her kingdom, while it remained in schism, was nothing less than damnable.[61] In a parallel letter to Pyning, the legate said that Mary should have marched as bravely into parliament as she had taken the field at Framlingham against the duke of Northumberland, in the previous July. God had not dissembled when he gave her the victory over Jane, and she should not act in a dissembling manner now, lest a great opportunity for God and the Church be lost. He had evidently heard from Pyning about Mary's desire to marry Philip, which did not appeal to him, and thought that she should have dealt with the Roman reconciliation first. Deliberately or not in his favourite role as a prophet, he told Pyning that she was being deceived and was in great danger, even before news of the conspiracies against her emerged.[62] As 1553, the year of Mary's accession, came to an end, her absent and impatient legate continued to be preoccupied with two of her policies of which he strongly disapproved, her slowness in ending the schism and her plan to marry Prince Philip of Spain.[63]

---

[60] Lutz no. 36; *CRP* 2 no. 764.

[61] *ERP* 4 no. 46; *CSP Ven*, V, no. 836; *CRP* 2 no. 765.

[62] *ERP* 5, pp. 171–181; *CRP* 2 no. 766.

[63] *CRP* 2 no. 767 (Pole to Thomas Goldwell, Dillingen, 2 December 1553, with further textual details); *CRP* no. 2 (Cardinal Giovanni Morone to Pole, Rome, 21 December 1553; Lutz no. 39).

On 1 January 1554, Pope Julius himself wrote a highly significant letter to Queen Mary, having heard of her intention to marry Philip from Charles V's ambassador in Rome, Juan Manrique de Lara. It was a *motu proprio* dispensation from consanguinity 'in the second and third degrees', due to their common descent from Isabella and Ferdinand of Spain, via Catherine and her older sister Juana respectively. The couple were also dispensed from the affinity that arose from Mary's having previously been betrothed to Philip's father Charles. The contract, *de futuro*, had been 'mutually' dissolved in 1526, when the emperor had married Princess Isabel of Portugal. Now, whatever Pole and some others may have thought, Julius freed Mary and Philip from any threat of excommunication and other canonical censure, and declared their public honesty, if they did indeed marry.[64] A week later, the pope sent a congratulatory letter to Philip, in which he said that a marriage with the queen of England would not only benefit the spouses themselves and their families, but also public affairs, and in particular the cause of returning England to the Roman obedience.[65] Whatever his doubts, the cardinal legate of England would have to accept the Anglo-Spanish marriage.

By the time that Mary wrote to her 'good cousin' again, from Greenwich Palace on 23 January, the feared rebellion had indeed broken out in England. News of the proposed Spanish marriage had spawned conspiracies in London from early November 1553, and while planned rebellions in the West Country, the Welsh Marches and the Midlands had come to nothing, Sir Thomas Wyatt, son of the poet, had raised part of Kent and was threatening London, on the basis of a mixture of anti-Spanish and general anti-Catholic sentiment.[66] In the midst of political turmoil that genuinely threatened her regime, Mary concentrated on ecclesiastical matters. She told Pole that there was still a great deal of progress to be made before the English Church could reunite with Rome. The clerical estate was full of heretics and schismatics, many priests were still married, under the dispensation granted by parliament under Edward VI, and some of these were enjoying the 'principal ecclesiastical benefices'. In her continuing canonical limbo, and without doing anything to offend Pope Julius, Mary wanted to place celibate Catholic priests in these benefices, and she was now asking Pole whether he could and would give her legal backing for such action, especially in Crown livings, and above all bishoprics, even before apostolic obedience was restored. She had already written to her ambassador at the Imperial court, Bishop Thomas Thirlby of Norwich, telling him to greet the legate, from her, when he

---

[64]    AGS Estado 879 no. 101, Estado 880 nos 141, 158; Tellechea, *El papado*, 1, no. III, pp. 7–10.

[65]    Tellechea, *El papado*, 1, no. IV, pp. 10–11.

[66]    Edwards, *Mary I*, pp. 159–169.

eventually arrived.[67] When Pole wrote again to Pope Julius, now from Brussels, on 28 January, he reported that the emperor had had fireworks there to celebrate Mary's victory over Wyatt, which seemed to have made him more positive about both of them, and the English situation in general. Characteristically, Pole told the pope that he believed Mary had won because she and her kingdom were under special divine protection. He reported that Charles was now ready to assist Mary with 20,000 gold ducats and 15 well-armed ships. He said that he had left Dillingen on 1 January, and reached Leuven/Louvain on the 19th, being received at the Imperial court on the 25th. He had been met by Bishop Thirlby and Sir John Mason, who were Mary's senior diplomats in the Netherlands, half-way between Leuven and Brussels, and when he arrived in the Imperial capital, he had first been received by the city's clergy, as legate, and then taken in solemn procession, under a canopy of estate, to the cathedral of St Michel. The next day he asked Granvelle for an audience with the emperor, and was told, somewhat unconvincingly, that he had been delayed in Dillingen because they had not expected a new legate so soon after the departure of Cardinal Dandino. More to the point, Charles and Granvelle still thought that the time was not ripe for Pole to cross to England, as there was a great deal of work to be done first in parliament.[68]

In March 1554, Henry Pyning was dispatched to England again, after Pope Julius had expressed to Mary, in a letter dated 15 February, his delight at the defeat of Wyatt. Nevertheless, Pole once again raised the issue of church goods, in the somewhat ominous form of an unflattering biblical analogy from the book of Daniel [5]. The Babylonian king Belshazzar had met the fate decreed for him in the writing on the wall in his banqueting hall, and interpreted by Daniel, because he had been using the gold and silver vessels that his father Nebuchadnezzar had looted from the Temple in Jerusalem.[69] In his mission instructions, issued in instalments to Pyning, Pole asked him to urge on Mary and her council the importance of preserving peace in Europe.[70] Pyning was also to deal with the issue of re-validating English bishops as Catholic. Mary was indeed able to make provisions to bishoprics, like any other Catholic ruler, with the authority of the pope in consistory. Pole would absolve them for schism, but only if they were duly repentant for what they had done since the break with Rome.[71] In accordance with these instructions, on 8 March the pope sent a further brief to Pole, confirming his legatine powers, and allowing him to delegate them.[72] A letter from Morone, dated on the following day, strongly

---

[67]   BAV MS Vat. lat. 6754 fol. 99r–v; *CSP Ven*, V, no. 849; *CRP* 2 no. 794.
[68]   Lutz no. 44; Tellechea, *Legación*, no. XVI pp. 86–88; *CSP Ven*, V, no. 850; *CRP* 2 no. 795.
[69]   Lutz p. 133n; *CRP* 2 no. 815.
[70]   *CRP* 2 no. 816 (further textual details).
[71]   *CRP* 2 nos 817–818 (further textual details for both).
[72]   *CRP* 2 no. 822 (further textual details).

suggests that, by this time, Pole thought it would be better for Mary to remain single, rather than marry Philip or Courtenay.[73] Then, on either 12 or 13 March, Mary wrote to tell Pole that parliament would reconvene on 2 April.[74]

At the beginning of this parliamentary session, a somewhat mysterious text was produced, which exists in manuscript and was also published by the royal printer, John Cawood.[75] This text purports to have been written by an author with the latinate name Iodochus Harchius (Josse de Harchies, c. 1500–80), who was a Netherlandish humanist and religious controversialist, who was later known for his writing on the Eucharist. There is no evidence of any direct link between Harchius and Pole, but they could of course have met in Brussels, and the piece, 'For the renewal of the commonwealth of England and for the return of Cardinal Reginald Pole. A speech to the most prudent senate (Parliament) of England', clearly reflects Pole's own views. The fact that it was printed by Cawood, suggests that it was regarded as an important statement, at a time when Mary and her advisers were anxious to clear the way for the Spanish marriage and the return to Rome. The speech opened with a lengthy exposition of humanistic political theory, followed by an equally detailed disquisition on the atrocities of Henry VIII and Edward VI in matters of religion. Pole's return would begin the process of restoring the English Church to its former happy state, and there was a great stress, entirely characteristic of the cardinal's own patrician views, on the destruction of 'true nobility' in the two preceding reigns. In a metaphor that Pole himself had used in *De unitate*, the speaker described England as a theatre, in which all the best men had been destroyed, and unprecedented tyranny ruled.[76] The current parliament, however, was not responsible for any of this, and should begin restoring lost piety and nobility by inviting Pole to return, as the loyal subject he was and not as an attainted traitor. If the members did this, foreign countries would become less suspicious of England, thus making the kingdom more respected ('noble') and more secure.

Meanwhile, Pole had had further correspondence with Stephen Gardiner. On 19 March, while in Saint-Denis, near Paris, on business concerned with his peace legation, he responded to a letter that Gardiner had written to him a week earlier, saying that in it he saw signs that its writer had shown repentance for his behaviour during the schism, though Gardiner firmly asserted that he had never fallen into heresy. Pole told him that he believed there to be few genuine Protestants in England, and that Pope Julius would be a good shepherd of the country, once it had submitted again to Rome, which he hoped would happen

---

[73]   Lutz no. 53; *CRP* 2 no. 823.

[74]   BAV MS Vat. lat. 6754 fols 113r–114r; *CSP Ven*, V, no. 859; *CRP* 2 no. 831.

[75]   BL Add. MS 32096, fols 236v–242r; [Iodochus Harchius] *Pro instauratione reipublicae Angl[iae] proque reditu R[eginaldi] Poli cardinalis. Oratio ad prudentissimum senatum Angl[iae]* (London: John Cawood, 1554); *CRP* 2 no. 839a.

[76]   Pole, *De unitate*, fol. XVIIIIv.

soon.[77] On 5 April, with parliament in session, Gardiner wrote once more to Pole, from his palace at Southwark, thanking him for his previous communication and, understandably, saying that he would be successful as legate in England if he overlooked past offences. He suggested that Pole should write a general letter to parliament, outlining the case for Church unity, but not referring to the pope's supremacy explicitly, or even suggesting that it might soon be restored in Mary's kingdom. Such a letter should also make it clear that former church property in lay hands would not be touched.[78] Gardiner was going to have to manage parliament on behalf of the queen, so that Pole would have been wise to listen to his tough and realistic political advice.

About a month later, on 6 May, Giovanni Morone, writing from Rome, raised another awkward issue. He said that it had gone down badly there that Pole, according to the information that had reached the Curia, had never personally congratulated Mary on her forthcoming marriage to Prince Philip of Spain. Pole might argue that the omission was a case of diplomatic tact, since he was on a legatine visit to France, bitter enemy of both England and the Habsburgs, when the news of the betrothal emerged, but nonetheless his silence was being taken, not unnaturally in view of his previously known stance on the subject, as disapproval.[79] By the time that he replied to Morone, on 25 May, Pole was in Dilighem, in the Netherlands, and hoping to be in England soon. He told his friend that the restoration of the kingdom to Rome was near, and that the only unresolved question was former ecclesiastical property. However, Gardiner had told him that there was no chance of this being restored in the current parliament, and he himself admitted that he still thought Charles V remained implacably opposed to his return to England, even though, while in Brussels, he had spoken favourably to the Emperor of Philip and Mary's marriage.[80] Three days later, Pole, now back in Brussels, poured his heart out to Morone. In his letter of 6 May, Morone had evidently offended him by returning to an old theme, which was that he preferred to withdraw from the front line when things became difficult. Pole indignantly rejected this suggestion, saying that although he did indeed return to his studies when public affairs did not require him, he would always respond to a call to action on God's behalf and was not afraid of rule as a magistrate, as he had shown in Viterbo and Bagnoregio. He had served the pope unstintingly, and would do so in the future if required, although he was willing to cede the problematic English legation to someone else, and had indicated this to Julius through his own secretary, Niccolò Ormanetto.[81] This

---

[77]   *ERP* 4 no. 48; Lutz no. 56; *CRP* 2 no. 840.
[78]   Muller, *Letters of Gardiner*, pp. 464–466; *CRP* 2 no. 847.
[79]   Lutz no. 62; *CRP* 2 no. 869.
[80]   *ERP* 4 no. 51; Lutz no. 63; *CSP Ven*, V, no. 882; *CRP* 2 no. 871.
[81]   *ERP* 4 no. 50; Lutz no. 65; *CSP Ven*, V, no. 884; *CRP* 2 no. 875.

was not the pope's intention, however, and on 28 May Gianfrancesco Stella wrote from Rome to tell Pole that he would reject attempts by Charles and Granvelle to have the legate recalled. On the contrary, Ormanetto would shortly return to Brussels with two papal briefs, one for Queen Mary, about Pole's provision of bishops for England, and the other for Philip, who was wrongly believed to be leaving Spain soon, on his way to his wedding, detailing the nature and importance of Pole's legation. Former church goods now in lay hands were not to be an obstacle to reunion.[82] During May, Pyning was called up for service again as Pole's messenger to England. His instructions indicated that news had reached Brussels of opposition to the legation and to reunion from prominent members of the English political establishment, who rightly saw the plan for Pole to confirm the provision of bishops to English dioceses as the not so thin end of the large wedge of restored papal supremacy, which they did not want at all. Pole urged Pyning to persuade Mary to reject the view of such counsellors, that nobody should be recommended for papal provision to English bishoprics until the whole kingdom was reconciled with the consent of parliament. He was to tell the queen that she was right to seek the provision of these bishops, in order to secure the restoration of the Church, and that the process could take place in stages. He suggested, in a characteristically dramatic image, that if this were not so, it would be as though England was a plague house, in which no patient could be cured unless they all were at once. As in the cases of Mary and Gardiner, it was canonically proper for individuals to seek absolution and reconciliation, before the kingdom as a whole followed suit.[83]

The cardinal of England remained, frustrated, in the Netherlands while Philip and his huge entourage landed at Southampton on 20 July 1554, and he married Queen Mary in Winchester cathedral five days later, on the feast of St James the Great, patron saint of Spain.[84] On 31 July, Niccolò Ormanetto reported to Alvise Priuli, from Valenciennes, that Charles V was still cautious, even after his son's wedding. He wanted to wait and see what happened in the English Church, and wondered whether the monarchs would take charge, ironically using their royal supremacy, or whether overall authority would be given to Pole as legate. Ormanetto's letter suggests that both the emperor and Pole viewed the situation with continuing uncertainty.[85] Coincidentally on the next day Pope Julius sent Pole a bull in which he confirmed his definitive ruling on the fate of English church goods. Although Pole had full powers to restore this property to the Church, Julius took account of the objections from Mary, and now stated that England could be reconciled, even if some goods

[82]  Lutz no. 66; *CRP* 2 no. 878.
[83]  *CSP Ven*, V, no. 883; *CRP* 2 no. 879.
[84]  Edwards, *Mary I*, pp. 185–192.
[85]  *CRP* 2 no. 915 (further textual details).

were still in the hands of lay impropriators. The matter was to be left to Pole's judgment.[86] On 3 August, however, Granvelle informed Pole that his departure to England was not going to be permitted by Charles until Philip and Mary had been consulted: a messenger was being dispatched at once to sound them out.[87] The English cardinal still had more than three months to wait before he saw his beloved homeland.

In August, Queen Mary and her new husband made their formal entry to London and started working out the new and unaccustomed project, in England though not in Spain, of dual monarchy. Also, it soon became clear that Philip wanted to become involved personally in the ending of the English schism. On 9 September his Franciscan confessor, Bernardo de Fresneda, wrote to Pole, saying that the Spanish very much wanted Pole in England, but that some of Mary's own councillors were still opposed to this.[88] Ten days later, Philip himself wrote, urging the cardinal to come to England as soon as possible, but while this letter was on its way to the Netherlands, Pole expressed his ever-mounting frustration to the new King of England, saying that he had been waiting on the other side of the ocean for more than a year, and could not understand why there was still so much resistance to the readmission to England of the Apostle Peter, in the form of Pope Julius and his legate. Philip had now inherited, by marriage, the title of 'Defender of the Faith', which Pope Clement VII had granted to Henry VIII, and he should act accordingly. Declaring that the refusal to admit him as legate was an insult to God as well as the pope, Pole daringly suggested that Philip and his Spanish advisers were even more scared of his arrival than were Mary and her council.[89] On 23 September, Pole wrote another letter, exuding frustration, to Anthony Browne, Viscount Montague, who was one of Mary's confidants, saying that he wanted to be a part of the action as soon as possible, and at the end of the month he expressed the same views in letters to Granvelle and the Emperor respectively.[90] Pole now decided to send Ormanetto as an envoy to Granvelle, who was effectively in charge of the Habsburg government because of Charles's illness, to persuade him to relent. The Italian was to tell the minister that the delay of the Church settlement in England was an insult to the pope and a dishonour to Charles and Philip. Like the king and queen of England, Pole promised to treat the possessioners courteously, and would work with them, both privately and in public, once he was in England.[91]

---

[86]    Tellechea, *Legación*, pt 2 no. 11, pp. 196–197; *CRP* 2 no. 916.

[87]    Pocock, ed., *History of the reformation*, 6, p. 340; *CRP* 2 no. 917.

[88]    BL Add. 25425, fols 302r–303r; *CRP* 2 no. 935.

[89]    *ERP* 4 no. 56; *CSP Ven*, V, no. 946; *CSP Span* XIII no. 63; *CRP* 2 no. 939 (c. 21–24 September).

[90]    Tellechea, *Legación*, no. XXVII, p. 108 (27 September 1554), no. XXVIII, pp. 108–110 (28 September 1554); *CRP* 2 nos 942, 943 (*CSP Ven*, V, no. 947).

[91]    *CRP* 2 no. 944 (fuller textual details).

Mary herself wrote to Pole, from Hampton Court, on 28 September. The letter to her 'good cousin' and signed 'Marye the Quene', was evidently of such importance that it was drafted by no mere secretary, but Gardiner himself. In it she said that she and her husband very much wanted Pole in England when all the circumstances were right. He should deal with their scruples of conscience, concerning the schism, and the treatment of clergy and places of worship. They were worried about the interdict, or prohibition of the celebration and administration of Catholic sacraments and offices in buildings and by clergy that had been part of the schismatical and heretical Church of England. A newly expressed concern was that the churches concerned had been 'polluted' by the burial within them of believers in the reformed religion, and Mary asked whether she and the king might, as Catholics, attend worship in such places.[92] On 6 October, Pole again wrote to Fresneda, acknowledging a lost reply from him and asserting that Philip would have to be Solomon to his father Charles's David, in the sense that while the father failed to build the Temple in Jerusalem, because of his sinfulness, the son succeeded in doing so [1 Kings 2:1–4, 6]. He urged Fresneda and two others among Philip's ecclesiastical advisers in England who were known to him, the Dominicans Pedro de Soto and Bartolomé Carranza, to put pressure on their king to act in this way.[93] It is clear, from a letter that Niccolò Ormanetto sent to another of Pole's circle then in England, Seth Holland, on 7 October, that there was growing tension in Westminster between the Spanish and English churchmen. Ormanetto referred to a suggestion from Carranza that Pole's orders from Pope Julius on the disposal of church goods should be altered, so that the whole matter was settled before the legate came to England and the country was reconciled to Rome. No doubt speaking for Pole, Ormanetto wanted Holland to tell the Spaniards to adopt a calmer attitude on the question of property and do nothing to delay or obstruct the reconciliation.[94] In a second letter to Seth Holland, dated 11 October, Ormanetto discussed further contentious questions that had been raised by Carranza. One was the use for Catholic worship of churches and churchyards in which heretics and schismatics were buried, about which Mary had already expressed scruples. Pole was inclined, for the primary purpose of saving souls, to allow such worship, as long as the individuals involved, and in particular the clergy, had previously been reconciled to the Roman Church. Similarly, though Pole agreed, according to Ormanetto, that canon law demanded the exhumation of the remains concerned, he ruled that this should not be done if the action would result in scandal and disturbance, which would hinder God's saving work.[95]

---

[92]   Tellechea, *Legación*, no. XL, pp. 130–131; *CRP* 2 no. 946.
[93]   *ERP* 4 no. 57; *CRP* 2 no. 950.
[94]   Tellechea, *Legación*, no. XXXII, pp. 115–119, app. II, no. 7, pp. 187–189.
[95]   Tellechea, *Legación*, no. XXXIII, pp. 119–120; *CRP* 2 no. 954.

On 14 October, Pole, now once again in Brussels, made yet another report to Julius. He had talked again to both Granvelle and Charles V, and was now optimistic about the religious situation in England. He nonetheless stated firmly that he would work only on the instructions of the pope and not those of Philip and Mary. He had met Charles on 10 October, in the presence of Granvelle and the current nuncio in Brussels, Girolamo Muzzarelli, and as a result needed yet more guidance from Julius on doctrine and on church property. He wanted the pope, through him, to give the King and Queen more discretion to reward those who assisted in the restoration of the Church. As far as the property was concerned, Charles V had talked in their meeting of his experience in Germany, and thought that such goods in England should not be permanently alienated to lay impropriators. Agreeing with Carranza, Pole suggested to Julius that his earlier brief on this subject might have to be broadened. He had shown it to Granvelle and feared further delay if it was not altered in this way. Meanwhile, the English parliament should meet at once to repeal the remaining religious laws of the previous two reigns, and now that Philip and Mary were married, everything possible should be done to end the potentially scandalous situation that the kingdom was in. It was no good waiting for everyone to come round to the Catholic restoration, since that would mean that nothing happened, and property would remain the biggest obstacle. Mary had judged that she needed a husband, since, in an amusing twist by Pole of God's words to Adam when creating Eve [Genesis 2:18], 'it is not good that the woman should be alone'. Despite the arrival of his son in England, the emperor still thought there was strong resistance in England to the sight of a red cardinal's hat, and he knew, as Pole did from Carranza, that the Spanish friars, Franciscan and Dominican, were afraid to wear their habits in the streets of Westminster and London, except within the precincts of the abbey.[96] That day, Pole also wrote to Cardinal Innocenzo del Monte, announcing the news of what was believed, wrongly as it turned out, to be Mary's pregnancy, which would greatly help to pacify the country. Secondly, parliament was due to reconvene in November, Pole also passed on the news of Bishop Gardiner's sermon on the feast of St Jerome (30 September), in which he had blamed himself for having previously supported the schism and the royal supremacy, as well as criticising those of his fellow Englishmen, and particularly Londoners, who were currently ill-treating Spaniards. Generally speaking, Pole saw all these as hopeful developments, though it would still be more than a month before he could return home.[97] Also on 14 October, Philip and Mary wrote to tell him, with supplementary information from the lips of Seth Holland, that they were sending Sir William

---

[96]  Lutz no. 75; *CSP Ven*, V, no. 951; Tellechea, *Legación*, no. XXIX, pp. 109–113; *CRP* 2 no. 955.

[97]  Tellechea, *Legación*, nos XXX, XXXI, pp. 113–115; *CRP* 2 no. 956

Paget and Sir Edward Hastings to brief him on the current situation in England
and to escort him home. The next day, the king and queen issued credentials for
the Imperial ambassador in London, Simon Renard, to go to Brussels to brief
Pole further.[98]

Negotiations over the former church property continued, and on 27 October,
Pole wrote again to Mary, thanking her for the inspired idea of sending Renard
to him in Brussels. He now felt reassured that he had not been putting excessive
pressure on her for a quick religious settlement, and that his knowledge and
understanding of his native land, which some had doubted because of his long
years of exile, were in fact accurate. He also had high hopes of her pregnancy
and the good that might follow from it.[99] The next day, the cardinal wrote to
Morone, expressing similar optimism, but nonetheless told his friend that if the
upcoming parliament did not readmit him, by removing his attainder, he would
not go to England. He had told Renard that in that case he did not expect the
reign of Philip and Mary to last long. He did not doubt their sincerity, but still
thought that the former church goods might wreck everything, and that Julius
III was prepared to cede too much on this issue. In his memoir of a conversation
with Renard in Brussels, he made his first recorded mention of his becoming
archbishop of Canterbury, a suggestion that the ambassador had apparently
made, no doubt with royal approval, on the grounds that such an appointment, in
place of the imprisoned Cranmer, would give him voice and vote in parliament.
He confirmed to Morone, as he had to Renard, that he would not accept that
appointment until England was once more in full communion with the Roman
See.[100] On the same day, however, he evidently felt confident enough to give
Henry Pyning and Seth Holland details of his return. He would land in Dover
not displaying his insignia as a papal legate, and would be met by some of his
remaining relations and an escort of a hundred cavalrymen for protection. He
also told his faithful servants that he was still not happy about the property issue,
and confirmed that he would not agree to replace Cranmer as archbishop until
the reconciliation had taken place.[101] On 6 November, Pole wrote to Cardinal
del Monte to confirm that Philip and Mary had finally agreed to receive him,
and he now asked for more funds from Rome, to assist him in his new task.[102]
Pope Julius replied to Pole on the same day, saying that he had consulted 12
of the cardinals on the matter of English church property, and also the curial
Segnatura, and all had agreed that the 'reduction' of the country to the Roman
obedience was far more important. Pole's powers were altered accordingly, but

[98]   *CRP* 2 nos 957, 959; Tellechea, *Legación*, no. XXXVII, pp. 120–121.
[99]   *CSP Ven*, V, no. 958; *CRP* 2 no. 971.
[100]  BL Add. 25425, fols 328r–329v; *CSP Ven*, V, no. 960; *CRP* 2 no. 973.
[101]  BL Add. 25425, fols 325v–328r; *CRP* 2 no. 974.
[102]  Tellechea, *Legación*, no. XXXIX, pp. 128–129; *CRP* 2 no. 980.

the whole subject, including the relevant documents, was to be kept secret for the time being, though copies were sent to him.[103] On 7 November, Julius sent a brief to Charles V, to tell him that the issue of English church property had been resolved, and in a separate letter confirmed the arrangement to Philip and Mary. These were evidently last-minute confidence-building measures, before Pole left for Dover.[104] Probably in the same post, Morone sent an encouraging letter to Pole, saying that he quite understood the conflicting emotions of hope and fear that his friend was feeling. The new bull from Julius should, however, deal with all remaining scruples, especially to do with the troublesome property question. For the ransoming of the kingdom it was worth giving up some property and, if Pole was less exacting on this subject, God would surely be able to restore things more fully in His own good time. Morone assured Pole that he now had the full support of Charles V, and of his ambassador in Rome, Juan Manrique de Lara.[105]

The process that finally brought Pole to Westminster began with the issuing by Philip and Mary, of letters patent, dated 10 November, which allowed him to exercise legatine authority in the kingdom.[106] The next day, the cardinal himself wrote to Pope Julius from Brussels, telling him that the king and queen had wanted him to be in London by the 12th, for the opening of parliament, but the emperor had thought that he should await the larger escort that Paget and Hastings would supply. Granvelle had meanwhile heard from King Philip that Pole should travel without his legatine insignia on display, but would nonetheless be treated as a legate by the Crown. Having been expected in Brussels on 10 November, the escort in fact arrived on the evening of the 11th, and it was now agreed that the company would leave on 13 November, and that, in order not to compromise the authority of parliament before the necessary legislative work had been completed, Pole would travel as though he was a papal ambassador, not a full legate.[107] This duly happened and on the 13th Pole wrote again to the pope from Dilighem, saying that on the day before he left he had an audience of Charles V, who was unusually ebullient, declaring that he believed Pole would avoid the disasters that had occurred in Germany. He urged the legate to consult his son and daughter-in-law about everything. Pole, meanwhile, told the pope that he planned to reach Calais in six days and London in another four, after the Channel crossing.[108] On 18 November, Philip and Mary wrote to Pole that they had received news from Paget and Hastings of the party's progress, and said that they would be met at Dover by Bishop Thirlby, now of Ely, and Viscount

---

[103]  *CRP* 2 no. 978 (further textual details).
[104]  AGS Estado 881 no. 67; Tellechea, *Papado*, 1, no. XII, p. 27.
[105]  *ERP* 4 no. 59; *CRP* 2 no. 979.
[106]  Hughes and Larkin, *Tudor proclamations*, 2, pp. 48–49; *CRP* 2 no. 984.
[107]  Lutz no. 78; Tellechea, *Legación*, no. XLI, pp. 131–134; *CRP* 2 no. 985.
[108]  Tellechea, *Legación*, no. XLIII, pp. 136–138.

Montague (Anthony Browne).[109] Then, in the nick of time, on 22 November, parliament repealed the act of attainder against Pole.[110]

Contemporaneous correspondence is lacking for the English cardinal's no doubt emotional arrival in Dover, and journey to Westminster, but once he was in Lambeth Palace, he described his journey in a letter to Cardinal del Monte. Having left Brussels on 13 November he had arrived in Calais six days later as planned, being met there by the marshal, Sir John Figge, and the Lieutenant, William, Lord Howard. The legatine party arrived in Dover on 20 November, after a good crossing, by sail, of three-and-a-half hours. On the 21st, he was formally greeted by Bishop Thirlby and Viscount Montague, who gave him a letter from the king and queen. Also there to meet him was the new archdeacon of Canterbury, Nicholas Harpsfield, who had replaced Thomas Cranmer's brother Edmund in that office. At this point Pole was asked if he wanted to enter England formally as a legate and he answered no. On 22 November he was escorted to Canterbury, where he met the cathedral chapter, and also dispatched Bishop Richard Pate to London with a reply to his sovereigns' letter. On the 24th, he stayed with Lord Cobham at Cooling Castle, after which he boarded the Queen's barge at Gravesend and sailed up the Thames to the landing stage beside the Palace of Westminster. It was at Cooling, which had been embarrassingly involved with Sir Thomas Wyatt's recent rebellion, that Pole was told, by the elderly Bishop Cuthbert Tunstall and the earl of Shrewsbury, that his attainder had been removed. The legate, in the role of ambassador, was received in Whitehall Palace by Bishop Gardiner, in his capacity as lord chancellor, and then at last met the king and queen. After this he rested in Lambeth Palace, across the river, while celebrations continued in Westminster, and awaited his first meeting with the parliament by which he felt he had been wronged for so many years. On 30 November, the feast of St Andrew the Apostle, England would be reconciled to Rome.[111]

---

[109]   Lutz p. 225n; Tellechea, *Legación*, no. XLV, p. 143; *CRP* 2 no. 988.
[110]   *SR* 1 & 2 Philip and Mary c. 18; *CRP* 2 no. 988a.
[111]   Lutz no. 79; Tellechea, *Legación*, no. XLIV, pp. 139–142; *CRP* 2 no. 989.

# Chapter 6
# Legate and Archbishop

On Reconciliation Day, 30 November 1554, Pole absolved England of the sin committed in its schism from the Roman Church, and its subsequent deviation from Catholic doctrine.[1] After this, he was able to take personal direction, if not exactly control, of developments in the English Church, in which much had already been done to restore Catholic practice and faith.[2] In December 1554, he consulted the bishops, both those of the old dispensation and those newly appointed, to discover the needs of their dioceses.[3] Then, in late January and early February 1555, he began work in earnest on the programme of restoration, dealing individually with the diocesans who would be responsible for carrying it out in much of England and Wales. Given that his earlier, intransigent position on church property in lay hands had had to be modified in the previous December, it was natural that he should turn to other matters, including heresy. To begin with, the restored bishops were required to swear an oath that 'from this hour forward I will be faithful and obedient to Blessed Peter the Apostle, and the holy, apostolic, Roman Church, and our lord, the lord pope Julius the Third, and his canonically elected successors'.[4] According to the later account of the martyrologist John Foxe, Pole sent the clergy to their parishes: 'exhorting them to entreat the people and their flock with all gentleness, and to endeavour themselves to win the people rather by gentleness than by extremity and rigour'.[5] Pastoral need clearly had priority over canonical correctness, since the position of some of the bishops, as well as numerous priests, was yet to be fully regularised in accordance with Roman standards, by means of repentance and absolution for their actions during the schism.[6]

Such anomalies did not prevent Pole from embarking at once on his campaign to restore and ensure doctrinal orthodoxy in the English Church. According to

---

[1]   Details of the various versions of Pole's address to Parliament are set out in *CRP* 2 pp. 366–367.

[2]   Scarisbrick, *Reformation and the English people*, p. 104; Haigh, *English reformations*, p. 206; A.G. Dickens, ed., 'Robert Parkyn's narrative of the Reformation', *English Historical Review*, 62 (1947), pp. 58–92, at p. 79.

[3]   Tellechea, *Legación*, XLVI, p. 146; *CRP* 2 no. 1000.

[4]   *CRP* 3 no. 1042 (Antony Kitchen); BMD MS 922, 1, fols 71v–74r.

[5]   Foxe, *A&M* 1583, p. 1482; Mayer, *PPP*, p. 225.

[6]   *CRP* 3 no. 1054; Pocock, *Burnet*, 6, pp. 366–369 (Pole's supplementary instructions to the bishops).

Foxe's reference to a document that is now missing, on 28 January 1555, Pole gave a new commission to Gardiner, who had led the action against heresy before the legate's arrival.[7] It gave him authority to 'sit upon, and order ... all such preachers and heretics ... as were in [his] prison [at Southwark]'. The document apparently named Bishop John Hooper, John Rogers and John Cardmaker, to whom were added, on 30 January, Rowland Taylor, Edward Crome, John Bradford, Laurence Saunders and Robert Ferrar. Justice was still, however, to be tempered with mercy. On 29 January, he began to delegate his powers to diocesan bishops and other appropriate authorities, including diocesan and university chancellors, all of whom had been absolved of heresy and schism, in order to speed up the full restoration of the Catholic Church. He told them that as his jurisdiction over Canterbury province covered most of the population of Mary's kingdom, he could not carry out his tasks alone. He therefore delegated many of them to the recipients of this letter, empowering them to reconcile individuals of any social rank to the Church, as long as they showed repentance, accepted the Catholic faith and did the appropriate penance. The letters detailed the offences that might have been committed by those who had officiated in the schismatical Church of England under Henry VIII and Edward VI. These included using services unauthorised by Rome, being ordained by heretical and/ or schismatical bishops, taking uncanonical oaths to the king as Supreme Head of the Church, and being presented to benefices outside Roman canon law, and in particular by lay patrons who possessed such livings. These men could be restored to their original canonical state if they did as they were required, and such concessions were made not only to secular clergy but also to former male and female religious who, at the dissolution under Henry, had left their houses without papal dispensation, and in the case of the men had become secular priests and accepted benefices in that capacity. Even if they had married, they might be restored to the ranks of the Catholic clergy as long as they abandoned their wives, and moved to a diocese other than the one in which they had lived in the married state. Pole was even prepared to trust rehabilitated members of the parish clergy, if authorised by their diocesan or chancellor, to use these powers which, as some of this batch of letters set out in full, were wholly derived from the ample grants which had been made by Pope Julius to Pole, in August 1553. Also included were the relevant parliamentary statutes, repealing Henry's Act of Supremacy and Edward's Act of Uniformity, and restoring the fifteenth-century laws against heresy and heretics, as well as Pole's legatine powers relating to clerical orders and benefices.

---

[7]   This commission is missing, see *CRP* 3 no. 1053, and Foxe, *A&M* 1583, p. 1483, where it is mentioned; Duffy, *Fires of faith*, p. 92; Loades, *The religious culture of Marian England* (London: Pickering and Chatto, 2010), p. 26.

It is evident from the documents that Pole issued in January and February 1555 that he was anxious that both clergy and people should be fully prepared, in spirit and in terms of canon law, to celebrate Easter as Catholics in 1555, the Sunday being 21 April. Bishops and chancellors, acting as Pole's delegates, were to announce local dates by which their clergy had to be fully absolved of their schismatical and heretical failings, have done due penance, and been reconciled to the Church. Only thus might they correctly administer the sacraments in Holy Week and at Easter, when the great majority of believers made their annual confession and communion. All, whether clergy or laity, were to be fully reconciled in time for that Easter and, in accordance with the growing tendency towards bureaucracy which at that time affected both Catholic and 'magisterial' Protestant churches in Germany and Switzerland, the names of the 'reduced' – those brought into line in this way – were to be registered. After this, general visitations were to begin in all dioceses and both universities, with particular attention being paid to the situation of clerical orders and of claims to benefices. The latter point indicated that the cardinal legate had certainly not lost his interest in pursuing the lay 'possessioners'. Also to be examined were the education of the clergy, the extent and quality of their preaching, if any, and their practice of the sacrament of reconciliation. In a detail which evidently reflected the bitterness that Pole had felt against King Henry since the mid-1530s, he instructed his delegates to ensure that not only the name of the pope was restored to Catholic service books but also that of St Thomas Becket of Canterbury. Finally, when these bishops and chancellors, and their own local delegates among the parish clergy, formally announced Pole's canonical instructions, he told them to stress the misery of schism, no doubt against those who thought that Mary's initial return to her father's 'national Catholic' Church was sufficient. The precise form of absolution was also included and, between the end of January and early March, copies of these documents were distributed to all those concerned.[8] This programme of action would be put into practice up to the end of Mary's reign, and although it was naturally a matter for the clergy in the main, it clearly had the explicit support, and indeed, motivation, of the queen herself.

In order for the campaign for universal orthodoxy to be effective, it was urgently necessary to resolve the situation of those English clergy who had married during Edward VI's reign. It might have been presumed that the reconciliation of England to the Roman See, on 30 November 1554, automatically implied an end to clerical marriage and the restoration of compulsory celibacy for those in major orders, whether they were seculars or former religious, women also being included in the latter category. In fact, Queen Mary had initiated action

---

8 BMD MS 922 fols 32r–35r; CUL Add. MS 4841 fols 26r–31v; OUA Wpß/M/22, in Bod. Twyne 7 fol. 147v.

on this point, using her much-disliked authority as Supreme Head on Earth of the Church of England, well before Reconciliation day. On 4 March 1554, and despite the fact that the 1549 Act permitting clerical marriage was still on the statute book, she had included in her injunctions to the bishops an order that all married priests should be deprived of their benefices. Nevertheless, given the acute pastoral need of the time, she had moderated the rigour of Roman canon law by instructing diocesans that those who abandoned their wives might resume their sacramental ministry at once, provided that they had previously received absolution for schism and heresy. They should, however, be required in future to work in a different diocese from the one in which they had lived in the married state, or else in a parish distant from their previous place of work. Mary and Pole had of course been in regular contact by correspondence, between August 1553 and March of the following year, and the queen's intervention over clerical celibacy corresponded closely to the legate's actions, and instructions, when he took up the reins himself, now under the provisions of Roman canon law.[9]

On 15 November, Mary had been able to report to Pole that her first parliament had repealed all her predecessor's religious statutes, including the act of 1549 allowing clerical marriage.[10] Then, on 22 January 1554, with Sir Thomas Wyatt's rebellion looming, she told her 'good cousin' that many married clergy were occupying some of the richest benefices and that she had used parliament to dispossess many of them. With her kingdoms still in schism from Rome, she nonetheless asked Pole if she might be allowed dispensation to provide replacements for these priests, without flouting his authority.[11] This was duly permitted, and eventually, between 11 March and 6 November 1555, Pole's legatine register records his absolution, on the above terms of 17 formerly-married priests in England and Wales.[12] It is not known how many others were dealt with in a similar manner by those, including diocesan bishops, to whom Pole had delegated his powers in this respect and in others, but it appears that a large proportion of clergy in southern and eastern England, and many in

---

[9]     E. Cardwell, *Documentary annals of the Reformed Church of England*, 2 vols (Oxford: Clarendon Press, 1839), 1, pp. 109–113; Helen Parish, *Clerical marriage and the English Reformation: precedent, policy and practice* (Aldershot: Ashgate, 2000), pp. 186–188; Thomas S. Freeman, 'Burning zeal: Mary Tudor and the Marian persecution', in *Mary Tudor: Old and new perspectives*, ed. Susan Doran and Thomas S. Freeman (Basingstoke: Palgrave Macmillan, 2011), pp. 171–205, at pp. 181–184.

[10]     *ERP* 4 no. 45; *CRP* 2 no. 757.

[11]     *CSP Ven*, V, no. 849; *CRP* 2 no. 794; Jennifer Loach, *Parliament and the Crown in the reign of Mary Tudor* (Oxford: Clarendon Press, 1986), pp. 77–78.

[12]     BMD MS 922, ii, fols 1r–v, 59v–60v, 62r–63r, 72r–73r, 79r–80v, 80v–82r, 118v–119v, 123r–124r, 132r–133r; BMD MS 922, iii, fols 6r–7v, 64v–65v, 65v–66v, 77v–78v, 111v–112v; BMD MS 922, iv, fols 4v–5r, 41v–42r, 84r–v [= *CRP* 3 nos 1110, 1149a, 1154, 1162, 1167, 1171, 1201, 1205, 1214, 1225, 1285, 1286, 1291, 1320a, 1333, 1380, 1424].

Wales (where the celibacy rule had never been highly regarded), did marry in Edward's reign.[13]

In May 1554, with the deprivation of married clergy by governmental authority well under way, a text justifying this reversion to traditional Catholic practice was published by Thomas Martin, a lawyer who had been educated at Winchester College and New College Oxford and who would later lead the prosecution in the Inquisition trial of Archbishop Thomas Cranmer.[14] Martin had gone into exile under Edward VI, denouncing from Paris the religious reforms of his reign. Returning to England after Mary's accession, as chancellor of Winchester diocese for the restored Bishop Gardiner, he quickly put his pen to use in her service as one of the most prominent early propagandists for her religious policies.[15] His treatise against clerical marriage combined religious teaching with polemic, including the introduction of a theme that become a constant in Catholic critiques of the reformed English Church after 1559. Early in his work, Martin linked the 'lechery' of clergy who married with Henry VIII's love for Anne Boleyn, which led both to the divorce of his wife Catherine and to the break with Rome. However he avoided mentioning Henry's name, which still had a positive resonance in 1554, even for the queen herself. Instead, he recounted the tale of Michael Cerularius (d. 1058), patriarch of Constantinople after 1043, from whose time in office the schism between the Western and Eastern Churches has conventionally been dated. In Martin's somewhat dubious account, the Byzantine emperor Michael VI Palaeologus had appointed Cerularius as patriarch in order to facilitate his own planned incestuous marriage, resulting in a split with the papacy. Martin commented obliquely: 'I would the lyke had never been practised synce els where.'[16] His meaning was plain enough. Deploying the Old and New Testament texts that had traditionally been cited in controversies over clerical celibacy and marriage, Martin took the view that the final judgment in the interpretation of Scripture rested with the bishops, as successors of the Apostles. Guided by the Holy Spirit, the bishops, and above all the pope, determined Christian doctrine, 'the Scriptures being witnesses, thei being iudges'. For this author, 'the holy ghoste dwelleth not in the dead letter [of the Bible uninterpreted] but in the lyvelye bodie of Jesus Christe, which is the Churche that he governeth'.[17] This 'enlivening' reading and understanding of Scripture should take place especially in general councils of the Church. Martin

---

[13]   MacCulloch, *Thomas Cranmer*, p. 129. Freeman suggests that those clerics who married were likely to have been sympathetic to reformed doctrines, but even traditionalists in the Church may also have sought this comfort (Freeman, 'Burning zeal', pp. 181–182).

[14]   Thomas Martin, *A traictise declaring and plainly proving that the pretensed marriage of priestes and professed persons is no marriage* (London, 1554).

[15]   Steve Hindle, 'Martin [Martyn], Thomas', *ODNB*.

[16]   Martin, *Traictise*, sigs iiii (r–v); *ODCC*, p. 1083.

[17]   Martin, *Traictise*, sigs D 3r–4v, F 1 r–v.

was enough of a Renaissance humanist to insist that the text of Scripture should be consulted, but this was in order to confirm the trustworthiness of unwritten truths. Martin quoted Jesus's words in John 21:25 ('if every one of them were written down, I suppose that the world itself could not contain the books that would be written'), commenting that he 'spake and didde manye thinges that be not penned in the Evangelistes'.[18]

Martin was equally sceptical of the prescriptive power of the other pillar of Church orthodoxy, apart from Scripture, this being the teaching of the Church Fathers, of which he said tartly: 'God forbidde we shoulde geve them more authoritie than to the worde of God.'[19] In this context, Martin criticised the Eastern churches for allowing priests to marry, and thus falling away from the standards of the earlier Eastern, or Greek, Fathers.[20] He fully supported the rule of compulsory clerical celibacy in the Western Church, as it had been asserted by Pope Gregory VII in the eleventh century, not as an innovation but as a re-affirmation of historic tradition.[21] On this historical basis, Thomas Martin launched into contemporary polemic. He pitilessly mocked the priests who had married under the terms of Edward VI's 1549 statute, ironically reiterating the argument included in its preamble, that they would be better to devote themselves solely to their service at the altar. They may have just wanted sex, but instead: '[t]hei found their wives ... to be their purgatory in this worlde, which thought in an other worlde to bee no purgatory at all'.[22] This mocking tone was taken up, in 1556, by possibly the most accomplished polemicist in the Catholic cause in Mary's reign, the London hosier Miles Hogarde (Huggarde). As well as lambasting those secular clergy and former religious who had broken their vow of chastity, he went after the 'purgatorial' wives, dividing them into two categories, former mistresses (in terms of canon law, 'concubines') who had previously had illegal but at least stable relationships, and other women of even less repute, who were, in a phrase that rings across the centuries, 'as common as the cartway'.[23]

Meanwhile, the re-enactment by parliament of the Lancastrian heresy laws, on 20 January 1555, opened the way for the trials, for heresy not treason, of those who had already been imprisoned under the authority of Gardiner.[24] Initially, the

---

[18]   Martin, *Traictise*, sig. B 2r.

[19]   Martin, *Traictise*, sig. D 3r.

[20]   Martin, *Traictise*, sigs N 3r–v, Q4r–v.

[21]   Martin, *Traictise*, sigs F 2r, G 1r–v, KK 1r, I 2r–4v, A 2r.

[22]   Martin, *Traictise*, sigs π A 3r–v, R3v; William Wizeman, *The theology and spirituality of Mary Tudor's Church* (Aldershot: Ashgate, 2006), pp. 36, 32, 40, 58–59, 66, 96, 123–124, 128–132, 139.

[23]   Miles Hogarde, *A displaying of the Protestants and sondry their practises* (London, 1556), pp. 73v–74r.

[24]   *SR* 1 & 2 Philip and Mary c. 6; H. Gee and W.H. Hardy, *Documents illustrative of the history of the English Church* (London: Macmillan, 1896), p. 384.

resulting investigation and trial of those accused of heresy was carried out by him and the other bishops under English statute law, though also under commission from Pole as legate. Thus there was direct continuity with the action which had been taken before the cardinal's arrival in the country against those who were believed to adhere to the teaching and practice of Edward VI's Church. By mid-January 1554, even before the beginning of the episcopal visitations of dioceses that had been ordered by Pole, the privy council had instructed the sheriffs and magistrates of Essex to arrest 'lewde' preachers and 'certain lewde persones' in Colchester and other places, who were urging people not to attend Catholic worship.[25] In February 1554, Bishop Edmund Bonner of London had targeted a wider circle of heretics, including some in Essex, when he ordered all Christians within his diocese to go to confession before Easter, and instructed his clergy to make lists of those who refused. The royal injunctions, issued in the following month, which ordered that married priests be deprived of their livings, also instructed diocesan bishops to remove from office preachers and teachers who were spreading 'evil' doctrine.[26] Bonner's diocesan visitation in September 1554 led to further examinations and arrests, with the result that by the time that the heresy laws were restored, there were already numerous suspects in the various London gaols, including King's Bench, Marshalsea, the Bread Street Counter, the Fleet and the Tower itself.[27]

John Hooper, former bishop of Gloucester and Worcester, was unusual among the 'heresiarchs', whose arrest the Queen and Gardiner hoped would put an end to Edward VI's Church settlement, even while the kingdom remained in schism. In July 1553, Hooper had sent a troop of horse to support Mary, but nonetheless his fiercely anti-Catholic views and his vigour in implementing reforming policies made him an obvious target. He was summoned before the privy council in August 1553, and by 1 September was in the Fleet prison. Given his open support for the legitimacy of Mary's title to the throne, it was evident that he could not be tried for treason, and he was instead charged with owing £509 5s. 5d. to the Crown in first fruits for his bishopric. It was equally clear, however, that much more serious charges awaited him if and when England's situation was regularised with Rome, and his family took the opportunity to escape, settling in Frankfurt. On 15 March 1554, Hooper was deprived of his see, under Mary's powers as Supreme Head on Earth of the Church of England, but he remained in prison thereafter until 22 January 1555, when he was interrogated by Bishop Gardiner in St Saviour's Southwark.[28] On the other hand, Nicholas

---

[25]   *APC* IV pp. 381, 395.

[26]   Houlbrooke, 'The clergy, the Church courts and the Marian restoration in Norwich', *CMT*, pp. 124–146, at p. 128.

[27]   Duffy, *Fires of faith*, pp. 90–92.

[28]   D.G. Newcombe, 'Hooper, John', *ODNB*.

Ridley, bishop of London, was clearly guilty of treason, in the eyes of Mary and her council. Earlier in 1553, when King Edward was already suffering from what would prove to be his terminal illness, Ridley, with his chaplain Edmund Grindal, a future bishop of London and archbishop of Canterbury, had gone to sound the Lady Mary out on religious matters. He was left in no doubt, by this abrasive encounter, that the reform would be eliminated if she came to the throne, and he thereafter devoted himself to securing the success of Edward and the duke of Northumberland's plan for the succession of Lady Jane Dudley, née Grey.[29] When Edward died, on 6 July 1553, Ridley had already accepted Northumberland's offer of the See of Durham, in succession to Cuthbert Tunstall, who had been deprived. Still as bishop of London, he preached at St Paul's, with his customary verve, in support of Queen Jane. In words that would come to haunt him, he declared that since both Mary and Elizabeth had been declared bastards by parliament during their father's lifetime, neither was eligible to succeed. After this, it was hardly surprising that Mary quickly had him arrested, once she reached London, and he was sent to join Archbishop Cranmer, Bishop Latimer and Prebendary John Bradford, who had been one of Edward's chaplains, in the Tower. Although he could have been tried for treason, Ridley was kept until Roman canon law had been restored, though in the meantime he was sent to Oxford, with the other two bishops, in March 1554, and took part with them in a public disputation there, in the following month, on the doctrine of the Eucharist. In this he forthrightly expressed his reformed views, continuing to write on the subject in the Oxford gaol, Bocardo, where he remained until his trial and death, with Latimer, on 16 October 1555.[30]

Hugh Latimer, who had been bishop of Worcester under Henry VIII and was latterly one of Edward VI's chaplains and court preachers, was, like Hooper, arrested by Mary's new regime for his religious views, though he was charged with sedition, rather than heresy, when committed to the Tower of London, in mid-September 1553. He had been allowed his liberty to attend his royal master's funeral, but had shown no sign of accepting the restoration of Catholicism. In January 1554 he was placed in the same cell as Cranmer, Ridley and Bradford, possibly in the vain hope that the 'heresiarchs' would somehow come to their senses, from the viewpoint of the queen and her advisers. In March, however, the three former diocesans were moved to Oxford, where Latimer suffered the same fate as Ridley.[31] In addition to the inmates of the Tower, other known reformists were inevitably threatened by Mary's accession. John Rogers, for example, who in the last years of Henry VIII had exercised a Lutheran ministry in north-western Germany and also acquired a Flemish wife and a family, returned to

---

[29]    Foxe, *A&M* 1583, p. 1396.
[30]    Susan Wabuda, 'Ridley, Nicholas', *ODNB*.
[31]    Susan Wabuda, 'Latimer, Hugh', *ODNB*.

England after Edward's accession and, on 27 August 1551, received the prebend of St Pancras, in St Paul's cathedral, from Bishop Ridley. The privy council ordered his arrest on 16 August 1553, in somewhat murky circumstances, given that he was preaching the legal, established religion of England, which Mary was at that stage still required to uphold, as Supreme Head. Despite this, and the continuing lack of heresy laws, Rogers was placed under house arrest as a seditious preacher, hence suspected of treason, and was deprived of his prebend on 10 October 1553, though he continued as incumbent of St Sepulchre's. Having remained in this confinement for five months, he became one of the first to fall under the provisions of the revived heresy statutes and the restored Roman canon law. On 27 January 1554, he was dispatched to Newgate prison, whence he was sent to be interrogated by Gardiner in Southwark. He was condemned on 29 January and on 4 February he was burned for heresy at Smithfield, near the church of St Bartholomew the Great, having the dubious distinction of being the first person to suffer that fate in Mary's reign.[32]

Given the traditional view, in Church and Inquisition, that most Christians would not deviate from orthodoxy unless they were led by an ill-disposed individual, it is perhaps not surprising that, of those who were accused of heresy at the beginning of Mary's reign, most were leading clergymen. It is notable, however, that almost as soon as the heresy laws were restored by parliament and the bishops came under direct legatine authority, laymen, some of them of relatively humble origin, also found themselves caught in the net. This pattern would continue for the rest of the reign, but one of the earliest cases, that of Thomas Tomkins, burned to death at Smithfield on 16 March 1555, suggests that defiance by individuals could provoke the ecclesiastical and secular authorities into action. Tomkins, a citizen of London and a weaver from Shoreditch, was one of eight 'moste constant wytnesses of the Christian doctrine', in Foxe's words, who were interrogated by the restored bishop of London, Edmund Bonner, while Gardiner was attempting to deal with Cranmer, Hooper, Latimer, Ridley and Bradford. The documents reproduced by Foxe, which appear to come from Bonner's episcopal register, suggest that in the autumn of 1554, Tomkins had pressed himself on his bishop, in order to debate his views on the two sacraments recognised by the reformers: Baptism and the Holy Communion. On 26 September 1554, Tomkins had agreed with Bonner that a document drawn up by the bishop represented his 'long-held views' on these subjects. He rejected the doctrine of transubstantiation, on the grounds that Christ was in heaven and could be nowhere else. He also thought that baptism should be administered only in 'the vulgar tongue' and without 'anye such ceremonies as customarily are used in the latine church' (such as exorcism and chrism). On this occasion Tomkins stated that that he had been 'many tymes and ofte called openly before my said Ordynary [Bonner] and talked withal'. He had also discussed his 'confessions and declarations' (evidently the September meeting was not the first) with other scholars and with the bishop's chaplains. As would happen on many other occasions in Mary's reign, Bonner and his agents had evidently worked hard to persuade Tomkins to change his views and return to Catholicism, though without success. The seriousness with which the weaver was treated is indicated by the fact that, in the session on 26 September 1554, Tomkins, and some others not named in Foxe's source, had been confronted not only by Bonner but also by Gilbert Bourne, bishop of Bath and Wells, and Henry Morgan, bishop of St David's. Even this high-powered team could not persuade Tomkins to budge, so, in the continuing absence of laws under which to try him as a heretic, he was simply condemned as such and sent to Newgate gaol, where he remained until March 1555. On 8 March he appeared before Bonner once more, who tried again to persuade him to return to the Catholic faith. When he refused, he was given a further set of documents, including articles of belief and a form of confession, to consider overnight, but when he returned to Bonner the next day he remained obdurate and was found guilty of obstinate heresy under the restored legislation. He died by fire at Smithfield on 16 March.[33]

Between 4 February 1555 and 10 November 1558, a week before both Mary and Pole died, nearly 300 men and women were burned alive for heresy. In addition, an unknown number died in prison, while awaiting trial or execution.[34] The four editions of the *Acts and monuments* that were overseen by Foxe himself, in 1563, 1570, 1576 and 1583, give some account, whether lengthy or brief, of the cases of 313 individuals, 263 male and 50 female, who died for their beliefs during these years, either by burning or in prison. The occupations of half of the males are recorded – 21 clergy, nine gentry, 123 artisans, craftsmen and tradesmen, and one lawyer, one constable and one schoolmaster. As was customary in early modern Europe, the women are mostly defined by their relationship to their husbands. The charges laid against these individuals can be roughly divided, as was customary in heresy trials throughout western and central Europe in the period, between the negative, in this case rejection of Catholic faith and practice and active opposition to it, and the positive, meaning the affirmation and spreading of reformed beliefs. Details of the charges are known in only 105 cases. Of these nearly half, 41, were accused of openly opposing Catholic teaching, notably on the Mass, in public or in private, and either absenting themselves from services or trying to disrupt them. Over 30

---

[33]   Foxe, *A&M* 1563, pp. 1170–1172.

[34]   Owing to the localised nature of the system for the judgment of heretics in Mary's reign, and the subsequent loss of records, it is essential to rely on Foxe and his sources. The discussion here of numbers and categories of those executed is mainly based on the table and editorial material in Doran and Freeman, *Mary Tudor*, pp. 224–271.

individuals were accused of leading or attending Protestant worship or reading the Bible in English, while other more miscellaneous charges included, in one case, assaulting a Catholic priest (committed by William alias Thomas Flower), visiting Protestants in prison, and in two cases trying to disrupt a burning, while one reconciled Catholic priest was charged with visiting his former wife, this being an offence under Roman canon law.

Mary's regime, like its Continental equivalents, placed heavy reliance on informers to instigate cases, and there do not appear to have been any inquisitorial visitations of areas of the country, looking for heresy, such as happened in the medieval Inquisition, and in sixteenth-century Spain. The names of such informers are known in 114 cases, according to Foxe. These included 11 clerics, often parish priests, but the vast majority of the cases were initially investigated and brought by laymen – members of Philip and Mary's council, 14 peers, 56 gentlemen and justices of the peace, and 21 local officials or townsmen. When it came to the judging of the cases recorded by Foxe, the names of those responsible are known in 297 cases. Here the clergy were active, including 18 bishops, three archdeacons, other clergy and eight diocesan chancellors. In a solitary case, the judge was a layman, Sir Anthony Browne, Viscount Montague.

Before examining the working of the system of religious repression that was unleashed in early 1555, it is useful to consider the moral values that underlay such violent persecution in sixteenth-century Europe. It has been estimated that, between 1525 and 1565, something in the region of 3,000 reformed Christians were judicially killed in Europe.[35] Since then, of course, many terrible persecutions have taken place, generally on behalf of secular ideologies, but a peculiar shock and revulsion tends to arise when such killings are justified on religious grounds. Also emotive, in the case of the Catholic inquisition in Mary's England, as in her husband and her father-in-law's territories, especially Spain and the Netherlands, is the method of execution ordained by Roman canon law for relapsed or obstinate heretics – to be burned alive. As a result of what happened in Mary's reign, as well as the activities of the Inquisition in Spain and the New World, the question has often been asked whether moral standards and values then were somehow different from those of more recent centuries. Explicitly religious persecution, leaving aside systematic violence in the cause of explicitly anti-religious ideologies, has certainly not been absent from modern times, but the moral question still needs to be addressed in the context of Marian England.

---

[35] William Monter, 'Heresy executions in Reformation Europe', in *Tolerance and intolerance in the European Reformation*, ed. Ole Peter Grell and Bob Scribner (Cambridge: Cambridge University Press, 1996), pp. 48–65.

In his general history of the English Reformation, the Catholic J.J. Scarisbrick wrote: 'We are horrified by these burnings', and left it at that.[36] A similar distaste, leading to a reluctance to confront the sordid details, may be found in the work of the Anglican historian of Puritanism, Patrick Collinson, who criticises the detailed accounts of horrible deaths by burning given by Foxe. For Collinson, Foxe's often lurid detail 'suggests an almost voyeuristic fascination rather than horror'.[37] Thomas Mayer is absolute on the subject: 'modern sensibilities abhor any execution for religion'.[38] Eamon Duffy agrees:

> Any civilised twenty-first century person will of course agree that burning men and women alive for their fidelity to deeply-held beliefs must be both obviously and profoundly 'the wrong weapon' in a struggle for religious reconstruction. But the consensus is a matter of moral hindsight, attained this side of the Enlightenment and strictly speaking is hardly a historical judgement at all.[39]

This appears to mean that sixteenth-century people, including both those who ordered the burnings and those who attended them, were generally more callous and heartless than the supposedly compassionate and sensitive souls of today. In this respect, all social classes of the period might be seen as being of one mind. Charles Parker expresses the thought thus, in his study of early modern religious persecution in the Netherlands:

> Men and women in the sixteenth and seventeenth centuries did not regard heresy, idolatry or apostasy as religious choices [even though that is exactly what the word 'heresy' originally meant]; rather they understood them as plagues of the soul, seductions of the devil, and portals to hell. Paradoxically, they believed that the religious choices they did make would free them from these terrors. Since all confessional groups regarded themselves as the true body of Christ, such denominations necessarily considered all others as sectarian, schismatic, heretical or idolatrous.[40]

This realistic view may be supplemented by that of Thomas McCoog SJ:

---

[36]    Scarisbrick, *Reformation*, p. 136.

[37]    Patrick Collinson, 'The persecution in Kent', in Duffy and Loades, *CMT*, pp. 309–333, at p. 309.

[38]    *PPP*, p. 277.

[39]    Duffy, *Fires of faith*, p. 79.

[40]    Charles Parker, *Faith on the margins: Catholics and Catholicism in the Dutch Golden Age* (Cambridge, MA: Harvard University Press, 2008), p. 6.

Toleration was not the norm; in the sixteenth century, it was at best extolled as expedient by the *politiques* [moderate sceptics] to the disgust [for example] of most Jesuits ...

The persistence of popery with its magical rituals and superstitious devotions, from a Protestant perspective, or the admission of heresy with its debasement of sacraments and iconoclastic destruction, from a Catholic one, threatened the body politic ...

The presence of a non-conforming minority posed a risk for the entire society, natural and supernatural threats so great that their demonisation is understandable.[41]

The great bulk of the available evidence for religious attitudes and policies in the period certainly appears to support such analyses, and yet even the very archives of the enforcing agencies, in particular the Inquisition, for example in late medieval France, Spain and Italy, suggest that by no means everyone accepted the arguments of Church and state. There was evidently an undercurrent of scepticism about unique truth claims made by specific religions – Christianity, Judaism and Islam – which refused to disappear and may have been strengthened by the experience of religious violence, often officially sponsored, in the sixteenth and seventeenth centuries.[42] Such principled rejection of religious persecution, on behalf of whichever cause, can even be found in the great martyrologist of the English Protestants, John Foxe himself. In his *Acts and monuments*, Foxe's overarching purpose was to demonstrate that, throughout the Middle Ages, the 'true' Reformed Church, based on apostolic principles, had always existed, in England and elsewhere, despite papal abuses and persecution. Yet he went further than condemning Catholic violence, believing that no Christian should

----

[41] Thomas M. McCoog SJ, *The Society of Jesus in Ireland, Scotland and England, 1589–1597: Building the Faith of Saint Peter upon the King of Spain's monarchy* (Farnham and Rome: Ashgate and Institutum Historicum Societatis Iesu (Rome), 2012), pp. 9–10. See also Benjamin Kaplan, *Divided by faith: religious conflict and the practice of toleration in early modern Europe* (Cambridge, MA: Harvard University Press, 2007), pp. 143–145 and Brad S. Gregory, *Salvation at stake: Christian martyrdom in early modern Europe* (Cambridge, MA: Harvard University Press, 1999), p. 14: 'Fundamentally were [the authorities] social control ideologues who imposed their constructions on an oppressed populace, or conscientious pastors who strove to rattle the complacent out of their deadly spiritual torpor?'

[42] Edwards, 'Religious faith and doubt in late medieval Spain: Soria, *circa* 1450–1500', *Past and Present. A Journal of Historical Studies*, 120 (1988), pp. 3–25, reprinted in Edwards, *Religion and society in Spain, c. 1492* (Aldershot: Variorum, 1996), III; Stuart B. Schwartz, *All can be saved: religious tolerance and salvation in the Iberian Atlantic world* (New Haven and London: Yale University Press, 2008), *passim*.

be persecuted for his or her faith, and linking all who died, even for what he regarded as the wrong religious cause, as successors to the proto-martyr Stephen [Acts 7:54–60]. Thus the range of human moral values was the same as today, but the application was somewhat different, with double standards applied to those who were punished for their religious beliefs. Pole could write lyrically of the sufferings of Fisher and More, while apparently blocking any feeling of compassion for the reformers who were burned to death under his authority in Mary's England. The trouble was that people on both sides of the sixteenth-century religious divide thought this, hence the plentiful supply of martyrs in the period. As long as the authorities were prepared to execute, there were plenty willing to suffer.

As far as Queen Mary herself was concerned, there can be no doubt that in respect of heresy, as in so many other matters, she was her father's daughter. She certainly did not lack tenderness in her character and personal relations, particularly with her servants and their family, and she had received a broadly humanistic Christian education which might have suggested a loving and relatively open-minded faith, but she does seem nevertheless to have drawn the line between true and false Christian belief very much in the way so pithily described by Duffy.[43] Whatever opening to tolerance may have appeared to be offered in her proclamation of 18 August 1553 on religion, long before the reconciliation to Rome it was clear to all, both at home and abroad, that Mary intended to restore and enforce Catholic orthodoxy, and use the full apparatus of Church and state to do so.

Medieval Continental inquisitions into heresy were ecclesiastical initiatives, with the lay authorities in a vital but subordinate role. Laymen might be involved in the denunciation and arrest of suspects, but inquisitors employed their own spies and police, known in Spain as 'familiars' (*familiares*) of the Inquisition. The Spanish example is particularly relevant to what happened in Mary's reign, because not only had her husband Philip become king of England, but he had brought with him Spanish churchmen who had both intellectual and practical experience of the battle against heresy. The Spaniards in Philip's household and Court, both lay and clerical, came to England in 1554 with the experience of over 70 years of operations by the Spanish Inquisition that had been founded by Pope Sixtus IV in 1478, at the request of Ferdinand and Isabella. From the start, this institution, although it was founded on canon law, with its tribunals

---

[43]    Edwards, *Mary I*, pp. 7–14, 226–231; Andrew W. Taylor, '"*Ad omne virtutum genus*"? Mary between piety, pedagogy and praise in early Tudor humanism', in Doran and Freeman, *Mary Tudor*, pp. 103–122; Aysha Pollnitz, 'Religion and translation in the Court of Henry VIII: Princess Mary, Katherine Parr and the *Paraphrases* of Erasmus', in Doran and Freeman, *Mary Tudor*, pp. 123–137; Aysha Pollnitz, 'Christian women or sovereign queens? The schooling of Mary and Elizabeth', in *Tudor queenship: the reigns of Mary and Elizabeth*, ed. Alice Hunt and Anna Whitelock (New York: Palgrave Macmillan, 2010), pp. 127–142.

staffed by ecclesiastics, relied heavily on the co-operation of the Crown and local authorities.[44] The same elements went into action in England, but in a different configuration. Here, before the reconciliation with Rome in November 1554, all policy initiatives concerning religion came from the queen herself, from her council and from parliament. As had been the case before 1547, while judgment on the orthodoxy or otherwise of the religion of individuals rested with the Church, joint commissions for heresy, consisting of laymen and clergy, were set up by central government to enforce the law of the land in towns and shires, with the active co-operation of urban officials, members of the aristocracy, and justices of the peace.

According to the information accumulated by Foxe, 31 nobles and gentlemen actively sought and arrested suspected Protestants between the beginning of February 1555 and the end of the reign. Some of these individuals were clearly committed Catholic supporters of Mary's cause from the beginning, when she first gathered her forces, in July 1553, to oppose and overthrow Queen Jane. Sir Henry Doyle joined her, with his two sons, at Framlingham in mid-July, and he brought to book one of Cranmer's inner circle, Rowland Taylor, rector of Hadleigh and archdeacon of Bury St Edmund's, who was one of the first to die at the stake, on 9 February 1555.[45] Sir Thomas Moyle, a Kentish gentleman and lawyer, who in 1543 had taken part in the unsuccessful Canterbury prebendaries' plot to remove Archbishop Cranmer, was accused under Edward VI of being a 'papist', and quickly rallied to Mary's support two years later. With Thomas Austen, he was responsible for the arrest of John Bland, a Yorkshireman and former fellow of St John's College Cambridge, who had been a strong supporter of Cranmer since the 1540s. As curate of Adisham in Kent, Bland physically resisted the restoration of Catholic worship there, coming into direct conflict with his churchwardens. Moyle, as the local justice, managed to revoke his bail, imposed for his earlier offence. Bland was interrogated in the chapter house of Canterbury cathedral, and kept in prison until the heresy laws had been restored. After this he was tried before Bishop Richard Thornden of Dover, who was then still technically Cranmer's suffragan but had ostentatiously returned to Catholicism. He was now taking a leading role in the harrying of the archbishop's remaining supporters, and had Bland burned at Canterbury on 12 July 1555.[46] In East Anglia, where Mary's coup had been launched, she received immediate and strong support from Sir John Tyrell and his cousin Edmund Tyrell, the latter being bailiff of St Osyth and Member of Parliament for Maldon, both in

[44]    Edwards, *Inquisition*, 2nd edn (Stroud: The History Press, 2009), pp. 31–47, 69–84; Edwards, 'A Spanish Inquisition? The repression of Protestantism under Mary Tudor', *Reformation and Renaissance Review*, 4 (2000), pp. 62–74.

[45]    Foxe, *A&M* 1583, pp. 2049, 2099–2100.

[46]    Patricia Hyde, 'Moyle, Sir Thomas', *ODNB*; Freeman, 'Bland, John', *ODNB*; Doran and Freeman, *Mary Tudor*, pp. 188–189, 232.

Essex.[47] According to Foxe, Edmund, in particular, was always keen 'to heape up mo[re] coales to this furious flame of persecution, whether of a blind zeale or of a parasiticall flettery [presumably of the Queen or Bonner], I knowe not'.[48] In 1556, Edmund led a sweep of Essex reformists, or 'gospellers', who had been cheekily meeting on his land, at Hockley, with the connivance of one of his herdsmen. In order to break up this group, Tyrell worked with Sir John Mordaunt, a privy councillor and heresy commissioner who had brought to book one of the earliest prominent targets of the campaign, Laurence Saunders, a leading supporter of Cranmer and a multiple benefice-holder, who was burned in Coventry on 8 February 1555.[49] Edmund and Sir John Tyrell more than once organised night raids to catch suspected Protestants, whom they dispatched for interrogation by Bishop Bonner as being 'not conformable to the orders of the Churche, nor to the reall presence of Christes body and bloude in the Sacrament of the aultare'.[50] In addition, one of Mary's judges, Sir Anthony Browne, had the distinction of being the only recorded lay judge of a heresy case, when he condemned a tailor from Colchester, George Eagles, for clandestine Protestant preaching. Being sentenced under English rather than Roman canon law, Eagles was not burned to death but hanged, drawn and quartered (as Catholics would be under Elizabeth), at Chelmsford on or about 2 August 1557.[51]

While Mordaunt and the Tyrells may have been genuinely devout, there were others who apparently sought to expunge their own Protestant past by vigorously pursuing people with similar views. An instance was Sir John Baker, a leading London lawyer who retained, and greatly expanded, his inherited property interests in Kent, where he was a justice of the peace. He had not only served Henry VIII and his son, but signed the engagement for acceptance of Edward's 'Devise', to replace Mary with Jane as his successor. He provided legal advice on the subject on 11 June 1553, and 10 days later signed the relevant letters patent. Nevertheless, he subsequently acquired a justified reputation as a heresy-hunter, being a commissioner for his home diocese of Canterbury, and he used his patronage of Kentish livings to harry Cranmer's supporters and replace them with clergy who upheld Marian orthodoxy.[52] Various noblemen made similar transitions from being supporters of the schismatical Church of England to upholding Catholic orthodoxy under the leadership of Mary and her agents.

---

[47]   Anna Whitelock and Diarmaid MacCulloch, 'Princess Mary's household and the succession crisis', July 1553, *Historical Journal*, 50 (2007), pp. 265–287, at pp. 281–283.

[48]   Foxe, *A&M* 1583, p. 1683.

[49]   Doran and Freeman, *Mary Tudor*, pp. 228, 229.

[50]   Foxe, *A&M* 1583, pp. 1895, 1896, 1912, 1917, 2006; Duffy, *Fires of faith*, pp. 95–96, 136–137.

[51]   J.H. Baker, 'Browne, Sir Anthony', *ODNB*; Doran and Freeman, *Mary Tudor*, p. 256.

[52]   J.D. Alsop, 'Baker, Sir John', *ODNB*; Freeman, 'Burning zeal', pp. 183–184; Foxe, *A&M* 1583, pp. 1584, 1979, 1981, 2112.

In August 1556, for instance, a new heresy commission was headed by John de Vere, earl of Oxford, a scion of the ancient aristocracy who had supported Mary quite early on, from his base in Essex, and had been rewarded with restoration to the office of lord chamberlain, and by Thomas, first Baron Darcy of Chiche, who had supported the succession of Jane Grey in July 1553. Now, in very different circumstances, this commission met in Colchester, a known centre of reformed Church activity, and planned to seize the property of fugitives and restore alienated property in Suffolk and Essex to the Church. In one case, their agents apparently came upon a 'conventicle' in session, and arrested 23 'gospellers' 'at one clap'. Their success turned against them, however, as first a pregnant member of the congregation had to be released, after a hearing before the municipal authorities of Colchester, and then there was further trouble when the rest were sent to London, for interrogation and sentencing by Bishop Bonner.[53] The complications which arose from this case would involve Pole personally, and highlight the contradictions within the leadership of the English Church at this time. First, though it is necessary to examine the Cardinal's succession to the see of Canterbury, as well as the fate of Cranmer.

When, at Christmastide 1554, Pole began to act as papal legate in a Catholic England, Bishops Cranmer, Latimer, Ridley and Hooper were still imprisoned in the Tower of London, awaiting trial for heresy. Cranmer was still archbishop, even though, having been attainted for treason, he was a dead man in law. In December 1553, while the legate was still trying to influence matters in England by means of correspondence from abroad, the archbishop had written to Queen Mary, appealing for her pardon for his 'heinous folly and offence' in sending troops to fight for Jane. His effort was in vain, and both he and his fellow bishops remained heresiarchs in the eyes of the government, who would have to be made an example of by conviction for heresy, if the Catholic faith was to be secured again in the kingdom. The combination of political danger, in the form of the Wyatt rebellion, with continuing religious dissidence, meant that London was not thought to be a suitable place for their trial. Therefore, on 8 March 1554, the privy council ordered that Cranmer, Latimer and Ridley should be taken to Oxford. They left on the 12th and were handed over at Brentford to the Sheriff of Oxfordshire, the soon to be ennobled Sir John Williams, who had from the start been one of Mary's leading supporters in the Thames Valley. They were imprisoned in the town gaol, Bocardo, on the city's north wall beside St Michael's church. This government action followed the issue of the queen's injunctions on religion on 4 March.[54]

---

[53]   Loades, 'Darcy, Thomas', *ODNB*; Foxe, *A&M* 1583, pp. 1971–1973; Duffy, *Fires of faith*, pp. 137–130.

[54]   MacCulloch, *Thomas Cranmer*, pp. 558–561.

Although Roman inquisitorial law had not yet been restored to England, the Crown appointed a delegation to examine the three bishops, who had now been deprived of their sees under the law of the kingdom. It was to be led by Dr Hugh Weston, who had formerly been Lady Margaret professor of theology at Oxford and was now prolocutor for the convocation of Canterbury. His team of Oxford scholars was supplemented by seven from Cambridge. There was to be a formal disputation, the proceedings of which were to be filed until it was possible to open full inquisitorial proceedings against the three. The disputation began in the university church of St Mary the Virgin on 14 April 1554, with the setting out of the agenda. Cranmer, Latimer and Ridley were to be asked for their views on whether the doctrine of transubstantiation was true, and whether every celebration of the Mass was a sacrifice. The actual sessions began on 16 April in the Divinity School, and Weston allowed them to deviate from the academic norm, with some proceedings in English rather than Latin and permission for the public to intervene vociferously. The debates lasted until 21 April, and produced no concession from the three former bishops, who stoutly maintained their reformed view of the Eucharist, as being no Mass. After this, the three remained in prison in Oxford, but not only were they regularly visited by Catholic persuaders, they also received support, in person and by tokens, from sympathisers. While Pole remained on the Continent, the Oxford process was effectively suspended. Then, on 28 December, Weston re-issued to the Canterbury convocation the unsurprising conclusion of the Oxford disputation, that Cranmer, Latimer and Ridley were not true members of Christ's Church.[55] After this, the three were removed from the houses of the mayor and bailiffs of Oxford, where they had recently been lodging in relative freedom and comfort, and returned to the Bocardo. They remained there when the inquisitorial campaign against heresy began, at the end of January 1555.

When Pole arrived in England, not only had his own act of attainder been repealed a very few days before, but he had a somewhat uneasy relationship with the Roman Inquisition, which was under the effective control of Cardinal Gianpietro Carafa, the future Pope Paul IV. Almost as soon as it began work, the renewed Holy Office had become concerned about the orthodoxy of Pole's Viterbo group, particularly when, in the year of its foundation, 1542, and no doubt in part as a consequence of its very existence, Piero Martire (Peter Martyr) Vermigli and Bernardino Ochino, fled to Reformed cities north of the Alps. Inquisition deputies, under the supervision of Cardinal Juan Álvarez de Toledo, quickly began an investigation of Pole's circle, and in particular of Marcantonio Flaminio. Because of this, and also because of his association with Gasparo Contarini and the Catholic-Lutheran colloquy at Regensburg in 1541, Pole evidently needed to display his orthodoxy, especially on the subject of

---

[55]    Lambeth Palace MS 751, p. 129.

justification. In his sermon at the opening session of the Council of Trent, on 7 January 1546, actually delivered by Angelo Massarelli, he proclaimed that one of the main aims of the council was to identify and extirpate heresy.[56] When, in 1550, Pole was himself appointed, by the new pope who had defeated him in conclave, Julius III, to a commission to supervise the Inquisition, he failed to support those of his friends who remained under suspicion of heresy, ceased, by the following year, to attend its meetings.[57]

When the cardinal legate reached England in November 1554, he found in London two Spanish friars, both known to him personally from Trent, who had strong views on how dissidents from the Catholic church should be treated. One of them, the Observant Franciscan Alfonso de Castro, who was King Philip's confessor in London, has, probably unjustly, achieved a reputation as being 'soft' on this subject, thanks to the unlikely praise of the Protestant martyrologist Foxe. Thus Loades writes of him:

> De Castro has earned himself a minor niche in English history by preaching in February 1555 against the burning of heretics, presumably on Philip's orders, since this does not correspond with what is known of his views.[58]

The point has been repeated more recently by Duffy, though with some scepticism.[59] It is indeed highly unlikely that Castro would have sought moderation in the treatment of obstinate heretics, given his previous published works on the subject, which were reprinted during Philip and Mary's reign.[60] He was born, in about 1495, at Zamora in north-west Spain, entered the Franciscan friary in Salamanca in 1510 or 1512, and studied at the university of Alcalá de Henares, until he went to a chair of theology at Salamanca. Before he reached England in 1554, Friar Alfonso travelled widely in Europe. He attended the papal coronation of the Emperor Charles V in Bologna in 1530 and circa 1533 he became chaplain to the Spanish community in the major Flemish port of Bruges. From there he travelled widely in Germany, witnessing the Reformation at first hand, and it was during this period that he published his catalogue of 'all' heresies (*Adversus omnes haereses*). As a member of the Spanish and Imperial delegation, he was present at the opening of the Council of Trent, and in March 1546 he joined the conciliar commission on the laity and Scripture.

---

[56] *CT*, 4, p. 548n.

[57] Mayer, *PPP*, pp. 132, 151, 187, 192–193; Fenlon, *Heresy and obedience*, pp. 234–235.

[58] Loades, *Mary Tudor: a life*, p. 255 n. 66.

[59] Duffy, *Fires of faith*, pp. 82–83.

[60] Alfonso de Castro, *Adversus omnes haereses libri XIV* (Paris: Josse Badius and Jean de Roigny, 1534, reprinted Antwerp: Joannes Steels, 1556); Castro, *De iusta haereticorum punitione libri III* (Lyon: Heirs of Jacopo Giunta, 1556).

In 1551, he returned to Trent for the second period of the council, and bitterly opposed its suspension by Julius III in March 1552.[61]

In later centuries, Castro became best known in Spain as a canon lawyer, but in his lifetime he was regarded as an expert on heresy and its extirpation. According to Foxe, in his sermon at Court in Whitehall on 10 February 1555, the Franciscan:

> did earnestly invay against the [English] bishops for burning of men, saying plainly that they learned it not in scripture to burne any for his Conscience; but the contrary that they should lyve and be converted, with many other things more to the same purpose.[62]

However, Castro's published works suggest that Foxe seriously misunderstood him. His 1547 work, *De iusta punitione* ('On the just punishment of heretics'), written for the Tridentine fathers, strongly asserted the Church's right to punish obstinate heretics but insisted that this should be done justly and correctly. Castro had apparently become concerned by some of the haphazard methods used by the lay authorities in the Low Countries to deal with such people, and his main anxiety seems to have been to ensure that the Church took full charge of such proceedings, in accordance with canon law. Speaking in London just six days after the first burning at Smithfield, that of John Rogers, and having observed for the first time the operation of the recently-restored Lancastrian heresy laws, Alfonso may well have expressed a concern that the campaign in England might turn out to be as chaotic and irregular, from the ecclesiastical inquisitor's point of view, as the procedures over which King Philip's father was then presiding on the other side of the North Sea.[63]

Also among Philip's ecclesiastical advisers in England was the Dominican friar Bartolomé Carranza de Miranda. In 1545, like Castro, he had been summoned to join the Imperial and Spanish delegation to the Council of Trent, and it was there that he first met Cardinal Pole, forming a friendship that would be renewed in England in 1554, after correspondence between the two men had taken place while the legate was still on the Continent.[64] Carranza is exceptional, among the inner core of Philip's entourage of churchmen, in being

---

[61]    Glyn Redworth, 'Castro, Alfonso de', *ODNB*.

[62]    Foxe, *A&M* 1583, p. 1529.

[63]    Redworth, 'Castro'; Edwards, *Mary I*, pp. 260–261; Virgilio Pinto Crespo, *Inquisición y control ideológico en la España del siglo XVI* (Madrid: Taurus, 1983), pp. 235–258.

[64]    Pocock, *Burnet* 3, p. 406; *CRP* 2 nos 909 (28 July 1554), 918 (5 August 1554, further textual details), 921 (10 August 1554, *ERP* 5 no. 54; Tellechea, 'Pole y Carranza', *CP*, pp. 183–184), 941 (27 September 1554, Tellechea, 'Pole y Carranza', *CP*, pp. 186–187), 951 (6 October 1554, *ERP* 5 no. 55; Tellechea, 'Pole y Carranza', *CP*, pp. 187–188); Edwards, 'Introduction. Carranza in England', in *RCEMT*, pp. 6–10.

exceedingly well documented, and this for a surprising reason. He, together with his Dominican brothers, Juan de Villagarcía and Pedro de Soto, and the Franciscans, Alfonso de Castro and Bernardo de Fresneda, advised Philip while he was England, but Carranza alone remained until 1557, after Philip had left for the Low Countries at the end of August 1555, following Mary's failed pregnancy. Eventually, Carranza joined his royal master, and in 1558 he was nominated and elected as Archbishop of Toledo, and hence primate of Spain. However, in August 1559 he was arrested by the Inquisition at Torrelaguna, near Madrid, and spent nearly 17 years in captivity, first in Valladolid and then in Rome. The collection of his papers that was made for his trial provides a large amount of important data on his time in England, as well as other periods in his life.[65] From these sources it is possible to reconstruct much of Carranza's role in the religious affairs of Mary's reign, as well as that of other Spanish servants of King Philip, both lay and clerical. What though of the cardinal legate and future Archbishop himself?

On the subject of Pole's attitude to heresy, Dermot Fenlon wrote, many years ago:

> Mary and Pole have been accused of excessive legalism in their fight against heresy, of relying too exclusively upon judicial weapons of suppression and punishment, too little upon persuasion and argument. Pole's experience in Italy, where he dealt mainly with educated and cultivated heretics, had given him no great hope of the success of persuasion.[66]

This accusation, that Pole adopted a dry and legalistic attitude towards his responsibilities in England, as legate and archbishop, partly reflected the prevailing view of his achievement at the time when Fenlon wrote. In particular, in R.H. Pogson's view: 'Pole ... did not worry much about heresy, because it did not seem an insuperable problem. The visitation articles of 1555 [see below] do not even mention it'.[67] This approach has largely been adopted since by Thomas Mayer:

[65]   José Ignacio Tellechea Idígoras, ed., *Fray Bartolomé Carranza: documentos históricos*, 7 vols (Madrid: Real Academia de la Historia, 1962–1994; Henry Kamen, *The Spanish Inquisition: an historical revision* (London: Weidenfeld & Nicolson, 1997), pp. 160–163.

[66]   Fenlon, *Heresy and obedience*, p. 285.

[67]   R[ex] H. Pogson, 'Cardinal Pole: papal legate to England in Mary Tudor's reign', unpublished Ph.D. dissertation, University of Cambridge, 1972, p. 173. See also Pogson, 'The legacy of the schism: confusion, continuity and change in the Marian clergy', in *The mid-Tudor polity, 1540–1560*, ed. Jennifer Loach and Robert Tittler (London: Macmillan, 1980), pp. 127–136.

Instead of attacking heresy head-on, Pole expected that Englishmen would docilely return to Rome. Pogson blames this on Pole's experience of Italian reform in the 1520s. This probably entered in, but much more important was Pole's personal interpretation of heresy and obedience from the time of *De unitate* forward. Accused of heresy several times, more often frustrated in his political designs, Pole usually fairly quickly bowed to pressure and relied on simple obedience. He could not see that others might not find the matter quite so straightforward.[68]

Since this was written, Pole has come to be seen as much more active in the campaign against heresy than was previously thought.

Loades has described the legate as 'a fierce enemy of heretics', seeing the early heresy trials, of John Hooper, John Rogers, Rowland Taylor, Robert Farrar and Laurence Saunders as being ordered by him, on 28 January 1555:

> in the hope, and probably the expectation, that [the accused] would submit when faced with the awful alternative which was now available. This was the test which was to determine whether heresy was to be a low-key nuisance or a highly visible system of defiance. When all the original defendants went to the fire, preferring their steadfast Protestant convictions, the writing was on the wall.[69]

Duffy, too, has recently seen Pole as an active persecutor, in his roles as legate and archbishop. Strangely, in view of recent scholarship and perhaps as an attack on an earlier Protestant enemy, Duffy described Pole, in 2009, as:

> for most historians of the reign a shadowy and non-integrated figure, eclipsed in practical leadership [of the campaign of burnings] by Gardiner, or Bonner or the Spaniards [Philip, or Carranza, perhaps?], even [why 'even'?] by Mary herself. It is hardly an exaggeration to say that the [unspecified] established narratives of the reign would not look very different if Pole were to be edited out altogether.[70]

Since then, Duffy has repeated this view, writing: 'Reginald Pole, by contrast [with Cranmer], is probably not much more than a name to most people', even though he 'masterminded the restoration of Catholicism under Mary Tudor'.[71]

Whether or not scholars have, up to now, properly recognised Pole's importance in the religious history of England and its dependent territories, and have let the general public in on that knowledge, there is in fact no shortage

---

[68]   Mayer, *PPP*, pp. 272–273.

[69]   Loades, *Religious culture*, pp. 81, 92.

[70]   Duffy, *Fires of faith*, p. 29.

[71]   Duffy, *Saints, sacrilege, and sedition: religion and conflict in the Tudor reformations* (London: Bloomsbury, 2012), pp. 180, 14.

of evidence from his own pen of his attitude to heresy, both before and during his time as legate to England and Archbishop of Canterbury. On 20 June 1554, while he was in Brussels awaiting the green light to return to England, Pole wrote to one of his regular correspondents, Cardinal Otto Truchsess von Waldburg of Augsburg.[72] He was reacting to the behaviour of one of the former fringe members of his Viterbo group, Pier Paolo Vergerio, who had recently attacked him as a fraud for abandoning the reformed views that he had previously held, and threatened to publish, without authorisation, his tract *De unitate*, in order to undermine his efforts in Mary's England and expose him to the Roman Inquisition.[73] Vergerio accused the cardinal of still holding Lutheran, or evangelical, views on justification, as he had done in the early 1540s, and of keeping them secret. Indignantly, Pole told Truchsess not only that Vergerio's charge was false, but also that those who subverted the true faith, as Vergerio had done, deserved death. However, even in such extreme cases, everything possible should be done to persuade them to repent, thus curing sick members of Christ's Body. Following the teaching of the Council of Trent, which was clearly accepted by his Spanish advisers and colleagues in England who had shared the experience of the council with him, Pole regarded heretics as errant children. They had to be disciplined, but the hope was that they would see the error of their ways and come to a fuller and more mature Christian faith, without the need for the ultimate and fateful penalty of burning. In England, the crucial test of Pole's own views and faith would be Archbishop Cranmer.

In a letter to Cardinal Giovanni Morone, written in Cranmer's last days, Pole recalled that when his messenger had brought from England the news of the archbishop's deprivation of his temporalities, on 13 November 1553, he was also told that Mary wanted him to succeed the attainted traitor, though at this stage he was one himself. Indeed, before his eventual arrival in England, Pole said that he had twice been urged to accept the post, first by one of his own supporters, unnamed, in the queen's household and then by Charles V's ambassador in London, Simon Renard. He knew that Mary herself had written to Pope Julius III in a similar vein. Pole told Morone that, with Cranmer now in gaol on heresy charges, he would, as he had always done, accept what God commanded. He felt, however, that he should remain in England and not come to Rome to receive the pallium. He reminded Morone of his long-standing views on the undesirability of bishops not residing in their dioceses, in which he coincided with his friends Giberti and Carranza, and declared that he would never abandon that scruple. If the pope decided not to grant him the See of Canterbury, knowing the difficult situation in which he found himself, Pole said that he would be quite content. He would be regretful only if he found himself in a job that he could not do

---

[72]    *ERP* 4 no. 53; *CSP Ven*, V, no. 901; *CRP* 2 no. 885.
[73]    Overell, *Italian reform*, pp. 145–166.

effectively. Thus he told Morone, who was one of his closest confidants, that he
really would be quite happy if he did not succeed Cranmer.[74] Wheels continued
to grind in Rome and, on 25 September 1555, Pole was able to issue a public
instruction, from Greenwich Palace, to John Clerk, bishop of Bath and Wells,
and Christopher Smith, an apostolic prothonotary in Lincoln diocese, in the
name of the king and queen, to conduct a process for heresy against Thomas
Cranmer, Hugh Latimer and Nicholas Ridley. This trial had in fact been begun
in Rome, on 19 June 1555, by Cardinal Jacopo Puteo on behalf of the new pope,
Paul IV Carafa, and the judge-delegate for the Roman Inquisition in England,
Bishop James Brooks of Gloucester. The relevant document had been served on
Cranmer on 7 September, he had appended his signature, and it was now to go
on public display. Clerk and Smith were to act as notaries in the forthcoming
trial.[75] The proceedings duly opened in St Mary's, Oxford, on 12 September,
with Bishop Brooks presiding, and Thomas Martin and John Story as royal
proctors. This was a new process, as the Apostolic See required, but material
from the 1554 disputation was re-used. The next day, witnesses' statements
for the prosecution were taken at New College, and the three defendants were
duly found guilty. Since they had been ordained in schism and not according to
the Roman rite, Latimer and Ridley could be dealt with quickly, but Cranmer,
having been consecrated as a catholic bishop and appointed to his see by Pope
Clement VII, was given 80 days to appear in Rome to answer the charges against
him. In the event, Latimer and Ridley were burned in Broad Street, outside
Balliol College, on 16 October, while Cranmer, who had been forced to watch
his friends die from Bocardo, remained there.[76]

In October 1555, Pole for the first time wrote personally to Cranmer. The
diplomatic and bibliographical history of this text is complicated, but the main
content is clear.[77] As in the Oxford disputation of April 1554, the Mass was
the focus of attention. In a letter to Girolamo Muzzarelli, dated 26 October,
Pole mentioned that he had written to Cranmer, and he now asked whether
his Roman friend thought that he should give the document concerned, which
is now generally known as *De Sacramento*, a wider circulation. With typical
conscientiousness, Pole mused that it might be best for him to ask the advice
of someone else who was not, like Muzzarelli, a personal friend.[78] In any case,
on 6 November Pole wrote again to Cranmer, from St James's Palace. Clearly
there was no intention that the prisoner should be allowed to go to Rome. Pole
condemned his errors in the sternest terms and urged him to repent, no doubt

[74]   *CRP* 3 no. 1104 (8 March 1555; *CSP Ven*, VI (i), no. 22).

[75]   *CRP* 3 no. 1384 (fuller textual details).

[76]   MacCulloch, *Thomas Cranmer*, pp. 574–575, 579.

[77]   *CRP* 3 pp. 181–182; Mayer, 'Reluctant author', pp. 55–56 (no. 7). This text was probably
amended after Cranmer's trial.

[78]   Lutz p. 285 n. 5; *CSP Ven*, VI (i), no. 255; *CRP* 3 no. 1415.

being fully aware that, if he did not appear in the Curia, the archbishop, as he still was in terms of Roman if not of English law, might be sentenced to burning as contumacious. Pole referred to the judges' verdict in Oxford, and also to Cranmer's subsequent appeal to the queen for mercy, which she had not answered but passed to the cardinal. In this letter, Cranmer had stated that, if anyone could prove to him that papal authority was not harmful to the kingdom, and that his views on the Eucharist were erroneous, he would humbly submit to the judgment of the Roman Church. On this basis, as well as praying daily for his repentance, Pole was willing to use reason to convince him. He saw a problem, however, in that reason had not brought Cranmer to his heretical views in the first place. Pole attacked him for his perjury, at the time of his appointment to Canterbury, in swearing allegiance to the pope when he in fact rejected his authority. With great bitterness, Pole accused the prisoner of fraud. Having become archbishop in this way, Cranmer had been rejected by God, and blinded against the truth. Pole then rehearsed the traditional arguments in favour of papal supremacy, saying that Cranmer's assertion, in his appeal to Mary, that England would be cursed if it re-admitted papal authority arose out of ecclesiological and historical ignorance. If he had been a good bishop, Cranmer should have made his case against the papacy to the nation, before any break took place. Now, however, the nation had to acknowledge that the schism was a curse. In his letter to Mary, Cranmer had also said that if he could see the writings of one ancient doctor, or Father of the Church, who shared the current papal teaching on the Mass, he would submit. To this Pole responded that William Pye, as a delegate from the convocation of Canterbury, had brought to him in prison a work by Bishop Cuthbert Tunstall which dealt with that very point.[79] Cranmer had apparently asserted that no English subject before him had ever been condemned by the pope, as a foreign ruler, and this could only be done by the Imperial Crown of England. Pole took this to mean that the archbishop preferred to die quickly, as a traitor, rather than await the pope's verdict on his heresy. Cranmer regarded the canon law of the Roman Church, which he had tried to replace during Edward VI's reign, as foreign, but Pole naturally rejected this view, putting the canons above and before the law of England, and upholding the procedures that Mary and her government had used against the primate. Cranmer was the prime mover in England's disastrous break with Rome, which he still upheld, despite everything that had happened since the 1530s. Pole had little hope for Cranmer, but would nonetheless pray for him, that Christ might forgive him.[80]

The 80-day interval, during which Cranmer was required to travel to Rome, expired on 3 December. The next day, Pole's secretary, Alvise Priuli, wrote to

---

[79]   Cuthbert Tunstall, *De veritate corporis et sanguinis Domini nostri Iesu Christi in Eucharistia* (Paris: Michel Vascosan, 1554); MacCulloch, *Thomas Cranmer*, p. 569.

[80]   BL Harleian MS 417, fols 69r–78v; *CRP* 3 no. 1421.

Gianfrancesco Stella in Rome, reporting that parliament had just voted for the restoration of church property from lay possession, adding that Pole's datary, Niccolò Ormanetto, would tell him about the English Synod, which was just getting under way (see Chapter 7). He confirmed that, on the day of writing, Cranmer's case had legally reverted to Rome for sentence.[81] In the event, Pope Paul and his Curia seem not to have waited for news from London, since Cranmer was formally deprived for heresy on 7 December.[82] Four days later, the pope issued a bull providing Pole to the See of Canterbury. It was carried to England, with two papal briefs, by Edmund Atkinson, Somerset herald, who left Rome on 27 December 1555.[83] In this bull of provision, Paul IV stated that he sought bishops who were not only learned but would set a good Christian example to the people of God. The See of Canterbury had become vacant owing to the errors of Thomas Cranmer, especially concerning the Eucharist and clerical orders, and his denial of papal authority. He was a Wycliffite and a Lutheran, who had published erroneous writings and defended his heretical views in public disputation. He had failed to appear before the Apostolic See and was now excommunicate and to be 'relaxed', or handed over, to the secular arm, this being the Inquisition's terminology for sentencing someone to be burned alive by the relevant lay authorities. Now, Pole was to be ordained priest, at the will (*motu proprio*) of the pope himself. Given the urgency of the situation in England, he was permitted to receive the orders of priest and bishop *extra tempora*, that is, outside the normal canonical seasons. As a special privilege, when Pole was added to the number of the cardinal priests, he would be allowed to keep his titular church in Rome, Santa Maria in Cosmedin, although it was normally served by a cardinal deacon. He was to hold both the spiritualities and the temporalities of the archbishopric, which the vacancy had placed in the Pope's hands rather than those of the 'Catholic Monarchs' Philip and Mary, thanks to the reconciliation on 30 November 1554.

On 11 December, Cranmer was moved from Bocardo to the lodgings of the dean of Christ Church, Dr Richard Marshall, who was a conservative, originally from Canterbury diocese, and also the university's vice-chancellor.[84] He would remain there for just over two months, under ever-increasing pressure to revert to the Catholic faith. Meanwhile in Rome, on 18 December, Paul IV summoned a further congregation to decide how exactly his deprivation should be carried out.[85] While the sentence on the man who could now be regarded as his legal predecessor remained to be carried out, Pole spent Christmas with

---

[81]    *CRP* 3 no. 1451.
[82]    *CSP Ven*, VI (i), no. 303.
[83]    LPL, Pole Register, fols 1v–2r; *CRP* 3 no. 1459.
[84]    MacCulloch, *Thomas Cranmer*, p. 585.
[85]    *CSP Ven*, VI (i), no. 319.

the queen, acting as a friend to her as well as a counsellor.[86] On 31 December, Cranmer began theological discussions with the Spanish Dominican Juan de Villagarcía, who was now regius professor of theology at Oxford and proved to be a formidable opponent.[87] Once the Epiphany had been celebrated, on 6 January 1556, the English Synod resumed its work in London, being prorogued about a month later, and then, on 22 January, Somerset Herald arrived from Rome with the bulls for Pole's provision as archbishop. While Villagarcía went to London to consult Pole, Carranza and perhaps the queen, Cranmer began to attend Catholic worship in Christ Church cathedral, even carrying a candle in the Candlemas procession on 2 February, a practice which until recently he had mocked.[88] The question was beginning to arise, in the minds of the royal and Church authorities, whether the life of the former archbishop should be spared, if he repented of his errors and returned to the Catholic fold.

In the meantime, the disgrading of Cranmer from his clerical orders went ahead in Christ Church Cathedral on 14 February, the leading roles being taken by Bishop Bonner of London, with great enthusiasm, and Bishop Thomas Thirlby of Ely, with considerable discomfort at this treatment of an old Cambridge friend and colleague. The ritual involved the dressing of Cranmer in parody versions of his vestments as deacon, priest and bishop, which were then torn from him amidst canonical cursing. The prisoner disrupted the proceedings, however, by loudly appealing against the papal sentence to a general council, which in the circumstances could only have meant the suspended Council of Trent, at which Pole, Castro, Carranza and others had developed their strong views on heresy. After this, Cranmer was returned to Bocardo, which he would only leave on 21 March, to be condemned in St Mary's and burned in the town ditch outside Balliol College.[89] Between 14 February and 18 March, Cranmer composed a series of ever more abject recantations, as well as one which appeared to have been written for him, perhaps by a Spanish hand – whether of Villagarcía, Carranza or De Soto.[90] Regardless of Cranmer's spiritual agonies at this time, on 24 February, the mayor of Oxford received a royal writ ordering Cranmer's burning. The date initially fixed was 7 March, but there was a further pause, as the prisoner gave every sign of a complete acceptance of the Catholic faith, this process culminating in his recantation of 18 March.[91] In the meantime, the transfer of the see of Canterbury to Pole was relentlessly continuing. He had

[86]   *PPP*, p. 242.

[87]   Nicholas Harpsfield (?), *Bishop Cranmer's Recantacyons*, ed. Lord Houghton, *Philobiblion Miscellanies*, 15 (1877–1884), pp. 53–58; MacCulloch, *Thomas Cranmer*, pp. 586–587.

[88]   MacCulloch, *Thomas Cranmer*, pp. 588–590.

[89]   MacCulloch, *Thomas Cranmer*, pp. 590–593.

[90]   Harpsfield (?), *Cranmer's Recantacyons*, pp. 72–81.

[91]   Harpsfield (?), *Cranmer's Recantacyons*, pp. 83–84; MacCulloch, *Thomas Cranmer*, pp. 594–598.

planned to go to Canterbury, for consecration and enthronement, on 23 March, celebrating his first Mass in his cathedral, as cardinal archbishop, on the feast of the Annunciation, 25 March. This was not to be, as Mary and her council insisted on his remaining in London, because of the current political tensions in the kingdom. Thus Pole was in fact ordained priest in London on 20 March, and consecrated bishop three days later, in the Observant Franciscan church alongside Greenwich Palace. In the meantime, his predecessor, having famously renounced his recantations in St Mary's church in Oxford, had died by burning as a Protestant, on 21 March. On that day, Pole received the temporalities of Canterbury and finally, on 25 March, he was given the pallium, which had been brought from Rome by Somerset herald, in the church of St Mary Arches in London, which was a Canterbury peculiar and hence technically within his new diocese.[92] A few years later, Friar Carranza remembered, during his own Inquisition trial, that he had been woken in the night of 21–22 March 1556, in Greenwich, on the Queen's orders, to be told that Cranmer truly was dead.[93]

---

[92]   *PPP*, p. 245; *CRP* 3 no. 1516 13 March 1556.

[93]   According to the procedures of the Spanish Inquisition, from which Cranmer, and others in England, did not apparently benefit, Carranza was permitted to name witnesses in his defence, and draw up a questionnaire to be put to them by the inquisitors. Question 58 asked witnesses to confirm that Carranza had sought the implementation of the Roman sentence against Cranmer and had been woken with news of his death as soon as the queen herself heard it. Although most witnesses, including King Philip, were vague on the subject, a royal chaplain, Cristóbal de Becerra, confirmed Carranza's statement. The interviews with witnesses were conducted in various places in Spain between 1562 and 1564 (Tellechea, *Documentos históricos*, 3, also in Tellechea, 'Bartolomé Carranza y la restauración católica inglesa (1554–1558)', in Tellechae, *CP*, pp. 95, 100, 102, 104, 107, 110).

# Chapter 7
# Consolidation and Crisis

When Reginald Pole finally became Archbishop of Canterbury with full powers, on 22 March 1556, he had already been in effective charge of the Church in England, Wales and Ireland for well over a year. Like his predecessor Cranmer, though with a different doctrinal approach, he had a strong international and ecumenical sense of what Christ's Body on earth should be, and had surrounded himself with suitable staff for that agenda. Having intervened frequently and extensively in the ecclesiastical affairs of Mary's kingdom before his return in November 1554, Pole had then taken direct charge, using the wide powers that Pope Julius III had given him and collaborating with existing bishops and officials, some of whom he had himself been involved in putting in place. Leading his team at Lambeth, along with his Venetian secretary Alvise Priuli, was his datary, Niccolò Ormanetto, a canon lawyer who had joined his service at Maguzzano, where Pole spent the summer of 1553.[1] It is possible that Ormanetto encouraged his master to be intransigent over the subject of ecclesiastical goods that had come into lay hands under Henry VIII and Edward VI, but the datary denied this and may indeed still have been in Rome when Pole launched his offensive on this subject against Mary and her council.[2] Ormanetto was a crucial right-hand man to Pole, possibly drafting his important letter to Cranmer, dated 6 November 1555, and certainly working alongside the cardinal during the English synod of 1555–6, and overseeing and intervening directly in legatine business concerning the English, Welsh and Irish dioceses.[3]

Thomas Mayer has described the English synod of 1555–6 as 'Pole's most important action as legate'. Nevertheless he regards it as a somewhat disorganised episode, blaming Pole's 'eagerness unrestrained by competence'.[4] This seems unduly harsh, especially if his efforts are compared with the previous synod to be held in London and Westminster, which had been presided over in 1537 by Thomas Cromwell, as vicegerent in spiritual matters for the Supreme Head on Earth of the Church of England, King Henry VIII, which effectively dissolved into the study groups that eventually produced the 'Bishops' Book' for

---

[1]   *CRP* 2 no. 610.

[2]   The question is referred to in a letter by Ormanetto from London to Gianfrancesco Stella in Rome, on 27 January 1555 *CRP* 3 no. 1047; *PPP*, p. 204.

[3]   *CRP* 3 nos 1421 (Lutz p. 285 n. 2), 1451, 1668, 1687 (BMD MS 922, i, fols 126r, 127r–128r; ii, fols 21r, 24r, 24r–v; *PPP*, pp. 235, 240, 258–259).

[4]   *PPP*, p. 236.

the ordering of the English Church.[5] The example was not especially propitious, in the situation of November 1555. In the summer of that year, with his programme of Catholic restoration well under way, Pole began to work towards a new synod. It was not, however, until 26 October, with the former bishops Latimer and Ridley already dead, that he broached the matter with King Philip, who by then was in the Netherlands. The context was Pole's continuing quest for the restoration of the Church's property. He had very reluctantly accepted legal advice that this could only be achieved through parliament, but was still engaged in negotiations on the subject with the convocation of Canterbury, which was then in session alongside the parliamentarians. Since the question of church goods involved both English provinces, York had to be represented as well, making a national synod the appropriate format for dealing with this question and the general reformation of the 'Anglican' Church (*reformationem ecclesiae anglicanae*).[6] Given that they were separated from each other by the North Sea, the reaction of the royal couple was notably rapid, which suggests that they had agreed their policy earlier. On All Souls' Day, 2 November, they issued, as monarchs and 'Defenders of the Faith', a licence authorising the convocation of the synod.[7] On 7 November, Pole reported to Cardinal Carlo Carafa, Pope Paul IV's nephew, that, on Monday 4 November, a Mass of the Holy Spirit had been celebrated by Bishop Bonner, in the chapel royal at Whitehall, after which the synod was formally opened. Proceedings took place in unspecified parts of the Whitehall-Westminster complex, and the participants lodged outside the royal precincts, except for Bishop Gardiner, who was allowed to stay in the palace itself, because of his extreme ill-health. In this letter, Pole told Carafa that he had asked the bishops to report on the state of their dioceses, and to work to regain the property of the Church.[8] In fact, Pole seems here to have been talking about the existing assembly of the convocation of Canterbury, rather than the synod, since it was not until 8 November that formal summonses went out to both provinces for the new gathering.[9] Its first act was to draft a document approving the plan which had been drawn up by Philip for ecclesiastical pensions, payable to the now thinning ranks of the former members of religious orders. On 11 November, Pole reported to the king that this had been done, adding that, since Archbishop Cranmer was imprisoned in Oxford, reform could not be achieved through the provincial administration of Canterbury, so that a legatine synod was required. The political climate in London was tense at the time, however, with rumours of what would later become known as the unsuccessful 'Dudley

---

[5]    MacCulloch, *Thomas Cranmer*, pp. 185–194

[6]    *CSP Ven*, VI (i), no. 256; *CRP* 3 no. 1414.

[7]    *CPR Philip & Mary*, III, p. 23; *CRP* 3 no. 1420.

[8]    *CSP Ven*, VI (i), no. 270; *CRP* 3 no. 1425.

[9]    *PPP*, p. 236.

conspiracy' against Mary and Philip, and there was immediate opposition when the draft decree on church goods was given its first reading in the Lords.[10]

The history of the text of the decrees of the 1555–6 synod, generally known by the title *De reformatione Angliae* ('On the reformation of England') was complex. Pole's surviving papers include various other documents, covering topics such as the role of bishops, preaching and education, which appear to be related to the synod, as well as sermons that he may have preached there.[11] The acts of the synod were first dispatched to Rome on 14 April 1556, in the custody of an Italian priest, Marino Vittori, who had recited the papal indulgence which had accompanied a solemn procession of the assembled synod, commemorating the feast of the Conversion of St Paul (25 January) and culminating in the celebration of a High Mass, in St Paul's cathedral, by Bishop Bonner.[12] Pole sent the decrees in the first instance to his friend Cardinal Giovanni Morone, who was promised a fuller account of proceedings, and the text in question remains in the Vatican Library.[13] In 1562, with Pole dead and the Council of Trent about to resume for what proved to be its final period, the English decrees were published in Rome.[14] The account of them which follows is based partly on the manuscript versions but mainly on the 1562 printed edition, which does not contain the fulsome explanations and exhortations of Pole's own drafts.[15]

The preface to the decrees (*Reformatio Angliae*, sigs A–Aii) referred to England's restoration to communion with the See of Rome, under Philip and Mary and with the co-operation of successive popes, Julius III, Marcellus II and Paul IV. Following this, the synod of English bishops had been convened by Pole, as legate, to find a remedy for abuses in the Church. The explicit model for the synod's proceedings was not, of course, Henry and Cromwell's effort in 1537, but the thirteenth-century gatherings convened by the papal legates, Cardinals Otto and Ottoboni, whose work had already been used by Bishop Bonner

[10]   *ERP* 5 no. 22; *CSP Ven*, VI (i), no. 275; *CRP* 3 no. 1430; *PPP*, pp. 236–237; Loach, *Crown and Parliament*, p. 135.

[11]   *PPP*, pp. 237–238; Mayer, 'Reluctant author', p. 89.

[12]   *CRP* 3 nos 1051 (*Avviso da Londra*, 28 January 1556), 1528 (14 April 1556); *PPP*, p. 306.

[13]   BAV Vat. lat. 5966, fols 27r–31v. Two manuscripts of the decrees exist in British libraries, CCCC MS 121 no. 11, pp. 7–31, and BL Cotton MS Cleopatra F.II, fols 72r–90r. There are two modern printed editions with English translations of the 1562 printed edition (see note 22), in T.E. Callahan, 'Reginald, Cardinal Pole's *Reformatio Angliae*, a critical edition with introduction and commentary: a thesis in history' (Buffalo: State University College at Buffalo, 1995); Gerald Bray, ed., *The Anglican canons* (Woodbridge: The Boydell Press and the Church of England Record Society, in association with the Ecclesiastical Law Society, 1998), pp. 69–137 (*Reformatio Angliae*), pp. 138–61 (collation of the Corpus Christi College, Cambridge and British Library MSS).

[14]   *Reformatio Angliae ex decretis Reginaldi Poli cardinalis, sedis apostolicae legati, anno M.D.LVI* (Rome: Apud Paulum Manutium Aldi F. 1562).

[15]   *PPP*, p. 239.

in his 1554 visitation articles for London diocese.[16] The first decree (sig. Aii) ordered a national celebration to be held to commemorate the reconciliation of England to Rome, on 30 November 1554. In thanks for this, the synod ordered, in addition:

> that throughout this kingdom, on all Sundays and Festivals, and also major Doubles [that is, special commemorations of saints in the Sarum and other liturgical uses], this [Reconciliation is] to be commemorated at Mass after the other collects. The relevant prayer was to be inserted [in liturgical books] and printed in them thereafter.

In addition, there were to be solemn processions throughout the kingdom 'in which the people of God are to give thanks for the benefits of peace received'. Thus, on each future St Andrew's Day, such a procession was to be held in every city, town and village in the kingdom, in which all the clergy, the lay authorities and the faithful should take part. On that day, special alms should be given, and other pious works should be done in the churches to which the processions headed, solemn Masses should be celebrated in them, and special sermons preached.

The second decree (sigs Aii–C) covered several subjects, beginning with a section on the sacraments, which reaffirmed the definitions made by the council of Florence in 1439. In order that Catholic teaching should prevail in England against heretical errors, examination and censorship of religious books should take place. In order that they might be clear about how they were to proceed, all bishops, deans, archdeacons and their officials who exercised ecclesiastical jurisdiction were to receive copies of the constitutions of Otto and Ottoboni, as well as the Latin Vulgate, both of which were to be carefully studied and applied, with the advice of experts if necessary. The synod 'damned and anathematised' all those who produced, imported and read heretical books, or other books that did not possess the licence of the Apostolic See.[17] In this second decree, the synod also warned those ordinaries (bishops and others) who up to then

---

16  Frere and Kennedy, *Visitation articles*, 2, p. 332; *PPP*, pp. 240–241.

17  This section of the decree somewhat resembles the wording in Queen Mary's proclamation of 18 August 1553: 'Her Highness therefore straightly chargeth and commandeth all and every her said subjects, of whatsoever estate, condition, or degree they be, that none of them presume from henceforth to preach, or by way of reading in churches or other public or private places (except in the schools of the universities) to interpret or teach any Scriptures or any manner points of doctrine concerning religion, neither also to print any books, matter, ballad, rhyme, interlude, process or treatise nor play any interlude except they have her Grace's special licence in writing for the same, upon pain to incur her Highness's indignation and displeasure' (Loades, *Chronicles*, p. 18). The Reconciliation returned such powers to the Church, though the government of Philip and Mary continued to intervene in such matters (see below).

had not been active in the extirpation of heresy to remedy this. The bulk of the decree consisted of the verbatim text on the seven sacraments which had been promulgated by the council of Florence, the main business of which had been to secure reunion between the Western and Eastern Churches. Some scholars, notably Marmion, Loades and Mayer, have suggested that, in using the 1439 Florence text, Pole and his advisers were deliberately by-passing Trent, where the legate and Friar Carranza had both been heavily involved.[18] However, both men would have been fully aware that the fathers at Trent had reaffirmed sacramental teaching precisely in the terms used by the Council of Florence, in their seventh session on 3 March 1547.[19] As the English decree of 1556 states, in the Florentine formulation, sacramental doctrine was 'briefly and clearly explained' (sig. Bii). Two short sections follow this exposition of the sacraments, the first of them dealing with the reservation of the Sacrament of the Altar. Here Pole introduced to the English Church, and eventually, through the last phase of the Council of Trent (1562–3) to the Catholic Church in general, the concept of a fixed tabernacle on the main altar to contain the reserved sacrament and encourage adoration. As already noted, the Cardinal's friend Bishop Giberti had pioneered this practice in his cathedral at Verona, abandoning the traditional arrangement of suspending the sacrament from the roof above the altar, in a pyx. The English synod ordered that the new type of tabernacle should be fixed to the high altar, though if this were not possible it should be attached to another altar nearby. Also, reversing the policy of Henry VIII and Edward VI, it was once again ordained that a light should burn perpetually before the reserved sacrament, since the body of Jesus Christ 'is the radiance of eternal light (*candor lucis aeternae*)' (sig. C). In addition, all existing Catholic constitutions and canons on the administration of the sacrament of the Eucharist were to be re-issued and enforced. The final section of Decree II dealt with Christian festivals, and in particular the annual celebration of the dedication of churches, which was commonly held on the last Sunday of October. The stern spirit of Catholic reform, as it was then being advocated in Italy and Spain by friends and colleagues of Pole and Carranza, is revealed in the decree's disapproving comment on the meals and dances, often in the nave itself, which had been a feature of such dedication festivals before the 1530s. Bishops were now to suppress such frolics: instead, the people were to confine their church attendance to the Divine Office, with the threat of canonical punishment for backsliders, this, ominously, to be administered by the lay authorities if necessary.

---

[18]    J.P. Marmion, 'The London synod of Reginald, Cardinal Pole (1555–1556)', unpublished MA thesis, University of Keele, 1974, 1, p. v; Loades, 'The piety of the Catholic restoration in England, 1553–8', in Loades, *Politics, censorship and the English Reformation* (London and New York: Pinter Publishers, 1991), pp. 200–212: *PPP*, p. 241.

[19]    *CT*, 5, p. 835.

The third decree dealt with another topic dear to Pole, Carranza, and their reforming friends and allies on the Continent, this being the requirement that bishops and other senior clergy should reside in their posts and carry out personally the duties required of them (sigs Cii–D). The tone here was fervent and urgent, with the synod fathers beseeching all clergy, in the mercy of Jesus Christ (*in Domini misericordiae Iesu Christi*), to tend their flocks, who had been gained by the blood of Christ. They should abandon secular duties elsewhere and return at once to their people. If they would not do so voluntarily, the censures and sanctions of canon law, dating back to Pope Gregory X at the council of Lyon (1274–5), should be used against them. Such provisions should apply to bishops, deans, provosts, archdeacons and also scholars. Here is clear evidence that Friar Bartolomé Carranza's views were being implemented. As Pole himself will undoubtedly have known, during the first two periods of the Council of Trent, the Spanish Dominican had produced two books in which precisely such a policy on clerical residence was powerfully advocated. In 1547, Carranza had published a powerful treatise, in Latin, concerning the personal residence of bishops and lesser clergy. This contained his exposition to the Tridentine fathers, as a theological consultant to the Emperor Charles V, of precisely the views that are contained in the relevant English decree of 1556.[20] During the second period of the Council of Trent, Carranza had written again on the subject of bishop's responsibilities, in a 'Mirror for pastors'.[21]

The fourth synod decree (sigs D–Dii) dealt with issues of preaching and teaching. Again following Carranza, who himself adhered to the canons of the Fourth Lateran Council (1215), it stated that the primary duty of pastors was to preach God's Word, and this should be done by the bishops themselves. Only in rare and special circumstances should the job be delegated to others. Bishops, rectors, vicars and others with pastoral responsibilities should preach on Sundays and major festivals. Those who felt unable to do so should appoint a deputy, by agreement in advance with their ordinary, and would face canonical censure and penalties if they failed to comply. Contrary to the view of some modern scholars, that Pole was not greatly concerned with the preaching of the Catholic faith as part of its restoration, this decree gave the importance of sermons the greatest possible stress, though it also noted that the people of God,

---

[20]   Carranza, *Controversia de necessaria residentia personali Episcoporum et aliorum inferiorum Pastorum Tridenti explicata per fratrem Bartholomeum Carranzam de Miranda instituti beati Dominici. Et regentem in collegio Sancti Gregorii eiusdem ordinis in Valle Oletana* (Venice: Ad signum Spei, 1547), also in Tellechea, ed., in facsimile with a Spanish translation, in Fray Bartolomé Carranza de Miranda, *Controversia sobre la necesaria residencia personal de los obispos* (Madrid: Fundación Universitaria Española and Universidad Pontificia de Salamanca, 1994).

[21]   Carranza, *Speculum pastorum. Hierarchia ecclesiastica in qua describuntur officia ministrorum ecclesiae militantis*, ed. Tellechea (Salamanca: Universidad Pontificia de Salamanca, 1992).

in order to be ready to hear and accept His Word, should first be prepared by means of the sacrament of penance and reconciliation.[22] As for the content of the sermons themselves, it was decreed that clergy who were not qualified to preach should instead read from books of homilies, as had happened, from a different theological viewpoint, in the previous two reigns. In addition, it was decreed, again following Lateran IV (1215), that children should be gathered in church, on Sundays and major festivals, to be instructed in the rudiments of the faith by the parish priest or someone delegated by him.

The atmosphere of continental Catholic reform, both before and after Mary's reign, may also be found in the fifth decree, which concerned the behaviour and discipline of the clergy (sigs Dii–E). What was envisaged was a quasi-monastic style of life for the secular clergy, resembling that of Pole's Viterbo group in the previous decade. Meals were to be simple, and 'the condiments of the table [were to be] charity, the reading of books about the saints and pious sermons'. Following many of its predecessors on the Continent, the synod decreed that the clergy should dress in a simple and identifiable way, avoiding garish secular fashions. They were to be 'the fathers of the poor, they should be the refuge of orphans, the destitute and the oppressed'. Senior clergy were to set an example in this respect that was to be followed by those of lesser rank. The decree went on to repeat, in forceful fashion, the Catholic policy on clerical marriage that had in fact been enforced since the queen's accession. The prohibition of such relationships with women, which were described as a public scandal, applied to all clergy from the order of sub-deacon upwards. Those who failed to reach this standard, or did not adopt correct clerical dress and the tonsure, would face severe canonical sanctions, including, in serious cases, deprivation of their benefices. Similar penalties would be applied to benefice-holders who failed to observe the canonical hours of prayer and worship, or to engage in Christian studies. To ensure that these standards were kept in future the sixth decree reaffirmed traditional discipline concerning clerical ordinations (sigs E–Eii). After the preaching of God's Word, the most important duty of a bishop was to choose suitable men as ministers in Christ's Church. If at all possible, bishops should ordain their own clergy, who were already known to them, rather than relying on a colleague elsewhere, as had often happened before the break with Rome, when bishops frequently acted as politicians in the royal council. Ordinations should take place in the correct canonical seasons, such as Trinity, Petertide and Michaelmas, though Pole himself sometimes allowed exceptions to this rule, using his legatine powers. Bishops and archdeacons, in particular, should ensure

---

[22] The view that Pole was not greatly concerned with preaching is expressed in Pogson, 'Reginald Pole and the priorities of government in Mary Tudor's Church', *Historical Journal*, 18 (1975), p. 16, and Loades, *RMT*, pp. 272, 276, 293. Argument for the contrary view is found in Duffy, *Fires of faith*, pp. 17–21, 30, 50–55.

that ordinands were of suitable quality, that they were not 'infected with heresy', were of legitimate birth, of canonical age (24 for the priesthood), without physical deformity (Leviticus 21:16–24), and of honest life and adequate learning. Candidates should be carefully examined for the five days preceding their ordination and, up to the last minute, if any problem emerged, they might be rejected or held back for amendment. It was noted that conditions would be less strict than this for men being admitted to minor orders, up to that of sub-deacon.

The seventh synod decree dealt with the vexed question of provision to ecclesiastical benefices, many of which, in 1556, were still in lay hands (sig. Eii). In the case of ordination, bishops were to examine candidates carefully, especially if the cure (care) of souls was involved. Prospective benefice-holders should be of 'sound doctrine', serious-minded and learned in the Faith. They would also be required to reside in their benefices, something that in many cases had not happened in the past. With a view to recruiting good graduate clergy in the future, the synod instructed bishops to collect from the universities of Oxford and Cambridge the names of men who would be suitable to occupy benefices. Finally, the bishops were to take particular care of benefices when they were vacant. The following three decrees were devoted to reaffirming traditional Catholic discipline against practices that had grown up under Henry and Edward. The eighth decree tackled the question of benefices in lay hands, resulting from the dissolution of the religious houses (sig. Eii). It re-stated the papal position affirmed by Lateran IV, in reaction to the lengthy and bitter conflict over investiture, between the German emperors and the pope, which had festered throughout the eleventh to thirteenth centuries. The ninth decree condemned once again the 'detestable' practice of 'simony', this being the purchase of ecclesiastical offices and benefices, on the model of the healer Simon Magus ('the Magician'), who had attempted to buy the power of the Holy Spirit from the first Apostles (Acts 8:18–24), (sigs Eii–F). With obvious relevance to the current situation in England, the tenth decree repeated Pope Paul II's fifteenth-century instruction for the keeping of a full inventory of church goods, as well as the prohibition of the hiring out of ecclesiastical offices by clergy to others, including laymen. Once again, the thirteenth-century constitutions of Otto and Ottoboni for the English Church were referred to.

Perhaps the most significant of the English decrees for the future of the Catholic Church in general was the eleventh, which dealt with the education of future priests, and created the seminary model that would be adopted a few years later by the Council of Trent (sigs Fii–G). The starting point was the current shortage of men suitable for the priesthood, after the upheavals of the two previous decades. To remedy this at a non-graduate level, which would be necessary to cover most of the country, seminaries ('seedbeds' of clergy) were to be established in some cathedrals – York, Lincoln, Salisbury and Wells being planned for a start – to teach boys from the age of 11 or 12. In order to be admitted, they should already be able to read and write, and there should be some expectation that they would eventually become priests. It was intended that some at least of the students would be from poor families, and they would all begin their studies with grammar, under the instruction of schoolmasters appointed by the diocesan chancellor, and overseen by the bishop, dean and chapter of the cathedral concerned. Two classes would be established in each seminary, according to age and level of education, and the teaching of grammar would be followed by instruction in the doctrine and discipline of the Church. Some of the boys would become acolytes and serve at cathedral services, and some of them would eventually progress through the orders to become priests. The new seminaries were also intended to act as town grammar schools for other boys who were not heading for the priesthood, who would be educated alongside those who were. Also envisaged was a version of 'student loans'. Although each diocese would fund its pupils' education and training, those who eventually obtained a benefice would be expected to compensate their home diocese with a share of its revenues, up to a limit of £20 per annum. Contributions would be lower in the case of less lucrative livings. Along with the rest of the programme outlined by the synod, which included plans for a new English translation of the Bible and a new catechism, which was to be written by Carranza, there was no time, before the deaths of Queen Mary and Pole on 17 November 1558, for much action to be taken.[23] However, the twelfth and last decree, on the legatine visitation of the Church in England and Wales, did have an effect, particularly in the universities.

This decree stated that, for the necessary remedying of abuses, such visitations were to take place according to the ancient custom of England (sigs Fii–Gii). They were to be carried out by the bishops themselves or by those whom they appointed, and were to be undertaken as soon as possible, beginning with the cathedral cities and then spreading out into the dioceses. Within the city, the bishop should first undertake a visitation of his cathedral, then of any collegiate churches with bodies of canons, and after that of parishes, schools (including universities), libraries and hospitals. While they carried out these visitations, bishops were to administer chrism (holy oil) and the sacrament of confirmation, as necessary, and also the sacrament of penance and reconciliation in cases that were reserved, because of their gravity, to the bishop himself. The visitations were thus to emphasise the spiritual development of the People of God, as well as inspecting church assets and the conduct of the clergy. Bishops should normally delegate their visitatorial powers to teams of four or five men, who should be of good character and serious-minded. They were to investigate moral conduct, liturgy and the discipline of lay marriage, on the subject of which the

---

[23] *PPP*, p. 242.

synod shared with the Protestant reformers an insistence that weddings should only take place in church. Any altars which were unconsecrated for Catholic worship, or were 'polluted' by their previous use for Cranmerian services, were to be reconsecrated. If necessary, churches, bells and sacristies were to be restored and repaired, under the appropriate faculties, and the liturgical equipment of churches was to be checked. On a note of reforming zeal, it was decreed that Masses and other parts of the Divine Office should be celebrated not just with ritual correctness but also 'piously and devotedly', with officiants clothed in the proper vestments. Once the churches had been inspected, the visitors were to turn their attention to the clergy themselves, checking that they had been properly ordained. The situation of benefices was also to be examined, to see if there were any illegitimate intruders or other unsuitable incumbents, or whether others were doing the benefice-holders' jobs for them. The visitors were to ensure that the festivals of the Christian year were being correctly celebrated in the churches, and that the children were being properly instructed. Indeed, everything about the lifestyle of the clergy was to be investigated and reported on.

Lastly, the visitors were to turn to the conduct of the whole People of God, to see if there were still any heretics among them, or any who had failed to make a Catholic confession, or else were living as moneylenders or were in illegitimate relationships with 'concubines'. The visitors were also to find out whether the Lenten fast was being observed, excluding those who had received canonical exemptions, such as were on occasions issued by Pole as legate, to continue consuming meat, eggs and dairy products during such periods. Everyone should be properly instructed in the faith and come devoutly to church, especially to Mass. As far as the other institutions were concerned, the visitors were to ensure that hospitals (in this context understood mainly as almshouses rather than medical establishments) were properly administered for the poor, who in turn should be living a devout and peaceful life. In the schools, which for this purpose included the two universities, the visitors were to examine the masters to find out what books they were lecturing on and whether they were doing their jobs properly. The visitors were also to ensure that no one was appointed to a teaching post without first being examined by the relevant bishop or his representative and receiving a licence. Anyone found to be unsuitable should be removed from his post. Libraries were to be checked for heretical or otherwise illegal books. In general, the visitors were to praise what was good and condemn what was not, and the results of their visits were to be acted upon by the diocesan authorities. This document was dated at Lambeth on 13 February 1556.

From the start of Mary's reign, reform of the two universities had been one of Mary's priorities, and in this she was actively supported by Pole and his advisers.[24] The synod decree, issued in February 1556, ordering a visitation of the University of Oxford, was not immediately implemented, almost certainly because of Cranmer's final trial and death. Thus it was in late July that a team of visitors, as outlined in the relevant decree but larger than many others, was appointed for Oxford, beginning work on or about the 20th of that month. They were Pole's datary, Ormanetto, who took a leading role, James Brooks, bishop of Gloucester, a doctor of divinity who had been the delegate of the Apostolic See who presided over the former archbishop's trial, Walter Wright, a civil lawyer who in late 1553 had represented Bishop Gardiner in investigating the colleges of which the bishop was visitor, Robert Morwen, president of Corpus Christi College in Oxford, and Henry Cole, also a civil lawyer and provost of Eton College, who had preached in the University Church of St Mary's on Cranmer's last day alive.[25] It seems probable that Carranza acted as a background adviser to the visitors, just as he had done at the London synod.[26] Pole drew up 30 articles under which the university was to be investigated. Under their terms the visitors were to ask whether the foundation statutes of the university and its colleges were being observed, and, if further statutes had been added during the period of the schism, the visitors were to inspect them. They were also to see whether statutory university lectures were being duly delivered, and whether all the university officers were fulfilling their daily and ceremonial duties. The election of university officers was to be scrutinised, and those in charge of the colleges were to be examined to see that they were educating their students properly. The university finances were to be investigated and, in particular, the visitors were to see if any of its property had been alienated in the preceding years. The provision of books in the university was to be investigated, to root out heretical works and if possible re-assemble collections of Catholic texts that had been scattered. The visitors were to ensure that disputations and other academic exercises were being carried out, and that degrees were being awarded in accordance with the traditional statutes. The visitors were also to turn their attention to student behaviour, ensuring that lectures were being regularly attended, and that students were not gambling and engaging in disputes with townspeople. The actual number of junior members was to be established, and if it had fallen in recent years, the causes were to be investigated.[27]

On 6 November, Pole sent a more detailed set of instructions for the governance of the university.[28] Four days later, the vice-chancellor, Dr Thomas

24     Andrew Hegarty, 'Carranza and the universities', *RCEMT*, pp. 153–172, at pp. 161–162.

25     Claire Cross, 'Oxford and the Tudor state from the accession of Henry VIII to the death of Mary', in McConica, *History of the University of Oxford*, 3, p. 146.

26     Andrew Hegarty, 'Carranza and the English universities', *RCEMT*, pp. 153–172, at p. 164.

27     Bodleian MS Twyne, VI, fols 155r–157v; *CRP* 3 pp. 322–323 n. 147.

28     *CRP* 3 no. 1768.

Reynolds and Dr Henry Cole, the latter acting alone as a visitor, formally presented to the university Pole's acceptance of the office of chancellor. Now that Pole was head of the university as well as legate, he instructed it to appoint a commission of delegates from each faculty, including that of canon law, which was now restored, to review all the statutes in accordance with his most recent set of injunctions, and amend them where necessary. Dr Cole and the vice-chancellor would enlighten them as to exactly what the cardinal wanted.[29] On 14–15 November, the provisional injunctions brought to Oxford by Henry Cole were read in Convocation, 14 delegates were elected to work on the university statutes, and they seem to have started at once. On 23 November, Reynolds wrote to Pole himself to report that Dr Cole had made a good start on the 'internal' visitation which was now preceding in accordance with the appropriate decree of the London synod.[30] The vice-chancellor and others hoped to continue the good work of reform in the university, though he admitted that their efforts were meeting some resistance. Although Oxford was generally perceived to be much more amenable than Cambridge to the Catholic restoration, this opinion was clearly by no means unanimous. Perhaps surprisingly, Reynolds was still awaiting the copy of Pole's injunctions that Ormanetto had promised to send him. Without it, Pole's wishes could not be enforced, and it appears from this letter that one of the vice-chancellor's preoccupations was the number of taverns in Oxford. A statute of Edward VI had exempted the two university towns from a national limit of two per town, but Reynolds thought that Oxford should have no more than three.[31] When it had been proposed, early in 1554, that Mary should hold her second parliament in Oxford, Stephen Gardiner, in his capacity as lord chancellor, had proposed allowing eight such hostelries in the city, and the abandonment of this plan had led to legal action by licensees, seeking compensation for the lost trade. Student drinking was clearly a preoccupation of Reynolds'. He was concerned that students were buying wine at exorbitant prices in establishments outside their colleges. Another three or four individuals had now asked him for licences to run taverns (provisioning of the town was under the supervision of the university) and he wanted Pole's authority for refusing them, as he did not think that he and his colleagues could resist them on their own. The visitation of the University of Oxford, which had begun in July 1556, was never formally concluded, but reform continued for the rest of Mary's reign, under Pole's jurisdiction, whether as legate or chancellor.

In addition to statutes, procedures and behaviour, the Catholic restoration and reform of the University of Oxford also involved changes to the curriculum, including the reconstitution of the faculty of canon law, which was noted above.

[29]   OUA NEP/supra/ Reg. 1, fol. 163v; Hegarty, 'Carranza', *RCEMT*, p. 165.
[30]   TNA SP 15/7/58; *CSP Dom*, Addenda pp. 440–447; *CRP* 3 no. 1776.
[31]   *Statutes of the Realm*, 12 vols (London: Eyre and Staham, 1810), 4 pt 2, pp. 169–170.

The university was seen as a provider of Catholic clergy for the Church, as well as servants of the law and the Crown, with the result that close attention was paid to the teaching of theology. In this, the Spanish Dominican friars in Pole's London circle played an active part. Bartolomé Carranza was almost certainly in Oxford in July 1556, with the visitatorial team, and thereafter supervised affairs in the university from London. Two of his companions, on the other hand, taught there as postholders. Juan de Villagarcía was a pupil and protégé of Carranza in Valladolid, where he became a bachelor of theology. He incorporated this degree in Oxford on 14 November 1555, after taking up a praelectorship (readership) in theology at Pole's old college, Magdalen, which he held until 7 July 1557, though he resided not in Magdalen but in Lincoln College, where no record of his stay survives. In the meantime, he was elected to succeed, after some interval, Pier Martire Vermigli as regius professor of theology, becoming a doctor of theology in Oxford in 1558.[32]

While Villagarcía had been hand-picked by Carranza and brought with him from Spain, the main instigator of Pedro de Soto's arrival in Oxford was Cardinal Pole himself. The legate and the Dominican had met in Germany in October 1553, when the former was on his slow and much-delayed journey across Europe to take up his two legations. At that time De Soto, who had been a confessor to the Emperor Charles V since 1542 and had attended the first two phases of the Council of Trent in that capacity, was helping to establish a Catholic university at Dillingen, near Augsburg, alongside its co-founder the prince bishop, Cardinal Otto Truchsess von Waldburg. This Spanish Dominican played an important part in the negotiations that eventually led to Pole's return to his native land. On 18 November 1553, Pole, who seems to have been in Dillingen since the last week in October, gave De Soto credentials to go on his behalf to the emperor in Brussels, in an attempt to overcome the resistance of both Charles himself and his chief minister, Cardinal Granvelle.[33] Although it would take a further year for Pole to succeed, it is clear that he came to hold a very high opinion of De Soto, in January 1555 urging Cardinal Truchsess to allow his transfer from Dillingen to England. The request was granted and, later in that year, the Venetian ambassador in London, Giovanni Michiel, would report to the Doge and Senate that Pole deferred greatly to the Spanish Dominican's judgment.[34] De Soto seems quickly to have become involved in the concern of

---

[32]   *CSP Foreign*, 1559–60, p. 3; Tellechea, 'Inglaterra, Flandes y España (1557–1559) en cartas inéditas de Carranza y otros', *CP*, pp. 243–292; Loach, 'Reformation controversies', in McConica, *HUO*, 3, pp. 363–396, at p. 378; G.D. Duncan, 'Public lecturers and professorial chairs', in McConica, *HUO*, 3, pp. 335–361, at p. 353; Hegarty, 'Carranza and the universities', in *RCEMT*, pp. 158–159.

[33]   Copies of Pole's instructions to Pedro de Soto are in TNA SP 69/1, fols 150r–153v and BAV Vat. lat. 6754, fols 89r–93r; *CRP* 3 no. 759, see also no. 758.

[34]   *CSP Ven*, VI (i), pp. 8–9 (6 May 1555).

the queen, Pole, and his Lambeth circle, for the health of the universities. In a letter to King Philip, dated 26 October, Pole reported that the friar was in Oxford, where he found, as a result of the upheavals of the previous two reigns, an acute lack of scholastic theology. By then, De Soto was engaged, with Friar Juan, in trying to bring Archbishop Cranmer back to the true faith, after the burning of Bishops Latimer and Ridley on 16 October. De Soto thought the study of Peter Lombard's 'Sentences', the staple text of medieval university theology in the West, should be resumed after a hiatus of about 20 years, and he suggested that funding for a lecturer in scholastic theology could be found by diverting the resources then allocated to the regius professor of Hebrew, Richard Bruerne, whose lectures were very thinly attended.[35] This arrangement was quickly adopted, and De Soto was recorded in the dean's register at Christ Church as Bruerne's deputy, between October 1555 and August 1556, when he was summoned to rejoin the emperor on the Continent. Bruerne continued to be paid a stipend, and would later receive the consolation of a canonry at St George's Chapel, Windsor.[36] A back-handed compliment to the efficacy of the two Spaniards' work in Oxford came from the future bishop John Jewel, then in exile. On 22 May 1559, now back in Elizabeth's England, and at his old university, Jewel wrote to the Zürich Reformer Heinrich Bullinger:

> Our universities are so depressed and ruined, that at Oxford there are scarcely two individuals who think with us, and even they are so dejected and broken in spirit that they can do nothing. That despicable friar Soto and another Spanish monk [Villagarcía], I know not who, have so torn up by the roots all that Peter Martyr [Vermigli] had so prosperously planted, that they have reduced the vineyard of the Lord into a wilderness. You would scarcely believe so much desolation could have been effected in so short a time.[37]

In Cambridge, on the other hand, in June 1553, shortly before King Edward's death, the Regent House had formally adopted the new Forty-Two Articles of Religion (to be reduced to Thirty-Nine in Elizabeth's reign) and resolved that all who supplicated for the degrees of master of arts, bachelor of divinity and doctor of divinity would have first to assent to them. Once it was clear that Mary had won, Regent House quickly persuaded Sandys to resign as vice-chancellor, and replaced him with a safe conservative, Dr John Yonge, who had previously opposed the reformer Martin Bucer, when he was regius professor

---

[35]   *CSP Ven*, VI (i), no. 256; *CRP* 3 no. 1414.

[36]   Hegarty, 'Carranza and the universities', pp. 157–158.

[37]   Hastings Robinson, ed. and trans., *The Zurich letters, comprising the correspondence of several English bishops and others, with some of the Helvetian Reformers, during the early part of the reign of Queen Elizabeth*, 2 vols (Cambridge: Cambridge University Press for the Parker Society, 1842), 2, p. 29.

of divinity. In effect, if not in law, all those who had supported the Edwardian religious establishment were now regarded as traitors and Mary and her council quickly restored Bishop Gardiner to his former office of chancellor, in place of Northumberland, with a brief to begin at once the removal of Protestants and their influence from the university. Sandys joined Northumberland in the Tower of London, though he avoided execution and eventually returned to Cambridge, then becoming a bishop, under Elizabeth. Gardiner quickly restored the Catholic statutes of the university and its colleges, and, as in Oxford, Mass was celebrated once again. In the autumn of 1553, the exodus of Protestants from posts in Cambridge was considerable. The successor of Paul Fagius as reader in Hebrew, Joannes Immanuel Tremellius, departed to the Rhineland, and in total 76 Cambridge men, 10 of them resident fellows, left for Switzerland or Germany. Gardiner became master of Trinity Hall once again, and the future bishop Thomas Watson was elected master of St John's. Sandys was replaced by Edmund Cosyn as master of St Catharine's, and Matthew Parker, the man who would succeed Pole as Archbishop of Canterbury, was removed from the mastership of Corpus Christi College. Only three heads of house remained in post after this purge, in Gonville Hall, and Magdalene and Jesus colleges.[38]

The build-up to the 1556–7 legatine visitation of Cambridge began in March 1555, when the burning of heretics was already under way around the country. The vice-chancellor was told that in future all those who supplicated for degrees or wished to speak in the Regent House would have first to affirm their belief in the Catholic faith.[39] Subsequently, on 26 July, Gardiner received a confession of faith, signed by about 130 regent masters and non-regent members of Cambridge University, which stressed the value of good works for salvation, the doctrine of the real presence of Christ in the Eucharist, the inerrancy of the Catholic Church, the value of the veneration of the saints and their relics, belief in purgatory, and the inviolability of religious vows. The document specifically rejected the teachings of Huldrych Zwingli, Johannes Oecolampadius, Martin Luther, John Calvin, Martin Bucer, and all other heresiarchs. On Gardiner's death, in November 1555, Pole was urged to become chancellor, and eventually he agreed.[40] On 1 April 1556, now archbishop of Canterbury as well as chancellor of the university, Pole wrote to Cambridge praising the good men who had been provided from there to preach before the queen during the recent season of Lent, and who had followed the fine examples of John Fisher and the late Stephen Gardiner. He professed reluctance to become chancellor of Cambridge

---

[38]  Cross, 'English universities', pp. 61–64; Hegarty, 'Cararnza and the universities', *RCEMT*, p. 156.

[39]  Muller, *Letters of Stephen Gardiner*, pp. 475–476.

[40]  Cross, 'English universities', *CMT*, p. 69.

but nonetheless accepted the offer of the post.[41] During much of that year, the main focus was the visitation of Oxford, which may have been regarded as a simple task, but on 13 November 1556, Yonge, who was master of Pembroke College, Cambridge, sent a report to Pole on the continuing influence of the late Martin Bucer's reformist views in his university. He clearly had a personal grudge against the previous regime. He had been expelled from his mastership and imprisoned for a year, as well as being condemned for his traditionalist views by Bucer, Archbishop Cranmer and Bishop Thomas Goodrich of Ely. He told Pole that in 1553 the Church of England had been in the same decayed and corrupt state as the Judaism once condemned by the prophet Joel (chs 1–2).[42]

Eventually, on 3 December 1556, Pole issued a citation for the visitation of the university to the current vice-chancellor, Andrew Perne. In it he stated that the London synod wished 'the old ecclesiastical discipline' to be restored in Cambridge and noted that Pope Paul IV was personally interested in the matter. Dr Perne was ordered to instruct all graduate members of Cambridge University, in the name of the commissioners, to prepare for the beginning of the visitation, which would take place on 11 January next, between eight and ten in the morning, in Great St Mary's church. In the meantime, they were to assemble all university and college statutes for inspection. The citation was read in Regent House, by the university orator, John Stokes, on 11 December. On Christmas Eve, the Convocation agreed that the expenses of the visitation, which John Foxe later estimated at about £100, should be shared by the university and the colleges. During the Christmas vacation, fellows, scholars and other university employees should only be allowed to leave town on condition that they returned by 11 January.[43]

A diary account of the Cambridge visitation was provided by the registrary, John Mere. When the Christmas, New Year and Epiphany celebrations were over, on 8 January the six existing commissioners of the queen in Cambridge, including the vice-chancellor, as well as the town recorder, Sir James Dyer, and constables and representatives of the parishes, were assembled in the town hall to hear the commission read. They were 'sworne to inquire of heresie, lollardie, conspiracie, seditious words, tales and rumors aginst the King and Queene' and to search out heretical books and any failings in the conduct of Catholic worship.[44] The next day, the visitors, or commissioners, were escorted into Cambridge by some of the heads of houses and were welcomed at Trinity College by its master, John Christopherson, who was bishop-elect of Chichester. They attended Mass, no doubt with the assistance of the choral foundation that had

---

[41]   *ERP* 5 no. 40; *CRP* 3 no. 1533.
[42]   Bod. Rawlinson MS C.45, fols 1r–4v; *CRP* 3 no. 1771b.
[43]   Foxe, *A&M* 1583, p. 1956; *CRP* 3 no. 1781 (further textual details); *PPP*, pp. 291–295.
[44]   Foxe, *A&M* 1583, p. 1956.

been newly re-established by Queen Mary. The high-powered team consisted of Cuthbert Scott, bishop of Chester, Niccolò Ormanetto, Pole's datary, John Christopherson, bishop of Chichester and Master of Trinity, Thomas Watson, bishop-elect of Lincoln, and Henry Cole, provost of Eton College. There were offers of accommodation from other colleges, but they settled at Trinity. They were welcomed with an oration by one of the college fellows, to which Bishop Watson replied, after which they rested, though they also placed interdicts, prohibiting all Catholic worship, on Great St Mary's, where Bucer was buried, and St Michael's, which contained the remains of Paul Fagius. Foxe observes that, up to that point, Catholic services, including the Mass, had been held in those churches without any apparent problem, since early in Mary's reign.[45]

The formal visitation got under way on 11 January, as planned. The vice-chancellor, the masters and presidents of the colleges, and all the graduates in the colleges and halls, were assembled before the commissioners, at the schools, in their academic dress. Foxe has a note that the scholars were told to wear their surplices but did not do so. The whole assembly, following the university cross, processed to Trinity College, where the commissioners were staying. The visitors sat on a bench, luxuriously furnished with cushions and placed on a carpet, inside the college gatehouse. The vice-chancellor, dressed in a rich cope, sprinkled the visitors with holy water and went to cense them, but this was refused. Then Stokes, the university orator, offered them a welcoming speech in Latin, in which he described the cardinal as 'truly our Moses (*vere noster Moyses*)', who had returned to his native land to restore a broken country and its Church, the faults of which were described in graphic detail, with the use of Classical analogies.[46] Bishop Scott replied to this speech, welcoming the good will that the university was showing to the commissioners, but leaving no room for doubt that inside this velvet glove there was a mailed fist.[47]

The next two months would test the truth of these assertions, but in the meantime, once the formalities at Trinity were completed, the commissioners went in procession to King's, where a Mass of the Holy Spirit was sung in the chapel. After this they continued to Great St Mary's where although the celebration of Mass was suspended under the interdict, there was a sermon. The preacher, one 'Mr Peacock', lambasted various Cambridge 'heretics' of previous years, notably Thomas Bilney, Thomas Cranmer, Hugh Latimer and Nicholas Ridley. The registrary, John Mere, then read the cardinal's visitatorial commission, after which the vice-chancellor made a speech in reply, displaying the letter of commission under Pole's seal, together with a document containing

---

[45]   Foxe, *A&M* 1583, p. 1957.

[46]   What is apparently the full text of John Stokes' oration is in Foxe, *A&M* 1583, pp. 1957–1958.

[47]   Foxe, *A&M* 1583, p. 1958.

the names of all the members of the university, which were read out. The plan was that the visitation should then begin in earnest, but there was a hitch. When the elderly provost of King's College, Robert Brassam, heard his name read, he said that all jurisdiction over his college was reserved to the bishop of Lincoln alone, by royal letters patent, presumably of the college's founder, Henry VI, and these could not be overridden. This naturally caused a stir, but the commissioners huffily replied that Cardinal Pole had given them full authority, received directly from Pope Paul IV, to carry out the visitation of the whole university. After this everyone went home, under orders to appear in the schools at 1 o'clock, for the examination of statutes to begin. This massive task involved the use of university and college archives. The next day, 12 January, the commissioners began work in King's, using a procedure that would be repeated in all the other colleges.

In each case, Scott, Ormanetto and their team ordered the head of house, fellows and scholars to appear in clerical dress and assemble at the outer gate towards the town. The master should wear priestly vestments and be preceded by a processional cross, with the rest of the college in order of seniority. The master was to sprinkle and cense the commissioners when they arrived, and say prayers, and all were then to process to the college chapel. At King's, a college noted in recent years for its reformist sympathies, there was another hitch, as Provost Brassam had not assembled the college by the main gate in time for the commissioners' arrival. The visitors came upon the King's men as they scrambled to put on their finery and Brassam was forced to apologise for this somewhat comic scene, though he spoiled the effect by again asserting that the visitors had no authority in his college unless they brought new and specific documents. Once again, Bishop Scott of Chester was furious, expressing doubts about King's orthodoxy, and pointing out that the pope's authority, under which Pole and they were acting, was greater than any other on earth. In this somewhat tense state, everyone adjourned to King's chapel for Mass, after which the main aisle and the side-chapels were searched for their complement of crosses, missals and vestments, all of which were brought for the commissioners' inspection. After this, every fellow and scholar was called before them by name, and then all, starting with the provost, were individually examined in his lodgings. Even at this stage, some refused to take the required oath, on the grounds that they had already sworn themselves to their college, and thought it wrong to have to swear against their conscience, thus suggesting that suspicions about their orthodoxy were not unfounded. It took the visitors three days to get through all the King's men, and after that they carried out the same procedure in other colleges.[48] The issue of Bucer and Fagius's bones, which had been raised at the very beginning, perhaps in order to intimidate the likes of the fellows of King's, had not been forgotten. On 15 January there was another gathering in Great St Mary's, during

---

[48]     Foxe, *A&M* 1583, pp. 1958–1960; Cross, 'English universities', *CMT*, pp. 70–71.

which the university formally repudiated the teachings of the two reformers, and the visitors publicly took possession of a new commission from Pole, which authorised them to make an inquisition into heresy.[49]

While the cold January days saw continuing interrogations of Cambridge men concerning their religious orthodoxy and their loyalty to King Philip and Queen Mary, legal moves were afoot to secure the burning of the remains of Bucer and Fagius, along with as many of their books as could be found in Cambridge. First, on 13 January, Dr Perne, the vice-chancellor, organised a meeting in the schools with the heads of the colleges, at which it was agreed that Bucer had indeed been a heretic and sectary, whose teaching had seriously damaged the university. The meeting petitioned the commissioners to have the former regius professor's corpse exhumed, so that an inquisition into his doctrine could be undertaken, because it was against canon law for him to remain buried in a Catholic church. The meeting came to the same conclusion concerning the remains of Paul Fagius, who had died soon after his appointment as reader in Hebrew, in 1549. The organisation of the two exhumations was placed in the hands of the vice-chancellor, who met the commissioners at seven the next morning, and was promptly given the sentences on the two reformers, which were drafted by Ormanetto, and confirmed that same evening by a convocation of the regent and non-regent masters.[50] There was some delay while the cases were referred to London for assent to the burnings, but confirmation of the sentences was eventually obtained from Pole, and it was decided that the judgement day should be 26 January. The vice-chancellor informed the mayor of Cambridge that he and his burgesses should all assemble on that day. When it arrived, the university and the townsmen duly gathered in Great St Mary's, to hear the sentences on Bucer and Fagius read once again by Dr Perne and to listen to a sermon by Bishop Scott, in which he said that while the commissioners could have proceeded against the reformers after the first citation by the university, on 13 January, they had wanted to allow Bucer and Fagius's defenders to make their case, hence the delay and the seeking of confirmation from London that the two men's remains might be handed over to the secular arm. After this sermon, the sentence against Bucer and Fagius was read, and Bishop Scott ordered that their bones should be dug up. Both men were then disgraded from their Catholic clerical orders (Bucer had been a Dominican friar) and their bodies were handed over to the mayor and his officers. Not content with this, Dr Perne also preached a sermon, denouncing Bucer and proclaiming the authenticity of the Catholic faith. While he was speaking, students pinned papers attacking Bucer to the church door.

---

[49]    Cross, 'English universities', *CMT*, p. 71.
[50]    Foxe, *A&M* 1583, p. 1959.

The next day, 27 January, the sentence on Bucer and Fagius was dispatched to London for confirmation, along with a letter from the commissioners to Pole, in which they asked him to instruct the mayor of Cambridge, by royal writ, to carry out the burnings. While awaiting a reply, the commissioners called in Bucer and Fagius's books, and also took part in the celebration of Candlemas on 2 February, with a militantly Catholic sermon by Thomas Watson. Finally, on 6 February, the two men were exhumed, Fagius first, and taken to the marketplace, where they were chained in coffins to a stake and burned, together with those of their books that had been assembled. As was customary in Continental *autos de fe*, a sermon was preached for the edification of the scholars and townsmen present, this task being undertaken by Dr Watson, but in Great St Mary's rather than at the site of the burning. This separation also corresponded to the custom in Spain at the time. Finally, on 7 February, the Blessed Sacrament was carried through the town in solemn procession and restored to St Michael's church and Great St Mary's.[51]

The ordinances issued by Pole on 18 March 1557, ostensibly at the request of the visiting commissioners, and not apparently delivered until the following May, were intended to lay down the ground-rules for a Catholic university in Cambridge as had been done in Oxford.[52] Statutes were published for the election of vice-chancellors and readers, as well as the regent masters of arts who formed the bulk of the university convocation, and other officials. As in Oxford, the avoidance of absenteeism was a preoccupation, as was the preservation and effective teaching of Catholic doctrine and practice. Discipline in dress and behaviour was also legislated for in detail, as well as teaching arrangements and the finances, which were not to fall into the ruin of Edward's reign. At about the same time, Pole, as chancellor of both universities as well as legate, issued injunctions for the proper conduct of worship in college chapels and impropriated chapels in both Oxford and Cambridge.[53]

Apart from London, both the English university cities were seen by Pole and his supporters as the main focus of the revival of the religious life, which had been regarded from the start as an important part of the restoration of Catholicism

---

[51]    Foxe, *A&M* 1583, pp. 1960–1963; the eucharistic procession is vividly represented, and conflated with the burning of the two Reformers' bones in Foxe, *A&M* 1570, p. 2151. In his description of the ceremony Foxe satirises the solemn eucharistic processions, particular to celebrate the Feast of Corpus Christi (the Body of Christ), which had been restored to England in 1555, under the influence of Pole, Bonner and Carranza (see John Edwards, 'Corpus Christi at Kingston upon Thames: Bartolomé Carranza and the Eucharist in Marian England', *RCEMT*, pp. 139–51).

[52]    CCCC MS 118 no. 8, pp. 183–203, printed in Frere and Kennedy, *Visitation articles and injunctions*, 2, pp. 415–421; abbreviated version of the Latin text, with partial English translation, in *CRP* 3 no. 1911.

[53]    CCCC MS 118 no. 11, pp. 209–215; *CRP* 3 no. 1912.

in Mary's kingdom, though one that brought into clear focus the issue of church property that had arrived in lay hands, as a result of the policies of Henry and Edward's governments. There was Spanish involvement too, particularly in the attempted restoration of religious orders. Before he came to England in July 1554, Bartolomé Carranza had been given powers by the Dominican General to restore the English province of the Order of Preachers, and even before that some English former friars had apparently re-adopted the habit spontaneously, although the kingdom was still in schism. Prominent among them was William Peryn (Perrin), who would later become prior of a Dominican community in the former Augustinian church and house of St Bartholomew the Great, Smithfield. This adjoined the site of the burning of many heretics in Mary's reign, and thus renewed the link between that Order and the Inquisition, which went back to its foundation in the thirteenth century.[54] In 1557, Peryn published a set of *Spiritual exercyses and goostly meditacions*, containing much material from the *Spiritual exercises* of Ignatius of Loyola.[55] Once Juan de Villagarcía and Pedro de Soto obtained academic posts in Oxford, it seemed natural that the former Dominican house there should be restored. At the time, the former 'Blackfriars', in Littlegate Street at the southern edge of the city, was in the possession of the mayor of Oxford. The restoration of religious houses was a slow business, and it was not until May 1557, when Carranza was no longer in charge of things in England, that Pole himself summoned Villagarcía to Lambeth, to begin arranging finance for a restoration in Littlegate.

One of the clearest examples of the restoration of papal jurisdiction in England was the return of religious houses of monks, nuns and friars. There was, however, no anticipation of Pole's arrival in England in the case of religious houses, and in the event it was Pope Paul IV, in his bull *Praeclara charissimi*, dated 21 June 1555, who gave the impetus for the renewal of the religious life in England, Wales and Ireland.[56] He formally wound up all the foundations that had been dissolved by Henry VIII, and gave Pole and his advisers a free hand in the restoration of old foundations, even though they were now technically new, if necessary diverting funds and personnel to new projects. This papal initiative was perhaps most conspicuously supported by Queen Mary herself in the case of the Observant Franciscan Order, to which both sides of her family, in England and Spain, had a strong historic attachment, going back into the fifteenth century. Thus the Order's friary alongside Greenwich Palace, east of London, where Mary herself had been baptised in 1516, was restored

---

[54]   Edwards, *Inquisition* (Stroud: The History Press, [1999] 2009), pp. 41–47.

[55]   William Peryn, *Spiritual exercyses and goostly meditacions, and a neare waye to come to perfection and lyfe contemplatyue, very profitable for Religious, and generall for al other that desyre to come to the perfecte loue of god, and to the contempte of the worlde* (London: J. Waley, 1557); Wizeman, *Theology and spirituality*, pp. 210–217.

[56]   BMD MS 922, iv, fols 44v–47v.

even before Pole's arrival in England, while the kingdom was still technically in schism. During Edward's reign, Mary had corresponded with two noted English Franciscans, William Peto and Henry Elson, in their exile on the Continent.[57] Peto had joined Pole's extended *familia* in Italy, living in the English Hospice in Rome, and once the legate arrived back in his native land, steps were taken to repair and re-open the Franciscan house. Eventually, in April 1555, on Palm Sunday, Maurice Griffiths, bishop of Rochester, installed the friars in their new, or renewed, community, which would turn out to be the largest of any order in Mary's England. To begin with there were 25 men and by November 1555 more had joined. Most of them were former English friars who had been absolved and renewed their vows, though some were Spaniards from King Philip's entourage, and there may also have been some Netherlanders. Mary herself spent no less than £1551 8s 6d on the Greenwich house, and would bequeath £300 to it in her will, when it was drawn up in March 1558. As she had done years before, she used the friary church for her own devotions, and Pole was consecrated there as archbishop.[58] Less successful was the attempt, strongly advocated by William Peto, to restore as an Observant house the main London Greyfriars, off Newgate Street, which in Edward's reign had become Christ's Hospital. In response to a petition from Franciscans, Philip's confessor, Alfonso de Castro, of the same order, with the Dominican Juan de Villagarcía, visited the hospital and school, being so delighted by what they saw that they urged the continuation of the new foundation, which indeed exists as a school to this day. More successful, at least temporarily, was the attempt to re-open the Observant Franciscan friary in Southampton, which began to function in January 1557, though its existence would of course be brief.[59]

Letters from Bartolomé Carranza to Juan de Villagarcía are a valuable source of information on the efforts made in Mary's reign to restore or establish Dominican houses. They survive because of Carranza's arrest and trial by the Spanish Inquisition on heresy charges, in August 1559. Villagarcía's side of the correspondence was collected when he too was arrested, but unfortunately it did not go to Rome with the rest of Carranza's trial documents, and cannot be found.[60] What does survive gives a deep insight into the atmosphere at the top of the English Church between 1554 and Mary's death, with some rare glimpses of Pole's own character. With Carranza still in London and Villagarcía in Oxford, as regius professor of theology, the correspondence frequently refers to the revival of the old Blackfriars in Littlegate, which was briefly achieved, in 1557–8, along

---

[57]   *CSP Ven*, VI (ii), no. 938.

[58]   Keith Duncan Brown, 'The Franciscan Observants in England, 1482–1559', D.Phil. thesis, University of Oxford, 1986, pp. 222–231; *PPP*, p. 286.

[59]   Brown, 'Franciscan Observants', pp. 231–233.

[60]   For the history of these texts, see Tellechea, 'Inglaterra, Flandes y España (1557–1559)', *CP*, pp. 245–282, at pp. 245–246.

with the establishment of a small convent of Dominican nuns, on an unknown site. The men's friary received funding from the Spanish Crown, paid by Francisco Lexalde, was also responsible for distributing Philip's pensions to various of Mary's councillors and other courtiers. The two Dominican post-holders in Oxford, Pedro de Soto and, more probably, Juan de Villagarcía, may have lived for a time in the men's house. In Cambridge, on the other hand, Carranza seems to have been happy to leave a university presence to the Franciscans, saying that one of their friars should go there, though he worried abou the students there being exposed to the theology of Duns Scotus, rather than the Thomism being taught by Villagarcía and Pedro de Soto in Oxford. By the end of Mary's reign, Carranza had succeeded in establishing two male Dominican houses, one in London and the other in Oxford, and two for females, one also in Oxford and the other at King's Langley, Hertfordshire.[61]

While the initiative in Dominican restoration arrived with King Philip, the notion of re-introducing to England the oldest Western monastic tradition, based on the Rule of St Benedict, began before Pole's arrival and the country's reconciliation to Rome. Perhaps inevitably, the main effort was focused on Westminster Abbey, which, being at the historic centre of English royal government, seems to have been regarded, from the start of Mary's reign, as a showcase of Catholicism, just as it had performed that function for Protestant reform in the previous reign.[62] As a part of this enterprise, in 1554, while her kingdom was still in schism, Mary ordered the restoration of the 'rogation' processions of prayer for good crops which traditionally took place on the Sunday before Ascension Day and the three following days up to that festival. The London diarist Henry Machyn records her own participation in the processions held in and around Whitehall and Westminster, from Monday to Wednesday:

> the quen['s] grace whent a prossessyon within sant James [palace] with harolds [heralds]and serjantsof armes, and iiii bysshops mytred, and all iii days they whent her chapell a-bowt the feldes, first day to sant Gylles [...] the nest day tuwyse-day to sant Martens in the feldes, [and there] a sermon and song masse, and so they dronke there, and the iii day to Westmynster, and ther a sermon and then masse, and mad good chere, and after a-bowt the [St James's] Parke.[63]

Evidently, there was much merry-making as well as liturgical activity.

---

[61]   *CP*, pp. 258, 260–267, 271; AGS Estado 811 no. 90; *CRP* 3 nos 2050a, 2054a; *PPP*, p. 286.

[62]   MacCulloch, *Tudor Church militant*, pp. 82–84, 111; J.F. Merritt, *The social world of early modern Westminster: Abbey, Court and community, 1525–1640* (Manchester: Manchester University Press, 2005), p. 54.

[63]   Machyn, *Diary*, p. 61.

At the time of the Queen's accession, Westminster Abbey was technically a cathedral, in the hands of a dean and chapter, although the diocese of Westminster, which had been carved out of London by Henry VIII in 1540, had been abolished in 1552. Technically, therefore, the abbey was a secondary cathedral for Bishop Edmund Bonner. As with other former religious houses, the attempt to re-found a Benedictine community at Westminster seems to have begun with the agreement over lay-impropriated Church lands which was made by the Crown and Pole, and enacted in statute in December 1554.[64] The first important development was on 19 March 1555, when John Feckenham, then dean of St Paul's but a former Benedictine monk, had an audience of the Queen, in his habit, along with 15 others similarly dressed. Mary accepted their petition that they should be allowed to resume the monastic life at Westminster. According to the Venetian ambassador, she instructed her then lord chancellor, Gardiner, to investigate the means by which this could be done, and by 14 April it was decided that Westminster Abbey could indeed be re-founded.[65] It quickly became apparent, however, that the current dean, Hugh Weston, and his canons, all of them enthusiastic Catholics, had no wish to give their church up, and Sir John Mason reported that they were threatening to resort to 'sore law'. The reintroduction of the monks was delayed during Thomas Cranmer's trial, but it is clear that Pole had a personal interest in restoring the Westminster community, and in linking it with the Benedictine Order on the Continent.

Back in 1537, as a newly-created cardinal, Pole had become the protector of the Cassinese Congregation, a Benedictine family which derived from the great monastery of Monte Cassino in central Italy. Having been actively involved with the Cassinese in Padua during the 1540s, after he had failed to be elected pope in the 1549–50 conclave, Pole spent more than one summer in Civitella San Paolo, north of Rome, which was a dependency of the Congregation's main Roman house, the famous monastery of St Paul-without-the-Walls (San Paolo-fuori-le-mura). In addition, immediately after the conclave, Pope Julius gave the cardinal of England the authority to reform another of the Cassinese houses in Rome, San Ambrosio, as cardinal protector of that Congregation.[66] When he returned to England, with the idea of restoring the country's monasticism, Pole did not forget the Cassinese. His correspondence indicates that, in November 1555, with the Westminster project under way, the cardinal was trying to have Cassinese monks sent to Mary's kingdom, bringing their experience in the capacity of monastic visitors.[67] The author of the relevant letter, Antonio Agustín, had produced the

---

[64]   *SR* 1&2 Philip and Mary c. 8.

[65]   *CSP Ven*, VI (i), no. 32.

[66]   *CRP* 2 no. 560 (14 February 1550).

[67]   TNA PRO 31/9/67; *CRP* 3 no. 1436: a letter from Antonio Agustín, at the Imperial Court in Brussels, dated 24 November 1555; *CSP Ven*, VI (i), no. 403 (p. 352).

necessary paperwork for such monks to go to England from Spain, and had shown it to the Spanish royal secretary Gonzalo Pérez. He had brought it to the Emperor Charles, who had put it before the council of his Chamber. Although the mission received approval, it came to nothing, even though the prospective visitors eventually, in 1557, when Westminster Abbey was functioning again without them, received a licence from the abbot of St Paul-without-the-Walls. The English monks would be left to work out their own salvation, for the brief time that was left to them.[68]

Before any of that happened, the existing dean and chapter had to be removed. On 7 September 1556, the Crown issued letters patent for the dissolution of the secular chapter of Westminster, making way for Pole, as legate, to establish a new Benedictine foundation.[69] Then, on 15 September, Pole gave the dean and chapter the instruction and authority to surrender the spiritualities and temporalities of the abbey, and informed the king and queen that he had done so.[70] This document stated, in accordance with Paul IV's bull, that the monastery of St Peter at Westminster was 'founded and erected anew (*de novo fundato et erecto*)'. On 18 September, the abbey's receiver-general, John Moulton, arrived in Westminster to carry out the legal transfer.[71] Five days later, pensions for the outgoing dean and chapter were authorised to be paid out of abbey funds until they received other employment.[72] On 25 September, Bishop Bonner formally agreed to relinquish his secondary cathedral to the monks.[73] The old dean and chapter had held their last formal meeting on the previous day, and on 26 September they resigned, leaving the precincts on the 28th, so that the monks could enter and take possession on the Feast of Michaelmas (29 September 1556).[74] The religious and financial activities of the Benedictine abbey began gradually. From 4 October, alms were distributed to the poor on the Sundays up to All Saints' Day (1 November) and three weeks later Abbot Feckenham and 14 monks were 'shorne' (tonsured) and installed by Archbishop Heath and Pole's datary, Ormanetto.[75] On 22 November there was a solemn monastic procession in the abbey, for the first time for over 15 years, and a week later Abbot Feckenham was consecrated at a solemn Mass,

---

[68]   *CRP* 3 no. 2020 (letter from Pole to the Abbot of St Paul-without-the-Walls, from Croydon on 28 May 1557; BAV MS Vat. lat. 6754 fol. 231 r–v; *CSP Ven*, VI, i, no. 904).

[69]   *CPR*, 1555–7, p. 546.

[70]   BMD MS 922, 6, fols 110v–111r; *CRP* 3 no. 1681.

[71]   WAM 37162 fol. 12, 37712, 37716–17, 37718, fols 2v, 3r; for fuller details of the restoration of Westminster Abbey, see C.S. Knighton, 'Westminster Abbey restored', *CMT*, pp. 77–123.

[72]   *CPR* 1555–7 547; BMD MS 922, 6, fols 121v–122r (25 September 1556).

[73]   WAM 12972; Knighton, 'Westminster Abbey', p. 82.

[74]   *CSP Ven*, VI (ii), no. 634.

[75]   *CSP Ven*, VI (ii), no. 723; Wriothesley, *Chronicle*, p. 136.

celebrated by Archbishop Heath.[76] Then, on Reconciliation Day, 30 November, Cardinal Pole himself came to the abbey, where there were now 26 monks, most of whom seem to have been over 40 years old and returning to their earlier profession.[77] Although the new community was technically not a restoration of the old, Feckenham and his monks seem to have wanted to regain all the rights of the former institution, including the administration of sanctuary in the abbey precincts. Thus on 6 December 1556 a procession of protected malefactors took place, which included a scholar of Westminster School who had killed a stall-holder in Westminster Hall.[78] Finally, on 20 December, the queen herself, having recovered from illness, travelled by barge to hear vespers in the abbey, now sung by 28 monks.[79]

Out of the re-establishment of the Benedictine community at Westminster came the notion of restoring other former abbeys of the order. When he reported on the success of St Peter's Abbey in the capital, in a letter written in his Croydon palace on 28 May 1557, Pole told the Abbot of St Paul-without-the-Walls, in Rome, that he intended to restore one of the former Benedictine foundations in Canterbury, meaning either the cathedral priory of Christ Church or St Augustine's Abbey.[80] This was not done, and equally abortive were the attempts, at about this time to send monks back to Glastonbury and St Alban's abbeys. In the case of Glastonbury, at an unknown date four of the abbey's former monks, probably now in the Westminster community, petitioned the lord chamberlain to be allowed to return to Somerset, saying that Queen Mary had promised this to them and that the cardinal supported the project. They got down to discussing finance, but nothing further happened.[81] Pole's personal enthusiasm for the Benedictine restoration is confirmed by Bartolomé Carranza in a letter sent to Juan de Villagarcía in Oxford on 18 May 1557. As well as commenting that the dean and chapter had approached their removal from Westminster 'with the desire of a merchant throwing his cloth into the sea in a storm, seeing that they would lose more by denying this to the Queen', he noted that Pole, whom both these Spaniards knew well, was 'really happy to have won this [restoration] for the monks of St Benedict'.[82] The necessitiess of Catholic worship had been accumulated in the abbey since Mary's accession,

---

[76]  Machyn, *Diary*, pp. 118–119, 119–120.

[77]  *CSP Ven*, VI (ii), no. 743.

[78]  Loades, 'The sanctuary', in C.S. Knighton and R. Mortimer, *Westminster Abbey reformed* (Aldershot: Ashgate, 2003), pp. 75–93.

[79]  *CSP Ven*, VI (ii), nos 771 (p. 879) and 884 (p. 1082); Knighton, 'Westminster Abbey restored', pp. 82–83.

[80]  *CRP* 3 no. 2020; *CSP Ven*, VI (ii), no. 904 (p. 1114).

[81]  BL Harleian MS 3881 fol. 38v; J.G. Clark, 'Reformation and reaction at St Alban's Abbey, 1530–58', *English Historical Review*, 115 (2000), pp. 320–321.

[82]  Tellechea, 'Inglaterra, Flandes', *CP*, pp. 259–260.

and now included a crozier for Abbot Feckenham, who also retrieved the former abbot's lodgings from the second Lord Wentworth.[83] Writing on Trinity Sunday (13 June) 1557 to Villagarcía, from Westminster, where he lived and worshipped regularly, Carranza mentioned a new missal that had been acquired for the abbey.[84] Its Benedictine community continued into the early months of Elizabeth's reign.

Though only briefly, houses of some other religious orders were restored in Mary's reign, in each case with both her own active involvement and that of Pole. An attempt was made to re-establish the Carthusian monastery at Sheen, near Richmond Palace, where the cardinal most probably received his early education. Another monastery with strong royal associations, was the Bridgettine convent at Syon, on the Thames west of London, where Mary's mother Catherine had been a regular visitor. At the dissolution this house had gone to John Dudley, duke of Northumberland, and it had reverted to the Crown after his execution for treason in August 1553.[85] Also, the restoration of the English properties, or commanderies, of the knights of St John of Jerusalem (the ordained knights also known as Hospitallers or Knights of Malta) was attempted on a larger scale, which befitted their strategic role in the combat against Ottoman Turkey and its allies in the Mediterranean. Here again, Pole was active, but in this case the main royal interest came from King Philip, and Pope Paul IV was also enthusiastic.

On 6 May 1557, Pole wrote in his capacity as legate, to the king and queen, the former being present in England at the time, urging the restoration of the priory of St John at Clerkenwell, just north of London.[86] After its dissolution by Henry VIII, this establishment had a chequered history. In 1549, most of the church itself had been blown up with gunpowder, on the orders of the duke of Somerset, and the materials transported for use in the building of his new family palace, Somerset House, on the Strand.[87] Despite this, Mary used the remaining accommodation at Clerkenwell priory as her residence, during her controversial visits to the London of Edward VI.[88] According to the chronicler John Stow, the remains of the priory church, as Pole found them, consisted of 'part of the choir ... with some side chapels'.[89] In this letter to the 'Catholic Monarchs', Pole stressed both the historic role of the Hospitallers, in the medieval crusading period, and in the current strategic situation in the Mediterranean. He described

[83]    Knighton, 'Westminster Abbey restored', pp. 94–95.

[84]    Tellechea, 'Inglaterra, Flandes', *CP*, p. 261.

[85]    Tellechea, 'Restauración', *CP*, p. 66; *PPP*, pp. 260, 287.

[86]    *CRP* 3 no. 1968 (further textual details).

[87]    Adrian Prockter and Robert Taylor, *The A to Z of Elizabethan London* (London: Henry Margary and Guildhall Library, 1979), pp. 48, 62.

[88]    *CRP* 3 p. 417, n. 13.

[89]    C.L. Kingsford, *A survey of London by John Stow reprinted from the text of 1603*, 2 vols (Oxford: Clarendon Press, 1908), 2, p. 85.

them, in the language of St Paul (1 Corinthians 9:24–27), as 'faithful athletes', striving in defence of the Cross of Christ, and using their naval resources and skills in war against the Muslim threat. By his own apostolic authority, delegated by Pope Paul IV, he now reconstituted the Clerkenwell priory, as the knights' English headquarters, along with nine of it former commanderies.[90] The new commanders (in Spanish *comendadores*) were to be named by Philip and Mary, who would add property to what had been confiscated under King Henry. On 1 December, Pole issued a legatine charter, this time to the brothers (knights) of St John of Jerusalem, stating that all the preceptories and commanderies named in the previous document had now been restored and distributed as detailed in the text.[91] In the following year, on 8 March 1558, Pole wrote to the grand master of the order, Jean de la Valette, acknowledging a letter that had been brought to him in London by Don Pedro de Mendoza, who was the knights' chancellor 'of the Castilian language (Spanish commanderies)'.[92] In this letter, Valette announced his appointment to the mastership, adding that he knew of the restoration of his order in England and fully approved of it. Another letter, sent by Pole to Valette on the same day, gave more details of progress. Three new knights had been created since the restoration of the Order in England, and were about to leave for Malta, with another possible candidate, no doubt so as to get nearer the action against the Turks. Also on 8 March, Pole sent a letter to King Philip, who had been corresponding with him about the order. The grand commander (*comendador mayor*) of León, Don Antonio de Toledo, would give him more details of Pole and Mary's activities in relation to the Knights of St John.[93] The next day, 9 March, Pole sent letters to the grand commander and to Philip, concerning the Hospitallers, and on 7 May he wrote again to the grand master in Malta.[94] In the early summer of 1558, it would have been hard, if not impossible, to imagine how drastically things in England would have changed by the end of the year, had the Catholic restoration continued.

Two of the reddest herrings in modern historians' assessments of Cardinal Pole's character and record are the notions, firstly, that he refused to receive Jesuits, members of St Ignatius of Loyola's Society (in Spanish *Compañía*) of Jesus, in England and, secondly, that this supposed refusal provides telling evidence of his 'backward-looking' approach to the revival of Catholicism in England. The case for these propositions was first made by Rex Pogson, particularly in an article derived from his thesis on Pole's second legation to England.[95] In the

---

[90]    *ODCC*, pp. 1584–1585.

[91]    *CRP* 3 no. 2131 (the original is in the National Library of Malta, Valletta, Arch. 17 (Zammit Gabaretta doc. 26)).

[92]    H.J.A. Sire, *The Knights of Malta* (New Haven: Yale University Press, 1994), p. 81.

[93]    *CSP Ven*, VI (iii), nos 1184, 1186, 1185, 1188, 1189; *CRP* 3 nos 2187, 2188, 2189.

[94]    *CRP* 3 nos 2193, 2194, 2225 (BL Add. 35830, fol. 26r).

[95]    Pogson, 'Cardinal Pole: papal legate', *passim*, and 'Pole and the priorities', pp. 3–20.

latter study of Pole's priorities as legate, between August 1553 and his death, Pogson takes the cardinal's supposed attitude to the Jesuits as an example of 'his legalistic approach and his rejection of the [unspecified] positive methods of the Counter Reformation'. He argues that, at the time of the reconciliation of England, on 30 November 1554, 'the Jesuits were proving expert in re-inspiring souls which [*sic*] had lost their obedience to Rome'. In particular, Pogson interprets a letter from Ignatius himself to Pole, dated in Rome on 1 May 1555, as 'suggesting that the time was right to develop a strong college of Jesuits to train men for Counter Reformation work under Mary'.[96] Pole's reply, a week later, though polite, gave 'no encouragement to Loyola's ideas'.[97] In addition, when reporting to Ignatius the work of the English synod of 1555–6, in a letter dated 15 December 1555, Pole, to Pogson's apparent surprise, makes no mention of the eleventh synodal decree, on the establishment of cathedral seminaries. Thus, as far as Pogson is concerned, Pole held back from consultation, let alone co-operation, with Ignatius. The historian asks: 'was this the result of indecision, incompetence, shortage of time or jealousy?'[98] There are, however, difficulties with this interpretation of Pole's correspondence. In his letter of 24 May 1555, Ignatius acknowledged one that he had received from Pole, which the cardinal had written in Brussels on 11 November 1554, just before his return to England. The Jesuit founder was delighted that the 'reduction' of Mary's kingdom to the Roman obedience was progressing so rapidly, and declared that his own 'tiny company' (*nostra minima compania* [the Jesuits]) was particularly happy about it all. This was the main message of the letter, and Ignatius continued with a report on his own progress. His German College in Rome was going well, and he mentions that he had one able English student in it, as well as one Irishman, and he suggested that other Englishmen might benefit from being there. He also stressed the good favour that his 'company' was enjoying with both Pope Julius and King Philip.[99] This could be regarded as a hint, but should probably be seen rather as another attempt to raise the status of the Jesuits, who had still not been fully recognised as a religious order. Pole's failure to take up Ignatius's suggestion about English students may well mean that he simply took his friend's letter in the spirit in which it was intended. As far as Pole's report on the English synod is concerned, the fact that it was dated as early as 15 December 1555 surely made it impossible to refer to specific decrees, whatever projects he and his advisers, including Carranza, may then have had in mind.

---

[96]   *ERP* 5 no. 59; McCoog, *Monumenta*, no. 73; *CRP* 3 no. 1036; Pogson, 'Pole and the priorities', p. 3.

[97]   *ERP* 5 no. 60; McCoog, *Monumenta*, no. 82; *CRP* 3 no. 1215; Pogson, 'Pole and the priorities', p. 4.

[98]   *ERP* 5 no. 61; *CRP* 3 no. 1462; Pogson, 'Pole and the priorities', p. 4.

[99]   *CRP* 3 no. 1036.

In any case, Pogson's interpretation of Pole's attitude to the future Society of Jesus was for many years accepted as orthodoxy, fitting, as it did, with A.G. Dickens' pronouncement that Pole 'failed to discover the Counter-Reformation'.[100] This view is accurately reflected in Loades' standard history of Mary's reign.[101] As far as the Jesuits were concerned, Duffy rightly pointed out that in personal terms at least, Ignatius was in fact 10 years older than Pole, and therefore was hardly the youthful future in comparison.[102] Since then, Mayer has supplied much detail of the international and local context of Jesuit development, and Pole's attitude towards it, but the question still needs further examination.[103] To begin with, as Mayer's work shows, Pole and Ignatius had known each other at least since 1540, when Pole was already a cardinal and, for the first time, legate to England, and the Jesuit 'company' received authorisation to minister publicly, from Pope Paul III.[104] At this time, with the English schism still recent, Ignatius and his early companions consulted Pole, then based in Viterbo, about a possible Jesuit mission to England, which never took place.[105] Thus it is hardly surprising that Ignatius should have been anxious to become involved with England after Mary came to the throne. On 27 October 1555, he sent a further letter to Pole, which was carried by Thomas Goldwell, who soon would be bishop of St Asaph. In it, he reminded Pole again of the existence of the Jesuit 'company', one of whose early and prominent members, Pedro de Ribadeneira, had intended to bring it in person, but did not do so in the event, remaining in Brussels at the court of King Philip.[106] Pole acknowledged this letter on 15 December 1555, saying, contrary to the impression given by Pogson and others, that he would be happy to welcome Ribadeneira in England.[107] Ignatius's response, however, from Rome on 19 February 1556, took a different line. While still reminding Pole of the 'company', he also expressed the wish that the cardinal should actually come to Rome in person, something that he had not done in the previous year, when Popes Marcellus and Paul were elected. This letter was brought to England

---

[100]  A.G. Dickens, *The English Reformation*, 2nd edition (London: Batsford, 1989), p. 311.

[101]  Loades, *Reign of Mary Tudor*, p. 372.

[102]  Duffy, *Stripping of the altars*, p. 520. It should nevertheless be noted that Ignatius did not set out on the spiritual path for which he is famous until he was in his thirties (John W. O'Malley, *The first Jesuits* (Cambridge, MA: Harvard University Press, 1993), pp. 23–28).

[103]  Mayer, 'A test of wills: Pole, Ignatius Loyola, and the Jesuits in England', in T[homas] M. McCoog, ed., *The reckoned expense: Edmund Campion and the early English Jesuits: essays in celebration of the first centenary of Campion Hall* (Woodbridge: Boydell and Brewer, 1996), pp. 21–37; *PPP*, pp. 252–253.

[104]  O'Malley, *First Jesuits*, p. 4 (*Regimini militantis Ecclesiae*, 27 September 1540).

[105]  McCoog, *Monumenta Angliae: English and Welsh Jesuits. Catalogues, Monumenta Historica Societatis Iesu*, 142–143 (Rome, 1992), I February 1541; *PPP*, p. 105.

[106]  *CRP* 3 no. 1413.

[107]  *ERP* 5 no. 61; *CRP* 3 no. 1462.

by Francisco Delgado, who played an unconstructive role in the rest of Pole's life, and also contained the news that Ignatius had ordered the Jesuits to pray specially for the English synod.[108] However, on 15 November 1556, Pole wrote to Diego Laínez, saying that he had heard of Ignatius's death, which had occurred on 31 July, adding that if Laínez were to succeed him as superior general, as he eventually did, this would be a sign of divine favour. Pole trusted that the Jesuits would continue their prayers for the state and future of the Christian religion in England.[109] This correspondence, though limited in quantity, certainly does not suggest that Pole lacked interest in, or enthusiasm for, the Society of Jesus and its work, but nonetheless, it does indicate tensions that may have made it appear that the arrival of working Jesuit missionaries was best delayed. These concerned both the Jesuits themselves and the Theatine order, to which Thomas Goldwell belonged.

The Theatines began life in 1524 as a group of secular priests under the leadership of Cardinal Tommaso del Vio (Cajetan), and the future Pope Paul IV, Gianpietro Carafa, who was then bishop of Chieti, or Theate, after which the order was named. This new congregation began as a direct response to Luther's critique of the Roman Church, attempting to reform abuses without schism, and it had many of the features of a traditional religious order. Like the Franciscans and others, its members were forbidden to own property, but Theatines were not allowed to beg. They led an austere life and dressed as secular clergy, apart from their distinctive white hose. By the mid-1530s, the Theatines had spread from Rome to other parts of Italy, though they had little influence elsewhere in Europe. Given these characteristics, it was perhaps inevitable that Carafa's congregation would engage in a certain rivalry with Ignatius's Jesuits, who shared its ideals and many of its ways of proceeding.[110] Relations between the two groups were not improved by a letter that Ignatius wrote to Bishop Carafa in 1536, while both were in Venice. In it the Spaniard, who was then very new to the life and organisation of religious orders, took it upon himself to give Carafa advice on how to direct his men. He pointedly claimed that his own 'company' avoided pomposity and showed love to all, and, in contrast, directly attacked Carafa for his lavish lifestyle, seeing the Theatines' failure to fulfil their ideal of poverty as an important reason for their lack of expansion.[111] Ignatius's Spanish nationality, much hated on patriotic grounds by the Neapolitan Carafa, made his advice fairly intolerable, and would have consequences that affected the Church in general and Pole in particular. Thomas Goldwell, who professed

---

[108]   *CRP* 3 no. 1500.

[109]   *ERP* 5 no. 62; *CRP* 3 no. 1773.

[110]   *ODCC*, pp. 1596–1597.

[111]   Joseph A. Munitiz and Philip Endean, ed. and trans., *Saint Ignatius of Loyola: personal writings* (London: Penguin Books, 1996), pp. 140–143, 385–386 (notes).

as a Theatine in Naples on 28 October 1550, and who like Pole had studied in Padua, became one of his closest associates in England under Mary, and his active presence there must have had some influence on the legate's response to Ignatius's hints and entreaties.[112]

Another important influence on Pole's attitude to the Jesuits, however many ideals and aspirations he may have shared with them, was the suspicion that they had aroused, particularly in Rome and in Spain, since the start of their work together in the 1540s. The first group of Ignatius's early companions to work in his native land, during the 1540s, had rapid and quite extraordinary success, in both reaching and influencing the leaders of society, including university scholars, churchmen, courtiers and royalty. However, they also excited considerable suspicion and even hatred, the latter tinged with not a little envy. Established religious orders were split in their attitude to the new group, many of whom were Spaniards like them. In particular, some Spanish Dominicans, including Bartolomé Carranza, admired the Jesuits' spiritual methods of prayer, based on their founder's *Spiritual Exercises*, and their concentration on Christian ministry in society rather than choir services (the Divine Office) in church, and were not deterred by their lack of a distinctive religious dress, or habit. Others of the Order of Preachers, notably Carranza's enemy Melchor Cano, held that Ignatius's followers were not in fact leading the authentic religious life, but instead were departing into a kind of mysticism which arrived at heresy by evading the hierarchical and sacramental system of the true Church. Worse, according to some of the Jesuits' opponents, notable among them Carranza's predecessor as Archbishop of Toledo, Juan Silíceo, they were verging on a Jewish or Muslim form of monotheism, and particularly the former, which was an extremely sensitive subject in Spain. Thus some of those sent to Spain by Ignatius in the 1540s and 1550s were regarded by their enemies there as crypto-Jews, or at least as followers of the 'illuminist' (*alumbrado*) groups which had been condemned by the Inquisition in the 1520s and 1530s. Such criticism and opposition helped to delay the recognition of the Society of Jesus as a full religious order, a privilege that would not be achieved until the final period of the Council of Trent, by which time Ignatius and Pole were dead.[113] With this background, Pole, who was himself suspected of not dissimilar views by Carafa's Roman Inquisition, might be pardoned for being cautious about Ignatius's men. Also, with Gianpietro Carafa as pope, things would only get harder, for him, for his king and queen, and for England. Much play has been made by English historians of the apparent condemnation of Pole, by Philip's councillor and confidant Gómez Suárez de Figueroa, count of Feria, after a meeting between

---

[112]   Mayer, 'Goldwell, Thomas', *ODNB*.

[113]   Feliciano Cereceda, SJ, *Diego Laínez en la Europa religiosa de su tiempo, 1512–1565*, 2 vols (Madrid: Ediciones Cultura Hispánica, 1945–6), 1, pp. 369–389, 396–404.

them in March 1558: 'The Cardinal is a good man, but very lukewarm, and I do not believe that the lukewarm go to Paradise, even if they are known to be moderate.'[114] It is less commonly noticed that the count was scarcely neutral since, along with others of Philip's senior courtiers, he had been a dedicated supporter of the Jesuits since the mid-1540s.[115] Even so, things might have been very different if Pole, not Carafa, had become pope in 1555.

When Pope Julius III died, on 23 March 1555, the 'cardinal of England' was in fact regarded as one of the strongest candidates to replace him, having narrowly missed election in the conclave of 1549–50. Yet he did not leave England and thus effectively, if not legally, disbarred himself from election. On 28 April 1555, he wrote to Queen Mary, from Richmond Palace, saying that he had just heard, the previous evening, of the election of his former collaborator Marcello Cervini, who unusually kept his baptismal name as Pope Marcellus II. He told Mary that this election gave him great consolation and joy, because of the new Pope's good nature and Christian doctrine.[116] Yet many thought that, rather than writing enthusiastically from England about the winner, Pole should have gone to Rome and become pope himself. Indeed, on 5 April, while the conclave was still in progress, the ill and exhausted Charles V had written from Brussels to Philip in London, telling him that he had consulted his sister Mary of Hungary, as well as other advisers, and they had drawn up a short-list for the papacy, which did not contain Cervini, but was headed by Pole. The conclaves of 1555 again demonstrated that such elections generally came down to a conflict between the French and Habsburg blocks, and Charles expressed doubts about Pole's governmental skills, though not about his goodness. Claiming to lack knowledge of the current situation in England, he told his son that he thought it should be left to Pole to decide whether he went to Rome or stayed at home. Three days later, Philip replied from Hampton Court, where he was attending his wife in what eventually proved to be her first false pregnancy, saying that Pole had told him that, if he did go to Rome, he would not be a candidate but simply a voter. If the majority of the cardinals wanted him, he could be elected in absentia, but he believed that his duty lay in England.[117]

Marcellus II had no time to influence Pole's situation in England before he died, on 1 May 1555, after a reign of only three weeks. The second conclave of that year was managed with great success, and again in the self-denying absence of the 'cardinal of England', by Gianpietro Carafa, who, as dean of the college of cardinals, was himself elected, as Pope Paul IV. A keen reformer since the

---

[114]   *CSP Span* XIII pp. 366, 370.

[115]   Cereceda, *Diego Laínez*, p. 373.

[116]   Lutz p. 256 n. 2; *CSP Ven*, VI (i), no. 65; *CSP Foreign*, no. 348; *CRP* 3 no. 1194; *CSP Ven*, VI (i), no. 65.

[117]   Manuel Fernández Álvarez, *Corpus documental de Carlos V*, 5 vols (Salamanca: Ediciones Universidad de Salamanca, 1970), 1, pp. 38–39.

beginning of the sixteenth century, Pope Carafa had also been an associate, and even a friend, of Pole, back in the reign of Paul III, though in the 1540s they had fallen out over theological matters, and in particular the respective roles of faith and actions ('works') in the salvation of Christians. Perhaps significantly, as well as possessing a Neapolitan hatred of all things Spanish, and a corresponding love of France, Carafa had had, in 1514, an unfortunate experience of England. He arrived as Pope Leo X's envoy in a vain attempt to break up the league of states then opposed to France, and was both snubbed by Henry VIII and fobbed off by Cardinal Wolsey and Bishop Richard Fox of Winchester.[118] That he had this unhappy memory of England may not have made his relations with Pole and the English Church any easier, but his love of France and hatred of the Habsburgs were undoubtedly the main causes of the difficulties that soon followed his election, at the age of 79.

The Imperial and Spanish cardinals and political agents in Rome, who were in practice allowed to associate fairly freely during the supposedly closed conclave, made every effort to prevent Carafa's victory, their three choices being, in order, Pole (despite his absence), Rodolfo da Carpi and Giovanni Morone.[119] An anonymous account of the 'conclave of Paul IV', written a few years later for King Philip and copied by his agent in Rome in the 1560s, Juan de Versoza, asserts that Carafa's election was largely a matter of accident and 'Fortuna'. As had been the case with the election of Marcellus, the French and Imperial groupings went to war, for and against the Cardinal of Naples. Pole was not seriously considered as a candidate because of a general recognition that he was fully occupied with affairs in England. Even so, Carafa's election was not quickly or easily achieved, taking the same length of time as Marcellus's reign.[120] In an alternative account of events, two other Italian aides at conclaves (*conclavistas*), Felice Gualtaro and Cipriano Saracinello, used Paul IV's election as a prime example of the characteristics of such processes. For them, Carafa's success should be studied by future *conclavistas* as a lesson in how one strong-minded individual could dominate proceedings and achieve the result that he desired. In particular, during both the 1555 conclaves, Carafa succeeded, as dean, in having the process of acclamation ('adoration') without a vote, which had so nearly brought Pole election back in 1549, ruled out completely. These hard-bitten curialists saw Pole's own high-mindedness as the best way to lose a papal election.[121]

Pope Paul's new reign soon brought troubles for Pole and the English Church, as well as for Habsburg, and hence English, political interests. On 24

---

[118]   *LP* I no. 2610; Scarisbrick, *Henry VIII*, pp. 51, 53.

[119]   AGS Estado 882 no. 151.

[120]   AGS Estado, Libros de Versoza, 2, fols 166r–171v.

[121]   AGS Estado, Libros de Versoza, 2, fols 14r–23r.

May 1555, just a day after his victory, Paul IV wrote to Charles V, then in poor health in Brussels, indicating that he might remove Pole's second legation, which was to work for peace between France and the Habsburgs. This had originally been delegated to him by Paul III, in 1537, as a cover for attempts to restore Roman authority in Henry VIII's kingdom, but between 1555 and 1558 it assumed ever greater importance. Even so, at this stage, the Pope assured Philip and Mary that he had no intention of reducing Pole's status in England, but this proved to be only a temporary respite.[122] Despite their earlier conflicts, over supposed heresy and papal elections, initial relations between Pole and the new pope gave every appearance of being friendly and constructive. In his posting on 24 May, Carafa sent letters to the English cardinal, telling him that he wished he had him in Rome as an adviser.[123] In his reply, dated 6 June, Pole said that he had been deeply affected by receiving news of Paul's election on the feast of Pentecost (2 June), seeing the news as a gift of the Holy Spirit. Evidently he expected the new reign to initiate further reform of the Church, on the lines that he and Carafa had pursued since the 1530s. He assured Paul that he would do everything he could to assist, adding that Philip and Mary's ambassadors, who had been dispatched after the reconciliation, originally to Pope Marcellus, and who were now nearing Rome, would give a full report of the English situation.[124] Pole's subsequent dispatch to Paul of his fellow Theatine, Thomas Goldwell, now bishop-designate of St Asaph, may be regarded as a gesture of peace and conciliation.[125] On 30 June, Paul sent another conciliatory letter to Pole, in which, contrary to what he had written to Charles V in the previous month, he professed that the best hopes for peace in Europe lay with Philip, Mary and Pole himself.[126] Instead, there would soon be further military conflict in Europe, involving France, the Habsburgs and the Papacy, and eventually dragging in England too.

The events that blighted Pole's last years of life began, if anyone had had the perceptiveness to realise it at the time, even before his return to England. They concerned the kingdom of Naples, Carafa's homeland. During the marriage of Philip and Mary, in Winchester Cathedral on 25 July 1554, the Spanish regent of Naples, Juan de Figueroa, read out Charles V's grant to his son of the title to that kingdom, which covered Sicily and much of southern Italy. Philip thus became a royal equal of his new wife, but his new territory was a papal fief, which meant that he should have been invested with it by not by his father but by Pope Julius III. This error, or omission, resurrected an ancient dispute which

[122] Tellechea, *Papado*, 1, pp. 43–45 (nos XXI, XXII).

[123] Lutz no. 99; *CRP* 3 no. 1231.

[124] *ERP* 5 no. 5; Lutz no. 100; *CSP Ven*, VI (i), no. 119; *CRP* 3 no. 1237.

[125] *CRP* 3 no. 1250 (24 June 1555; *ERP* 5 no. 7; Lutz p. 269n; *CSP Ven*, VI (i), no. 139).

[126] Lutz p. 273; *CRP* 3 no. 1260.

involved France, as well as Spain and the papacy.[127] It seems that it was only the arrival on the papal throne of a Neapolitan aristocrat, in May 1555, that jogged the memory of someone in the Habsburg bureaucracy. Even then, action was delayed, and it was not until 1 October of that year, with Philip back in Brussels, that a document was drafted in the Imperial chancery, in which he formally accepted investiture as King of Naples from Pope Julius, who by that time had died.[128] Ever helpful to the project of Mary and Philip in restoring England to the community of Catholic nations, Julius had in fact granted the king the crown of Naples as early as 23 October 1554, yet it would not be until more than a year later that Philip at last swore fealty to the pope, as his feudal suzerain.[129] Paul IV would not be so obliging. He was fully aware that, by signing the Brussels document on 1 October, Philip had made himself a papal vassal, thus giving the Holy Father the legal right to intervene in Habsburg affairs in one of the most strategically sensitive areas of Europe. Pope Carafa would not forget that, by the terms of the agreement made between his predecessor, Pope Julius II, and Philip's grandfather, Ferdinand of Spain, successive Spanish rulers were obliged to do personal homage to the pope.[130] Almost at once, Carafa announced that he intended to sue both Philip and his father for failing to fulfil this obligation.[131]

The fact that Pope Paul had retained Pole's services as legate *a latere* for securing peace between France and the Habsburgs, despite threats to withdraw that power from him, meant that the cardinal of England was bound to become involved in the conflict that ensued. On the same day as Paul's election, a peace conference, between the French and the Habsburgs had opened on English territory at La Marque, between Calais and Gravelines. At last it had appeared that Pole's peace legation was coming to fruition. The position of the English as neutral parties and mediators was not unreasonably questioned by the French, but Pole, who had not yet become archbishop, was able to chair the conference in his capacity as papal legate. The discussions opened on Ascension Day, and Pole and the English delegates, who purportedly represented only Mary and not Philip, sat at the 'head' of a large, round table, with the Habsburg team on their right and the French on their left. Henry II of France was represented by two great rivals, the cardinal of Lorraine, Charles de Guise, and the constable of France, Anne de Montmorency, while the leading Habsburg delegates were the duke of Medinaceli, Juan de la Cerda, and the cardinal bishop of Arras, Antoine Perrenot de Granvelle. Pole worked hard, spending days two to four of the conference in separate, private negotiations with the French and the Imperialists.

---

[127]    John Edwards, *Ferdinand and Isabella* (Harlow: Pearson Longman, 2005), pp. 109–114.

[128]    Tellechea, *Papado*, 1, pp. 52–53 (no. XXVIII). On Mary's pregnancy see Edwards, *Mary I*, pp. 266–268.

[129]    Tellechea, *Papado*, 1, p. 25 (no. X).

[130]    Tellechea, *Papado*, 1, p. ix.

[131]    Tellechea, *Papado*, 1, p. xii.

He was accompanied in these meetings by the English team, which was led by the lord chancellor, Bishop Gardiner. Much time was spent on the problems between these two major powers in the Mediterranean, especially in Italy, but there was no will for a solution, and on 9 June the French left, accusing Pole and the English team of bias in favour of the Habsburgs.[132] The French stance seemed reasonable enough at the time, given that Henry II and his representatives still believed that Mary was pregnant, and would soon produce an heir who might also secure the future of Charles and Philip's line. In any case, Pole would never have another opportunity to broker affairs on an international stage.

At first, the failure of the La Marque peace conference seemed to have no unfortunate consequences for Philip, Mary or Pole. On 30 June, Paul IV wrote to the king and queen, with an account of the long-awaited arrival of their ambassadors in Rome. Four popes had died since such a formal event had last occurred, and the primary purpose of the ambassadors, led by Bishop Thomas Thirlby of Ely and Sir Edward Carne, was to swear their kingdom's obedience to the Holy See. In an eloquent speech, Bishop Thirlby declared that the reconciliation sealed on 30 November 1554 was genuine, and Carne took charge of having the documents that had been issued by Julius III updated and re-issued in Pope Paul's name. At this stage, it still appeared that the pope was very enthusiastic about what was happening in Mary's kingdom.[133] Within a few weeks, however, Pope Carafa had had one of his characteristically violent changes of mood and policy. On 12 August, he sent Pole a letter in which he virtually, though not precisely, ordered him to abandon his legation in England and return to Rome. According to the Venetian ambassador in London, Giovanni Michiel, who provides the only surviving evidence of this communication, Pole obediently, and equally characteristically, placed himself in the Holy Father's hands.[134] This exchange would soon be superseded by a further outbreak of war in Europe.

Philip abandoned his still childless wife at the end of August 1555, and travelled to Brussels, where his father was beginning to abdicate from his many crowns and titles, something unprecedented among medieval and early modern rulers. The resulting uncertainty about the future of the Habsburg territories gave cheer both to the French and to Pope Paul, who was happy to tell anyone who would listen that the emperor was both a physical and an emotional cripple. It is clear that Pole and Queen Mary were equally anxious to keep England out of any conflict that might arise from the failure of the La Marque peace conference, and initially Paul IV confined himself to ecclesiastical rather than

---

[132]   *CRP* 3 nos 1242 (*ERP* 5 no. 6; *CSP Ven*, VI (i), no. 136), 1251 (Pole to Pope Paul IV, 9 June and c. 24 June 1555; Lutz no. *9a; *CSP Ven*, VI (i), no. 140).

[133]   Tellechea, *Papado*, 1, pp. xxvii, 46–49 (no. XXIV).

[134]   *CSP Ven*, VI (i), no. 182; *CRP* 3 no. 1339.

military measures. He accused Charles and Philip of seeking 'monarchy', which in sixteenth-century Europe meant the hegemony of a single ruler over the whole continent. Not only this, he accused the Emperor of being an enemy of Christ, and even of actively encouraging heresy in his dominions, and particularly in Germany. Then he announced that he was going to excommunicate both father and son, as rebels, because of their conduct in relation to the kingdom of Naples. In what would prove to be a precedent for action by his successors against the England of Elizabeth, he made himself the 'protector' of all the Habsburgs' subjects. Although these actions did not apply directly to England, they were bound to have repercussions, at least for the political class, and this became obvious when, soon afterwards, war threatened Italy yet again. In October 1555, talks between the papacy and the French led to the formation of a league, aimed at expelling the Habsburgs from Italy. If this happened, Siena and some Milanese territory would go to the See of Rome, while the historic, and strategically vital, duchy of Milan as well as the kingdom of Naples would be granted by the pope to Henry II of France, who would in turn give them to his sons, Francis and Charles, respectively. As its feudal overlord, Pope Paul would authorise a French invasion of Naples, and the island of Sicily would be partitioned between France and the papacy. It is impossible to understand what happened to England between 1555 and the deaths of Pole and Mary without giving due attention to these continental developments. Paul's volatile manoeuvres must have weighed heavily on the cardinal, as well as the king and queen, since his hopes for the English Church depended very largely on his relations with the pope whom he represented. Philip tried to frustrate Pope Paul's scheme by offering further peace negotiations with France, but he met with refusal, and the opportunity for Pole to act once again as peace legate was taken away.[135]

Paul now revealed himself unambiguously as a violent enemy of the Habsburg dynasty. On 8 October 1555, he harangued the Imperial, English and Venetian ambassadors in Rome on the prerogatives of the Roman See that he was determined to defend. He reminded them of the horrors of the 1527 Sack, for which he held the Emperor Charles personally responsible. A week later, he publicly expressed his view that all Spaniards were *marranos*, in other words false Jewish converts to Christianity and announced that he intended to punish the whole nation. Although this did not in fact happen to the Spaniards, he did act against Jews within the papal territories, ordering them to wear yellow badges and establishing the first ever ghetto in Rome itself.[136] On 27 July, Carlo Carafa, the pope's nephew and now secretary of state, had written to Pole to

---

[135] M.J. Rodríguez-Salgado, *The changing face of empire: Charles V, Philip II and Habsburg authority, 1551–1559* (Cambridge: Cambridge University Press, 1988), pp. 147–148.

[136] *PPP*, pp. 303–304; Kenneth Stow, *The Jews in Rome*, 2 vols (Leiden: Brill, 1997), 1, pp. 742–743.

report gleefully that these moves were the first, easy measures in the planned reform of the Church.[137] At least the accusation of crypto-Judaism was unlikely to be made against England, even by Pope Paul, since the kingdom's Jews had been expelled by Edward I, back in 1290. But, in any case, during the autumn and winter of 1555–6, papal pressure grew on the Habsburgs, and by proxy on Mary and Pole. In Brussels on 25 October, Charles handed over to his son, with great ceremony, his rule over the Habsburg Netherlandish territories. Although this move no doubt infuriated the Pope, he initially appeared to accept it, even writing to Philip on 28 November, to urge him to renew his efforts for European peace.[138] On the same day, Paul wrote to Queen Mary, again praising her and Pole for their efforts to restore the Catholic faith in England, but asking her to do more to stop her husband and father-in-law making war in Europe. Of course he made no mention of his own military plans, in alliance with France.[139] Nevertheless, as 1555 ended, with Pope Paul taking the necessary steps for Pole to replace Cranmer as archbishop, there seemed to be good relations between Rome and the English Church. During the transfer of Canterbury, Pole did however express anxiety to Pope Paul about the warmongering climate that seemed to prevail in Europe. As legate, he sent one of his staff, Vincenzo Parpuglia, to Brussels to work for peace.[140] The Pope's response initially seemed to be positive. Just before Christmas, he reassured Pole that he was still his legate in England, he praised the restored and newly-created Catholic hierarchy there, and showed his approval of the initial work of the English synod, promising to do everything he could to help restore the 'primitive', truly apostolic, Church in Mary's realm.[141] Events were soon to reveal a very different picture.

As the year 1556 began, King Philip once again followed the path of negotiation. In February, he offered a truce with France, to be negotiated by Pole, as legate for peace, with his Spanish ambassadors in Rome, French representatives, and the mediation of the pope. This plan came to naught, but nonetheless a truce was negotiated by the Emperor Charles and Henry II at Vaucelles, with Mary's English representatives, led by Pole, acting as go-betweens. It seems clear that Philip personally had scruples about making war in Italy, particularly against the pope, and as both the Habsburgs and the French were short of money, the argument for peace won the day. Even so, the Vaucelles truce failed to solve any of the long-term problems between the main powers of Europe. Firstly, it infuriated Pope Paul, who, on hearing of it, in Rome on 14 February, flew into one of his customary rages. He removed Pole's peace legation, giving it instead

---

[137] *CRP* 3 no. 1320.

[138] Tellechea, *Papado*, 1, pp. 56–57 (no. XXXI); *CRP* 3 no. 1442.

[139] Tellechea, *Papado*, 1, pp. 58–59 (no. XXXII).

[140] *CRP* 3 nos 1463 (Pole to Cardinal Carlo Carafa, 15 December 1555; Lutz p. 294 n. 2; *CSP Ven*, VI (i), no. 313), 1469 (Pole to Pope Paul IV, 20 December 1555).

[141] *CRP* 3 no. 1472 (further textual details).

to Cardinal Scipio Rebiba, who was an ally of the Pope's nephew, Carlo, and equally committed to the French cause.[142] Yet still, on 8 June 1556, Paul wrote to King Philip, praising him for his efforts in the cause of peace.[143] Pole, on the other hand, was fully aware of his own isolation, as an archbishop and legate who had been effectively abandoned by the pope, just as his queen had been left alone and childless by her husband, on the verge of a new European war. In a letter dated 14 July, the English cardinal confided in Giovanni Morone, who was himself now being accused of heresy by Paul IV. In this sad and perceptive analysis, Pole told Morone that, while he was still working for peace, despite the removal of his legation for that purpose, he and the queen greatly feared that she and her kingdom would be caught in the middle of a conflict between her husband and the Pope. He wanted Philip to settle as soon as possible his quarrels with the papacy.[144] His letter crossed with one from Morone to him, expressing the view that war was the most likely outcome.[145] In September, Morone was proved right. Cardinal Carlo Carafa had gone to France to goad Henry II into action, while Philip's senior commander, the duke of Alba, set out with an army from Naples, on 1 September, to invade the papal states. This move not only produced panic in Rome but also led King Henry to send troops both into Italy and to France's northern frontier with the Habsburg Netherlands. The fighting in Italy continued into November, and although Rome escaped another sack, largely thanks to Alba's unwillingness to repeat the events of 1527, Pole and his queen found themselves in the impossible position that they had feared.[146]

Still active in the Roman Curia, despite the suspicion he was under, Morone wrote to Pole, on 28 November 1556, to tell him that the pope now wanted him to abandon Mary and come to Rome. Under threat from the Spanish army, Paul had been forced to make a truce with the Habsburg enemy, and this seems to have sent him into a depression. According to Morone, he blamed King Philip for everything that had happened, and would not listen to Pole's appeals for peace, or his defence of Queen Mary as a loyal Catholic monarch. Indeed, the pope was now so angry that the cardinals thought it best to keep English correspondence from him. He was proclaiming to all and sundry that he would rather be martyred than have peace without honour, and that, if the Vicar of Christ was not to be respected, it would be impossible for the Church to deal with the Protestants or with the Turks.[147] Pole was not, however, willing to abandon his duty, either to care for the queen in her husband's absence or to ensure the

---

[142]   Tellechea, *Papado*, 1, pp. xxx, 162–163 (no. XXXV); *PPP*, p. 306.

[143]   Tellechea, *Papado*, 1, pp. 65–66 (no. XXXVI).

[144]   Lutz p. 326n; *CRP* 3 no. 1615.

[145]   *CRP* 3 no. 1624 (18 July 1556; *ERP* 5 no. 51).

[146]   On the campaigns in Italy in 1556, see Frederic J. Baumgartner, *Henry II, King of France, 1547–1559* (Durham, NC and London: Duke University Press, 1988), pp. 179–184.

[147]   *CRP* 3 no. 1778; Rodríguez-Salgado, *Changing face*, pp. 157–158.

survival of the restored Catholic Church in England. Thus despite his friend Morone's warnings, he sent his servant Henry Pyning to Rome to try to arrange appointments to the episcopal sees that were then vacant.[148] As 1556 ended, both Mary and her archbishop were left in isolation in London, condemned by the Pope for their supposed support of the queen's husband, whose return she longed for vainly.[149]

The New Year saw the arrival of the French army in Italy and the official breakdown of the truce of Vaucelles. Worse still, from England's point of view, there was a new threat of military action on the border between France and the Netherlands, which also posed a real threat to Calais and its Pale, and they would only remain in English hands, as a last enclave in France, for another year.[150] In these new circumstances, and after an abortive, and possibly French-sponsored, attempt to seize the English throne by Thomas Stafford, grandson of the late duke of Buckingham, who landed at Scarborough on 28 April 1557, war was declared on France, by Mary and Philip, who was also present once again in England, on 7 June. Thus everything that Mary and Pole had been working for, during the previous two years, crumbled to ruins. Neither queen nor archbishop would see peace for the rest of their earthly lives. Initially, fighting continued in Italy but France's northern frontier was not affected. Then, fortified by a rare good harvest and a resulting increase in royal revenue, Henry II decided to send an army north against Philip. At the end of July 1557, the Habsburgs reacted to the French moves by besieging Saint-Quentin, and achieving a major victory over Henry's garrison and reinforcements on St Lawrence's Day, 10 August. Although Philip himself took no direct part in the action, he was so affected by the victory, which involved the capture of numerous French nobles, that when he later built his mountain palace-monastery of El Escorial, north-west of Madrid, he dedicated it to that third-century deacon and martyr.[151] The effect on the French of their defeat at Saint-Quentin, followed some days later by the fall of the town itself, as well as the excitement behind the lines in Brussels, are vividly conveyed by Friar Bartolomé Carranza, in a letter to Juan de Villagarcía in Oxford. On 28 August Carranza wrote to his Dominican brother:

> You will already have heard of the victory that our men gained on St Lawrence's Day against the French, in which the leading men of the kingdom of France were captured. Each day they bring French prisoners here. On Monday 23rd they took the Constable [Anne de Montmorency] and a son of his to Ghent, and they are

[148]   *CRP* 3 no. 1783 (Pole to Pope Paul IV, 6 December 1556; *ERP* 5 no. 11; *CSP Ven*, VI (ii), no. 753).

[149]   *CRP* 3 nos 1789, 1794 (*CSP Ven*, VI (ii), no. 772), 1797.

[150]   Rodríguez-Salgado, *Changing face*, pp. 157–159; Baumgartner, *Henry II*, pp. 185–192.

[151]   Baumgartner, *Henry II*, pp. 192–196; Rodríguez-Salgado, *Changing face*, p. 178.

distributing dukes and counts of France among all these [Habsburg] castles. Yesterday, the count of Hornes, who had captured him, sent the duke of Longueville to his house, and the day before yesterday they brought three hundred French soldiers, and cartloads of prisoners are passing all the time.[152]

English involvement in the conflict on the Franco-Netherlandish border would only create further problems for Mary and for Pole.

While war continued between France and the Habsburgs, Pole maintained his struggle to placate the pope, and thus save his work in England. In April 1557, for instance, he wrote to ask Paul to give some consolation to English Catholics, and recognise Philip's part in achieving the restoration of the traditional faith.[153] Carafa's response was certainly not what Pole wanted or expected. On 10 April, he deprived Pole of his legation to England and appeared, although the relevant document is unclear, to remove even his residual legatine powers as Archbishop of Canterbury, which automatically came with that office (as *legatus natus*). On 25 May, Pole responded indignantly. Both he and the queen were horrified at Paul's action, though they assured him of their continued loyalty. Even so, the archbishop undertook to give his full support to any replacement as legate, adding that one would certainly be needed.[154] On the same day, Pole wrote a longer letter to Cardinal Carlo Carafa, based on the reports that he had received from Henry Pyning in Rome. In it, he clearly expressed his upset at the pope's action, and detailed all the efforts that he and King Philip had made, in the preceding months, to seek peace in Europe. As he had done before, he urged that Paul should allow Mary to mediate between him and her husband. As for the English legation, he stated that Paul could only have behaved as he did if he was badly informed about the current situation in the kingdom.[155] In a reply, dated 20 June, Pope Paul recognised that Pole had taken very badly the revocation of his legation but described himself as a true father to Queen Mary, though he rather spoiled the effect by comparing England to the 'prodigal son' of the New Testament parable (Luke 15:11–32). Pole was summoned back to Rome, and in the meantime told that that he would be replaced as legate by the elderly Franciscan, William Peto, who was then a member of the Greenwich Observant community. Presumably, Paul's beloved spiritual daughter was to be abandoned to her own devices, without her husband, her 'good cousin' – or a child.[156]

[152] Tellechea, 'Inglaterra, Flandes', *CP*, p. 263.
[153] *CRP* 3 no. 1939 (undated; *ERP* 5 no. 29).
[154] *ERP* 5 no. 14; *CSP Ven*, VI (ii), no. 899; *CRP* 3 no. 2010; *PPP*, p. 309.
[155] *CSP Ven*, VI (ii), no. 900; *CRP* 3 no. 2111.
[156] *CSP Ven*, VI (ii), no. 1024; *CRP* 3 no. 2048.

Whatever the Holy Father may have thought, all the available evidence suggests that Pole generally behaved correctly, during the political and military crisis of 1557. When Philip had returned to England, in March, to seek military aid, the cardinal had stuck to protocol and refused to meet him publicly, though admittedly the two did talk in private, as Pole later claimed, about a possible peace plan.[157] A further crisis loomed, however, when Cardinal Giovanni Morone was arrested by the Roman Inquisition on 31 May on charges of 'Lutheranism'. Not only did this arrest threaten Pole's intimate circle, but it also removed his and King Philip's most useful adviser in the Roman Curia. Ever since the Papal Inquisition had been established in the thirteenth century, heretical leaders and their groups of followers had been targeted together, so Pole's own recall to Rome now took on an even more sinister aspect. Mary's response to these developments was vehement and perhaps surprising. From then on, she behaved as Queen of England first, and a Catholic ruler second. When Paul's nuncio approached the Channel, in early July, bearing letters for both Mary and Pole, he was at first refused entry to the English territory around Calais. On 6 July, Mary travelled to Dover to say farewell, for the last time as it turned out, to her husband, and after that the nuncio was allowed into England. Nevertheless, Mary still refused initially to allow Pole to have the pope's letters. Despite this, he was determined to see them and she eventually gave way, so that he could see written proof that his legation was indeed to be taken from him. Although he felt bound to obey the pope, he initially wanted to go to Rome to justify himself, but then Sir Edward Carne, Mary and Philip's English resident ambassador there, reported that Pole was being actively investigated by the Inquisition, as part of the process against Morone. When she heard this, Mary ordered Pole, as her subject, not to leave England. On 26 July she sent a strongly-worded protest to Pope Paul, saying, not unreasonably, that Pole was vital to the restoration and continuance of Catholic religion in her kingdom.[158] Peto pleaded his age as grounds for his not becoming papal legate, while the queen told Carne, in words that would probably have delighted her father and Archbishop Cranmer, that he must inform the pope that any trial of Pole for heresy would have to take place within the boundaries of her kingdom.[159]

It may well be that it was in response to the pope's actions, in the summer of 1557, that Pole composed what has become known as his 'Apologia', to justify his beliefs and practice as a Catholic Christian (Appendix 3).[160] With vehemence and some bitterness, this text, which Pope Paul probably never

---

[157] *CSP Ven*, VI (ii), pp. 858, 862.
[158] *CSP Ven*, VI (ii), pp. 1161, 1166, 1240.
[159] *CSP Ven*, VI (ii), p. 1248.
[160] Inner Temple Petyt MSS vol. XLVI, fols 391–426, edited in Tellechea, 'Pole y Paulo IV', *CP*, pp. 201–241, and summarised in *CRP* 3 no. 2076.

saw, took him back to the 1530s, when the two men had worked together for the reform of the Catholic Church, 'in head and members'. What flies off the page is Pole's sense of betrayal, as an aristocrat and as a patriotic Englishmen. He claimed that no cardinal had ever been treated so badly by a pope, and he protested at the injustice of being condemned unheard. He set out, in no uncertain terms, the awful consequences that would follow if he was forced to leave England, and heaped on Paul the resentment felt by a hurt and embittered ex-friend. He accused him of following, not divine precept but the evil example of secular rulers, conduct that was condemned by Jesus in the Gospels. The Pope was wrong to condemn Morone, and, less alluringly, Pole also tried to detach himself from the now dangerous views of his old Viterbo circle. As far as the legation in England was concerned, he had undertaken it out of duty to God and the Church, and was indignant at being falsely accused. He went on to detail recent events in England, including Mary's hiding of the papal letters, and his own efforts to obtain and read them. This text clearly indicates that Pole was kept in England not just by the queen herself but also by her councillors, though he worked hard, in July 1557, to abide by canon law and obey the pope. Eventually, at the end of that month, he sent his datary, Ormanetto, to Rome to secure his vindication against charges of heresy. He attacked Paul's conduct of the process against Morone and concluded with a graphic description of the currently sad state of Queen Mary, who had once again been entrusted to his care by King Philip. She had relied on Philip and the pope for support, but was now abandoned and desperate.[161]

Despite this breakdown between Pole and Pope Paul, from June 1557 until the cardinal's death, the programme of Catholic restoration, including the burning of convicted heretics, continued unabated. In addition, despite the revocation of Pole's legatine powers, and the refusal of Friar Peto to take them up, Pole continued to act as both legate and archbishop. Appeals from lower ecclesiastical courts still reached his legatine court and his archiepiscopal Court of Arches, thus ironically bringing back, in a new form, the 'Catholic' schismatical Church of Henry VIII.[162] It appeared that, for Pole as for Cranmer, service to the Crown and the Church in England ultimately trumped loyalty to the pope, though in Pole's case without any abandonment of Catholic belief and practice. There was paradox on the Roman side as well, since Paul IV continued to appoint bishops who had been recommended by Pole, including the preacher

---

[161]   Tellechea, 'Pole y Paulo IV', *CP*, pp. 201–209, 213, 219–223, 225–241.

[162]   Mayer, 'The success of Cardinal Pole's final legation', in *CMT*, pp. 149–175, at p. 153 (table 5.3).

and polemicist Thomas Watson, to Lincoln, and David Pole to Peterborough.[163] Almost to the end of both their lives, Mary fought for Pole's rehabilitation in Rome.

---

[163] Loades, 'The Marian episcopate', in *CMT*, p. 47.

# Chapter 8

# Dying

On 30 November 1557, the English Church commemorated not only the feast of St Andrew the Apostle but also the third anniversary of the reconciliation of England to Rome. In the capital, the official ceremonies of the day started with a procession, High Mass and a sermon, preached by Bishop Edmund Bonner, at St Paul's cathedral, with a priest from every parish in London diocese in attendance. There were equivalent liturgical celebrations in Westminster, and in the evening, Cardinal Pole preached in the Chapel Royal at Whitehall Palace, before the Queen, the court, judges and the London corporation.

Much has been made by some historians of Pole's supposed unwillingness to preach, despite all evidence to the contrary, and his views on the use and value of sermons need to be placed in their proper context.[1] Thomas Mayer rightly stresses that, for many years before his return to England, Pole had affirmed the vital importance of preaching, in communicating the Gospel to the people and persuading them to believe and practise it.[2] Much of the controversy hangs on the interpretation of a letter that Pole wrote, on 20 June 1558, to his old friend Bartolomé Carranza, who was then in Brussels awaiting his return to Spain as the new archbishop of Toledo.[3] Initially, Pogson based his view, that Pole was against frequent preaching of the Catholic faith in England, on his translation of a crucial passage in the letter, which in general was an answer to a critique, by one primate of another, of Pole's failure to reside in his Canterbury diocese, or even in one of the 13 London parishes that were subject to his jurisdiction as 'Canterbury peculiars'. The sentence in question reads, according to Pogson: 'I think that it is better to check the preaching of the Word rather than proclaim it, unless the discipline of the Church has been fully restored.'[4] This certainly seems to imply that the re-establishment and enforcement of Catholic discipline should come before preaching, but Pogson's reading is problematic. In the version

---

[1]   Pogson, 'Pole and the priorities', pp. 17–19; Loades, 'Reign of Mary Tudor', pp. 272, 276, 293; Haigh, *English Reformations*, p. 224; MacCulloch, *The later Reformation in England, 1547–1603* (Basingstoke: Palgrave Macmillan, 2000), p. 20.

[2]   Mayer, *PPP*, pp. 246–251; Duffy, *Fires of faith*, pp. 50–55, including summaries of three of Pole's English sermon texts: BAV Vat. lat. 5968, fols 277r–303v, 419r–441r, 446r–482v.

[3]   The full text is transcribed in Tellechea, 'Pole, Carranza y Fresneda. Cara y cruz de una amistad y de una enemistad', in *CP*, pp. 121–197, at pp. 191–196. The letter is summarised in *CRP* 3 no. 3225.

[4]   Tellechea, 'Pole, Carranza y Fresneda', *CP*, p. 193; Pogson, 'Pole and the priorities', p. 16.

included in his biography of Pole, Mayer has his subject saying, in this crucial passage, that his reservations about frequent sermons arose from his concern that, particularly in the context of London, the pulpit might be abused by 'carnal men'. 'More preaching was the last thing London needed, but Pole stressed [the capital's] peculiarity [in this respect].'[5] While agreeing with this revision, Duffy suggests that Carranza may have just wanted to get Pole out of London, and away from his governmental responsibilities, and Dermot Fenlon takes a similar view.[6] A closer translation of the vital passage of Pole's letter might read:

> Truly I, who daily acquire greater experience of the infected and sick state of this body, find that, where there is greater abundance of the Word, there men profit less; which we see happening nowhere more than in London. And neither do I deny that the preaching of the Word of God is necessary, but [it should] only [happen] if ecclesiastical discipline is either there beforehand or established at the same time. I say that [otherwise] the Word departs, rather than advances, because carnal men receive it to the empty delight of their senses and not as the saving discipline and food of their souls.[7]

Whether or not he was unfairly critical of Pole's attitude to preaching in 1558, Bartolomé Carranza undoubtedly had a strong record in that particular ministry, as befitted a member of St Dominic's Order of Preachers, for whom this has always been a special charism. In his *Speculum pastorum* ('Mirror of Pastors'), which he had completed in connection with the second phase of the Council of Trent (1551–2), Carranza had listed preaching as the pastor's second duty in priority, after praying for God's people, and before the celebration of the Eucharist. Although the decrees of Trent would not be promulgated for some years, Carranza and Pole brought to England, in 1554, its draft instruction, already approved by the Tridentine fathers, that bishops, or if necessary qualified deputies, should always preach on Sundays and major festivals, this provision being duly included in the decrees of the English synod. In addition, according to the Tridentine draft, Scripture and the Divine law were to be proclaimed to the people on days of fasting in Advent and three times a week in Lent. According to Carranza, bishops who failed in this respect were 'dumb dogs' (Isaiah 56:10: 'His watchmen ... are all dumb dogs, they cannot bark'). Carranza quoted a relevant canon of the eleventh Council of Toledo (675), which stipulated that a bishop had to preach, if necessary leaving other tasks, because his flock must not be left hungering for the Word of God. Several years before his now famous letter to

---

    5   *PPP*, pp. 246–251.

    6   Duffy, 'Cardinal Pole preaching', *CMT*, p. 179; Dermot Fenlon, 'Pole, Carranza and the pulpit', *RCEMT*, pp. 81–97, at pp. 85–87.

    7   Tellechea, 'Pole, Carranza y Fresneda', *CP*, p. 193, ed. and trans. Edwards.

Pole, Carranza also criticised, in his *Speculum pastorum*, the bishops of his own day who did not preach, instead spending their time with law cases, and leaving sermons to subordinates.[8] This was a shrewd hit against contemporary lawyer bishops, for example in Mary's England, including Stephen Gardiner. Given Carranza's views on this subject, as well as Pole's, it is perhaps not surprising that episcopal appointments increasingly went to qualified theologians.

It is sometimes hard to assess whether the texts surviving in Pole's papers, which have a tone of instruction and exhortation, were sermons, drafts for sermons, or tracts of another kind. Even so, Mayer has identified 13 texts and fragments, to be found in a manuscript in the Vatican Library, which do appear to have been preached as sermons on particular occasions.[9] Although there is no definite proof, internal evidence does suggest that some of them were associated with the synod of 1555–6, with Pole's consecration as archbishop of Canterbury, or with St Andrew's Day (30 November), now also the 'Day of Reconciliation'. It was one of the St Andrew's Day sermons, that of 1557, which, as well as proving to be his last preached on that festival, became innocently embroiled in the modern historical controversy over Pole's attitude to preaching. In that year, the feast of St Andrew fell at an unhappy time for both the cardinal archbishop and the queen, with England involved in continental war and Pole suspected of heresy by the Roman Inquisition. The surviving version of the sermon, which was perhaps a transcript produced after the event, survives only in a later, printed edition, which may have come from a now lost manuscript, possibly once in the papers of the martyrologist John Foxe.[10]

Pole took his text, suitable for the coming season of Advent, from Matthew's Gospel, where John the Baptist said to the Jewish Pharisees and Sadducees:

> You brood of vipers! Who warned you to flee from the wrath to come? Bear fruit worthy of repentance. Do not presume to say to yourselves, 'We have Abraham as our ancestor', for I tell you, God is able from these stones to raise up children to Abraham. Even now the axe is lying at the root of the trees; every tree therefore that does not bear good fruit is cut down and thrown into the fire [3:7–10].

These verses came from the mouth of a former Cardinal Inquisitor, who was presiding over the burning of unrepentant English heretics, and who was now

[8]    Carranza, *Speculum pastorum*, pp. 22, 228–230.

[9]    BAV Vat. lat. 5968, fols 1Ar–4v, 6r–8v, 16r–17r, 18r–21r, 22r–23r, 35r–42v, 227r–247v, 277r–303v, 379r–399r, 419r–441r, 446r–482v; Mayer, 'Reluctant author', pp. 68–74 and *CRP* 3 no. 1524.

[10]    John Strype, *Ecclesiastical memorials relating chiefly to religion and its reformation under the reigns of King Henry VIII, King Edward VI and Queen Mary* (Oxford: Clarendon Press, 1816), 3, part 2, pp. 482–510; Duffy, 'Cardinal Pole's preaching', *CMT*, p. 187, n. 31; Mayer, 'Reluctant author', p. 72.

himself evading trial in Rome for heresy. They were directed at the authorities of England, especially in London, and introduced a sermon that urged them to repentance. On the way, and this gives a clue to the context of the sermon, which otherwise is unclear, he also alluded to the Gospel for St Andrew's Day (Matthew 4:18–22), which recounted Jesus's calling of Andrew, by the Sea of Galilee, to become his disciple. What followed was effectively another 'Apologia' by Pole for the conduct of the restoration of Catholicism in England in the current reign, together with a rigorous assessment of the spiritual state of the kingdom, particularly in the capital, and an outline of what still needed to be done.

First, Pole tackled the question of church property, which was of great interest to his congregation of lawyers, councillors and courtiers. Sticking to the hard-won agreement made in December 1554, he repeated that they would not be required to hand back all their former church goods as their own 'fruits of repentance', but he nonetheless urged them to restore to religious use any former monastic churches on their property, in order to supplement the creaking parochial system. He reminded his listeners that, in any case, they only held these properties thanks to the grace of the Church and he rather unkindly compared the 'possessioners' to a greedy child, who had been given a large apple by its mother. Thinking that it would do her child harm, she asked for at least a piece of it back. The analogy was not over-subtle. The 'mother' was evidently the Church, and the child was a lay beneficiary of ecclesiastical property, such as many who were seated in Pole's congregation. Perhaps reflecting the social values of his age, and its theology, the preacher then turned to Christ Himself, portraying him as the angry father of the family, who threatened to intervene, by taking the apple away altogether, and throwing it out of the window. Pole told his listeners that he did not think that Christ's vicar, Paul IV, would really behave like this, though in doing so he displayed an optimism that probably neither he nor they felt, given the current tensions between himself and the pope, and the poor political relations between England and Rome. On this occasion, he suggested that the papacy would be willing to allow the possessioners to retain their goods, at least for the time being, but the whole passage is intriguing. It almost seems to suggest that Pole was inviting the 'great and the good' of Marian England to join him in securing the future of English Catholicism with or without the help of the pope.

At this point in the surviving text, the cardinal archbishop turned to the vexed question of medical and social provision in the capital, which was then growing rapidly as, in poor economic conditions combined with a rapid rise in population numbers, immigrants flocked into London from other parts of England. In an effort to compensate for the loss of the public work of the dissolved religious houses, five new hospitals, on the traditional medieval pattern which combined medical and social purposes, had been established in London during Edward

VI's reign. These were St Bartholomew's, St Thomas's, Bethlehem, Bridewell and Christ's Hospital. Religious reformers saw these foundations as a demonstration that the traditional Catholic Church did not hold a monopoly of the provision of medical and social care, but Pole was contemptuous of their efforts. He bluntly suggested to his rich and powerful listeners that they might use some of their ill-gotten gains from the Church to improve what he evidently regarded as a fairly grim and disgraceful situation. Using his considerable experience of Italy, which was one of the most urbanised areas in Europe, he pointed out that, while there were fewer than 10 hospitals currently operating in London, any major Italian city, such as Milan or Rome, had dozens, if not hundreds, of such establishments. He regarded this social failure as characteristic of the defects of the whole reforming enterprise under Henry and Edward, which had begun by despoiling religious houses and the clergy. Warming to a familiar theme, he told his congregation that this decline in social provision had resulted from the schism, which had caused a general decline in the morals and values of English society. They should be grateful for the kingdom's reconciliation to Rome on that day in 1554, which they were assembled to commemorate, and here he moved into the still-controversial territory of religion. As his later correspondence with Carranza would show, he was fully aware of the continuing strength of reformed religion, and even general scepticism about religion, in the capital, and he tackled the subject head-on. The authorities and citizens of London should accept the burnings of unrepentant heretics, most of which were taking place at Smithfield. Having eulogised those who had become his greatest Christian models, John Fisher and Thomas More, he directly attacked those, some of whom were probably listening to him at that moment, who still rejected the religious policies of the king and queen. He not only blamed young people for continuing to attack the Catholic faith and its practices, but turned on their elders and supposed betters, who might incite their violence and abuse even if they themselves did not take part. In the surviving version of this sermon, Pole concluded with an attack on the commonly-held notion that those who died on the bonfires were 'true' martyrs, and with an emotional appeal to all to return to Catholic orthodoxy and loyalty, despite the grim situation in which the kingdom then found itself.

Pole's public preaching may have been a relatively rare event, but this was partly because he had colleagues in the episcopate who also fulfilled this role. Notable among them was Thomas Watson, who was born near Sedgefield, in County Durham, in 1513. Watson became a fellow of Fisher's college, St John's, Cambridge, in 1533, and was appointed chaplain to Bishop Stephen Gardiner in 1543, assisting him in opposing the religious reforms under Edward VI. Under Mary, he devoted himself to preaching and religious controversy. In August 1553, he preached a sermon, under heavy guard at St Paul's Cross on the Sunday following the attack, in the same location, on the future bishop of Bath and Wells, Gilbert Bourne. Watson returned to Cambridge in late September that year, to begin implementing Gardiner's plans for the restoration of Catholicism in the university, becoming master of St John's and receiving a doctorate in theology. He went back to London to defend the Catholic cause at the abortive convocation of Canterbury, held in St Paul's cathedral on 18 October 1553, and a month later he became dean of Durham. In Lent 1554, he gave sermons before the Queen on the third and fourth Sundays, concentrating on the real presence and the sacrifice of the Mass, thus anticipating Carranza's efforts in the following year.[11] In May 1554, Watson resigned from St John's and took an active part in the repression of heresy, including the trial of John Hooper in February 1555. In December 1556 he became bishop of Lincoln, taking up the post in the following year, on the feast of the Assumption (15 August). He continued to propagandise for the Catholic Church, and in March and April 1557, he preached before the queen, and finally, in 1558, he produced a collection of 30 of his own sermons, which were intended for the use by parish priests who did not feel able or qualified to write their own.[12]

The need for such collections had been recognised and acted upon by the 1555–6 synod, which decided that preaching would be a good way to persuade the faithful to abandon the 'errors' of the previous 20 years. The initial plan, approved by the synod, was to produce four books of 'homilies' for general use. One would concentrate on issues of doctrine that were currently being disputed between Catholics and reformers, and the second would concentrate on historic teachings of the Church, covering the Ten Commandments, the Lord's Prayer, the Hail Mary, the Creed and the seven sacraments. The third volume was meant to provide commentaries on the passages from the epistles and gospels that were read at Mass on Sundays and major festivals, and the fourth was to cover the rites and ceremonies of the liturgy, and the moral vices and virtues, as traditionally defined by the Church.[13] These categories bear a marked resemblance to those of the catechism, a commentary on which was duly compiled by Bartolomé Carranza, at the synod's request, in the latter part of Mary's reign. Before Cardinal Pole took a direct hand in the Catholic restoration in England, Bishop Edmund Bonner and others had identified the need to counteract the official, and mandatory, collection of homilies that had been issued in 1547 and to which, ironically, Bonner had himself contributed, on the subject of Christian charity. In 1555, Bonner, together with John Harpsfield and Henry Pendleton,

---

[11]    Thomas Watson, *Twoo notable sermons ... concerninge the reall pesence of Christes body and bloude in the blessed sacrament; also the masse, which is the sacrifice of the Newe Testament* (London: John Cawood, 1554).

[12]    Watson, *Holsome and catholyke doctryne concerninge the seven sacramentes ... set forth in maner of shorte sermons* (London: Robert Caly, 1558); Wizeman, *Theology and spirituality*, p. 29; Kenneth Carleton, 'Watson, Thomas', *ODNB*.

[13]    Frere and Kennedy, *Visitation articles*, 2, p. 402.

produced such a collection, which appeared in at least 10 editions in Mary's reign, most of them in company with a catechism, also written by Bonner.[14] Like their Edwardian predecessor, the 1555 *Homilies* were written by various authors, and covered salvation history, charity, the Church, papal primacy and the Eucharist.[15] These official collections were accompanied by numerous other individual works, all aimed at counteracting the reformed theological currents of the previous two reigns, and bringing the English people back to the Catholic faith. But in 1558, this programme was finally overtaken and obstructed by the secular, political considerations which remained an important part of Pole's life, as he counselled the queen, and attempted to end England's alienation from the Continental powers and the papacy.

As the year 1557 drew to a close, there appeared to be stalemate between France and the Habsburgs. Few, other than those who were planning it, appear to have expected the New Year French attack on Calais, though rumours of it were reaching the neighbouring Netherlands by mid-December. For Henry II of France, the capture of England's last remaining Continental possession would not only bring an end to the Anglo-French conflict, which had begun in 1337, but also help to expunge the dishonour of the French defeat at Saint-Quentin, earlier in the year. By the feast of the Epiphany, on 6 January 1558, Calais and its Pale, the former English enclave, were in French hands, Pole may have lost his peace legation, but he continued to be involved in the work of Mary and her council, as they reacted to this humiliating blow. Initially, the lord deputy of Calais, Thomas, Lord Wentworth, was blamed for the surrender, with some suggesting that he was a Protestant sympathiser, who may have acted treacherously. The available evidence, though incomplete, suggests that Philip, although he was as surprised as his English wife and subjects by Henry II's Christmas campaign, had monitored the situation in Calais since mid-September, and had attempted unsuccessfully to reinforce Wentworth by both land and sea.[16] For the rest of Mary and Pole's lives, he continued to urge the English to mount a counter-attack, but with little or no success. The cardinal was close to Mary and her council throughout this period, but evidence does not survive of any specific activity on his part in relation to Calais. He did, however, remain in charge of the Church in England, Wales and Ireland.

---

[14]  Edmund Bonner, John Harpsfield and Henry Pendleton, *Homelies sette forth by the right reverende father in God, Edmunde Byshop of London* (London: John Cawood, 1555); Bonner, *A profitable and necessarye doctryne, with certayne homelies adioned therunto set forth by the reverende father in God, Edmonde byshop of London, for the instruction and enformation of the people beynge within his diocese of London, and of his cure and charge* (London: John Cawood, 1555).

[15]  Wizeman, *Theology and spirituality*, p. 29.

[16]  *CSP Domestic Mary*, pp. 97–98; C.S.L. Davies, 'England and the French war, 1557–9', in Loach and Tittler, *The mid-Tudor polity*, pp. 159–185, at p. 174; Edwards, *Mary I*, pp. 309–312.

It is now clear, thanks to the work of Thomas Mayer, that Pope Paul IV's revocation of Pole's legatine powers, in 1557, did not bring an end to his work in hearing appeals to him as legate, as well as archbishop, against the verdicts of lower ecclesiastical courts. Although Pole's legatine register (BMD MS 922) is incomplete, it has proved possible to piece together much of his work, in this respect, during his last year of life.[17] Between January and November 1558, Pole received 14 recorded appeals to his legatine court of audience, which by then should have been wound up on Paul IV's orders, and 11 to his 'audience' as archbishop of Canterbury, and it may still be possible to find others in the records of diocesan courts and registries. These figures were indeed lower than those of the previous year, but the question that remains is why such business was still being transacted at all. One explanation suggested by Mayer is that the relevant English and Welsh lawyers were not satisfied that the pope ever did revoke Pole's legatine powers with full canonical force, but it is also possible that they followed the example of the queen and council, for whom business evidently continued as usual in this period.

In the latter part of 1557, some, including Cardinal Alessandro Farnese, had indeed expected Pole to be restored to his former status, but Pope Paul himself, on 14 July 1557, firmly told both Mary and her bishops, who had protested strongly at the revocation, that it would not be proper, under any circumstances, to make such a restoration. Even so, legatine business continued within England, and it could reasonably be argued that this was entirely appropriate, as long as Pole was still appealing to Rome against the revocation of his powers.[18] As already noted, in the summer of 1557, Pole did in fact send his datary, Niccolò Ormanetto, to Rome, arriving there on 23 August. He bore typically contradictory messages from the cardinal archbishop, both expressing Pole's willingness to submit to the pope and at the same time asking him to restore his position. At the end of August, Ormanetto relayed through the pope's nephew, Cardinal Carlo Carafa, Pole's willingness to submit, like a child to his father.[19] The datary was not allowed to see Pope Paul himself until 4 September, which was the day of a meeting of the council of the Inquisition, at which Pole's case was discussed. The cardinal of England's allies in the Curia apparently had great difficulty in persuading the pope to see Ormanetto until this meeting at last took place, unusually for him, in the evening. Ormanetto did not immediately make conduct with the resident English ambassador in Rome, Sir Edward Carne, and this may well have been deliberate.[20] According to a curial observer, Bernardo Navagero, Ormanetto was ill when he went to this interview and

17    Mayer, 'The success of Cardinal Pole's final legation', *CMT*, pp. 149–175, at pp. 149–151.
18    Mayer, 'The success', pp. 150, 159–161.
19    *CSP Ven*, VI (ii), no. 1002.
20    *CSP Foreign*, no. 662.

had to terminate it early. Nonetheless, he managed to speak up for Pole, telling Paul that his achievements had been great in restoring the Catholic religion in England, and going on to complain bitterly about the revocation of the cardinal's legatine powers. But crucially, according to Navagero, no mention was made of Pole's formal recall to Rome, apparently because the relevant brief (*breve*), if it existed, had not been seen in England. In response, the pope apparently confined himself to blaming King Philip for everything that had gone wrong, in his opinion, on the continent and in his and Mary's island kingdom. Although he spoke vehemently, it appears that Ormanetto did not take the opportunity to deliver Pole's 'Apologia' to the pope.[21]

As far as Pole's administration of the Church was concerned, the reduction in the number of appeals heard by his legatine and archiepiscopal courts may well be explained by the clearing, in the previous two years, of a backlog of business that built up during the schism. In any case, it is certain that, whatever was thought in Rome, Pole was still regarded at home as having the authority that had been granted to him by Julius III in 1553. As in the reign of Henry VIII, and no doubt earlier, the level of activity in ecclesiastical courts had fluctuated before the split with Rome, and there is no doubt that Pole was still functioning as a legate in 1558.[22] Many of these cases concerned excommunication and other ecclesiastical penalties under Roman canon law, against which individuals protested. Other pleas that might reach Pole's courts concerned dispensations to clergymen to hold multiple benefices, a practice that Pole's friend Carranza particularly deplored. This practice of 'pluralism' went against many medieval papal measures, dating back to Pope Innocent III, as well as the constitutions of the thirteenth-century legates to England, Cardinals Otto and Ottoboni, who had provided the basis for Pole's own synod of 1555–6. The relevant decree of the council of Trent, which in 1557–8 was still to be ratified, followed the Fourth Lateran Council of 1215, as well as Pope John XXII's definitive bull *Execrabilis*, issued in 1317, in declaring that any cleric who held more than one benefice should be deprived of all. As far as England was concerned, according to Ormanetto, Pole approved of this hard line, even though the need to restore full clerical coverage in England and Wales, and also to fund higher education for potential Church leaders, forced him to depart on numerous occasions from the principle of personal residence in a single post.[23]

During 1558, another continuing aspect of Pole's governance of the English and Welsh Church was the burning of those convicted as unrepentant heretics.

---

[21]   *CSP Ven*, VI (ii), no. 1024; *PPP*, pp. 316–317.

[22]   Martin Ingram, 'Regulating sex in pre-Reformation London', in *Authority and consent in Tudor England: essays presented to C.S.L. Davies*, ed. G.W. Bernard and S.J. Gunn (Aldershot: Ashgate, 2002), pp. 71–95, at pp. 85–86.

[23]   *CRP* 3 no. 1047; Mayer, 'The success', pp. 162–165.

From January to 17 November of that year, when such proceedings stopped on news of the death of the queen and the cardinal archbishop, 45 men and women died in this way. The great majority of them were burned in two centres of continuing attachment to reformed religion, London (19) and Norwich (13), followed by five in Canterbury, together with one person each in York, Ely, Winchester, Gloucester, Exeter and St David's. Prominent among them were artisans, tradesmen and their wives, all being of this lower social rank except for one clergyman and one 'gentleman'.[24] Also, in what proved to be the last months of his archiepiscopal reign, Pole himself became personally involved in the arrest and burning of heretics in his own diocese, no longer leaving such activity to his suffragan, Richard Thornden, bishop of Dover, or the archdeacon of Canterbury, Nicholas Harpsfield, and other local commissioners for heresy.[25] Given Pole's current status in the Roman Church, himself under vehement suspicion of heresy, in the terminology of the Inquisition, this activity in Kent might either appear ironical, or else as a very material way of demonstrating his innocence to his former colleagues in the Curia.

Pole's renewed involvement with the Roman Inquisition, now as a suspect rather than one of its commissioners, became more direct as a result of Ormanetto's visit to Rome in August and September 1557. Pope Paul's revocation of Pole's legatine powers, had been the first step in what came increasingly to look like a campaign against him, his friends and members of his household. On 14 June, Friar William Peto was nominated, despite his protests, to replace Pole as legate *a latere* in England, and the way seems to have been cleared for this move by the arrest, a fortnight earlier, of Cardinal Giovanni Morone, on charges of heresy. At the same time, two other friends of Pole, Bishops Tommaso Sanfelice and Giacomo Soranzo, were detained on similar charges. Then, also in June 1557, Pope Paul attacked Pole's secretary, the Venetian aristocrat, Alvise Priuli, who was one of his closest collaborators in Lambeth Palace. Paul revoked a grant of Priuli's right to succeed, at the next vacancy, to the episcopal see of Brescia, which he had received from Pope Julius III, with the official support of the Venetian Republic. At that time, Priuli's close friendship with Pole had counted in his favour, both in Venice and in Rome, but now things were very different.[26]

Mary's ambassador in Rome, Sir Edward Carne, hoped that the truce of Vaucelles, made in September 1557, would lessen Paul's hostility to all things English, and he even fondly imagined that the Franco-Habsburg treaty might contain, among its many secret clauses, the restoration of Pole's legations, both

---

[24]   Doran and Freeman, *Mary Tudor*, pp. 260–265.

[25]   Patrick Collinson, 'The persecution in Kent', in *CMT*, pp. 309–333, at p. 321.

[26]   Tellechea, 'Pole, Carranza y Fresneda', *CP*, p. 138; *ERP* 5 no. 15; *CRP* 3 no. 2211 (introduction); Fenlon, *Heresy and obedience*, pp. 270–271; *PPP*, p. 339.

on the Continent and in England.[27] The basis for Carne's hopes may have been the clause which stipulated that ecclesiastical corporations in general would be pardoned by the Pope for their behaviour during the conflict, but nothing was specifically said about Pole.[28] In reality, it was soon revealed that the peace appeared to make Pope Paul even angrier with Pole than he had been before. This was why Mary's messenger was kept waiting for so long and why Carne himself got hardly a word out of the Holy Father, when he did eventually gain an audience with him.[29] At the end of September and the beginning of October 1557, the duke of Alba, who still posed a potential military threat to the papal states, tried to intercede for both Pole and Morone, but was rebuffed, as was Carne, once again.[30] When Alba met the Pope once again, he learned that Paul was still vowing vengeance on Pole.[31]

The reason for the Pope's venom was clearly revealed when, on 4 October, Pole's friend and confidant, Morone, was formally charged with heresy. The second and third charges against him referred to his views on the justification, or salvation, of Christians, accusing him of having opposed the decree on the subject which had been drawn up at Trent in 1546. The seventh charge against Morone referred to his understanding of the papal office, accusing him of believing and stating that the pope should be obeyed only in his capacity as a temporal ruler in Italy, and not as Christ's Vicar, while the fifteenth charge accused Morone of holding the proposition, which was more than implicitly critical of sixteenth-century popes, that Christians should not make war on one another.[32] At about this time, another of Pole's close associates, Pietro Carnesecchi, was summoned to Rome for investigation.[33] Dangerous for Pole was the evidence given to the Roman inquisitors, on 12 October, by the Dominican, Gabriel Martinet. The Inquisition was traditionally happy to receive hearsay evidence, and in this case Friar Martinet testified that a fellow Dominican, Michele Ghislieri, the future Pope Pius V, and a former member of the same order, Ioannes Arnesius, had claimed to him that, in the 1540s, Pole used Vittoria Colonna's money to bribe men to join his 'school of angels', the Viterbo circle. Other witnesses, Gelido and Orazio Ragnotti, testifying under the equally venerable inquisitorial principle of judging a person's guilt by association, stated that they had received such money. Martinet, perhaps speaking the words of the absent Arnesius, also claimed that he had heard the late Pope Marcellus, when he was legate at Trent alongside Del Monte and Pole, condemn the English cardinal for heresy. Whether true or not,

---

27   *CSP Foreign*, 1558–9, nos 672, p. 339, and 678, p. 341; *PPP*, p. 330 and n. 161.
28   *PPP*, p. 330 n. 16 (BAV MS Barbarini lat. 5115, fols 96v–97r (article 6 of the treaty)).
29   *CSP Foreign*, 1558–9, pp. 334, 337
30   *CSP Ven*, VI (ii), nos 1042, 1043.
31   *CSP Foreign*, 1558–9, no. 672, p. 339.
32   Firpo and Marcatto, *Processo*, 2 part 2, pp. 390–391, 393.
33   Firpo and Marcatto, *Processo*, 5, p. 314; Fenlon, *Heresy and obedience*, p. 279.

this was damning evidence, in the circumstances of late 1557.[34] In mid-October of that year, an insider, Pietro Bertano, sent to one of Pole's long-standing friends and supporters, Cardinal Ercole Gonzaga, a list of the enemies (*oppositarii*) of the Englishman, and of Morone, in Rome. These were the men who believed the Inquisition prosecutor's charges, most of which were based on hearsay and guilt by association. According to this school of thought, Pole, like Morone, had kept the company of suspicious individuals, and even favoured them. On the list was the late Marcantonio Flaminio, who had in fact been brought back to the Catholic faith by Pole, to such effect that the future Pope Paul IV had attended him sacramentally on his deathbed, if only to check on his orthodoxy. In the conditions of 1557, history was readily re-written. Yet it was clear that anyone associated with the *Beneficio di Cristo* was suspect, and Priuli, too, was drawn into the net. It was asserted by witnesses that the future Paul IV had regarded Pole, in the 1540s and early 1550s, as a saint and angel in his moral conduct, but unsound in Christian doctrine.[35] Although it was never acted upon, a set of 18 charges against Pole was prepared at this time, on the basis of this testimony, which had primarily been directed against Morone. In it, Pole was accused of being averse to the true Faith, of having preached heresy and tried to persuade others to do so, of having promoted heretical preachers and obstructed orthodox ones, and generally of having been an aider and abettor (*fautor*) of heresy and heretics.[36] If found guilty, Pole would have been liable to burning, just like those who were being thus condemned under his authority in England.

The history of this action against Pole, which was formally part of the trial of Morone, goes back to his original appointment by Pope Paul III as a cardinal, soon after which he had been named to the papal reform commission for the Church, which was intended as a preparatory step before a general council. The divisions in the higher councils of the Church that became evident to much of Europe, in the reign of Paul IV, were already identifiable in the 1537 commission. It had contained some zealous seekers after reform, all friends of Pole – Gasparo Contarini, Jacopo Sadoleto, Gian Matteo Giberti, Gregorio Cortese, abbot of San Giorgio Maggiore in Venice, Tommaso Badia, Master of the Sacred Palace, and Federigo Fregoso, formerly archbishop of Salerno – who sought to repair the increasingly fractured unity of the Church by removing the abuses of which Luther and other evangelical reformers complained. However, Pope Paul attempted to balance the commission by also including in it two bitter opponents of all things 'Protestant', Girolamo Aleandro, archbishop of

---

[34] Firpo and Marcatto, *Processo*, 6, pp. 287–292.

[35] Firpo and Marcatto, *Processo*, 5, p. 307n; Mayer, *PPP*, pp. 331–332.

[36] Firpo and Marcatto, *Processo*, 1, pp. 15–90.

Brindisi, and Gianpietro Carafa.[37] In the event, when the commission reported, its recommendations concerned the reform of the Curia, and not of Christian doctrine.[38] They were not implemented, and neither was the council convened until 1545.[39] The trial of Morone and his associates was evidently intended to be the settling of accounts by the former at the expense of the latter.

The records of the Roman trial of Cardinal Morone are not the only source for information about the papal undermining of Pole which took place in the last 18 months of his life. Material collected by inquisitors, between 1559 and 1563, for the trial of Carranza, inevitably touched on Pole as well. The relevant evidence went back to the first phase of the Council of Trent, between 1545 and 1547, when the two men first met and worked together. In 1547, in a letter written to Charles V on 19 July, Mendoza had made explicit his suspicions about Pole's theology. The context was the question of the Englishman's suitability for the papal throne, which was then becoming an issue because of Paul III's poor health. Here too, the ambassador praised Pole's personal conduct, but questioned his orthodoxy on the matter of justification.[40] Testimony in Carranza's trial, from one of Philip's chaplains, Francisco Delgado, gives some insight into life at Lambeth Palace in Pole's time. One of the main grounds for the arrest and trial of Carranza was the inclusion of supposedly heretical statements in his catechism, which had been commissioned by the 1555–6 synod for use in the English Church. Delgado, who was in a good position to observe, while he was with the king at Westminster, testified that Alvise Priuli, who was Pole's secretary, helped to revise the catechism, when it was in its first draft. The witness acted as a messenger between Carranza and Priuli, actually taking the text to Lambeth, where the latter read it, section by section, in his study, and even on the boat between Westminster and Greenwich. Priuli suggested amendments and, according to Delgado, indicated dubious passages without actually crossing them out. In addition, Carranza went to Lambeth for meals with Priuli, at which the catechism would be read and discussed. Another member of Pole's household, Gian Battista Binardi, was always present at these sessions, which sometimes lasted from ten in the morning until 7 o'clock at night. Delgado told the Valladolid inquisitors that these goings-on had made him suspicious at the time, 'because they said that, of the aforementioned Priuli, Pope Paul IV said that the business of Priuli was not at all clean ... and that from then on he suspected that what the aforesaid Priuli was amending was not good, and especially since he

---

[37] J. Martin, *Hidden enemies: Italian heretics in an Italian city* (Berkeley, Los Angeles and London: University of California Press, 1993), p. 38.

[38] 'Consilium delectorum cardinalium et aliorum praelatorum ad emendanda Ecclesia Sancti Domini Nostri Paolo III ipso iubente conscriptum et exhibitum', in *CT*, 12, pp. 131–145.

[39] Michael Hutchings, *Reginald, Cardinal Pole, 1500–1558. The last* [sic] *Archbishop of Canterbury* (Midhurst: The Saint John Press, 2008), pp. 31–32.

[40] Fenlon, *Heresy and obedience*, p. 219; Tellechea, 'Pole, Carranza y Fresneda', *CP*, p. 124.

has seen the archbishop of Toledo [Carranza] imprisoned'.[41] During this period, Delgado, although evidently trusted by Carranza, Priuli and, of course, Pole, appears to have acted as a kind of spy for the Franciscan Bernardo de Fresneda, while going in and out of Lambeth Palace. According to further evidence, given by Delgado as a witness for the prosecution of Carranza, some theological questions, arising out of the draft catechism, were referred back to the author by Priuli. When asked who else, apart from Carranza, Priuli, and himself, was present at these sessions, he listed Binardi, Francesco Estelle, who was another of Pole's household, and Ormanetto. Nevertheless, when pressed further by the inquisitors, Delgado admitted that he did not actually hear anything 'that he could judge to be bad or good' during the meetings at Lambeth. However, he did hear Priuli say to Carranza that he should not publish the catechism in Spanish, as he eventually did, 'because it was a profound and serious thing'. He added that Pole's secretary asked Carranza for a collection of extracts from the work, for his personal use.[42]

It is probable that Delgado reported his observations of the Pole household to Fresneda, who was then in Brussels. When his trial began, Carranza took the opportunity, allowed by the canon law of the Inquisition, to name those whom he regarded as his enemies, and among them he included Delgado, characterising him as a 'judaizing' *converso*, a convert from Judaism, though in this period the term was habitually used of those who were Christians from birth, but had Jewish ancestry. When he gave evidence himself, Carranza denied having entrusted his catechism to anyone who had been accused of heresy (*infamado de herejía*), though he had shown it to some of the Spanish theologians who had come to England with King Philip in 1554. As for Pole, Carranza told the inquisitors that he could not remember which parts of the catechism he had shown him, though the cardinal, 'seeing that it had been ordained in a synod, told him several times to finish it'.[43]

Cardinal Carlo Carafa's mission to Brussels, in 1557, had ostensibly been concerned with keeping the peace between France and the Habsburgs, but he also took with him a copy of all or part of the Morone trial. The aim of this somewhat irregular manoeuvre, which broke inquisitorial secrecy, was to put pressure on Philip to end his support for Pole, against his recall for investigation in Rome. At about this time, Pope Paul told Navagero that Priuli was definitely a heretic, because 'he is of the damned school, that apostate house, of the cardinal of England', in other words, Lambeth Palace. This was the reason why

---

[41]   Tellechea, *Documentos históricos*, 2, p. 945; Tellechea, 'Carranza, Pole y Fresneda', *CP*, pp. 137–138.

[42]   Tellechea, *Documentos históricos*, 2, pp. 948–949; Tellechea, 'Carranza, Pole y Fresneda', *CP*, pp. 138–139.

[43]   Tellechea, *Documentos históricos*, 5, p. 242; Tellechea, 'Carranza, Pole y Fresneda', *CP*, p. 139.

he had removed Pole's legatine powers earlier in the year. In Paul's view, Pole was the master heretic and Morone his disciple, and Priuli was just as bad. Also, if Marcantonio Flaminio had still been alive, he would have been burned. His brother Cesare, who was a friend and companion of Priuli, had indeed been burned as a 'Lutheran' outside the main Dominican church in Rome, Santa Maria sopra Minerva, in a public *auto de fe*. His friend Galleazzo Carciolo had suffered a similar fate. During this tirade, Pope Paul told Navagero that 'were our father a heretic, we would carry the faggots to burn him'.[44] When he got to Brussels, towards the end of 1557, Carlo Carafa explained to Philip exactly why his uncle was pursuing Pole and said that he had part or all of the Morone papers with him, including the charges that would be preferred against Pole. He offered to show them to the king, who duly set aside a date for this, but in fact Carafa showed the whole dossier to Fresneda.[45] Later, giving evidence against Carranza, Fresneda stated that he had indeed seen these documents in Brussels.[46]

Mayer discusses at length whether a process against Pole had by this stage been launched, in addition to that which was under way against Morone. Certainly, by March of the following year, his last on earth, Pole himself thought that there was, and he seems always to have supposed that Carlo Carafa's mission to Brussels was directed mainly against him. In a letter to the pope, dated at Greenwich on 30 March 1558, Pole was extremely direct. First, he appealed to Paul to restore Priuli's *accessus* to the see of Brescia, now that it was vacant as a result of the death of Cardinal Durante Duranti. However much, or little, he knew about the plotting then going on in Rome and Brussels, Pole was undoubtedly right to state that there was an inquisitorial process against him, which might discredit anything he had to say. He had accepted the revocation of his two legations as necessary to separate the Church's business from that of King Philip, but now feared, because of the Roman Inquisition's activity, that the pope had other motives. He stoutly defended his own achievement, as legate in England, and even suggested that, by his current behaviour, Paul was re-writing Scripture, so that Abraham slew his son Isaac, instead of the boy's being saved by the Lord (Genesis 22:1–19).[47] The Morone trial papers show that Pole was indeed one of those accused, but if a formal trial started against him, it is now lost.[48]

This letter from Pole seems to have been a response to the sending to Brussels, by Pope Paul, of Gianfrancesco Stella. He arrived there in mid-

---

[44] Firpo and Marcatto, *Processo*, 5, pp. 301–212; *PPP*, p. 332, with detailed references in n. 173.

[45] *PPP*, pp. 333–334, with detailed references in n. 178, based on BAV Barbarini lat. no. 5115, fol. 145r, no. 5302, fol. 93v, and no. 5211, fols 168r–170r.

[46] Tellechea, *Documentos históricos*, 2, pp. 560–562 and 563–564.

[47] *CRP* 3 no. 2211.

[48] Firpo and Marcatto, *Processo*, 6, pp. 425–431; *PPP*, pp. 34–35.

December 1557, and in January received instructions to inform Cardinal Carafa that Pole would indeed have to come to Rome and defend himself before the pope.[49] Pole's protests, as well as the efforts of Philip and Mary's ambassadors in Rome, could not prevent Paul from increasing the pressure on Pole in the early months of 1558. Still, the main target was the Viterbo 'crypto-Lutheran' circle of the 1540s. Cardinal Michele Ghislieri summoned all survivors from it to Rome for interrogation, and proceedings were even started against those who had died. As in the cases of Bucer and Fagius in Cambridge in the previous year, it was perfectly possible, under the canon law of the Inquisition, for the dead to be condemned for heresy and have their bones exhumed and burned. This campaign was pursued with even greater enthusiasm after Ottaviano Raverta reached Rome on 20 January, with a report from Carlo Carafa, in Brussels, which included details of his actions against Pole.[50] Allegedly, Philip was still, at this stage, trying to save his English archbishop from the Roman Inquisition, even offering it the opportunity to set up a tribunal in Medici Florence, over which he had political hegemony.[51] Navagero was the source for much of this information, which could not be proved because of the secretive ways of the Holy Office, even though the pope himself took no trouble to conceal his own views on the supposed heretics in general, and Pole in particular.

Interestingly, early in 1558, Carlo Carafa seems to have begun to play a double game, publicly supporting his uncle's actions against the 'Lutherans', but covertly doing what he could, by means of backstairs influence, to help both Pole and Morone. Carlo seems to have realised what a crucial role Pole was playing in the English government, particularly as Philip and his agents tried to persuade Mary and her council to react militarily to the French capture of Calais, at the beginning of January.[52] Even so, as spring arrived, the threat of a trial of Pole was not lifted and, indeed, two further witnesses in the Morone case implicated the English cardinal in his friend's supposed heresy. Pole was fully aware of the dangerous documents that Carlo Carafa held in Brussels, and tried to defend himself in writing, both there and in Rome.[53] Soon, however, another extremely unhelpful storm blew up in relations between the Habsburgs and Pope Paul. On 14 March, at a Diet in Frankfurt-am-Main, Charles formally passed his Imperial crown to his brother Ferdinand of Austria, as the final stage of his abdication from all authority, with a view to retirement to Spain. No one consulted the pope, and his reaction was furious. His anger only grew because it was not until mid-May that the Imperial high steward, Martín de

---

[49]    *CSP Ven*, VI (iii), no. 1135; *CRP* 3 no. 2157 (10 January 1558).

[50]    *CSP Ven*, VI (iii), no. 1156.

[51]    *CSP Ven*, VI (iii), no. 1155 [= Firpo and Marcatto, *Processo*, 5, p. 320]; *PPP*, p. 337.

[52]    *PPP*, pp. 338–339.

[53]    Firpo and Mocatto, *Processo*, 5, p. 326 and 2, pt 2, pp. 744, 754

Guzmán, arrived in Rome to give formal notice of the Diet's action. In the meantime, the Curia had done its research in the Vatican archives, by order of Pope Paul's March consistory, and retrieved all available documents concerning Imperial–papal relations, a subject that had been a source of conflict for many centuries. Guzmán's main purpose was to do homage on behalf of the new emperor, Ferdinand, but Paul refused him a formal audience, in his capacity as an Imperial ambassador, instead having a private meeting with him. Perhaps surprisingly, given his normal, autocratic, style, Paul asked the cardinals for their views on how he should proceed, and their varied and nuanced opinions survive. Each of the 17 'voters' had to answer four questions. They were to say whether they were willing to accept the action of the Frankfurt Diet, and agreed that the Holy See had not been consulted about it. If they agreed with these two statements, they were thirdly asked if they thought that Ferdinand's election as emperor should be declared invalid. The fourth question was more emollient, however, asking what would be best 'for the public good, peace and tranquillity of the Christian Commonwealth (*res publica*)'.[54] The voting cardinals, including Carlo Carafa, who was now back in Rome from Brussels, were in favour of recognising Ferdinand as the new emperor.[55]

In the Vatican archives is a letter, written at this time by Philip to his subject, Cardinal Pedro Pacheco, in which the king offered an evidently heartfelt critique of Pope Paul IV's conduct, and its likely consequences. Firstly, he defended his uncle's claim to succeed to the Holy Roman Empire, stressing the harm that would be done in Germany by further papal intransigence. Such an approach had turned out badly there in the past, and if Rome resisted the transfer of power now, the consequences would affect 'all of Christendom'. He added:

> And it would be in the hands of His Holiness to take another, shorter way to promote the aim which he so much desires, to reduce them [the Germans, to full obedience to Rome], if, as he has always shown the longing to reform the Church, and remove the scandals, he truly set his hands to them. [He should] treat with the German prelates, who, in accordance with the request that they have made to him so many times, should place in the universities of Flanders, Spain, Italy and France, and even in that of Cologne, some men of their dioceses, who should acquire the true foundation of sacred theology, and could instruct the people of their dioceses, which today have such a lack of teaching, and ask for it and desire it, and have been lost through the ignorance and disordered life of the parish priests (*curas*) ... Through the neglect there of matters of religion, every day there

---

[54]   BAV Barbarini. Lat. 2545; Tellechea, *Paolo IV y Carlos V: la renuncia del Imperio a debate* (Madrid: Fundación Universitaria Española, 2001), pp. 13–16.

[55]   Tellechea, *Paolo IV y Carlos V*, pp. 16–17.

is seen in the ministers less doctrine and more corrupt habits. This other way would make them turn back, and would bring them to knowledge of the truth.

In this letter, Philip went on to emphasise the extraordinary nature of his father's abdication, and pointed out that Ferdinand had been properly elected under the terms of the 1356 'Golden Bull' of the Emperor Charles IV.[56] England is not mentioned in this letter, but might well have been, given the danger to the Catholic religion there. In any case, despite the cardinals' vote, relations between Rome and the Habsburgs did not improve over the summer of 1558, and the row only ended when Charles V died, in the Hieronymite friary of Yuste in Spanish Extremadura, with Carranza at his bedside, on 21 September of that year.[57] But while all this was going on, it was becoming ever clearer that King Philip's confessor, the Franciscan, Bernardo de Fresneda, was now Pole's enemy.

Back in March 1558, Pole evidently still trusted in Fresneda's good faith. On the 30th of that month, he sent Gianfrancesco Stella to Brussels with letters to the pope and to Cardinal Bernardino Scotti, with a covering letter to Fresneda, in which he said that he wanted the Franciscan to read and approve them before they were forwarded to Rome. He also asked Fresneda to speak to Philip on his behalf, though it is not clear whether this was done out of innocence or desperate calculation.[58] In his letter to Scotti, Pole adopted a tone of injured innocence, with his customary historical perspective, saying that he wanted Pope Paul to treat him as well as Gregory the Great had treated Augustine of Canterbury, as a loyal and effective representative of the Roman Church in a hostile land. Fresneda, however, had already turned against Pole, apparently because he was a friend of Carranza, with whom he had quarrelled while they were together in London, in 1554–5. On the surface, Fresneda did not want Pole to be seen as guilty because of his association with Carranza. This was evidently untrue, however, and by the summer of 1558, Pole seems to have understood clearly that Fresneda was his enemy. At that time, there were rumours that Pope Paul was dying, but on this occasion, Pole was not included among the likely candidates to replace him.[59] It was only after Pole's death, and the arrest by the Spanish Inquisition of Carranza in August 1559, that Fresneda gave details of the link that he had made between the accused and Pole, as suspected heretics. He testified that he had indeed seen the whole 'process' against Pole, by the Roman

---

[56]   BAV Vat. lat. 6206, fols 180v–185r, transcribed in Tellechea, *Paolo IV y Carlos V*, pp. 158–161.

[57]   Tellechea, *Paolo IV y Carlos V*, pp. 57–58; Tellechea, 'Carlos V y Bartolomé Carranza. Un navarro junto al lecho de muerte del Emperador', in Tellechea, *Fray Bartolomé Carranza de Miranda (investigaciones históricas)* (Pamplona: Gobierno de Navarra, Departamento de Educación y Cultura, 2002), pp. 313–377 at pp. 366–367.

[58]   *CRP* 3 nos 2209–2211; *PPP*, p. 339.

[59]   Firpo and Marcatto, *Processo*, 5, pp. 387–388; *CSP Span* XIII no. 469; *PPP*, p. 343.

Inquisition, when Carlo Carafa brought it to Brussels in order to try to persuade Philip to allow Pole to be extradited from England to Rome.[60]

On 6 and 14 October 1559, in his cell in the now-vanished convent of San Francisco in Valladolid, Bernardo de Fresneda gave evidence to an inquisitor, Diego González. One of the basic principles of the Inquisition, in Spain and in Rome, was that only a full confession, or testimony, could achieve absolution, and avoid or mitigate ecclesiastical sanctions. Fresneda, who acted as the king's confessor, was all too aware that the Inquisition's work was based on the sacrament of penance and reconciliation. Thus he will have expected González to ask him why he had not come to the Inquisition when his suspicions about Pole first arose, in October 1557. The Franciscan carefully told the inquisitor that all he had received was second- or third-hand information. This was somewhat disingenuous, as such testimony was a staple of the Holy Office's work, but now he would spill the beans in any case. He said he had been told by one Julián, a 'wandering' Bernardine friar, who had served in northern Europe as a chaplain to various hospitals and to the Habsburg armies, that he, Julián, had heard from Dr [Juan] Morillo, an Aragonese theologian, 'who was a great heretic', and had been at Trent and also in the University of Paris, that 'if he [Morillo] was a heretic, Cardinal Pole of England and Friar Bartolomé Carranza had made him [one]'.[61] Friar Julián, from whom Fresneda claimed to have received this rather damning information, acted as Dr Morillo's 'chancellor', and was known as 'the heretics' pimp (*alcahuete*)', had himself been denounced by Carranza to Philip. Morillo's involvement with Pole, as well as Carranza, was undoubtedly close. In the early 1540s, he had served the bishop of Chiaramonte, and he had taken messages to Pole and the other papal legates at Trent, Del Monte and Cervini, before joining the English cardinal's circle, after he had abandoned the Tridentine debates on justification.[62] This evidence was evidently damning for Carranza, but it also reflected on Pole, whose successor, Matthew Parker, obtained and used it.[63] According to another witness in Carranza's trial, Friar Baltasar Pérez, Juan Morillo stayed with Pole for some time, in Venice, and Rome, though his claim that the Aragonese accompanied him to England seems to be false. By then, Morillo had in fact fled to Protestant Frankfurt, joining a Lutheran church there, and Julián may have gone there too, and perhaps married.[64] Basing his evidence on that of Julián, another witness, Don Felipe de la Torre, asserted to the inquisitors in Valladolid that Pole had indeed been a 'heretic', at the time of

---

[60]  Fenlon, *Heresy and obedience*, pp. 271–272; Tellechea, 'Pole, Carranza y Fresneda', *CP*, p. 153.

[61]  Tellechea, *Documentos históricos*, 2, pp. 561–562; Tellechea, 'Pole, Carranza y Fresneda', *CP*, p. 154.

[62]  Fenlon, *Heresy and obedience*, pp. 127, 172–173; *PPP*, pp. 156, 162, 165.

[63]  *PPP*, p. 364.

[64]  Tellechea, 'Carranza, Pole y Fresneda', *CP*, pp. 155–157.

the first sessions of the Council of Trent. Also, he had heard that Dr Morillo was 'a great friend (*muy amigo*), not only of the cardinal of England himself, but also of suspect members of his Viterbo circle, such as Flaminio and Priuli, as well as Carranza, who was currently on trial in a separate case. De la Torre said that he knew Morillo had written two letters to Pole while in Paris, in 1546–7, though he did not know their contents.[65] Carranza was sufficiently concerned about Friar Julián, and the damage he might do him, to 'recuse' the Bernardine to the Valladolid inquisitors, asserting that any testimony he gave would be false because of personal enmity.[66] This did not prevent the Inquisition from collecting Julián's evidence by other routes.

In his testimony of October 1559, which came early in Carranza's lengthy trial, Bernardo de Fresneda stated clearly that he had indeed suspected the archbishop of Toledo, as he now was, of heresy, because 'he saw him many times in England, closeting himself thus in the houses at Lambeth, and Richmond, and Hampton Court'. Evidently he saw Carranza as guilty by association with Pole, who also frequented these palaces. As for the cardinal archbishop himself, Fresneda was blunt. Pole 'found himself vehemently suspect concerning justification'. What was worse, his friend Carranza had 'close friendship and familiarity' with Pole's secretary, Priuli, who, as the Franciscan reminded his interrogator, had been deprived by Pope Paul IV of his right to the see of Brescia as a result of the heresy process in Rome against Cardinal Morone, in which Pole was also implicated. Fresneda now made it clear, speaking after Paul's death and before the election of Pius IV, in December 1559, that he had become convinced of Pole's guilt when Carlo Carafa showed him the Morone trial papers, in Brussels at the end of 1557. The whole matter concerned justification, and Fresneda also named, as a suspect, the Dominican Pedro de Soto, co-founder of the Catholic university at Dillingen, near Augsburg, who also taught at Oxford as part of Mary and Pole's reform of the English universities. De Soto was accused on the basis of his 'many closetings and close friendships' with Pole and Priuli. For Fresneda, Pole and Priuli were evidently the sources of the 'heresy' that had affected Carranza and brought him to trial, and his suspicion of them had sprung from his reading of the Morone trial, which had been deliberately shown to him in Brussels in late 1557. From this he concluded that 'with a large number of witnesses, the two cardinals [Morone and Pole] were condemned as heretics', and, once he realised this, he evidently went over in his mind his time in England, in 1554–5, seeing events of that period in a new and unfavourable light.

The Carafas had wanted Fresneda to persuade King Philip to repudiate Pole and submit him for trial in Rome, but their attempts did not succeed. Instead, the king supported the determination of his wife and her council to keep the

---

[65]   Tellechea, *Documentos históricos*, 2, pp. 852–853.
[66]   Tellechea, *Documentos históricos*, 3, p. 476.

cardinal archbishop of Canterbury in England, and also had Carranza named as archbishop of Toledo. When a Spanish royal secretary, Pedro de Hoyos, argued with him about his negative view of Pole and Carranza, after the latter had become archbishop, Fresneda claimed later to have said that Carranza's friendship with Pole was the main stain on his character. To the Valladolid Inquisition in October 1559, Fresneda recalled the conditions in which he and the other Spanish churchmen had lived, while they were with King Philip in London. They had been at Westminster Abbey, in 'some lodgings that gave onto the cloister', and sometimes they had played games together – bowls, cards, and *las argollas*, which involved getting balls through rings, in a little garden (*huertecillo*) nearby. When Fresneda's evidence was put to other prosecution witnesses for corroboration, as the Inquisition's procedures required, the bishop of Almería, Antonio de Corrionero, suggested what may have been another motive for the Franciscan's hostility to Carranza, his desire to replace him in the king and queen's inner counsels.[67]

A further indication of the dark cloud under which Pole lived in his last years also came to light later, during the Inquisition trial of Bartolomé Carranza. In March 1569, the Roman inquisitors identified as genuine a document, written by Licentiate Alonso Merchante de Valeria, titular bishop of Sidon, dated at Toledo on 5 March 1560, and composed by Cardinal Francisco de Mendoza. It was a denunciation of three cardinals, Contarini, Pole and Morone. As the first two had died, in 1542 and 1558 respectively, and Morone had been released and rehabilitated after the death of Pope Paul IV, in August 1559, it is hard to see why Mendoza composed his document, if it was not intended to condemn Carranza by association. The main, explicit target of the memorandum was, however, Pole, and particularly his views on the doctrine of justification. Mendoza first attacked Contarini for conceding too much on this subject to the Lutherans at Regensburg, in March–May 1541. The Spanish cardinal claimed that, before he died, on 24 August 1542, Contarini had been reproved by Paul III and some cardinals for his conduct in Germany. Mendoza added that Pole and Morone regarded Contarini as an oracle and asserted that, after the Venetian's death, it became public knowledge that they agreed with him, and hence with Luther, on justification by faith. When it came to the justification decree at the Council of Trent in 1546–7, Mendoza supported the view, held by many conservatives at the time, that Pole had left the council, without signing the decree on the subject, because he disagreed with its contents. His 1560 letter also mentioned prominent friends and associates of Pole in his Viterbo period, Vittoria Colonna and Marcantnio Flaminio, who died as suspected crypto-Lutherans, and the two Italian preachers who openly became Protestants, Piero Martire Vermigli

---

[67]  Tellechea, 'Carranza, Pole and Fresneda', *CP*, pp. 161, 163, 167; Tellechea, *Documentos históricos*, 2 (i), pp. 547–549.

and Bernardino Ochino. According to Mendoza, Paul III had wanted Pole to return to Trent to vote on the justification decree, but he refused, and had to be summoned to Rome, though he did submit to the terms of the decree when the council agreed it. The Spanish cardinal also mentioned the conclave of Julius III in 1549–50, at which Pole's orthodoxy had been impugned by the future Paul IV. Mendoza added the important information that Julius, once he was on the papal throne, had ordered Pole, and other cardinals, to write in support of the justification decree. Pole was initially reluctant but eventually agreed to do so, but not until he had been appointed legate to England, in August 1553. This time, he was approached by Pope Julius and by one of own his friends, Girolamo Muzzarelli, bishop of Conza. He submitted the result to the dean of Leuven/Louvain University, Ruard Tapper, who himself came under suspcion as a supposed 'crypto-Lutheran'. According to Mendoza's statement, Muzzarelli found that Pole's statement 'fell short in some things, and [was] even confused'. In fact, the bishop of Conza held the document back, apparently so that it would not further delay and hinder Pole's return to his homeland.[68]

By the time that all this information was collected by the Inquisition, in Valladolid and Rome, Reginald Pole and his queen were both dead. Before that happened, apart from Friar Bernardo de Fresneda, one other Spaniard, Gómez Suárez de Figueroa, fifth count of Feria and relative of King Philip, had had opportunities to see both of them, during their last, difficult months. He had been in England in 1554–5, fallen in love with one of Mary's ladies-in-waiting, Lady Jane Dormer, and made a serious effort to learn and speak English. At the time of the fall of Calais to Henry II of France, at the beginning of 1558, he was with his master in Brussels, as captain of the royal guard and an intimate and trusted counsellor. Even before then, Philip had been worried about the situation in England. He was well aware of his wife's loneliness and distress, especially after the public failure of her imagined second pregnancy, earlier in that year, as well as the continued obstinacy of those who resisted the Catholic restoration, and the cardinal archbishop's travails with Pope Paul. In such circumstances, Philip needed a trusted Spanish eye on proceedings in his island kingdom, and Feria was the obvious choice. He was duly dispatched, and arrived in London at the end of January 1558. His initial reaction to the beleaguered Pole was extremely negative. He complained that the cardinal was too compliant with the hesitations of Mary and her council, in the wake of the loss of Calais.[69] Feria's attitude to the cardinal, which may have been influenced by the gossip of Fresneda and others in Brussels, as well as his own personal commitment to the Jesuits, was ambiguous. On the one hand he accused Pole of interfering

---

[68]    Tellechea, 'Contarini, Pole, Morone, denunciados por el Cardenal Francisco de Mendoza (1560). Un documento del proceso de Carranza', *CP*, pp. 285–302.
[69]    *CSP Span* XIII nos 397, 402, 404, 406, 485, 444.

in government, having financial reports made to him, but at the same time he claimed that he was a 'dead man', demoralised and lacking in enthusiasm for the Church and even his own life. He claimed to be trying to re-animate the cardinal by talking to him each day, in and around Westminster.[70] Feria remained in England until July 1558, before leaving the ambassadorship in the hands of Don Alonso de Córdoba, and returning to the Continent.[71]

The death of Charles V, at Yuste in Spain on 21 September, would confine Philip to the Netherlands, while he also attempted to control his massive territorial and political inheritance, but, by October, he knew that both his wife and Pole were seriously ill, the latter with quartan fever. On 22 October, the king wrote to tell Pole that he could not come to England but would send instead the count of Feria, who left Philip at Arras, on 7 November, arriving in Dover by the 8th and London on the 9th.[72] He was accompanied by the Jesuit Pedro de Ribadeneira, who had been one of Ignatius's early companions, something that must have put further pressure on Pole. The count's dispatch to Philip, dated 14 November, details his discussions with the English council, and with the Lady Elizabeth ('Madama Ysabel') herself, concerning the succession, which was evidently imminent.[73] He also visited the cardinal, who was gravely ill.

As early as 6 September 1558, Pole had written to Philip, telling him that Queen Mary had an 'unusual fever', which had lasted four days (a 'quartan'), but her doctors expected her to recover soon. This was ominous, since there was a particularly severe influenza epidemic in England that year, from which people of all social classes died.[74] In this letter, Pole also reported that he himself had been suffering from a 'double quartan ague', and had now realised that this was indeed serious, something that he had previously been reluctant to admit. Later in that month, he was sufficiently anxious about his health to commend his Italian servants to the king, in a letter dated 23 September. By this time he had received a reply to his earlier letter, and now said that his fever was bothering him intermittently.[75] The count of Feria's meeting with the dying Pole, in November 1558, was unlikely to be easy. The two men had never seen eye to eye, and Feria had probably aggravated matters by bringing with him a leading Jesuit. More importantly and urgently, Philip wanted the count to facilitate Elizabeth's succession, and Pole had never got on with her either,

---

[70]   *CSP Span* XIII nos 413, 415.

[71]   M.J. Rodríguez-Salgado and Simon Adams, ed. and trans., 'The Count of Feria's dispatch to Philip II of 14 November 1558', *Camden Miscellany*, 28 (London: Royal Historical Society, 1984), pp. 302–344, at pp. 306–307; *PPP*, p. 338.

[72]   *CSP Span* XIII no. 482; AGS Estado 811 no. 88; *CRP* 3 no. 2293.

[73]   Rodríguez-Salgado and Adams, 'Dispatch', *passim*.

[74]   *PPP*, p. 343; Wriothesley, *Chronicle*, 2, pp. 90–91; Loades, *Reign of Mary Tudor*, p. 389 and n. 112.

[75]   *CRP* 3 nos 2276 (*CSP Ven*, VI (iii), no. 1264), 2282 (LPL Pole's register, fol. 81v).

only two meetings between them being recorded.[76] Also, at this time, one of Pole's more suspect associates, Pietro Carnesecchi, who would himself be tried by the Roman Inquisition, wrote to tell Giulio Gonzaga about rumours that the cardinal of England was now in trouble with Philip and his ministers, who blamed him for all the king's problems in England.[77]

Ominously, Feria also brought with him to England King Philip's confessor, Bernardo de Fresneda, who had apparently been sent to view and report on Queen Mary's physical health and spiritual state. On 10 November, he dispatched a report to Brussels, addressed not to the king himself but to his confidant, Ruy Gómez de Silva. In it he not only urged his master to take more emotional care of his wife, but also stressed that he needed to watch closely the English succession. He gave a detailed and pessimistic account of Mary's condition, and asked him to send her detailed instructions for the conduct of affairs, because her council, with whom the count of Feria was negotiating, was currently allowing her very little say in what happened.[78] As for Pole, by mid-November, he seems to have understood that her death was near, and that Elizabeth would soon succeed her half-sister as queen. On the 14th, he wrote to Elizabeth from Lambeth Palace, saying that although he himself was now mainly focused on the world to come, he wanted to leave everyone 'satisfied' with him, including her. He sent this letter to Hatfield House, where the princess resided, by the hand of his former servant Seth Holland, who was now dean of Worcester. Holland was given the cardinal's credentials to negotiate.[79] In parallel, the count of Feria went in person to talk to Elizabeth, meeting her at Brocket Hall, the home of the Lord Admiral and Lady Clinton, and reporting the result to the king in his dispatch of 14 November.[80] Both the archbishop and his queen were now preparing for death, on either side of the Thames, surrounded by a mixture of loyal friends and impatient enemies. What could not have been anticipated was that they would both die on the same day, 17 November, Mary at about seven in the morning, and Pole at about seven at night.

Four days later, the count of Feria reported the news in detail to King Philip. On what proved to be his last day alive, Pole was 'was very weak and with a continual temperature'. Both he and the queen had received all the Catholic rites in preparation for death, but an effort was made to conceal from the cardinal the news of Mary's passing. An unnamed servant broke the embargo, perhaps as the bells of Westminster rang out for Elizabeth's accession, and Pole went rapidly downhill. Feria's unsympathetic verdict was that:

[76] *CSP Ven*, VI (ii), no. 743.

[77] Giacomo Manzoni, ed., 'Il processo Carnesecchi', in *Miscellanea di Storia italiana*, 10 (1870), pp. 189–573, at p. 301.

[78] AGS Juntas y Consejos de Hacienda 34–482; Edwards, *Mary I*, pp. 328–329.

[79] BL Cotton Vespasian F. III, fol 28r; *ERP* 5 pp. 275–276; *CRP* 3 no. 2308.

[80] *CSP Ven*, VI (iii), no. 1285.

God did him a mercy in taking him, and Your Majesty lost very little in him, as far as I can understand, because of some things that they tell me, though I believed it all before.[81]

Evidently, Feria was referring to the inquiries and suspicions of the Roman Inquisition.

A very different tone was adopted by Pole's fellow suspect, Alvise Priuli, when he wrote to his brother Antonio, on 27 November, giving more details of his friend and master's last hours. He said that both cardinal and queen had made their confession regularly, in the month preceding their deaths, and had received extreme unction, the last rites, on 15 November. He confirmed that, on the 17th, the intention had been to keep the news of Mary's death from Pole, but a servant had told him, and he reacted by saying to Priuli and the bishop of St Asaph, Thomas Goldwell, that it was appropriate that they should depart this life together, since they had shared in each other's struggles for so many years. Now, he said, in words which show no sign of a belief in purgatory, Mary was 'assumed to the Kingdom [of Heaven] (*assunta al Regno*)'. After he heard the news, Pole could still speak, but was deeply affected and tearful. Having finished articulating his reaction to Mary's departure, he remained silent for about 15 minutes. To those around his bed, it seemed that his spirit was still strong, although, physically, he became ever weaker. By the time that he was hit by another of the feverish fits which regularly afflicted him, he had also acquired a chill. At this point, he ordered the prayers for the dying to be brought, and the evening offices of vespers and compline were said. This was at about 5 o'clock and two hours later he died.[82]

In a second account of the archbishop's death, also written by Priuli, on the same day, to Antonio Giberti, in Rome, some of the details of Pole's last days were varied. In this version, both Mary and Pole received the last rites on 16 November, and, on the same day, the cardinal had a Mass of the Holy Spirit celebrated at Lambeth, and then on the 17th he was accompanied to a 'very quiet and very calm death' by the recitation of the Angelus, in which he apparently took part. At the hour of his death, Pole had been surrounded by Bishop Goldwell, Dean Holland, and many members of his own *familia* at Lambeth.[83] Few details are known of Pole's funeral, which took place in Canterbury cathedral, after, with the permission of the new queen, he had lain in state for 40 days at Lambeth. According to the diarist Henry Machyn, who, being himself a funeral director, took a professional interest, the order for Pole's obsequies, including

---

[81]   Tellechea, 'Inglaterra, Flandes y España', *CP*, p. 275 (doc. XVIII).

[82]   *CSP Ven*, VI (iii), no. 1286; *CRP* 3 no. 2311.

[83]   *CSP Ven*, VI (iii), no. 1287; *CRP* 3 no. 2312.

his place of burial, was agreed by Elizabeth's new council.[84] For the journey to Canterbury, the late cardinal archbishop's body was carried on a 'chariot' or hearse, surrounded by four gilded banners, which may have depicted doctors of the Church, as well as his personal coat-of-arms.[85] The cortège travelled via Rochester, where the west door of the cathedral was especially opened for its entrance, and the funeral took place in Canterbury cathedral on 15 December, the day after Queen Mary was laid to rest in Westminster Abbey. The eulogies delivered at Pole's funeral, one in Latin and the other in English, would serve as prototypes for his biographers.[86]

Pole had wished to be buried in the 'Corona' of St Thomas Becket's former shrine in his cathedral, and this was permitted. The 'Corona', which represented the 'crowned' head of the martyred Thomas, is to the east of the cathedral's high altar and in the north-western corner of St Thomas's chapel. Pole's simple, stone tomb was placed on the left-hand side of its entrance, surrounded by an Italian-style painting in oil, in fact on the flat wall but giving the false perspective of a narrow apse, to form the 'monument' of the tomb itself. What is visible today is a late nineteenth-century restoration, requested and largely paid for by the Catholic Truth Society.[87] The original work was done by Dominick Lampson (Dominicus Lampsonius, 1532–99), a Flemish painter, poet and humanist, who was born in Bruges but spent much of his life in the prince-bishopric of Liège. Lampson no doubt received this commission as a result of his having worked for three years at Lambeth, as a secretary, up to Pole's death. The tomb itself was a plain stone slab, with no effigy, and it may well be that this simplicity reflected the reforming ideas picked up by Pole during his time in Italy. His friend and mentor, Gian Matteo Giberti, had, for example, believed that large and ostentatious tombs obstructed worship and thus hindered the faithful. Although Lampson himself never visited Italy and only knew its art from reproductions, his teacher, Lambert Lombard, who came from Liège and served its successive diocesans, did go to Italy in 1537, while Pole was taking refuge from Henry VIII's agents with the then bishop of Liège, his friend and correspondent Everard de la Marck. Lombard thus had direct experience both of Italian art and of the cardinal on whose tomb his pupil Lampson worked.[88]

The 'monument' surrounding the tomb bears Pole's apt motto, *Estote ergo prudentes sicut serpentes, et simplices sicut columbae* ('Be wise as serpents and innocent as doves' (Matthew 10:16b)). The composition (*invenzione*), which may well have been designed by Lampson and Pole's faithful retainer,

---

[84]   Machyn, *Diary*, p. 178.

[85]   Machyn, *Diary*, p. 185.

[86]   *PPP*, pp. 345–346.

[87]   *PPP*, pp. 345 and illustration 17; p. 348 and note 279 provide fuller details of this restoration.

[88]   *PPP*, pp. 348, 354.

Gianfrancesco Stella, consists of two 'stories', with a strong emphasis on the liberation of the cardinal's soul from its earthly prison, and on the Resurrection of Christ, a state also promised to His faithful. About 1580, when the tomb seems still to have been more or less intact, Francis Thynne, who wrote a short 'Life' of Pole but disliked Lampson's work, reported that on the tomb itself there was an emblem ('device') representing the cardinal's scriptural motto in the form of a globe with a snake twisted around it, on the snake's head a white dove, and attached to it the words *prudens simplicitas* ('prudent simplicity').[89] Eighteenth-century engravings of Pole's monument, although not making it easy to distinguish detail, indicate a painted Classical structure, with false perspective suggesting a recess, but also show a previous painting underneath, in which a large figure of St Christopher, together with a fish, an early Christian symbol, remained visible.[90] The Lampson ensemble included pairs of cherubic boys, or 'sprites', and the Hebrew symbol of God's name, the Tetragrammaton, as well as the text, *Beati mortui qui Domino moriuntur* ('Blessed are the dead who from now on die [or "will die"] in the Lord' (Revelation 14:13)).[91]

To anyone in Rome, or elsewhere in Europe, who was familiar with the iconography of the late medieval and Renaissance prophetic groups associated with Abbot Joachim of the twelfth century and the 'spiritual' Franciscans of the 1300s and later, this quotation from the New Testament 'Apocalypse' would have attracted immediate attention. When combined with the style and content of Lampson's 'monument', such a viewer, whether friendly or hostile, would almost certainly have recognised at once an allusion to the 'Angelic Pope', which Pole had so nearly become, in the conclave of Julius III. What can still be discerned of the Fleming's work in Canterbury bears a striking resemblance to the painting, also in oil on plaster, in the Borgherini chapel in the Franciscan church of San Pietro in Montorio in Rome, by Sebastiano del Piombo who also painted Pole himself, during his time in Viterbo.[92] In the real, not virtual, apse or recess of the first chapel from the west, in the south aisle of the 'other' St Peter's in Rome, Sebastiano unusually combined a portrayal of Christ's flagellation at the pillar, during his Passion (John 19:1) with his transfiguration on Mount Tabor (Matthew 17:1–8). The message, associated with those who longed for an end to the corruption of the Roman papacy, basing much of their thought and prayer on the Book of Revelation, was that, after much suffering, the Church would itself be transfigured. Many, including the painter and very probably Pole himself, believed that this task would be carried out by an 'Angelic

[89]  Francis Thynne, 'Reginald Pole', in Raphael Holinshed, *Chronicles of England, Scotland and Ireland* (London: J. Johnson et al., 6 vols, 1807–8), 4, pp. 745–746.
[90]  *PPP*, pp. 350–351 (illustrations 18, 19).
[91]  *PPP*, pp. 352–354.
[92]  *PPP*, pp. 386–391.

Pope', who would restore the purity of the Gospel and the Christian life.[93] It had been thought by some that Pope Marcellus would bring in this era, but his early death had ushered in a very different approach to papacy, in the irascible form of Gianpietro Carafa.[94] Perhaps he who 'died in the Lord', as was written on Pole's tomb, would achieve the reward of his faithfulness to this 'spiritual' Christianity, but as soon as he was dead, as in life, his character and reputation began to be fought over, in ecclesiastical politics and in print.

[93] Josephine Jungić, 'Joachimist prophecies in Sebatiano del Piombo's Borgherini chapel and Raphael's *Transfiguration*', in *Prophetic Rome in the High Renaissance period*, ed. Marjorie Reeves (Oxford: Clarendon Press, 1992), pp. 321–343.

[94] William Hudon, 'Epilogue: Marcellus II, Girolamo Seripando, and the image of the Angelic Pope', in Reeves, *Prophecy*, pp. 373–387.

# Chapter 9

# Legacy

Even in less fraught circumstance, the death of an archbishop of Canterbury would have been a matter of national importance, and Pole's departure confronted the new Queen Elizabeth with the need for immediate decision and action. On 21 November 1558, the count of Feria reported to Philip, who, in accordance with the 1554 marriage treaty, was no longer king of England, that two days after the cardinal died, a delegation of royal commissioners, consisting of the earl of Rutland, Nicholas Throckmorton, and George Carew, had arrived at Lambeth, with instructions to 'embargo all his goods, and they made an inventory of them'.[1] It was made clear to Feria, and to Pole's household, that the commissioners expected to find great wealth.[2] They eventually had to admit that they had failed to do so, but the question of Pole's personal finances is an interesting one, particularly in view of his known reforming ideals.

As a young man, still favoured by King Henry VIII, Reginald had been what has been described as an 'egregious pluralist', in terms of ecclesiastical benefices from which he received income without performing any duties.[3] Beginning at Magdalen College, Oxford, in 1512, with a royal pension of £12 per annum, he had an increase in the following year, and in 1518–19 started acquiring livings, including the deanery of Wimborne minster and two successive canon's stalls, or prebends, in Salisbury cathedral. Between 1523 and 1526, he was an absentee fellow (*socius compar*) of Corpus Christi College, Oxford, in addition to the pension that he received from Henry, while he was in Italy. This amounted to 300 *lire* or about 500 *scudi*. At this time, his income from all sources seems to have totalled about £170 sterling, which befitted a nobleman of royal descent. Once back in England, in 1527, Pole began collecting benefices once more, including a stall in the collegiate church of Knaresborough, Yorkshire, as well as a prebend of Exeter, which in August of that year was replaced by the deanship of that cathedral, again *in absentia*. When the property and income of the English Church, as a whole, were valued by the Crown, in the *Valor ecclesiasticus*, during

---

[1]  On 19 November 1558, the commissioners made an inventory of the horses in Pole's stables at Lambeth, Canterbury Park and Ford, while the next day they listed his bedding and his wardrobe (*CSP Dom Queen Elizabeth*, 1, nos 10 (i), 10 (ii) and 10 (iii)).

[2]  Tellechea, 'Inglaterra, Flandes y España', in Tellechea, *CP*, p. 275; TNA SP 12/1, fols 20r–29r; *CSP Dom 1558–70*, no. 102.

[3]  John B. Gleason, *John Colet* (Berkeley and Los Angeles: University of California Press, 1989), p. 44.

the dispute with Rome over King Henry's divorce and papal authority, Pole was recorded as having an income of about £200, which was substantial. This rose to about £250 in 1532, when he acquired the rectory of Puddletown in Dorset.[4] Such happy pluralism, which suggested a smooth path towards even higher office in the Church, was abruptly ended when Pole finally came out publicly against the divorce.

By the end of 1536, Henry's former protégé had lost all his English benefices, and, when Paul III made him a cardinal, he gave him the relatively small pension of a 'poor cardinal', which amounted to 200 *scudi* per month (about £67), so that he could live, if only parsimoniously, among the princes and merchant dynasts of Italy. His income rose when he was made legate to Viterbo in August 1541, to the equivalent of about £120 a month, but his outgoings were substantial too. Fortunately for him, in 1542, he began to receive legacies from his 'spiritual' friends, and these strengthened his financial position. Bishop Giberti of Verona bequeathed to him two substantial pensions drawn from Spanish cathedrals, Burgos and Granada, as well as one from the cathedral schoolmastership (*capscolania*) of Valencia cathedral, though Pole would have great difficulty in obtaining the money owed from Spain. Yet at least some of it did arrive to swell his coffers, and tragedy again brought him financial advantage when his friend and penitent, Vittoria Colonna, died in 1547, leaving him 9,000 *scudi*, although the money was primarily intended as a dowry for Vittoria's daughter. In July of that year, Pole moved from his legation at Viterbo to be papal governor in nearby Bagnoregio, but although he received a stipend in this post, he probably lost on the transaction. There he remained into the 1550s, still receiving the pension of a 'poor cardinal' at the time of the conclave of Julius III, at which he was almost elected pope. In June 1550, he was receiving a papal pension of 1,800 *scudi* per annum, but by this time he was also being paid one by the Emperor Charles V. In addition, in 1549, Pope Paul III had granted him the abbey of Gavello/ Canalnuovo, which he held *in commendam* for 300 scudi (c. £100) per annum. The practice of commendation, whereby the wealth of monastic communities was extracted by absentees, was seen by many as a scandal, and even Leo X's conservative Fifth Lateran Council had tried to ban it, but a reformer such as Pole still did not feel able to resist its attractions. As a result, by the time that Edward VI died, Mary won the English throne, and the cardinal of England was appointed as legate to his homeland, it seems that he was receiving as income approximately 4,800 *scudi* (£1,600) a year, or even more. When Julius III made him his legate, he automatically doubled his stipend.[5]

Once Pole arrived in England, in November 1554, and started to administer the English, Welsh and Irish churches directly, it is curiously difficult to discover

---

[4]   Mayer, 'Cardinal Pole's finances: the property of a reformer', in Mayer, *CPEC*, XV, pp. 1–4.

[5]   Mayer, 'Cardinal Pole's finances', pp. 4–8.

how much revenue ended up in his hands. Potential sources of income included the fees payable for his legatine absolutions and dispensations, but, when he died his loyal secretary and executor, Alvise Priuli, claimed that he had virtually no money left, and this may well have been true. Similarly, Pietro Carnesecchi stated that, when he died, Pole had only about 4,000 *scudi* in total, which will have been a disappointment to Elizabeth and her agents. Once he was installed as archbishop of Canterbury, in March 1556, he did however receive £5,000 per annum, by order of the king and queen, as well as £2,600 a year in ordinary revenues from his diocese and its outlying 'peculiars'. It was the job of the lord treasurer, William Paulet, marquess of Winchester, to find Pole's income as archbishop, to add to what his diocese could produce. This was done partly by assigning to him a pension of £1,000 from the diocese of Winchester, to be paid in six-monthly instalments, and partly from the revenues of lands in Kent, Sussex and Surrey which had earlier been confiscated by the Crown from the diocese of Canterbury.[6] If these funds proved to be insufficient, Queen Mary told Paulet to make up the difference with Treasury receipts. This order was executed on 13 March 1556, just over a week before the burning of Cranmer, and Pole continued to receive this money until his death, apart from the last instalment, due at Michaelmas (29 September) 1558, which may have been held back because of Pole's illness, rather than a premonition of his demise.

One of the difficulties in assessing the cardinal's finances is the hopeless mixing of public and private funding in his budgeting. Nevertheless, it is clear that the vast majority of his income was consumed by the expenses of his household, which included the funding of trips home for his Italian servants. Also, while in England, he and his receiver, Henry Pyning, often had difficulty in laying hands on the Continental revenues to which he was entitled, including the Spanish pensions and the income from his commendatory abbey of Gavello, in Italy. Pole himself must have been aware that, in receiving income from many of these sources, he was going against his reformist conscience, which had been evident since the late 1530s, when he sat on Paul III's commission, but he could no doubt assure himself, or try to, that the work in England demanded such a sacrifice of ideals. In his last year of life, it became particularly awkward for Pole that he needed money from Burgos cathedral, since its bishop was Cardinal Francisco de Mendoza, who by this time was convinced that both he and his friend Carranza, along with Priuli, were 'Lutheran' heretics. When he died, Pole was also still owed 6,000 *scudi* (£2,000) by the papacy in legatine expenses. It is not therefore surprising that Elizabeth's men quickly realised that he had not been sitting on heaps of money.[7]

[6]  Corpus Christi College, Cambridge MS 127, no. 1; *CSP Ven*, VI (i), no. 482; Mayer, 'Cardinal Pole's finances', *CPEC*, XV, p. 10 and n. 67.

[7]  Mayer, 'Cardinal Pole's finances', *CPEC*, XV, pp. 10–15.

One source of confusion, in the winter of 1558–9, was the fact that Pole never produced a definitive will, the best available version having been made on 4 October 1558.[8] In addition, according to Alvise Priuli, who was Pole's main executor, he had a list of benefactions prepared, but was too ill to sign it, though he did give the Venetian oral permission to use it. The will itself was proved with remarkable rapidity, on 8 December 1558, allowing Pole's affairs to be wrapped up in the next few months.[9] This relatively simple document begins with a devout preamble, in which Pole commended his soul to God, without mention of the Virgin Mary and the company of saints in heaven. He also expressed his devout obedience to the Roman See, including its current occupant, Paul IV, and this shocked some of his reformist friends. Pietro Carnesecchi, for example, agreed with another of Pole's Italian circle, Giulia Gonzaga, that this humble submission was ill-timed, given that the pope was pursuing Pole for heresy up to his dying day, and his reputation was still being besmirched, in and around the Roman Inquisition. Later, Carnesecchi added bitterly that, fortunately, faith in God, and its reward, were not judged by men.[10]

As was the custom for dying cardinals, Pole remitted to the Apostolic See any debts he still owed, for example in the form of annates, ever since he was elected to the college under Paul III. A total of 6,000 ducats from his expenses during his English legation were to go to pay this debt. As was indeed done, he instructed that his body should be buried in Canterbury cathedral, in the chapel of St Thomas Becket's head, and, in the manner of older tradition, two chantries were to be established there, to pray for his soul, those of his relatives, and of all the faithful departed. Mass was to be celebrated daily at one or other of these altars. Priuli, as heir and executor, was to distribute his designated benefactions, since he had no living family members. Priuli was to take charge of all his goods, whether in England, Italy or Spain: 'He is to act as me.' He was to accept as much of his master's residue as he wished, after the benefactions had been made, while Henry Pyning, 'my faithful and most dear chamberlain and receiver-general', was to deal with the accounts. It was customary for property 'dilapidations' to be paid out of a deceased archbishop's estate to his successor, and Pole noted, in this context, that he had spent £1,000 on building works at Lambeth Palace.[11] This statement was important, since, according to Pyning's accounts as receiver, in 1556 and 1557, Pole had had new apartments built onto the palace, at a cost of approximately £600. No detailed accounts of the work itself survive, but it seems that this project absorbed at least a fifth of Pole's income, as legate and archbishop. Because of the many changes made since in the palace, it is impossible

---

[8]  *CRP* 3 no. 2286.
[9]  *CRP* 3 no. 2311; TNA PROB 11/42A, fols 107r–108r; SP11/14, no. 1.
[10]  Manzoni, 'Processo Pietro Carnesecchi', p. 294; Mayer, *PPP*, p. 294.
[11]  *CRP* 3 no. 2286.

to establish exactly what was done, but eighteenth-century engravings appear to indicate a range of rooms, with a gallery, on the east side of the palace, and open arches underneath, forming a *loggia*, in the Italian style that would have been so familiar to the cardinal, though not ideally suited to the London climate.[12] Still surviving, in splendour and useful as a backdrop for photographs, is one of the two fig trees that were supposedly planted during Pole's time as archbishop, and perhaps includes the remains of the other.

Although Alvise Priuli was the main executor of Pole's will, he was given a committee of Englishmen to supervise him, all of them faithful servants of what was now, after 17 November 1558, the *ancien régime*. They were Nicholas Heath, archbishop of York and lord chancellor, Thomas Thirlby, bishop of Ely, Sir Edward Hastings, chamberlain to Queen Mary, John Boxall, secretary to Mary's privy council, Sir Edward Waldegrave, chancellor of the duchy of Lancaster, Sir William Cordell, master of the rolls, and Henry Cole, vicar-general of Canterbury diocese. When this document was drawn up, Pole evidently assumed that the queen at the time of its execution would be Mary, and he asked her to remove any impediments to the execution of his will, also granting £50 to each of his executors and asserting that any future codicils to it should have full legal force. The document was witnessed by Bishop Thomas Goldwell of St Asaph, Dean Seth Holland of Worcester, Pole's chaplain Maurice Clynnog, and his auditor, Gianfrancesco Stella. The will was sealed by his secretary, Marcantonio Feita, and written by Dominick Lampson, who painted his tomb in Canterbury. The list of those who received legacies from Pole's estate, administered by Priuli, was lengthy. The former almonry of Canterbury cathedral, which may have been Pole's private oratory there, was granted to the King's School, and some ecclesiastical plate, including a silver-gilt cross and large candlesticks, went to the cathedral. Pole had wanted to give some of his books and manuscripts to the revived Dominican house in Oxford, but he evidently doubted, correctly, whether it would survive, and the bequest in fact went to New College. Another part of his library, mostly his Greek books, was bequeathed to what became the English College in Rome, over which Pole had had personal oversight for many years, when it was still the English pilgrims' hospice. Perhaps ironically, whether consciously or not, Pole left an inkstand to Elizabeth's new secretary, Sir William Cecil, and other small gifts went to the earl and countess of Rutland, the former having come to rummage in Lambeth Palace for the cardinal's imagined treasure. As well as making various payments to his household, to relatives and to Priuli himself, Pole left a property in Rome to Carlo Gualteruzzi and made a small benefaction to the Knights Hospitallers of St John.[13] In his letter of 27 November 1558 to his brother Antonio in Rome, Alvise Priuli said that he really

---

[12] Mayer, *PPP*, pp. 321, 330; LPL MS 3563, fols 12, 26r–27v.

[13] *CRP* 3 no. 2286.

did not want to take anything from Pole, and that all his estate should go to pious causes.[14] In his parallel letter to Antonio Giberti, Priuli said that the late cardinal had made nothing out of his legation to England, and had spent all his income, including funds from Spain and Italy.[15]

Almost immediately after her half-sister's death, Elizabeth began to give indications of her future course in matters of religion, which would also be central to England's foreign relations, especially with the Habsburgs and the papacy. Sermons preached at St Paul's Cross, in London, continued to reflect official views and policy, as in the previous reign, and the first sermon of Elizabeth's reign was preached by William Bill, a Protestant who had been marginalised under Mary. Although, while Queen Mary and her cardinal had continued their work, the long-term prospects for the reformed religion had looked bleak, the count of Feria was evidently right to tell King Philip, in November 1558, that the English expected Elizabeth to change policy drastically, in favour of a Protestant settlement. Significantly, as soon as the news from London spread, all trials and planned executions of 'heretics' were halted, and imprisoned suspects were released.[16] When Mary came to the throne, in 1553, she had implicitly and explicitly encouraged the restoration of the Sarum rite, even though it was still illegal under parliamentary statute, and it was probably expected by many that Elizabeth would act in the same manner. In reality, she took a strictly legal line, allowing, and indeed requiring, the Catholic liturgy to continue as the sole legal form of worship in her kingdom, until parliament decided otherwise. Yet this legalistic approach did enable her to make a few small, but significant, changes, in the use of her own Chapel Royal, in cases where earlier liturgical experiments in the vernacular, made under Henry VIII and Edward VI, had not been specifically forbidden by the Act of Repeal passed by Mary's first parliament, in November 1553. Famously, the new queen retained a crucifix and two candles on the holy table in her chapel, but she also made adjustments to the service, which for the time being, was still following the Catholic cycle of Office and Mass, from matins and lauds in the morning to the last votive antiphon at night.[17] Although the rest of the Catholic clergy were initially left undisturbed, immediately after her accession, Elizabeth removed the dean of the Chapel Royal, Bishop Thomas Thirlby, and replaced him with George Carew, who had remained unobtrusive in the previous reign, but was evidently expected to be amenable to changes in a reformed direction.[18] The only illegal action authorised by Elizabeth at this time was the omission of the elevation of the

---

[14]   *CRP* 3 no. 2311.

[15]   *CRP* 3 no. 2312 (27 November 1558).

[16]   Haigh, *English reformations*, pp. 238, 225.

[17]   MacCulloch, *Later Reformation*, p. 29.

[18]   *CSP Span* 1558–1567, p. 6.

consecrated bread and wine at the culmination of the Mass. In any case, it seems clear that the queen intended to abandon the Latin liturgy, even if she insisted on waiting for parliament to act, and her initial moves all exploited loopholes to restore vernacular uses that had been legal in the last year of Henry VIII's reign (1546–7) and in the first two years of Edward VI. Thus on Sunday 16 December (*O Sapientia*), the English litany was restored in the Chapel Royal, to replace the procession before the High Mass. In a proclamation issued on 27 December, the feast of St John the Evangelist, again using a loophole in her predecessor's legislation, Elizabeth extended the optional use of the English litany to the parishes, as well as another practice which had already been re-introduced in her chapel, which was the reading in English, apparently in addition to Latin, of the Epistle and Gospel at the High Mass. In the last years of Henry VIII, the lessons had been read in English at matins and evensong, but the use of the vernacular in the Mass itself was in fact a return to the practice of the first two years of his son's reign.

Meanwhile, the former King Philip of England spent that Christmas and New Year in the monastery of Grunendal, in the Netherlands, where he received news of the new queen's doings from Feria. On 29 December 1558, the feast of St Thomas Becket, whose commemoration had been restored by Mary and in whose chapel at Canterbury Pole was now buried, the count dispatched a report to Philip of the Christmas liturgical events at the English court. The first major incident had occurred at the High Mass on Christmas Day, which was celebrated by Owen Oglethorpe, bishop of Carlisle. After the service had begun, the queen indicated that there should be no elevation of the consecrated elements. According to Feria, Bishop Oglethorpe replied that 'Her Majesty was lady of the person and life, but not of the conscience'. When Elizabeth realised that the bishop was going to defy her, and perform the prescribed rite, she got her retaliation in first, by leaving the chapel after the reading of the Gospel. According to Feria, on 28 December, the feast of the Holy Innocents, a different celebrant, perhaps George Carew, omitted the elevation of the bread and wine.[19] Carew was certainly the celebrant at the first major public ceremony of Elizabeth's reign, which was her coronation in Westminster Abbey on 15 January 1559. The Benedictine community was still in place and the ritual, including the High Mass, was traditional, but there were two obvious signs of things to come. The queen refused to allow the monks to process before her, carrying tapers, and the eucharistic elevations were omitted. All the existing bishops having refused to officiate, the faithful Carew obliged, and it is possible that Elizabeth received communion in both kinds, though as she did so behind

---

[19]  AGS Estado 811, nos 101–103.

curtains, as was customary for European royalty, this is not certain.[20] The absence of the English bishops was a clear indication of the conflict that had already broken out, in the first few weeks of the reign, between Elizabeth and the existing Church establishment.

Crucial to the achievement and nature of Elizabeth's religious settlement was William Cecil, the future Lord Burghley, who had conformed in the previous reign and kept close to power, even though he had played no significant public role. At the end of March 1558, Cecil had met Elizabeth at Somerset House, in London, apparently in his capacity as surveyor of her estates, but by the time of Mary's death, he had become her half-sister's secretary. On 20 November, he attended her council at Hatfield House. Immediately, he became active in religious, as well as general political matters, and at about this time, he seems to have received a letter of advice on the future of the English Church from Edward Guest, who would later become one of Elizabeth's new bench of bishops. The document, which has been dated to 1552 but seems to fit much better the context of 1558–9, was a revision of the first Prayer Book of Edward VI (1549), concentrating on the most contentious aspects of the book, in terms of the religious situation at the time. These were the use of liturgical ceremony and the Eucharist.

In December 1558, William Cecil also asked the advice, on church matters, of his old friend from Gray's Inn, Richard Goodrich. As was inevitable, given England's situation at the time, still technically a Catholic country with Spain as an ally, but threatened by conflict with the papacy, France and Scotland, Goodrich took a wide-ranging view, stating, on the basis of Henrician political thought and ecclesiology, that there was no need for the kingdom to continue to submit to papal authority. Given the dreadful state of relations between England and Pope Paul IV, during Mary and Pole's last years, it seemed certain that Elizabeth, being the bastard daughter of Anne Boleyn, would have had to sue humiliatingly, and quite possibly unsuccessfully, for a papal dispensation to succeed her half-sister as a Catholic monarch. Goodrich adopted a robustly independent line, asserting, not implausibly in view of recent events, that England had done nothing but suffer from the pope's authority and 'curse'. Nevertheless, Pope Paul should not be unnecessarily provoked, given that the two great powers of Europe, France and the Habsburgs, were negotiating a peace that might leave Elizabeth in dangerous isolation. Goodrich therefore advised Cecil that the government should prepare very carefully before it brought religious proposals to parliament. The first stage should be to repeal just a few laws relating to the powers of bishops, which had been restored under Mary in accordance with Roman canon law. As far as the liturgy was concerned, things

---

[20]   C.G. Bayne, 'The coronation of Queen Elizabeth', *English Historical Review*, 22 (1907), pp. 650–673.

should carry on as they currently were in the Chapel Royal, with the Sarum Mass but excluding the elevations.[21]

More radical was an anonymous 'Devise for the alteration of religion', which appeared in Mary's last days, and was very probably written by Cecil himself. It certainly reflected the radical Protestant views of his circle, many of whom had known each other since Cambridge days. For them, it was a basic tenet that Roman religion could never be 'true' religion, and Edward VI's reign was the only model for how things should be, although it would have to be improved upon. At this stage, with English negotiators still in the Franco-Habsburg peace conference at Câteau-Cambrésis, hoping vainly to recover Calais, Cecil seems to have regarded Spain as an ally. Not unreasonably, he was mainly concerned by the threat of Paul IV and France. He feared that, if what he regarded as 'true' religion was restored in England, France would be able to attack on grounds of heresy, as well as traditional enmity. Pope Paul would excommunicate Elizabeth, and put her kingdom under interdict, thus bringing about a crisis in both Church and state. In these circumstances, which would indeed occur after 1570, England would be 'prey to all princes that will enter against it'. Scotland would invade with French help, and Ireland would become a dangerous centre of dissidence, 'by reason of the clergy [there] that is so addicted to Rome'.[22] The new regime in England also faced internal enemies. Mary's officials, apart from members of her council who could be removed at once, would try to cling to power, while her remaining bishops, along with the great majority of the lower clergy, would urge their flocks to oppose any reformation of religion. Most of the judges and justices of the peace would probably aid and abet them, refusing to enforce any new laws on worship that might be enacted by parliament. If Elizabeth's government asked for financial aid from her subjects, there might well be rebellion in the shires, and protest might come not only from traditionalists but also from radical Protestants, who would feel that the regime's reform of the Church had not gone far enough.

To confront all these difficulties, Cecil proposed to begin by reducing the external threats to Elizabeth's England. Rather than trying to regain Calais, the kingdom should sue for peace with France, although there was also the possibility of meddling in the growing religious conflict across the Channel, in both French and Habsburg territory. Given the intransigence of Paul IV, whose demise had been often predicted but still had not materialised, Cecil saw no point in trying to conciliate Rome, with its 'evil will, cursing and practising'. With or without the French threat, it would be necessary to re-fortify the border with Scotland, and extra funds and troops would be needed to secure Ireland from the interference

---

[21]  TNA SP 12/1, fols 156r–158r; Stephen Alford, *Burghley: William Cecil at the Court of Elizabeth I* (New Haven and London: Yale University Press, 2008), pp. 80–82, 90–92.

[22]  BL Add. MS 48035, fols 144r–146v; Alford, *Burghley*, pp. 92–93.

of Catholic powers. Those of Mary's councillors who were primarily there because of their devotion to the papacy should be removed, as indeed occurred, but the religious test was to remain essential in new appointments. Elizabeth's councillors were to be chosen on the basis both of their long service to her in her 'wilderness years' and of their good, in other words Protestant, religion. This 'Devise' was referred to Cecil's Cambridge circle for amendment as necessary, and duly examined by that group at the house of Cecil's old tutor, Sir Thomas Smith, in Cannon Row, Westminster. After this, the document was put before Elizabeth, with a view to its being considered subsequently in parliament. The religious climate at court, as the year 1559 began, was graphically illustrated in a Twelfth Night masque in which the Roman cardinals were portrayed as crows, and a statue of Henry VIII's bugbear, St Thomas Becket, whose feast had just been commemorated in the churches, was beheaded and ejected from the scene.[23] Such was the recently-deceased Cardinal Pole's legacy in the court of the new queen, as he lay in his new tomb near Becket's shrine in Canterbury.

With the queen's coronation accomplished, in a somewhat polemical religious atmosphere, the first parliament of the reign assembled on 25 January 1559. It was opened by the new lord keeper of the privy seal, Nicholas Bacon, who was a close friend and ally of William Cecil, and at once introduced the main item on the agenda, which was 'an uniform order of religion'. The penitential season of Lent was about to begin, with the traditional ceremonies of Ash Wednesday, but the preachers chosen for Paul's Cross in that season, including Pole's successor Matthew Parker, were strongly reformist. Their message, which was generally understood to be that of the government, was that papal authority in England was over and done with: true religion would triumph, with the overthrow of idolatry and superstition. On 9 February, the first ecclesiastical bill, for the restoration of the Royal Supremacy over the Church, was introduced for its first reading, not in the Lords, whose attitude was uncertain, but in the Commons, where reformists were reckoned to be dominant. Things did not go entirely smoothly, however, and the second reading took three days, to the annoyance of Cecil and his parliamentary business managers, who eventually succeeded in having it sent up to the Lords. Even so, it now seemed likely that the bill would not pass in its initial form, and a second version was drafted, and introduced to the Commons on 28 February. While it was still in the Lower House, the bishops issued, on 3 March, a robust statement of the Catholic position, which was still, of course, the law of the land at this stage, but Cecil and his allies brushed this intervention aside. Ten days later, the revised Supremacy bill reached the Lords, where Archbishop Nicholas Heath of York, the most senior bishop in the hierarchy since the death of Pole, declared that no woman could be Head of the Church.

---

[23]     *CSP Ven*, 1558–80, p. 11; Alford, *Burghley*, pp. 92–94.

Notable in this debate, in that it was given by a lay peer, was the speech delivered by a relative of the late cardinal, Anthony Browne, who, in September 1554 had chosen the title Viscount Montague, in honour of the executed Henry Pole, baron of the same name. Browne, the only lay peer to vote against the Royal Supremacy in this committee debate, analysed the perilous political and strategic position of England in a manner remarkably similar that of William Cecil and his allies, but drew the opposite conclusion, when it came to matters of religion. He made a blistering attack on the Supremacy bill, seeing it clearly as undermining the whole of Mary and Philip's religious settlement:

> the matter in hande, to the body wherof exhibited unto us I have to speake and not to the particularitie of the title, which only toucheth the Scripture, carying awaye by generall wordes the whole estate of Christ's religion. For as in the first parte the supremacie is only intreated of, even so in the bodie of the bill, all that ever was made for the defence of the [Catholic] faith against the malignitie of wicked heresies, are wholly repealed, and the confusion lately used in religion, newely received and established: the Masse abrogated, the sacrifice of the Churche rejected, the sacramentes prophaned, the holie aultars destroyed, temples vyolated, mariage of preistes allowed, their children made legitimate; lybertie given to them by purchase or other meanes to procure to their posteritie, lands and hereditamentes, and thus I conceive the effect of this bill.

Having got this off his chest, Viscount Montague explicitly proclaimed his own allegiance to the religion:

> which I professed in my baptisme, wher I was made a member of Christs misticall bodie, and vowed to beleeve the holy Catholique Churche, as the spowse and only beloved of Christe, by unitie in the which I am to bee saved or damned.

In these words, Montague not only represented the late Cardinal Pole's views, but also prefigured what would become the Roman Catholic case against Elizabeth and her successors.[24]

Holy Week was approaching, and the government realised that, given opposition in the Lords, the Supremacy bill would not be enacted until after Easter. Parliament would need to be prorogued until after the solemn season, but, although the full Catholic observance, including confession, liturgy and Easter communion, would continue, the frustrated government rushed through parliament a bill which stipulated that there would be no penalty for those who preferred to use the 1552 Prayer Book instead, thus omitting virtually all the

---

[24]  Michael C. Questier, *Catholicism and community in early modern England, c. 1550–1640* (Cambridge: Cambridge University Press, 2006), pp. 119–122.

traditional ceremonies of the season. At 9 o'clock in the morning on Good Friday (24 March), Queen Elizabeth herself went to parliament, with the hope of being able to assent to the revised Supremacy Act, but, with last-minute advice, she instead prorogued Parliament until the Monday after Low Sunday (3 April). In the meantime, in order to move things along, Cecil suggested that there should be a debate between Catholic and Reformed clergy, on the pattern of some Continental cities in the early Reformation. This duly began in Westminster Abbey, on 3 April, before the Lords and Commons, and was chaired by Nicholas Bacon. The intention was that the Catholics would be publicly out-argued, and parliament would agree to a new reformation settlement, but in the event the traditionalists, who were already under considerable personal pressure from the government, refused to accept the debating conditions, which involved their producing a set of questions for the reformers to answer, and Cecil's friend Bacon, the lord privy seal, quickly ended the proceedings. Bishops Watson of Lincoln and White of Winchester were then arrested for disobedience to the 'High Court of Parliament', and sent to the Tower, while their London residences were searched for incriminating material, on the orders of Elizabeth's council.[25]

On 10 April, a week after parliament re-assembled, a third Supremacy bill was introduced to the Commons, and this contained what appeared to be a concession to the more cautious and conservative among English Christians. To make it clearer that the Headship of the English Church was under the true supremacy of Christ, the term 'head', for the monarch, was altered to 'governor', as it remains to this day. The new measure also restored the Edwardian licence for communion to be received in the forms of both bread and wine, and repealed the Catholic heresy laws, which had been restored under Mary. Perhaps because of these adjustments, as well as heavy government pressure, the new bill was better received than its predecessors. A week later, it went to the Lords, and was scrutinised in committee, with the result that a few minor changes were made to reduce the possibility of punishment for those ordinary English people who remained loyal to the Catholic faith and liturgy. Finally, on 29 April, the bill was ready for the royal assent (1 Eliz. 1 c. 1). At the same time, things seemed to have moved on liturgically, with efforts now being made to restore the 1552 Prayer Book, which was favoured by Cecil and his circle, rather than that of 1549, as the queen may have wanted. In the final debate in the Lords, Abbot John Feckenham of Westminster spoke against the Supremacy bill, and no fewer than 18 peers voted against it. The measure passed by just three votes, and this would not have been possible if Bishops Watson and White, or other bishops who were under house arrest by this time, had been present.[26] On this thread hung the future of the Church of England.

---

[25]   Alford, *Burghley*, pp. 95–100.
[26]   *SR* 1 Eliz. 1 c. 2; Alford, *Burghley*, pp. 100–101.

It seems clear now that the main force behind the religious settlement that eventually emerged, in 1559, was William Cecil. This was evident, both in the case of the Supremacy bills, which began their course in January, and in the draft for the Act of Uniformity, which was first introduced in the following month. The two versions of the Uniformity measures reflected the evolution of policy in Elizabeth's inner circle, the first envisaging the restoration of the 1549 Prayer Book, and the second that of 1552. Active on the case were the queen's strongest supporters, including Nicholas Bacon, Anthony Cooke, Francis Knollys, Edmund Grindal and Richard Cox, and the overwhelming desire to produce a settlement led to the granting of concessions to traditionalists, for example over vestments and communion, which sowed the seeds of future conflict, with more radical reformers as well as Catholics. By Easter 1559, the government seems to have abandoned any attempt to conciliate the existing English bishops, and the only sops to tradition in the Act of Uniformity, as it eventually reached the statute book, were the highly ambiguous clause on 'ornaments', which has caused dispute in the Church of England ever since, and the use of the phrases 'Body of Christ' and 'Blood of Christ' in the administration of the Holy Communion, which might allow some to believe that they were attending a 'true Mass', even though that word was now excised from the book.[27] The Act of Uniformity set out the changes made in the 1559 Prayer Book:

> with one alteration or addition of certain lessons to be read on every Sunday of the year, and the form of the Letany altered, and corrected, and two sentences only added in the delivery of the Sacrament to the Communicants, and none other.[28]

In the litany, Elizabeth's book made an important deletion, noted as a correction in the act. From the 1552 petition ('From all sedicion and prieuie conspiracie, from the tyranny of the bysshop of Rome and all hys detestable enormities, from all false doctrine and heresy, from hardnesse of hearte, and contempte of thy woorde and commaundemente, Good lord, deliuer us'), the references to the pope and his 'tyranny' and 'detestable enormities' were removed.[29] As for the words of administration of the Holy Communion, there did appear to be a slight move, limited and ambiguous as it was, from the blunt 1552 affirmation of the Swiss 'memorialist' doctrine of the Eucharist to some sense of the real presence of Christ in the sacrament, which Lutherans shared, at least in part,

---

[27]   Felicity Heal, *Reformation in Britain and Ireland* (Oxford: Clarendon Press, 2003), pp. 359–360.

[28]   Reproduced in Brian Cummings, ed., *The Book of Common Prayer: the texts of 1549, 1550 and 1662* (Oxford: Oxford University Press, 2011), p. 187.

[29]   *The first and second Prayer Books of Edward VI* (London: The Prayer Book Society, 1999), p. 362; Cummings, *Book of Common Prayer*, p. 118.

with Catholics.[30] Although Elizabeth had been persuaded not to restore the more obviously ritualistic 1549 book, the amendments of 1559 at least provided her with a legal loophole for the devotional practice of her youth, but without the elevation of the elements, which she regarded as idolatrous.[31]

With its own religious settlement in place, Elizabeth and her government, with Cecil as the main motivator, could turn their attention to the appointment of new bishops, who would work for the 'Supreme Governor' and enforce the 1559 Prayer Book. By the end of 1558, no fewer than 10 diocesan sees were vacant through natural causes: Rochester, Gloucester, Ely, Bath and Wells, Lincoln, Oxford, Norwich, Chichester, Bristol and Bangor. Oxford had been vacant for a year, while the other incumbents had died during 1558. Thus, even if the remaining bishops, apart from the elderly and compliant Anthony Kitchin of Llandaff, had not adopted a totally intransigent attitude to the proposed religious changes, a major overhaul of the episcopate would have been essential. By the time that the Acts of Supremacy and Uniformity were in place, the holders of other major sees, York, London, Lincoln and Winchester, had rejected the settlement and were being punished for it, while the now very elderly Cuthbert Tunstall of Durham could only hope to end his days in peace. Nevertheless, the government moved only slowly to appoint new diocesans, including a new archbishop of Canterbury to replace Pole. But first, it is perhaps worth considering the options if Elizabeth, against all probability, had decided to keep her kingdom Catholic.

Paul IV was pope until his death, on 18 August 1559, being succeeded, on Christmas Day of that year, after a very long conclave, by Giovanni Angelo Medici, who took the name Pius IV. Given this chronology, any new legate to England in 1559 would have to have been chosen by the Carafa pope, who by this time had no love for the country. The cardinal protector of England in Rome, Giovanni Morone, was at the time being tried by the Inquisition on suspicion of heresy, and there was no Englishman available to do that job. In the fraught political and religious situation of 1558–9, this would undoubtedly have created major problems. As for the post of archbishop of Canterbury, if Queen Mary had survived Pole, and England had remained Catholic, she and Philip would have had the power to nominate a replacement, but given the poor state of their relations with Pope Paul IV, it seems unlikely that he would have been co-operative. Against this, it should, however, be noted that, in the summer of 1558, Paul had agreed to the Spanish king's nomination of Bartolomé Carranza to the archbishopric of Toledo. Yet, even if Paul had co-operated with England's 'Catholic Monarchs', it would have been hard to find a suitable English

---

[30]    MacCulloch, *Later Reformation*, pp. 30–31.

[31]    Susan Doran, 'Elizabeth I's religion: the evidence of her letters', *Journal of Ecclesiastical History*, 51 (2000), pp. 699–720; Heal, *Reformation*, 361.

candidate. As far as the 'job specification' was concerned, it was inevitable that a Catholic successor to Pole would have had to continue the programme to restore and bed in the traditional religion, in its new, reformist form, against continuing opposition from a vociferous minority at home and abroad, and probably still deploying the penalty of burning. He would have had to liaise with Mary and Philip and their councillors during the peace negotiations between France and the Habsburgs, including the need to decide what to do about Calais. Another urgent task would have been to replenish the depleted episcopal bench, in order to implement more fully the decrees of the English synod of 1555–6, which had still not been supported by the definitive canons of the Council of Trent. As for the required qualifications for a new Catholic archbishop, a graduate of Oxford or Cambridge would have been expected, and probably one qualified in theology, rather than the traditional civil and canon law. Cranmer and Pole had both broken the succession of lawyer archbishops, and the climate of the 1550s and 1560s, on both sides of the religious divide, favoured training suitable for the spiritual rather than the administrative aspects of the job. Previous episcopal experience was not a necessary qualification for becoming Primate, as Parker would demonstrate, just as his two predecessors had done.

Bonner of London, Turberville of Exeter and Tunstall of Durham would have been disqualified by their age. On the other hand, a shortlist for consideration by monarchs and pope would probably have included Bishop John White of Winchester, who had solidly Catholic views, despite having been head of Winchester College under Edward VI. His reign would have been short, however, as he died on 12 January 1560.[32] In principle, Pole's old associate Richard Pate, bishop of Worcester, could have been a candidate. He was an Oxford theologian, and an experienced diplomat, who was well known in Rome, but his friendship with Pole might well have counted against him with Pope Paul.[33] Another possible candidate would have been Nicholas Heath, archbishop of York, though he had a reformist, Cranmerian past, and a traditional background in law at Cambridge and political activity, latterly as Philip and Mary's lord chancellor. His public opposition to the Elizabethan settlement indicated that he was now solidly Catholic, and his age, 59, would have been acceptable (he would live until 1578).[34] Also a possible candidate was Bishop Cuthbert Scott of Chester, a Cambridge theologian who was a leading propagandist for the Catholic religion under Mary and Philip. In the event, his views led him to leave England for Leuven/Louvain, in 1564.[35] The three remaining possibilities for the shortlist were Owen Oglethorpe of Carlisle, an

---

[32]   Carleton, 'White, John', *ODNB.*
[33]   Kenneth Carleton, 'Pate, Richard', *ODNB.*
[34]   David Loades, 'Heath, Nicholas', *ODNB.*
[35]   Kenneth Carleton, 'Scott, Cuthbert', *ODNB.*

Oxford theologian and former president of Magdalen College, David Pole, bishop of Peterborough, and, perhaps the best-qualified of all, Bishop Thomas Goldwell of St Asaph, a member of Paul IV's Theatine order and an enthusiastic Catholic reformer, who would later work with St Carlo Borromeo, archbishop of Milan.[36] In reality, it was of course Elizabeth's task to find a new archbishop, who would implement the Church settlement that had been enacted by her first parliament. He would be Matthew Parker, doctor of divinity and former master of Corpus Christi College, who had remained quietly in Cambridge during the previous reign.[37]

As Elizabeth's settlement was gradually established in the country, not without resistance from the Catholic and more radical Protestant sides, it became clear that everything possible was being done to remove what might have been regarded as Pole's legacy. The new royal visitation of the dioceses, carried out by commissioners in 1559, allowed the more zealous reformers to push the Queen's balanced and nuanced concepts to extremes, reviving the iconoclastic approach that had been adopted in Edward VI's reign.[38] In 1562–3, the first Canterbury convocation of Elizabeth's reign took place, with the new, reformist bishops in place. The 39 articles of religion, based on the 42 of Edward's reign, were duly enacted, showing considerable influence from Swiss reform, especially that of Geneva, and the assembly asked for a major revision of canon law, something that Cranmer had failed to achieve, and also for further revision of the liturgy, to remove the nods in the direction of tradition. This scheme for the future, which would only be achieved in part, may well have originated from the new bishops themselves, rather than radical outsiders.[39]

In all the difficulties of his time as archbishop, Parker did not forget his predecessor, instead helping to provide the basis of a Protestant 'Black Legend' about him that would be influential for centuries. Even before he went to Canterbury, Parker may well have been the instigator of a sermon denouncing Pole, which had been preached in December 1558, when he was hardly dead.[40] Much later, in 1572, after Elizabeth had been excommunicated by the pope, a major historical compendium, aimed at demonstrating that the Church of the British Isles was linked to the first apostles without the involvement of the Roman papacy, was published by Parker, John Joscelyn and George Acworth,

---

[36] Margaret Clark, 'Oglethorpe, Owen', *ODNB*; T.F. Mayer, 'Pole, David', *ODNB*; T.F. Mayer, 'Goldwell, Thomas', *ODNB*.

[37] David J. Crankshaw and Alexandra Gillespie, 'Parker, Matthew', *ODNB*.

[38] Frere and Kennedy, *Visitation articles*, 2, pp. 176–189; Margaret Aston, *England's iconoclasts: laws against images* (Cambridge: Cambridge University Press, 1988), pp. 298–303.

[39] David Crankshaw, 'Preparations for the Canterbury provincial convocation of 1562–3', in Susan Wabuda and Carl Litzenberger, eds, *Belief and practice in Reformation England* (Aldershot: Ashgate, 1998), pp. 50–93; Heal, *Reformation*, p. 362.

[40] *CSP Ven*, VII, no. 2.

from the presses of John Day.[41] In it were included some thoroughly-researched and vitriolic pages about Pole, on which Acworth, in particular, seems to have worked.[42] The writers apparently used the Roman printer and publisher Paolo Manuzio's edition of some of Pole's letters, in his *Epistolae clarororum virorum selectae*, as well as the biographies of the cardinal archbishop by his former servants, Ludovico Beccadelli and Andras Dudic. Parker and his friends were also not above using contemporary satires on Pole, one of which accused him, somewhat implausibly, of having fathered two children by the abbess of Santa Chiara in Viterbo, when he was papal legate there in the 1540s. Parker and Acworth, as scholars of 'Divinity', were keen to portray Pole as being a Classical rhetorician rather than a theologian, and hence excessively influenced by Renaissance style, rather than solid doctrinal content. For the section on Pole in *De antiquitate*, Parker and his co-authors consulted some of the English Protestants who had been in exile under Queen Mary, and in this way learned of the story of his supposed conversion to 'Lutheranism' of Juan Morillo, which had been used against him by the late cardinal's enemies in Italy and Spain.[43] Parker also alleged that the previous archbishop had made a simoniacal transaction with bishop John White. This supposed offence against canon law concerned White's transfer from the see of Lincoln to that of Winchester, for which Parker even alleged a bribe to Pope Paul IV. In fact, the 'crime' involved a transfer of ecclesiastical benefices on the orders of the Crown, but, by the 1570s, anything would do to blacken Pole's name.[44]

In general, Parker's account seems to have followed Henry VIII's line against Pole, after they had quarrelled. In 1563, another of the printer John Day's clients, the Protestant martyrologist John Foxe, had reproduced, in his *Acts and monuments*, the letter which Cuthbert Tunstall and John Stokesley had written against Pole, in early 1537, after they read his *De unitate*.[45] This controversy was used by Parker, and his associates, to suggest that, in the late 1530s, Pole had chosen Italian degeneracy over patriotism and gratitude to his king, an accusation that would remained attached to him for centuries, in non-Catholic circles. At this stage (1536–7), according to this interpretation, Pole had gone through a 'monstrous metamorphosis', thus giving cause for Parker's famous maxim that his predecessor was *inglese italianato, diavolo incarnato* ('Englishman

---

[41] Matthew Parker, *De antiquitate Briannicae ecclesiae et priuilegiis Cantuariensis cum Archiepiscopis eiusdem LXX* (London: John Day, 1572).

[42] Parker, *De antiquitate*, pp. 406–423.

[43] Parker, *De antiquitate*, pp. 410–411; Gordon Kinder, 'Juan Morillo – Catholic theologian at Trent, Calvinist ruler at Frankfurt', *Bibliothèque d'Humanisme et Renaissance*, 38 (1976), pp. 345–350, at p. 349.

[44] Parker, *De antiquitate*, p. 418.

[45] Foxe, *A&M* 1563, pp. 613–620; *CRP* 1 no. 144.

italianate, devil incarnate').[46] For Parker, Pole, by turning against his king, had become inconstant, and would remain so for the rest of his days. He became chameleon-like, changing his opinions to suit those around him, and thus he could not be counted either as a true Catholic or a true reformer, which was a lonely and isolated position in which to be.[47] Despite all this, in his peroration, Parker acknowledged Pole's exemplary and singular learning and his personal virtue, which would have shone more brightly had he not been seduced by the 'pontifical mores' of Rome. Above all, by presiding over the burning of Cranmer, he had become a 'tyrant' in his episcopal role.[48]

This fairly damning portrait of Pole was taken up by other Elizabethan writers. Holinshed's *Chronicles* used Parker, as well as Foxe, although the latter offered a more balanced view of the cardinal. Holinshed concluded that although Pole was 'malignant', he was nevertheless 'of more lenity than many other popelings'.[49] John Foxe's own treatment of Pole, in successive editions of his *Acts and monuments*, was balanced, in the sense that he did not regard him as the main instigator of the burning of Protestants under Mary, but nonetheless, he concluded, in his 1563 edition, that the late cardinal was 'a man of noble birth, but yet an arch-enemy unto God, and to Christ's true religion, yea, altogether given to papistry, ambition and hypocrisy'.[50] In 1570, on the other hand, Foxe, who was now himself disillusioned by the conservatism of the Elizabethan Church, praised Pole for his restraint in handling heretics, as he saw them.[51] Pole's future reputation in Catholic circles would be very different.

Within three years of the deaths of Pole and Mary, many prominent people, especially in the universities, left England rather than accept the new religious settlement. In Oxford, a third of the fellows of New College refused to swear the oath of Supremacy, and even some of those who were elected after 1559 were eventually deprived for their religious views Many of them moved to Catholic universities in France (Douai) and the Netherlands, where they gathered with colleagues from most of the other Oxford colleges and from several in Cambridge. At Leuven/Louvain, they lived in two separate lodging houses, nicknamed 'Oxford' and 'Cambridge' respectively. In addition, in 1564, Bishop Cuthbert Scott of Chester left England for the same university, by which time, the old hierarchy in England, with the exception of the elderly Kitchin of Llandaff, had been removed from office. In addition, Bishops Pate of Worcester and Goldwell of St Asaph, who had been close to Pole, left for the Continent.

---

[46]   Parker, *De antiquitate*, p. 406.

[47]   Parker, *De antiquitate*, pp. 410–411.

[48]   Parker, *De antiquitate*, p. 423; Mayer, *PPP*, pp. 364–365.

[49]   Raphael Holinshed, *Chronicles of England, Scotland and Ireland*, 6 vols (London: S. Johnson and others, 1817–18), 4, p. 144.

[50]   Foxe *A&M* 1563, p. 656.

[51]   Foxe, *A&M* 1570, pp. 1525–1526.

Meanwhile, in Oxford, 10 colleges received new heads, and in Cambridge eight.[52] The senior bishop in England after Pole's death, Archbishop Nicholas Heath of York, initially tried to co-operate with the new government, remaining on the council, though he was no longer lord chancellor. In early 1559, he even helped Bacon to organise the religious disputation in Westminster Abbey, and rebuked his Catholic colleagues when they refused to participate, by failing to produce the requested list of questions. Nevertheless, he spoke and voted in the House of Lords against the Supremacy and Uniformity bills, and refused to swear the oath of Supremacy when it was enacted. He was deprived of his see on 5 July 1559, and sent to the Tower of London, whence he was freed two years later and allowed to retire to his estate at Chobham, in Surrey, where he remained until his death in 1578. During these years, he was banned from public life, but still had Mass celebrated illegally in his house.[53] The argumentative bishop of London, 'bloody' Edmund Bonner, was unlikely to receive gentle treatment from the new regime, given his record of actions against reformed ideas and their adherents, after having initially supported them. Even so, he continued to work for the queen, in his former role as a diplomat, and helped to entertain visiting French envoys on 23 May 1559: they stayed with him in his episcopal palace for five days. However, when he refused, on 30 May, to swear the oath of Supremacy, he was deprived of his see, though he initially remained at liberty. In April 1560 he was confined to the Marshalsea gaol, under the jurisdiction of the new bishop of Winchester, Robert Horne, and there he remained until his death, in 1569, having refused once again to take the oath, when offered it by Horne in 1564. Bonner regarded Parker's, and hence Horne's, consecration as invalid, and this resistance, which was shared by others, eventually led Elizabeth and her government, in 1567, to pass an act that retrospectively validated all the episcopal consecrations that had taken place since the beginning of the reign.[54] Evidently Bonner had touched a sore, legal spot.

Bishop Thomas Watson of Lincoln had been a lively Catholic controversialist during Mary's reign, and might have expected a turbulent time under her successor. He was naturally one of the Catholics appointed to take part in the Westminster debate with Protestants, in April 1559, but, as has already been noted, his 'contumely', or defiance, led to his arrest and imprisonment in the Tower, along with Bishop White of Winchester. Watson's health thereafter declined, though he and White seem to have been well treated, on the orders of the council. However, on 25 July, Philip and Mary's wedding anniversary, he was deprived of his see, and placed in the private custody, first of the new bishop of

---

[52]   Penry Williams, 'Elizabethan Oxford', in *History of the University of Oxford*, iii, pp. 397–440, at pp. 405–406; Duffy, *Fires of faith*, pp. 199–202.

[53]   David Loades, 'Heath, Nicholas', *ODNB*.

[54]   Carleton, 'Bonner, Edmund', *ODNB*.

London, Edmund Grindal, then of Edmund Guest, Cecil's adviser, who was now
bishop of Rochester, and finally of Richard Cox, bishop of Ely, with whom he
seems to have remained until January 1565. He was evidently still regarded as a
potential dissident, as he was then sent back again to the Tower of London, where
he remained until 5 July 1574, being further interrogated after the papal bull of
excommunication against Elizabeth was issued in 1570. He lived long enough,
until 1584, to suffer all the new injunctions against real or suspected Catholics
that were imposed after this final breakdown in Anglo-papal relations. In 1580,
he was imprisoned, with other recalcitrant Catholic clergy, including the former
abbot of Westminster, John Feckenham, in Wisbech Castle in Cambridgeshire,
a former palace of the bishops of Ely, and there he died.[55] Mary's former chaplain,
and bishop of Bath and Wells, Gilbert Bourne, also refused to take the oath of
Supremacy, and was duly deprived of his see in the latter part of 1559. It was
likely that he was kept on while it was still hoped that he might take part in
the consecration of Matthew Parker, but when it became clear that he would
not, he was removed, arriving in the Tower of London on 18 June 1560, though
released from there in the following year. He spent the rest of his life, until 10
September 1569, in the custody, first of Nicholas Bullingham, now bishop of
Lincoln, and then of the former dean of the Chapel Royal, George Carew, who
had by then collected a plurality of fine livings, as archdeacon of Exeter, dean of
Bristol, and dean of St George's Chapel, Windsor.[56]

Despite all these developments, it seems that, at least for the first few years
of Elizabeth's reign, there was still some hope, in Catholic circles, that the new
Queen might not, in the end, separate England from the Roman See. Although
he now had no official function, Mary and Philip's ambassador there, Sir
Edward Carne, remained in the Eternal City, despite being summoned home by
Elizabeth. Pope Pius IV appointed him as warden of the English Hospice, but
he held the post for only a year, dying in 1561, and being buried in the church
of St Gregory the Great (Gregorio Magno), which was for ever associated with
St Augustine of Canterbury's mission to England.[57] More significantly, the new
papal reign saw certain moves to preserve links between Elizabeth's church
and Rome, perhaps even envisaging a renewal and continuance of the Catholic
hierarchy there, despite all evidence of moves towards reform, in parliament and
the dioceses. A paper in the Vatican archives, found in the nineteenth century,
appears to have been written by Bishop Thomas Watson, in 1560, and suggested
how the Holy See might fill the vacancies in English bishoprics, as though
the remaining Catholic bishops were still in legal possession. It suggested that
Archbishop Heath of York should go to Canterbury, and that Watson himself

[55]   Carleton, 'Watson, Thomas', *ODNB*.
[56]   Angelo J. Louisa, 'Bourne, Gilbert', *ODNB*.
[57]   David Rundle, '*Bonae litterae*: the English in Rome', bonaelitterae.wordpress.com.

should replace him in York.[58] Also at this time, Pius IV dispatched one of Pole's former associates, the Piedmontese Vincenzo Parpaglia, abbot of Santa Salute, Turin, on a mission to England.[59]

Parpaglia had first known Pole in the late 1530s, when he was engaged in his legation to France and Spain.[60] At the colloquy of Regensburg, in 1541, he ran the household of Cardinal Gasparo Contarini, and between December 1541 and January 1546, when he and Pole left for Trent, he governed the 'Patrimony of Peter', as vice-legate of Viterbo. When Pole left Trent, Parpaglia acted as a go-between in his negotiations with his fellow legates at the council, and he stayed with the English cardinal until he left Viterbo in the summer of 1553. During Pole's time as legate and archbishop, Parpaglia was involved, as Pole's agent, in the restoration in England of the Knights Hospitaller of St John of Jerusalem.[61] Referring later to Parpaglia's mission to Elizabeth, the Jesuit Juan de Polanco described him as the cardinal's *maestro di casa* (steward).[62] Having become involved, during the latter part of Mary's reign, in vain attempts to negotiate with the French, Parpaglia appears to have left Pole's service, though he remained in touch with some of his faithful servants and supporters, including Ludovico Beccadelli and Pietro Carnesecchi. He seems to have moved to Rome in or about January 1558, and in December of that year was in Flanders, where he was under suspicion, because of his earlier involvement with France. He was in fact arrested on Granvelle's orders, with the approval of Philip and of his own sovereign, Duke Emmanuel Philibert of Savoy. Once released, he returned to Italy, and in the spring of 1560, he became involved in the efforts of Pope Pius to restore links with England, which began with the setting up of a commission of five cardinals, including Pole's old friend Cardinal Morone, who had now been rehabilitated.

By 4 May 1560, Parpaglia had been appointed as nuncio to England, leaving Rome 10 days later. In a move which appeared to reflect the growing bitterness between Pole and the Spaniards, which had afflicted his last years, the Spanish ambassador in Rome, Francisco de Vargas, acted immediately to thwart the mission, though he could not prevent the abbot from reaching Flanders. He did, however, succeed in obtaining an order for his detention in the Netherlands, and even Parpaglia himself expressed the view that he was very unlikely to succeed

---

58    Cited in Carleton, 'Watson, Thomas'.

59    For a detailed account of Parpaglia's English mission, and its historiography, see Mayer, 'Rome and England in the early 1560s. Cardinal Pole's legacy and Vincenzo Parpaglia's mission (1560)', an unpublished paper kindly provided by the author.

60    *CRP* 1 nos 248, 252, 260, 277, 285, 289.

61    *CRP* 3 nos 1392, 1032, 1033.

62    Thomas M. McCoog and László Lukács, eds, *Monumenta Angliae*, 3, *England, Scotland and Wales: documents (1541–1562)* (= Monumenta Historica Societatis Iesu, 151) (Rome: Institutum Historicum Societatis Iesu, 2000), p. 338 (I June 1560).

in England, because Elizabeth had already imprisoned the remaining English Catholic bishops.[63] On 21 September, the Pope recalled him to Rome, thus admitting that the mission had achieved nothing, but this failure was mainly due to Philip and his agents, rather than Elizabeth herself. It has been argued that the Parpaglia mission was intended to put the English queen on the spot, by inviting her, through his nuncio, to send representatives to the forthcoming final sessions of the Council of Trent, but the choice of envoy seems to have represented a mistaken attempt to conciliate her, by sending her an associate of Pole. In reality, having no direct and reliable contact with English political circles at this time, Pius was unaware of the solidly Protestant direction in which the Church there was moving, or of how far Pole's stock with the government had fallen since his death. Meanwhile, the odour of sanctity was increasingly surrounding the late cardinal in Catholic circles on the Continent.

Tributes to Pole had begun even while he was still alive. In 1554, the composer Orlando di Lasso (Lassus, 1530–94), from Mons in Hainaut, who was in England with King Philip, wrote a five-part motet, with a text apparently also by him, in which he praised the legate's work:

> The heavens[64] bless you, Reginald,
> The stars smile on you, the mountains exult,
> Because you send forth auspicious fires
> And draw tears from their stone.

Whether or not the composer was here predicting the cardinal's violent assault on heresy, his assessment was undoubtedly positive, and, as Pole's life drew to its close, work began to portray his life and achievement in as positive a manner as possible, with a hagiographic tone. Mayer has devoted much effort to demonstrating that Pole, as a typical, prominent figure of the Renaissance period, formed his own self-image in his writings, and Paolo Simoncelli, also, speaks of the 'myth of sanctity' surrounding him.[65] Writers who had known him well, for example his archdeacon in Canterbury, Nicholas Harpsfield, might be seen, on this interpretation, as collaborators in the process. Working on their 'lives' of Pole between about 1557 and 1562, Beccadelli and Dudic, in particular, produced what Mayer has trenchantly called 'plainly hagiography'.[66] They both evidently believed that their master's sanctity was on a par with that of the English martyrs whom he most revered, Thomas More and John Fisher.

---

[63]   *CSP Rome* nos 43, 52, 56.

[64]   The Latin, *poli*, is of course a play on Pole's family name.

[65]   Paolo Simoncelli, *Il caso Reginald Pole: eresia e santità nelle polemiche religiose del Cinquecento* (Rome: Edizioni di storia e letteratura, 1977), pp. 17, 241.

[66]   Mayer, 'A sticking plaster saint? Autobiography and hagiography in the making of Reginald Pole', *CPEC*, XII, p. 209.

Another collaborator in the enterprise, and suspect in the eyes of the Roman Inquisition, was Giovanni Battista Binardi, who, with Alvise Priuli, took Pole's papers to Paris and began a project to publish his works – something that Pole had never willingly done during his own lifetime.[67] In the event, the only result of this publication effort, but a highly important one, was the edition by the Roman printer Paolo Manuzio, of a version of the decrees of Pole's English synod of 1555–6.[68] Manuzio's prologue to this edition of the decrees was the first published biography of Pole, and the first of many to portray him as a holy man, and an inspiration to Catholic Christians. In the same year, Beccadelli's Italian *Vita del cardinale Reginaldo Polo* appeared, and in 1563 this was followed by Dudic's Latin *Vita Reginaldi Poli*, which, being composed in an international language, was distributed more widely, even though its author later became a convinced Protestant. Dudic both translated and edited Beccadelli's work, which was not published in the sixteenth century, although it was known to later Catholic writers, such as Nicholas Sander.[69] In that way, the positive account of the cardinal archbishop was transmitted to the beleaguered Catholics of England, Wales and Ireland, for several centuries.

Important in the spreading of Pole's fame and achievement in the Catholic world, despite all efforts by his Protestant detractors and his Catholic enemies, was Bishop Thomas Goldwell. Initially, he seems to have expected to continue under Elizabeth, and he was indeed allowed to attend his master's funeral in Canterbury. He even complained to Sir William Cecil, when he was not summoned to parliament in January 1559, but after this he seems to have understood the true situation, and left for Rome, though owing to illness he initially got no further than Leuven/Louvain. His subsequent career, in what later became known as the 'Counter-Reformation' Church, was testimony not only to his own ability but also to what he and Pole had experienced and learned together. From 1560 until his death, in 1585, he was superior of the Theatine house in Rome, San Silvestro, until 1564 *custos* of the English hospice, active in the final sessions of the Council of Trent, and vicar-general to Archbishop St Carlo Borromeo of Milan. In the 1570s, he was involved in the development of the English hospice into the English College (the 'Venerabile'), and he also became personally involved in preparing and operating the mission to England, for which its students were trained. He himself did not however, reach his homeland again, and died in Rome on 3 April 1585, being buried in San Silvestro. By then, he was not well viewed by William Allen, cardinal and missioner, who would take a leading part in organising the English seminaries

---

[67] Mayer, 'A sticking plaster saint?', pp. 210–211; Mayer, *PPP*, pp. 358–361.

[68] *Reformatio Angliae, ex decretis Reginaldi Poli Cardinalis, Sedis Apostolicae Legati, anno MDLVI* (Rome: Paolo Manuzio).

[69] Mayer, *PPP*, pp. 356–359.

on the Continent, which might be seen as Pole's most important memorial.[70] Being born in 1532, Allen, a Lancashire man who became a fellow of Oriel College, Oxford, was too young to be personally associated with Pole, in his *familia*, or household. In Mary's reign, Allen strongly supported the Catholic restoration in the university, and he seems to have admired the Spanish friars who came to teach there, Juan de Villagarcía and Pedro de Soto. His respect for Spaniards seems never to have left him, despite the part that some of them had played in undermining his reputation during his lifetime. Under Elizabeth, and up to his death, in Rome on 16 October 1594, Allen had laboured with one of the greatest benefactions of Pole and his circle to the Church, the establishment of special seminaries for the training of priests, as the English synod of 1555–6 had decreed. Thus the English Colleges, especially in Douai, Rheims, Rome and Valladolid, may be seen, at least in part, as memorials to Pole.[71]

The religious divisions which developed during his lifetime, and still exist today in not so different a form, have inevitably polarised perceptions of Reginald Pole's character and achievement. Yet, during his lifetime and still in modern historiography, this bifurcation has partly been blamed on the character of the man himself. From the 1540s, Pole acquired a reputation for ducking out of difficult situations at vital moments. In 1546, when he was papal legate and could have taken a lead towards Catholic acceptance, at least in part, of Lutheran teaching on the salvation of the sinful by faith, he pleaded illness and left the Council of Trent. Then, in the conclave of 1549–50, which eventually elected Julius III, he obstinately refused to campaign for himself as pope, even though, in December 1549, he was only one vote short of being elected. When, partly as a consequence, the Roman Inquisition began to put pressure on supposed crypto-Lutherans in high Catholic circles, including some of his close friends, Pole largely boycotted the supervisory committee of the Inquisition, to which Julius had appointed him in 1550. All this gave him a reputation, among the more strong-minded reformers, both Catholic and Protestant, for being indecisive and even cowardly, yet in other respects no one could have been more determined and resolute.

One important fact about Pole, which is sometimes neglected but in reality dominated his whole life, is his consciousness of his royal origins. Whether or not he was descended from Welsh princes on his father's side, Pole was undoubtedly a Plantagenet of the Yorkist branch. It is impossible to understand Henry VIII's violent reaction to him and his family, once they quarrelled in the mid-1530s, without recognising the threat that he and his relatives posed to the king and his

---

[70]   Mayer, 'Goldwell, Thomas', *ODNB*.

[71]   Duffy, 'Allen, William', *ODNB*; Katy Gibbons, *English Catholic exiles in late sixteenth-century Paris* (Woodbridge: The Boydell Press, The Royal Historical Society, 2011), pp. 15, 31, 33, 56.

descendants. This might well have been a problem even if there had not been a split between England and Rome, over the divorce of Catherine of Aragon. The lengthy, surviving drafts of Pole's speech to parliament, eventually delivered in November 1554, are replete with high aristocratic views, not to say prejudices, and provide a more than usually accurate insight into the author's mind, and his values. Despite his intense involvement in some of the most interesting and radical spiritual and theological currents of mid-sixteenth century Catholicism, it seems that Pole never forgot his royal status, and expected others to appreciate it. In this respect, at least, Pole's Catholic England, if it had taken root, would indeed have been nostalgic and backward-looking. This was not so in the religion that was also central to his existence, which in general looked forwards as well as back.

One of the most interesting aspects of Pole's time as legate and archbishop is the fact that, like his predecessor Thomas Cranmer, and indeed his successor Matthew Parker, he was a theologian, and not a lawyer, as most bishops had been up to that time. It has to be admitted that, thanks to his somewhat chequered academic career, around but not formally in the University of Padua, he lacked the theological qualifications of Cranmer and Parker, but he balanced this by his extraordinary association with so many of the leading spiritual and creative people of his day, from Michelangelo to Ignatius Loyola. Parker was undoubtedly right to characterise Pole, at least in part, as 'italianate', but utterly missed the point, as nearly everyone since has done, that he was in many respects, a reformer, with a personal life of austerity and purity, whatever rumours there may have been to the contrary, in his own day and since. While being 'gay' should not, in any case, be a matter for criticism, let alone condemnation, there is no specific evidence that Pole went beyond warm friendships with other men, as was condoned, and even required, in the Church and society of his day. His building works at Lambeth Palace suggest that, had he lived longer, in a Catholic England, he would have pioneered the aristocratic interest in Italy and its culture that only in fact emerged during the reign of Elizabeth's successor James I.

Given that his time as legate and archbishop was so short, it is extraordinary how much he achieved, and although Protestant efforts to undo his work began as soon as he was dead, his faith and achievement lived on, through his own followers, through the model for the Church set out in his synod and amplified by the Council of Trent, and in the Catholic recusant and missionary movements of the decade after his death. Today, it is still asked whether a genuinely holy man can hold high office in the Church with success in matters of mammon as well as God, but Pole, as a very exceptional archbishop of Canterbury, argues strongly that it is. His part in Queen Mary and King Philip's attempt to repress reformed ideas in their island kingdom by means of inquisition and the stake will always blacken his name, but he was nonetheless close to being, in some respects, the holy man that his friends and servants, such as Priuli, Beccadelli and Dudic, claimed him to be. At least according to the criteria of his own day, in Dermot Fenlon's words, 'Pole's sanctity was not a "myth". It was the real thing'.[72]

---

[72] Dermot Fenlon, 'Pietro Carnesecchi and Cardinal Pole: new perspectives', *Journal of Ecclesiastical History*, 56 (2005), pp. 529–533, at p. 532.

# Appendix

## 1. Pole Breaks with King Henry VIII (1536)

Pole's great treatise in defence of the unity of the Church defines his views on papal authority, monarchy, and the history of England, as well as praising those who died for their refusal to accept Henry's Supremacy over the Church of England. Originally intended to be read in manuscript, perhaps by Henry alone, the treatise later acquired the title *Reginaldi Poli ad Henricum octavum Britanniae regem pro ecclesiasticae unitatis defensione libri IV* ('Four books by Reginald Pole to King Henry the Eighth of Britain in defence of the unity of the Church'), but is commonly known as *De unitate* ('On unity').

The textual history of *De unitate* is complicated (for a full account see Mayer, 'Reluctant author', pp. 43–47). A good manuscript version, in fair copy, is BAV MS Vat. lat. 5970 fols 1–125. Against Pole's wishes, the version of the text used here was printed in Rome in 1539 by Antonio Blado (reprinted Farnborough: Gregg International, 1965). The text is available in English in Joseph C. Dwyer, ed. and trans., *Reginald Pole: Pole's defense of the unity of the Church* (Westminster, MD: Newman Press, 1965), used here with some revision.

The three extracts presented here illustrate Pole's main points of argument with his king and former friend: papal authority, the limitations of secular monarchy, and his own status and rights as an English aristocrat.

### A. Pole's Self-Assessment

'By my own natural accord, I tend to avoid all strife and contention. My custom of acting in this way extends from my boyhood to the present. I have avoided all public and private contention and I have not had any litigation before the judges. This is a very unusual circumstance in the case of one who has justly owned some degree of worldly goods. To such an extent have I avoided arguments with others that I do not think there is a word that causes greater distress to my soul than the word contention itself' (Dwyer: 16).

### B. Pole's Love for King Henry VIII

'If a faithful servant should be called to the bedside of his kindly master who was seriously ill, would not this servant be filled with doubt as to the appropriate manner in which to address his master? ... May God be my witness that never has the love of a mother for her only son been greater than the love that I have always had for you. No child has ever cherished his parent with affection greater than mine. No-one has ever been subject to a king more just and merciful than you' (Dwyer: 4, 6).

## C. *The Nature of Papal Authority*

'Here [Matthew 16:18] we can understand the magnitude of the power given to Peter. How clear the words are in this passage, how much they point in every respect to the person of Peter when it is said: "I will give you the keys of the kingdom of heaven". This is so evident that if nothing else had been presented, this very great authority conferred upon Peter in that passage saying: "you are Peter [Greek: *petros*], and on this rock I will build my church" would alone have shown most clearly the magnitude of the position entrusted to Peter. It would have shown most clearly that he had been made head of the Church' (Dwyer: 123).

## D. *The Possibility of Bad Popes*

'How does the wickedness of pontiffs pertain to me, since I know it cannot impede me unless I so desire? For all their power is for edification, none of their power is a hindrance to anyone's soul. But what if the wickedness of one man who is pontiff is truly not a hindrance to Christians but instead a benefit? What if it displays even more the glory of Christ? For what a great and remarkable thing would we do by bestowing honour upon a bad pontiff ... By the very fact that we do not seem to be deterred, however by human vices, by the very fact that we, nonetheless, venerate the image of Christ in him he sits on the throne of Christ and maintains the unity and harmony of the Church, by this very fact we show ourselves to be true Christians. In this way the glory of Christ is especially demonstrated' (Dwyer: 245–246).

## E. *Monarchy and its Limitations*

'There can be no great change in any state without accompanying serious injustice and disturbance to the commonwealth. If any change in government involves some injustice and danger, how much greater will that injustice and danger be where the change is made from the best to a poorer condition? It is this type of injustice that you have now inflicted upon the Church. For wherever men have assembled together, wherever the opinion of many ages has been consulted, a community of men with the government under the control of one man has always been written into their customs as the best possible condition of life. You now propose to overthrow this condition in the Church and to substitute many heads in the Church. Now is this [only] a slight injustice?' (Dwyer: 10).

'You [Richard Sampson] certainly cannot prove that any special power not previously possessed by kings had now [with Christ's coming to earth] been conferred upon them by the Scriptures. Nor can you call upon the testimony of the Scriptures to show that any special honour that had not belonged to kings before the advent of Christ should now be conferred upon them. If in any discussion concerning the honour that should be given to kings you can only say that the Scriptures have in no way detracted from the honour due to them, this fact at least should be clearly established for you on the authority of the Scriptures' (Dwyer: 32).

## E. Pole's View of English History

### (i) The Recent Past

*(The beginning of Henry VIII's reign)*

'I recall how you were once the occasion of great hope to all, in your youth. You gave great hope not only for your own happiness but for that of all who would be in any way associated with your kingdom. All proposed to themselves a happy life with you as king. They looked forward to a golden age during your reign. For what did your distinguished virtues not promise, what did not shine forth in you especially during your first years as prince? Among all your virtues a certain devout piety displayed itself, to which were added those virtues men customarily hold in great esteem: justice, clemency, liberality, and such prudence as befitted your youthful age. And beyond these was added a certain innate modesty, as if given by nature to guard your other virtues ... All causes of sedition had, in you alone, been extinguished. If previously there had been other controversies concerning the lawful right to the kingdom, if there had been titles that might occasion the rise of sedition, all of these were so joined together in you that all said, with the highest degree of justice, that you were king. No factions now flourished, all titles of every kind appeared to be bound together harmoniously in you' (Dwyer: 194).

### (ii) The Current Situation (1535–6)

*Anne Boleyn*

'You, a man of your age and with such experience, are miserably burning with passion for the love of a girl. She, indeed, has said that she will make herself available to you on one condition alone. You must reject your wife

[Catherine] whose place she desires to hold. This modest woman does not want to be your concubine, she wants to be your wife. I believe she learned from the example of her sister [Mary, who had previously been Henry's mistress], if in no other way, how quickly you can have your fill of concubines. She, however, was anxious to surpass her sister by retaining you as a lover. This woman, pleasing to the one by whom she appeared to be so ardently loved, desired to be joined to you by an indissoluble bond. She desired to remain with you perpetually. And to this passionate longing you responded mutually. In fact you actively surpassed her, so that you thought it would be the greatest achievement of your fortunes, the height of happiness, if your legitimate and just wife were cast out of your marriage and it were permitted you to be united with this woman in matrimony and to live with her for ever' (Dwyer: 185–186).

### Pole's Family: The Execution of the Earl of Warwick

'There was certainly only one thing that impelled your father [Henry VII] to the murder of my uncle [the earl of Warwick], who was, in the general opinion of all, as innocent in his whole life as a one year-old infant, as the Scriptures commonly say. This one thing was the fact that he was the son of the brother of King Edward IV [George, duke of Clarence]; he was the sole male descendant remaining in this branch of the family. Your father saw how easily my uncle might be the occasion of new seditions, concerning the right to his kingdom, that might arise against your father's house. Even while your father lived, he had experienced some of these dissensions. For the people, on several occasions, were in arms on behalf of my uncle and they were often in the habit of being tumultuous. When your father had disposed of this man, he thought that he and his heirs might live securely and reign without fear. He thought all impediments had been removed. He then thought that God's providence played no part in the succession of kings, that human prudence did everything. But how differently events actually turned out, contrary to what his very great prudence had foreseen. Where he would have feared the greatest danger to his succession, there now exists no danger but rather a very strong defence. Where there would have been safety, according to his plans, the greatest danger has been created for him, that is for his house [the split with Rome]' (Dwyer: 197).

### The Likelihood of Rebellion

'When you remove the succession with which all men of every rank, except you, the parent, are now marvellously in accord [that of Princess Mary], you are arming all for mutual slaughter, to the utmost of your power. When that succession is removed, who will be quiet among all those who might find even a pretence of right for an invasion of your kingdom? How many, however, will there be who have such a pretence? ... Even now, you are stirring up a greater and much crueller sedition than the one from which you freed the people amidst great rejoicing [at Henry's accession in 1509]. Before you became king, the people were harassed by continual slaughters within the confines of the kingdom [the Wars of the Roses], as if in their very entrails. Whichever side triumphed, the opposing side lived in the greatest misery. Those seditions, however, cannot be compared with the ones you are currently kindling' (Dwyer: 198–199)

[The Pilgrimage of Grace soon followed the completion of Pole's *De unitate*.]

### Henry VIII's Failings as a Ruler

'During the twenty-seven years of your reign [1509–36], have [your people] not had sufficient experience in observing ... your plundering? However, if during that time you had given any sign of liberality, they would have recognised this in all other matters, as well as those pertaining to the public good. For in the early years of your reign you poured out large sums of money. To regain your inroads ino the Treasury, you afterwards despoiled all kinds of men. You always regarded the nobility with scorn. You never loved the people. You plundered and molested the clergy in every possible way. Most recently, though, more like a raging wild animal than a man, you have torn to pieces some worthy men [the monks executed in 1535]. These men had lived very long lives. They were a credit to your realm, pillars of the Church of God, flowers of mankind. They merit these titles, for they showed themselves outstanding among men, not only in their lives but also in the way in which thy left this life' (Dwyer: 287).

### G. Pole's View of Martyrdom

### John Fisher and Thomas More

'People of London, behold the head of Fisher, that most holy man. Severed from his body, it was fixed to a pike in the common view of all in London, near the bridge over the Thames. Behold the head of More, that most guiltless of men. It was set up in the same place and given the same home. Oh, what a mournful sight, not only for the city of London alone but for all England. Oh, what a miserable spectacle, not only for the country of England but for the whole world where the Christian name extends. Were these not the very men from whose virtues and literary talents England derived such great enjoyment? By their lives, they provided England with a singular, saintly example' (Dwyer: 204).

*The Significance of Martyrdom for the Church*

'Through these men the Church can know more about the will of God than through any books written by hand. These things written on paper were dictated by the same [Holy] Spirit, for without doubt the written memorials of the Evangelists and the Apostles that we have, written in the New Testament, were inspired by the Spirit of God. Nevertheless, as the original always has greater authority than all other things that are described in books, so also those books written in the blood of the martyrs are to be preferred to all others. These were the original books in which the finger of God appeared. The hand of man appears in all others that were written with ink on paper. Although the hand of man followed the hand of God and could not err, nevertheless it has less dignity and is subject to more accidents. The books can be distorted by the perverse reasoning and interpretation of men, and can be imagined in many forms. Those that are written in the blood of martyrs cannot be adulterated. These indeed are uncorrupted and are always asserted strongly in the collected writings of the Church. By their means, the Church greatly increases knowledge of divine things. For God, in his compassion, never ceased writing books of this kind until the Church would abound with a knowledge of all things necessary for salvation. Afterwards, there were many other ways in which the most excellent God carefully declared His will for us. But, indeed, the particular method of teaching this was always through the book of the martyrs. In the beginning, Christ, the Son of God, was first, then this teaching was continued in his other members, so that the most kindly God always produced his holy martyrs in concluding all great controversies. These were original things in his own hand: they could not be contradicted' (Dwyer: 234–235).

## 2. Pole Approaches the Duke of Somerset (1549)

The precise history of this text is uncertain. Internal evidence suggests that it was composed in the summer of 1549, and was completed in October of that year. It may well be that it was never despatched to England, but it forcefully expresses Pole's views on religious and political questions. Addressed to Edward Seymour, duke of Somerset and lord protector, it was a vain attempt to exploit the death of Henry VIII by bringing his kingdom back into the Catholic fold, and refers to a rejection by Somerset of earlier ventures (*CRP* 2 no. 549: Somerset to Pole, 4/6 June 1549). Had the letter reached its planned recipient, it would have found Seymour no longer in post, having been replaced, with the title of Lord

President of the Council, by John Dudley, earl of Warwick, with whom Pole had also corresponded earlier (*CRP* 2 no. 538: Pole to Warwick, 6 April 1549).

There are several surviving manuscript versions of this text (for full details see *CRP* 2 p. 31).

These extracts are translated by the author from Italian.

### A. Henry VIII's Reception of De unitate

'It was that king, whom I had loved above all other men, who, having had occasion to know my sincere view on this subject, which was very contrary to his own, did not want to have a row with me, or to scoff at me as you [Somerset] do. It happened in this way. The aforesaid [Henry] had received a document of mine which treated of the divorce that he wanted to have from his first wife [Catherine]. And because that document of mine was very much opposed to his intention and desire, I was made to understand from my lord, by my brother of good memory [Sir Henry Pole, Baron Montagu] that the lord duke of Norfolk [Thomas Howard] had told him that the king had conceived a bad feeling towards me for this reason, telling him that [the document] would be my complete ruin.

Then I said to my lord brother that I was sure that could not be true, once the king had read everything that I had written to him knowing that it was impossible that, with my declaring my mind to him, with such sincerity and affection of heart, when His M[ajesty] read it, he could have conceived ill will against me, and that, when he did so, I could take it as a most certain argument that His M[ajesty] had not read everything that I had written. Clearly, if he did read it, I was absolutely sure that there could be no offence from me in a document that was not given to anyone else to read other than the one for whom it was intended. This is why I spoke with so much greater confidence, knowing above all that His M[ajesty] had not given it to other people to read. Thus, firmly persuading myself that such an approach [as mine] could not be despised, or received with such disdain, I asked that same lord, my brother, by discovering the king's mind, to find out what effect my reply had had on His M[ajesty]. And he answered that, finding it convenient to discuss with His M[ajesty] in a secret garden where, having been commanded to enter, he told him the whole story from the beginning ... Henry said that reading my [text] could have induced his mind to conceive some anger against me, but although the document was very contrary to his will, he nevertheless knew from it my love for him, and the sincerity with which he had written it. But in the end my opinion did not please him, and he very much wanted me to change it. If I did this, I would know how dear my person was to him' (*CRP* 2 pp. 34–35).

## B. Pole's Social Attitudes: Disparagement of the Duke of Somerset

'In your reply ... I saw and judged in such a way that it seemed to me that you wanted to be held to be a person of honour and prudence, and of gravity, not foolhardy but discreet, and full of gentility, and I saw that your letter gave the totally opposite impression, looking more like [one from] those who, coming from a low condition to some degree of honour, know no other way to employ to show that they are honoured than despising all those whom they think not to be their equals in authority, just as they themselves were despised when they were in a base condition, and beyond that, I saw this letter [of yours] as abandoning all the gravity and humanity required for you to discuss such important matters, such as those appertaining to your government'.

## C. A Story told to Pole by Queen Catherine

'I told you [Somerset] of the great troubles that the Most Serene Queen Catherine, aunt of His Majesty [Charles V], had to suffer, and the distress that she had to suffer, and what that same lady chose to say, thinking always of this [trouble], that is, she thought that a large proportion of the troubles from which she suffered came to her from the hand of God, not for some fault of hers but for the salvation of her soul, and that in this way the divine justice punished the sin of King Ferdinand her father, who, having begun to negotiate to marry her to Prince Arthur, the eldest son of the king of England, there being some disturbances at the time, caused by the favour and good will that the people had conceived for the earl of Warwick, my mother's brother ... because he was the grandson of the due of Clarence, brother of King Edward [IV], he had come, through the death [of the "Princes in the Tower"], to be the closest heir in the male line, to have the Crown of England at that time. King Ferdinand, seeing that the negotiations were coming to a conclusion for the marriage of his daughter, began to make a difficulty, saying that he did not want to give her to someone who was insecure in his kingdom. Thus the king [of Spain] incited [Henry VII], who was so inclined on his own account, to be the cause of the death of that innocent earl, who had no guilt for those disturbances.

Once Henry VIII was on the throne, with Catherine [as his wife] she therefore confessed that she was totally obliged to recompense and make restoration to us for the damage that we had received from her plan [against Warwick], although she had had no responsibility for it ... She had found proof that, in all her troubles and annoyances, she had never had greater consolation from any family in the kingdom than from ours, even though we had suffered so much distress because of her (*CRP* 2 pp. 49–50).

### 3. Nearing the End of his Life, Pole Unburdens Himself to Pope Paul IV

This lengthy text, in which Pole expressed his despair and frustration at his treatment by Paul IV, was apparently taken from England to Rome by his datary, Niccolò Ormanetto, but was probably never read by the pope. Nonetheless, it illustrates not only Pole's state of mind, as his death approached, but also his recognition of the damage that the Carafa papacy was doing to the attempted restoration of Catholicism in Mary and Philip's island kingdoms.

The version in the library of the Inner Temple (Petyt MS 538/46) is edited and transcribed by Tellechea in *CP* pp. 199–241 (summary in *CRP* 3 no. 2076), and here translated by the author.

### A. Paul IV as a 'Satanic' Pope?

'To [Pole's charges] Your Holiness says that, in this clamour, I am throwing out curses which are of such gravity that I must have been led to it by the spirit of Satan. Yet in truth are not the things I throw against you quite otherwise? I utterly abhor cursing, especially from Your Holiness, so I should far more willingly endure the curses of everyone else than one word, with the force of a curse, said by Your Holiness ... For if this is said as a curse, how much more would it be so if made by someone whom Satan named as Vicar of Christ. For Christ Himself, who, as Scripture says, when he is cursed does not curse [in reply], even called Peter by that name [Satan], to whose to whose office Your Holiness succeeded, when He was persuading him that, he might be exposed to suffering, and death for the human love that he professed for Christ: "Get behind me, Satan! ... For you are setting your mind not on divine things but on human things". Indeed this curse should not be spoken, even less should it be said by someone who is tempted by Satan and conquered, who arguably does not know what is of God, but what is of men, that is, something done against the honour of Christ and the good of one's neighbour' (*CP* p. 235).

### B. A Pope must take Counsel from Cardinals and Bishops

'For by the institution of God and his high providence towards his Vicar the pastor is provided, nor should one be lacking who may raise him up from falling into infirmity. First [popes] have in their support the cardinals, who if possible are not only called to a part in the concerns of ruling the universal Church, and perpetually to assist in its councils, but are also given by God as guardians of [the pope's] soul, and watchmen against all the tricks of Satan, who is accustomed to approaching and tempting the supreme pontiff more frequently and vehemently than the rest. He perpetually studies to sow many and ever more serious offences, like tares among the wheat.

From this it is clear not only that it is proper for cardinals to admonish a supreme pontiff freely, should they know that his actions are not of God but of men; in truth they must do this and use clear words, because if they do nothing, they will have to give Christ a good reason for it' (*CP* p. 236).

# Bibliography

**Primary Manuscript Sources**

Archivo General de Simancas      Estado, legajos 505, 506, 806, 811,
     879, 880, 881, 882, 1321
     Estado, Libros de Versoza 2
     Juntas y Consejos de Hacienda 34

Biblioteca apostolica vaticana      Barbarini 2545, 5115, 5211, 5302
     Vat. lat. 5827, 5966, 5967, 5968,
     5970, 6206, 6754

Bibliothèque municipale de Douai      MS 922
Bodleian Library, Oxford      Rawlinson MS C.45
     Mith MS 67
     Twyne MSS VI, VII

British Library, London      Additional 25114, 32091, 32096,
     35425, 35839, 35840, 41577,
     41781, 48035
     Cotton: Cleopatra E.V, E.VI, F.II
     Nero B.VI, B.VII
     Titus B.II
     Vespasian B.XVIII
     Vitellius B.XIV
     Egerton 985
     Harleian 41, 3881, 6989
     Lansdowne 115
     Royal XVIIB, XXXV

Cambridge University Library      Add. MS 4841
Corpus Christi College,
     Cambridge: Parker Library      MSS 105, 106, 118, 121, 127
Inner Temple, London      Petyt MS XLVI
Lambeth Palace Library, London      MSS 751, 1135, 3563
     Archbishop Pole's Register

Oxford University Archive      NEP/Supra/Register 1
     Wpβ/B Wpβ/M/22

The National Archives, Kew      C.2/38
     E.404/79

The National Archives, Kew                PRO 31/9/67
                                           PROB 11/42/A
                                           SP 1/106, 114, 116, 120, 138, 240
                                           SP2/N 1550160
                                           SP10.6, 7
                                           SP11/1/7, 12.1, 14.1
                                           SP69.1
Westminster Abbey Muniments               MSS 12972, 37162, 37712, 37716,
                                           37717, 37718


## Primary Printed Sources

Beccadelli, Ludovico, revised by Andras Dudic, with Giovanni Binardi, *Vita Reginaldi Poli, Britanni S. R. E. Cardinalis, et cantuariensis archiepiscopi* (Venice: Ex oficina Dominici Guerrei et Joannis Baptistae fratrum, 1563).

Bonner, Edmund, *A profitable and necessarye doctrine with certayne homilies adioined thereunto set forthe by the reverende father in God, Edmunde bishop of London, for the instruction and information of the people beynge in his diocese of London, and of his care and charge* (London: John Cawood, 1555).

Bonner, Edmund, John Harpsfield and Henry Pendleton, *Homelies sette forth by the right reverende father in God, Edmunde Byshop of London* (London: John Cawood, 1555).

Bray, Gerald, ed., *The Anglican Canons* (Woodbridge: The Boydell Press and the Church of England Record Society, in association with the Ecclesiastical Law Society, 1998).

Callahan, T.E., 'Reginald, Cardinal Pole's *Reformatio Angliae*, a Critical Edition with Introduction and Commentary. A Thesis in History' (Buffalo: State University College at Buffalo, 1995).

Cardwell, E., *Documentary Annals of the Reformed Church of England*, 2 vols (Oxford: Clarendon Press, 1839).

Carranza, Bartolomé, *Controversia de necessaria residentiali personali Episcoporum et aliorum inferiorum pastorum Tridenti explicata per fratrem Bartholomeum Carranzam de Miranda instituti beati Dominici. Et regentem in collegio Sancti Gregorii eiusdem ordinis in Valle Olitana* (Venice: Ad Signum Spei, 1547).

Carranza, Bartolomé, *Controversia sobre la necesaria residencia personal de los obispos*, ed. and trans., with facsimile, by José Ignacio Tellechea Idígoras (Madrid: Fundación Universitaria Española and Universidad Pontificia de Salamanca, 1994).

Carranza, Bartolomé, *Speculum pastorum, hierarchia ecclesiastica in quo describuntur officia ministrorum ecclesiae militantis*, ed. Tellechea (Salamanca: Universidad Pontificia de Salamanca, 1992).

Castro, Alfonso de, *Adversus omnes haereses libri XII* (Paris: Josse Badius and Jean de Roigny, 1534, reprinted Antwerp: Jeremias Steels, 1556).

Carranza, Bartolomé, *De iusta haereticorum punitione libri III* (Lyon: Heirs of Jacopo Giunta, 1556).

*Christopheri Longolii orationes duae* ['Vita Longolii'] (Florence: Heirs of F. Giunta, reprinted Farnborough: Gregg International, 1967).

*Collection of Ordinances and Regulations for the Government of the Royal Household* (London: John Nicholas, 1790).

Corrie, G.E., ed., *Sermons by Hugh Latimer, Sometime Bishop of Wocester, Martyr 1555* (Cambridge: Cambridge University Press, 1844).

[Corycius, Janus] *Coricianus*, ed. Joseph Ijswijn (Rome: Herder, 1997).

Courtenay, Edward, trans., *A treatise most profittable of the benefite that true Christians receve by the dethe of Jesus Christ* (London, 1548).

Cummings, Brian, ed., *The Book of Common Prayer: The Texts of 1549, 1559 and 1662* (Oxford: Oxford University Press, 2011).

Delicado, Francisco, *Retrato de la Lozana andaluza*, ed. Claude Allaigre (Madrid: Cátedra, 1985).

Dickens, A.G., 'Robert Parkyn's Narrative of the Reformation', *English Historical Review*, 62 (1947), pp. 58–82.

Fernández Álvarez, Manuel, ed., *Corpus documental de Carlos V*, 5 vols (Salamanca: Ediciones Universidad de Salamanca, 1970).

Firpo, Massimo and Dario Marcatto, eds, *Il processo inquisitoriale del Cardinal Morone*, 6 vols (Rome: Istituto storico italiano per l'ete moderna e contemporanea, 1981–9).

*First and Second Prayer Books of Edward VI, The* (London: Prayer Book Society, 1999).

Frere, W.H. and W.M. Kennedy, eds, *Visitation Articles and Injunctions of Periods of the Reformation*, 3 vols (London: Longman, 1900).

Garnett, Richard, ed. and trans., *The Accession of Queen Mary, being the Contemporary Narrative of Antonio Guaras, a Spanish Merchant Resident in London* (London: Lawrence and Bullen, 1892).

Gee, Henry and William John Hardy, eds, *Documents Illustrative of English Church History Compiled from Original Sources* (London: Macmillan, 1896).

Hamilton, W.D., ed., *A Chronicle during the Reigns of the Tudors from 1485 to 1559 by Charles Wriothesley, Camden Society*, 2nd series, 11, 2 vols (1875–7).

Harpsfield, Nicholas (?), *Bishop Cranmer's Recantacyons*, ed. Lord Houghton, *Philobiblion Miscellanies*, 15 (1877–84).

Hay, Denys, ed. and trans., *The* Anglica Historia *of Polydore Vergil, A.D. 1485–1537, Camden Society*, 3rd series, 74 (1950).

Hearne, Thomas, ed., *Joannis Lelandi Antiquarii de Rebus Britannicis Collectanea*, 4 vols (Farnborough: Gregg International, [1799] 1971).

Hogarde, Miles, *A displaying of the Protestants and sundry their practises* (London: Robert Caly, 1556).

Holinshead, Raphael, *Chronicles of England, Scotland, and Ireland*, 6 vols (London: S. Johnson and others, 1817–18).

Hughes, P.L. and J.F. Larkin, *Tudor Royal Proclamations*, 2 vols (New Haven and London: Yale University Press, 1964–9).

Kingsford, C.L., ed., *A Survey of London by John Stow reprinted from the Text of 1603*, 2 vols (Oxford: Clarendon Press, 1908).

Kingsford, C.L., 'Two London Chronciles', *Camden Miscellany*, 12 (1912).

Loades, David, *The Chronicles of the Tudor Queens* (Stroud: Sutton Publishing, 2002).

McCoog, Thomas M., ed., *Monumenta Angliae: English and Welsh Jesuits. Catalogues, Monumenta Historica Societatis Iesu*, 152–153 (Rome: Institutum Historicum Societatis Iesu, 1992).

McCoog, Thomas M. and Lasló Lukács, eds, *Monumenta Angliae*, 3, *England, Scotland and Wales. Documents, 1541–1562* (Rome: Institutum Historicum Societatis Iesu, 2000).

McCulloch, Diarmaid, ed. and trans., 'The *Vita Mariae Angliae* of Robert Wingfield of Brantham', *Camden Miscellany*, 4th series (London: Royal Historical Society, 1984), pp. 181–301.

Mantova, Benedetto da, *Il Beneficio di Cristo*, ed. Salvatore Caponetto (Floence: Sandini, 1972).

Manzoni, Giacomo, ed. 'Il processo Carnesecchi', *Miscellanea di Storia Italiana*, 10 (1870), pp. 189–573.

Marsilius of Padua, *Defensor Pacis*, ed. C.W. Prévité-Orton (Cambridge: Cambridge University Press, 1928).

Muir, Kenneth, *Life and Letters of Sir Thomas Wyatt* (Liverpool: Liverpool University Press, 1963).

Muller, James Arthur, *The Letters of Stephen Gardiner* (Cambridge: Cambridge University Press, 1933).

Munitiz, Joseph A. and Philip Endean, ed. and trans., *Saint Ignatius of Loyola: Personal Writings* (London: Penguin Books, 1996).

Nichols, J.G., ed., *Chronicle of Queen Jane and of the First Two Years of Queen Mary, The, Camden Society*, 1st series, 47 (1850).

Nichols, J.G., ed., *Chronicle of the Greyfriars of London, Camden Society*, 1st series, 48 (1851).

Nichols, J.G., ed., *The Diary of Henry Machyn, Citizen and Merchant-Taylor of London. From A.D. 1550 to A.D. 1563, Camden Society*, 1st series, 42 (1848).

Parker, Matthew, and others, *De antiquitate Britannicae ecclesiae et priuilegiis Cantuarensis cum Archiepiscopis eiusdem LXX* (London: John Day, 1572).

Peryn, William, *Spritual exercyses and goostly meditacions, and a neare waye to come to perfection and lyfe contemplatyue very profitable for Religious and general for al other that desire to come to the perfecte loue of god and to the contempte of the worlde* (London: J. Waley, 1557).

Pocock, Nicholas, ed., *The History of the Reformation of the Church of England, by Gilbert Burnet*, 7 vols (Oxford: Clarendon Press, 1865).

Pole, Reginald, *Reformatio Angliae ex decretis Reginaldi Poli Cardinalis, sedis apostolicae Legati, anno MDLVI* (Rome: Apud Paulum Manutium, 1562).

Pole, Reginald, *Regnaldi Poli Cardinalis Britanni ad Henricum Octavum Britanniaeregem libri IV* (Rome: Antonio Blado, [1536] 1538).

Robinson, Hastings, ed., *Original Letters Relative to the English Reformation*, 1 (Cambridge: Cambridge University Press for the Parker Society, 1864).

Robinson, Hastings, *The Zurich Letters, comprising the correspondence of several English Bishops and Others, with some of the Helvetian Reformers, during the Early Part of the Reign of Queen Elizabeth*, 2 vols (Cambridge: Cambridge University Press for the Parker Society, 1842).

Rodríguez-Salgado, M.J. and Simon Adams, eds, 'The Count of Feria's Dispatch to Philip II of 14 November 1558', *Camden Miscellany*, 28 (London: Royal Historical Society, 1984), pp. 302–344.

Roper, William, *The Life of Thomas More*, in R.S. Sylvester and D.P. Harding, eds, *The Collected Works of Sir Thomas More* (New Haven: Yale Univesity Press, 1962).

Sampson, Richard, *Oratio qui docet hortatur admonet omnes, potissimum Anglos regiae dignitati cum primis ut obedient* (London: Thomas Berthelet, 1534/5).

Sanudo, Marin, *I diariidi Marin Sanudo*, 59 vols (Venice: F. Visentini, 1879–1903).

Starkey, Thomas, *A Dialogue between Pole and Lupset*, ed. T[homas] F. Mayer, *Camden Society*, 4th series, 37 (1989).

*Statutes of the Colleges of Oxford*, 3 vols (London: Royal Commission on the Universities, 1859.

*Statutes of the Realm*, 12 vols (London: Eyre and Staham, 1810).

Stow, Kenneth, *The Jews in Rome, 1536–1557*, 2 vols (Leiden: Brill, 1997).

Strype, John, *Ecclesiastical Memorials relating chiefly to Religion and its Reformation under the Reigns of King Henry VIII, King Edward VI and Queen Mary* (Oxford: Clarendon Press, 1816).

Tellechea Idígoras, José Ignacio, ed., *El Papado y Felipe II*, 3 vols (Madrid: Fundación Universitaria Española, 1999–2002).

Tellechea Idígoras, José Ignacio, *Fray Bartolomé Carranza: documentos históricos*, 7 vols (Madrid: Real Academia de la Historia, 1962–94).

Thynne, Francis, 'Reginald Pole', in Raphael Holinshead, *Chronicles*.

Tunstall, Cuthbert, *De veritate corporis et sanguinis domini nostri Iesu Christi in Eucharistia* (Paris: Michel Vascosan, 1554).

Valdés, Alfonso de, *Obra completa*, ed. Ángel Alcalá (Madrid: Fundación José Antonio Castro, 1996).

Watson, Thomas, *Holsome and catholyke doctrine concerninge the seven sacraments... set forth in maner of shorte sermons* (London: Robert Caly, 1558).

Watson, Thomas, *Twoo notable sermons concerning the reall prsence of Christes body and bloode in the blessed sacrament, also the masse, which is the sacrifice of the newe Testament* (London: John Cawood, 1554).


## Secondary Printed Sources

Alford, Stephen, *Burghley: William Cecil at the Court of Elizabeth I* (New Haven and London: Yale University Press, 2008).

Alsop, J.D., 'Baker, Sir John', *ODNB*.

Anglo, Sydney, *Machiavelli – the First Century. Studies in Enthusiasm, Hostility and Irrelevance* (Oxford: Oxford University Press, 2005).

Aston, Margaret, *England's Iconoclasts: Laws against Images* (Cambridge: Cambridge University Press, 1988).

Baker, J.H., 'Browne, Sir Anthony', *ODNB*.

Baumgartner, Frederic J., *Henry II, King of France, 1547–1559* (Durham, NC and London: Duke University Press, 1988).

Bernard, G.W., 'The Dissolution of the Monasteries', *History*, 95 (2011), pp. 390–409.

Bernard, G.W., *The King's Reformation: Henry VIII and the Remaking of the English Church* (New Haven and London: Yale University Press, 2005).

Bernard, G.W., *The Late Medieval English Church: Vitality and Vulnerability before the Break with Rome* (New Haven and London: Yale University Press, 2012).

Brigden, Susan, '"The Shadow that you know": Sir Thomas Wyatt and Sir Francis Bryant at Court and in Embassy', *Historical Journal*, 39 (1996), pp. 1–31.

Brigden, Susan, *Sir Thomas Wyatt: The Heart's Forest* (London: Faber & Faber, 2012).

Brown, Keith Duncan, 'The Franciscan Observants in England, 1482–1559', unpublished D.Phil. Thesis, University of Oxford, 1986.

Brundin, Abigail, *Vittoria Colonna and the Spiritual Practice of the Italian Reformation* (Aldershot: Ashgate, 2008).

Cameron, Euan, 'Italy', in Andrew Pettegree, ed., *The Early Reformation in Europe* (Cambridge: Cambridge University Press, 1992), pp. 188–214.

Carleton, Kenneth, 'Bonner, Edmund', *ODNB*.

Carleton, Kenneth, 'Pate, Richard', *ODNB*.

Carleton, Kenneth, 'Scott, Cuthbert', *ODNB*.

Carleton, Kenneth, 'Watson, Thomas', *ODNB*.

Carleton, Kenneth, 'White, John', *ODNB*.

Cereceda, Feliciano, *Diego Laínez en la Europa religiosa de su tiempo, 1512–1565*, 2 vols (Madrid: Ediciones Cultura Hispánica, 1945–6).

Chibi, Andrew A., 'Sampson, Richard', *ODNB*.

Chibi, Andrew A., 'Richard Sampson, his "Oratio", and Henry VIII's Royal Supremacy', *Journal of Church and State*, 39 (2007), pp. 543–560.

Chrimes, S.B., *Henry VII* (New Haven and London: Yale University Press, [1972] 1999).

Clark, J.G., Reformation and Reaction at St Alban's Abbey', *English Historical Review*, 115 (2000), pp. 297–328.

Clark, Margaret, 'Oglethorpe, Owen', *ODNB*.

Clough, Cecil H., 'Clement VII and Francesco Maria dell Rovere, Duke of Urbino', in Kenneth Gouwens and Sheryl E. Reiss, eds, *The Pontificate of Clement VII: History, Politics, Culture* (Aldershot: Ashgate, 2005), pp. 75–108.

Collett, Barry, *Italian Benedictine Scholars and the Reformation: The Congregation of Santa Giusta of Padua* (Oxford: Oxford University Press, 1985).

Collinson, Patrick, 'The Persecution in Kent', in *CMT*, pp. 309–333.

Crankshaw, David [J.], 'Preparations for the Canterbury Provincial Convocation of 1562–3', in Susan Wabuda and Carl Litzenberger, eds, *Belief and Practice in Reformation England* (Aldershot: Ashgate, 1998), pp. 50–93.

Crankshaw, David J. and Alexandra Gillespie, 'Parker, Matthew', *ODNB*.

Cross, Claire, 'The English Universities, 1553–58', in *CMT*, pp. 57–76.

Cross, Claire, 'Oxford and the Tudor State from the Accession of Henry VIII to the Death of Mary', in James McConica, ed., *History of the University of Oxford*, 3 (Oxford: Oxford University Press, 1986), pp. 117–149.

Daniell, David, 'Rogers, John', *ODNB*.

Daniell, David, *William Tyndale: A Biography* (New Haven and London: Yale University Press, [1994] 2011).

D'Ascia, Luca, 'Un erasmiano italiano: Note sulla filosofia della religione di Niccolò Leonico', *Rivista di Storia e Letteratura Religiosa*, 26 (1999), pp. 242–264.

Davies, C.S.L., 'Bishop John Morton, the Holy See, and the Accession of Henry VII', *English Historical Review*, 102 (1987), pp. 2–30.

Davies, C.S.L., 'England and the French War, 1557–9', in Jennifer Loach and Robert Tittler, eds, *The Mid-Tudor Polity, c.1540–1560* (London: Macmillan, 1980), pp. 159–185.

Davies, C.S.L., 'The "Tudors": or not?', *The Oxford Historian*, 9 (2011), pp. 6–10

Davies, C.S.L., 'Tudor: What's in a Name?', *History*, 97 (2012), pp. 24–42.

Dickens, A.G., *The English Reformation*, 2nd edn (London: Batsford, 1989).

Dickens, A.G. *Reformation Studies* (London: Hambledon, 1982).

Dillon, Anne, *Michelangelo and the English Martyrs* (Farnham: Ashgate, 2013).

Doran, Susan, 'Elizabeth I's Religion: the Evidence of her Letters', *Journal of Ecclesiastical History*, 51 (2000), pp. 699–720.

Doran, Susan and Thomas S. Freeman, eds, *Mary Tudor: Old and New Perspectives* (Basingstoke: Palgrave Macmillan, 2011).

Dowling, Maria, *Fisher of Men: A Life of John Fisher, 1469–1535* (Basingstoke: Macmillan, 1999).

Duffy, Eamon, 'Allen, William', *ODNB*.

Duffy, Eamon, 'Cardinal Pole Praching: St Andrew's Day 1557', in *CMT*, pp. 176–200.

Duffy, Eamon, *Fires of Faith: Catholic England under Mary Tudor* (New Haven and London: Yale University Press, 2009).

Duffy, Eamon, *Saints, Sacrilege and Sedition: Religion and Conflictin the Tudor Reformations* (London: Bloomsbury, 2012).

Duffy, Eamon, *The Stripping of the Altars: Traditional Religion in England, 1400–1580*, 2nd edn (New Haven and London: Yale University Press, 2005).

Duffy, Eamon, *The Voices of Morebath: Reformation and Rebellion in an English Village* (New Haven and London: Yale University Press, 2001).

Duncan, G.D., 'Public Lecturers and Professorial Chairs', in James McConica, ed., *History of the Unversity of Oxford*, 3 (Oxford: Oxford University Press, 1986), pp. 335–361.

Dunn, T.F., 'The Development of the Text of Pole's *De Unitate Ecclesiastica*', *Papers of the Bibliographical Society of America*, 70 (1976), pp. 455–468.

Edwards, John, 'Corpus Christi in Kingston upon Thames: Bartolomé Carranza and the Eucharist in Marian England', in *RCEMT*, pp. 139–151.

Edwards, John, 'Experiencing the Mass anew in Mary I's England: Bartolomé Carranza's "Little Treatise"', *Reformation and Renaissance Review*, 9 (2007), pp. 265–276.

Edwards, John, *Ferdinand and Isabella* (Harlow: Pearson Longman, 2005).

Edwards, John, 'Fray Bartolomé Carranza's Blueprint for a Reformed Catholic Church in England', in Thomas F. Mayer, ed., *Reforming Reformation* (Farnham: Ashgate, 2012), pp. 141–159.

Edwards, John, *Inquisition* (Stroud: The History Press, [1999] 2009).

Edwards, John, *Mary I: England's Catholic Queen* (New Haven and London: Yale University Press, 2011).

Edwards, John, 'A Spanish Inquisition? The Repression of Protestantism under Mary Tudor', *Reformation and Renaissance Review*, 4 (2000), pp. 62–74.

Edwards, John, 'The Spanish Inquisition Refashioned: The Experience of Mary I's England and the Valladolid Tribunal, 1559', *Hispanic Research Journal*, 13 (2012), pp. 41–54.

Fenlon, Dermot, *Heresy and Obedience in Tridentine Italy: Cardinal Pole and the Counter Reformation* (Cambridge: Cambridge University Press, 1972).

Fenlon, Dermot, 'Pietro Carnesecchi and Cardinal Pole: New Perspectives', *Journal of Ecclesiastical History*, 56 (2005), pp. 529–533.

Fenlon, Dermot, 'Pole, Carranza and the Pulpit', in *RCEMT*, pp. 81–97.

Fincham, Kenneth and Nicholas Tyacke, *Altars Restored: The Changing Face of English Religious Worship* (Oxford: Oxford University Press, 2007).

Firpo, Massimo, *Inquisizione romana e Contrareforma: Studi sul Cardinale Giovanni Morone e il processo di eresia* (Bologna: Il Mulino, 1992).

Fletcher, J.M., 'The Faculty of Arts', in James McConica, ed., *History of the University of Oxford*, 3 (Oxford: Oxford University Press, 1986), pp. 157–199.

Fragnito, Gigliola, 'Ercole Gonzaga, Reginald Pole e il monasterio di S[an] Benedetto Pilitone', *Benedictina*, 37 (1987), pp. 253–271.

Fragnito, Gigliola, 'Gli "spirituali" e la fuga di Bernardino Ochino', *Rivista Storica Italiana*, 74 (1972), pp. 777–811.

Freeman, Thomas F., 'Bland, John', *ODNB*.

Freeman, Thomas F., 'Burning Zeal: Mary Tudor and the Marian Persecution', in Doran and Freeman, *Mary Tudor*, pp. 171–205.

Gibbons, Katy, *English Catholic Exiles in Late Sixteenth-Century Paris* (Woodbridge: The Boydell Press, The Royal Historical Society, 2011).

Ginzburg, Carlo and Adriano Prosperi, *Eresia e Riforma nell'Italia del Cinquecento* (Florence and Chicago: Sansoni and the Newberry Library, 1974).

Gleason, Elizabeth G., *Gasparo Contarini: Vence, Rome and Reform* (Berkeley and Los Angeles: University of California Press, 1993).

Gleason, Elizabeth G., *Reform Thought in Sixteenth-Century Italy* (Chico, CA: Scholars Press, 1981).

Gleason, John B., *John Colet* (Berkeley and Los Angeles: University of California Press, 1989).

Goodman, Anthony and Angus MacKay, 'A Castilian Report on English Affairs in 1486', *English Historical Review*, 88 (1973), pp. 92–99.

Gordon, Bruce, 'Italy', in Andrew Pettegree, ed., *The Reformation World* (London: Routledge, 2000).

Gouwens, Kenneth, 'Clement and Calamity: The Case for Re-evaluation', in Kenneth Gouwens and Sheryl E. Reiss, eds, *The Pontificate of Clement VII: History, Politics, Culture* (Aldershot: Ashgate, 2005), pp. 3–14.

Greenblatt, Stephen, *Renaissance Self-Fashioning: From More to Shakespeare* (Chicago IL: Chicago University Press, [1980] 2005).

Gregory, Brad S., *Salvation at Stake: Christian Martyrdom in Early Modern Europe* (Cambridge, MA: Harvard University Press, 1999).

Gunn, Steven, 'Prince Arthur's Preparation for Kingship', in Steven Gunn and Linda Monckton, eds, *Arthur Tudor, Prince of Wales: Life, Death and Commemoration* (Woodbridge: The Boydell Press, 2009), pp. 7–19.

Guy, John, *Thomas More* (London: Arnold, 2000).

Haigh, Christopher, *English Reformations: Religion, Politics and Society under the Tudors* (Oxford: Clarendon Press, 1993).

Hall, Basil, 'The Colloquies between Catholics and Protestants, 1539–1541', in G.J. Cuming and D. Baker, eds, *Studies in Church History*, 7 (1971), pp. 235–266.

Harris, Barbara J., *Edward Stafford, Third Duke of Buckingham, 1478–1521* (Stanford: Stanford University Press, 1986).

Heal, Felicity, *Reformation in Britain and Ireland* (Oxford: Clarendon Press, 2003).

Heal, Felicity, 'What can King Lucius do for you? The Reformation and the Early British Church', *English Historical Review*, 120 (2005), pp. 593–614.

Hegarty, Andrew, 'Carranza and the English Universities', in *RCEMT*, pp. 153–172.

Hindle, Steve, 'Martin [Martyn], Thomas', *ODNB*.

Höllger, C., 'Reginald Pole and the Legations of 1537 and 1539: Diplomatic and Political Responses to the Break with Rome', unpublished D.Phil. thesis, University of Oxford, 1989.

Houlbrooke, Ralph, 'The Clergy, the Courts and the Marian Restoration in Norwich', in *CMT*, pp. 124–146.

Hoyle, R.W., *The Pilgrimage of Grace and the Politics of the 1530s* (Oxford: Oxford University Press, 2001).

Hudon, William V., 'Epilogue: Marcellus II, Girolamo Seripando and the Image of the Angelic Pope', in Marjorie Reeves, ed., *Prophetic Rome in the High Renaissance Period* (Oxford: Clarendon Press, 1992), pp. 73–87.

Hudon, William V., *Marcello Cervini and Ecclesiastical Government in Tridentie Italy* (DeKalb: Northern Illinois University Press, 1992).

Hughes, Jonathan, *Arthurian Myths and Alchemy: The Kingship of Edward IV* (Stroud: Sutton Publishing, 2002).

Hutchings, Michael, *Reginald, Cardinal Pole. The Last* [sic] *Archbishop of Canterbury* (Midhurst: Saint Joan Press, 1558).

Hyde, Patricia, 'Moyle, Sir Thomas', *ODNB*.

Ingram, Martin, 'Regulating Sex in Pre-Reformation London', in G.W. Bernard and S[teven] J. Gunn, eds, *Authority and Consent in Tudor England: Essays Presented to C.S.L. Davies* (Aldershot: Ashgate, 2002), pp. 71–95.

Jones, Michael and Malcolm Underwood, *The King's Matter* (Cambridge: Cambridge University Press, 1992).

Jungić, Josephine, 'Joachimist Prophecies in Sebastiano del Piombo's Borgherini Chapel and Raphael's *Transfiguration*', in Marjorie Reeves, ed., *Prophetic Rome in the High Renaissance Period* (Oxford: Clarendon Press, 1992), pp. 321–343.

Kamen, Henry, *The Spanish Inquisition: An Historical Revision* (London: Weidenfeld & Nicolson, 1997).

Kaplan, Benjamin, *Divided by Faith: Religious Conflict and the Practice of Toleration in Early Modern Europe* (Cambridge, MA: Harvard University Press, 2007).

Kinder, Gordon, 'Juan Morillo – Catholic Theologian at Trent, Calvinist Ruler in Frankfurt', *Bibliothèque d'Humanisme et Renaissance*, 38 (1976), pp. 345–350.

King, M.L., *Venetian Patriotism in an Age of Patrician Dominance* (Princeton: Princeton University Press, 1986).

Knecht, R.J., *Renaissance Warrior and Patron: The Reign of Francis I* (Cambridge: Cambridge University Press, 1994).

Knighton, C.S., 'Westminster Abbey Restored', in *CMT*, pp. 77–123.

Lander, J.R., 'The Treason and Death of the Duke of Clarence', *Canadian Journal of History*, 2 (1967), pp. 1–28.

Lethead, Howard, 'Cromwell, Thomas', *ODNB*.

Levine, Mortimer, *Tudor Dynastic Problems, 1460–1571* (London: Allen & Unwin, 1973).

Loach, Jennifer, *Edward VI*, ed. George Bernard and Penry Williams (New Haven and London: Yale University Press, 1999).

Loach, Jennifer, *Parliament and Crown in the Reign of Mary Tudor* (Oxford: Clarendon Press, 1986).

Loach, Jennifer, 'Reformation Controversies', in James McConica, ed., *History of the University of Oxford*, 3 (Oxford: Oxford University Press, 1986), pp. 363–396.

Loades, David, 'Darcy, Thomas', *ODNB*.

Loades, David, 'Heath, Nicholas', *ODNB*.

Loades, David, *Henry VIII: Court, Church and Conflict* (Kew: The National Archives, 2007).

Loades, David, 'The Marian Episcopate', in *CMT*, pp. 33–56.

Loades, David, *Mary Tudor: A Life* (Oxford: Blackwell, 1989).

Loades, David, *Oxford Martyrs, The* (London: B.T. Batsford, 1970).

Loades, David, 'The Piety of the Catholic Restoration in England, 1553–8', in Loades, *Politics, Censorship and the English Reformation* (London and New York: Pinter), pp. 200–212.

Loades, David, *Politics and the Nation, 1450–1669*, 3rd edn (London: Fontana, 1988).

Loades, David, *The Reign of Mary Tudor: Politics, Government, Religion in England, 1553–58*, 2nd edn (London and New York: Longman, [1979] 1991).

Loades, David, *The Religious Culture of Marian England* (London: Pickering and Chatto, 2010).

Loades, David, 'The Sanctuary', in C.S. Knighton and R. Mortimer, eds, *Westminster Abbey Reformed* (Aldershot: Ashgate, 2003), pp. 75–93.

Louisa, Angelo J., 'Bourne, Gilbert', *ODNB*.

McConica, James, 'The Rise of the Undergraduate College', in McConica, ed., *History of the University of Oxford*, 3 (Oxford: Oxford University Press, 1986), pp. 1–68.

McCoog, Thomas M., *The Society of Jesus in Ireland, Scotland and England, 1589–1597: Building the Faith of St Peter upon the King of Spain's Monarchy* (Farnham: Ashgate, and Rome: Institutum Historicum Societatis Iesu, 2012).

MacCulloch, Diarmaid, *The Later Reformation in England, 1547–1603* (Basingstoke: Palgrave Macmillan, 2000).

MacCulloch, Diarmaid, *Thomas Cranmer: A Life* (New Haven and London: Yale University Press, 1996).

MacCulloch, Diarmaid, *Tudor Church Militant: Edward VI and the Protestant Reformation* (London: Allen Lane, The Penguin Press, 1999).

McGrath, Alister E., *Iustitia Dei: A History of the Christian Doctrine of Justification from 1500 to the Present Day* (Cambridge: Cambridge University Press, [1986] 1993).

McNair, Philip, 'Benedetto da Mantova, Marcantonio Flaminio, and the *Beneficio de Cristo*: A Developing Twentieth-century Debate Reviewed', *Modern Language Review*, 82 (1987), pp. 614–624.

McNair, Philip, *Peter Martyr in Italy: An Anatomy of Apostasy* (Oxford: Clarendon Press, 1967).

Marmion, J.P., 'The London Synod of Reginald, Cardinal Pole (1555–1556)', unpublished M.A. thesis, University of Keele, 1974.

Marshall, Peter, 'Catholic Exiles', in Marshall, *Religious Identities in Henry VIII's England* (Aldershot: Ashgate, 2005), pp. 225–261.

Marshall, Peter, 'Religious Exiles and the Tudor State', in Kate Cooper and Jeremy Gregory, eds, *Studies in Church History*, 43 (2007), pp. 263–284.

Martin, J., *Hidden Enemies: Italian Heretics in an Italian City* (Berkeley, Los Angeles and London: University of California Press, 1993).

Martines, Lauro, *Scourge and Fire: Savonarola and Renaissance Italy* (London: Jonathan Cape, 2006).

Mayer, Thomas F., 'Becket's Bones Burnt! Cardinal Pole and the Invention of an Atrocity', in Thomas S. Freeman and Thomas F. Mayer, eds, *Martyrs and Martyrdom in England, c.1400- 1700* (Woodbridge: The Boydell Press, 2007), pp. 126–143.

Mayer, Thomas F., 'Cardinal Pole's Finances: The Property of a Reformer', *CPEC* XV.

Mayer, Thomas F., 'A Fate Worse than Death: Reginald Pole and the Paris Theologians', *CPEC* XI.

Mayer, Thomas F., 'Goldwell, Thomas', *ODNB*.

Mayer, Thomas F., 'Lupset, Thomas', *ODNB*.

Mayer, Thomas F., 'Marco Mantova and the Paduan Religious Crisis of the Early Sixteenth Century', *CPEC* IX.

Mayer, Thomas F., '"Nusery of Resistance": Reginald Pole and his Friends', *CPEC* II.

Mayer, Thomas F., 'Pole, David', *ODNB*.

Mayer, Thomas F., 'Pole, Geoffrey', *ODNB*.

Mayer, Thomas F., 'Pole, Henry', *ODNB*.

Mayer, Thomas F., 'Pole, Reginald', *ODNB*.

Mayer, Thomas F., 'A Reluctant Author: Cardinal Pole and His Manuscripts', *Transactions of the American Philosophical Society*, 89, pt 4 (1999).

Mayer, Thomas F., 'Starkey, Thomas', *ODNB*.

Mayer, Thomas F., 'A Sticking Plaster Saint? Autobiography and Hagiography in the Making of Reginald Pole', *CPEC* XII.

Mayer, Thomas F., 'The Success of Cardinal Pole's Final Legation', *CMT*, pp. 149–175.

Mayer, Thomas F., 'A Test of Wills: Pole, Ignatius Loyola and the Jesuits in England', in T[homas] M. McCoog, ed., *The Reckoned Expense: Edmund Campion and the Early English Jesuits. Essays in Celebration of the First Centenary of Campion Hall* (Woodbridge: Boydell and Brewer, 1996), pp. 21–37.

Mayer, Thomas F., 'When Maecenas was Broke: Cardinal Pole's Spiritual Patronage', *CPEC* XIV.

Merritt, J.F., *The Social World of Early Modern Westminster Abbey: Court and Community 1525–1640* (Manchester: Manchester University Press, 2005).

Monter, William, 'Heresy Executions in Reformation Europe', in Ole Peter Grell and Bob Scribner, eds, *Tolerance and Intolerance in the European Reformation* (Cambridge: Cambridge University Press, 1996), pp. 48–65.

Moorhouse, Geoffrey, *The Pilgrimage of Grace: The Rebellion that shook Henry VIII's Reign* (London: Weidenfeld & Nicolson, 2002).

Morgan-Guy, John, 'Arthur, Hari Tudor and the Iconography of Loyalty in Wales', in Steven Gunn and Linda Monckton, eds, *Arthur Tudor, Prince of Wales: Life, Death and Commemoration* (Woodbridge: The Boydell Press, 2009), pp. 50–63.

Nagel, Alexander, 'Experiments in Art and Reform in Italy in the Early Sixteenth Century', in Kenneth Gouwens and Sheryl E. Reiss, eds, *The Pontificate of Clement VII: History, Politics, Culture* (Aldershot: Ashgate, 2005), pp. 385–409.

Newcombe, D.G., 'Hooper, John', *ODNB*.

Niccoli, Ottavia, *Prophecy and People in Renaissance Italy*, trans. Lydia C. Cochrane (Princeton: Princeton University Press, 1999).

Nieto, José C., *El Renacimiento y la otra España: Visión cultural socioespiritual* (Geneva: Librairie Droz, 1997).

Olin, John C., *The Catholic Reformation: Savonarola to Ignatius Loyola* (New York: Fordham University Press, 1992).

O'Malley, John W., *The First Jesuits* (Cambridge, MA: Harvard University Press, 1993).

O'Malley, John W., *Trent and All That: Renaming Catholicism in the Early Modern Era* (Cambridge, MA: Harvard University Press, 2000).

O'Malley, John W., *Trent: What Happened at the Council* (Cambridge, MA: The Belknap Press at Harvard University Press, 2013).

Orme, Nicholas, 'Latimer, William', *ODNB*.

Overell, Anne, 'Cardinal Pole's Special Agent: Michael Throckmorton, c.1503–1558', *History*, 94 (2009), pp. 265–278.

Overell, Anne, 'An English Friendship and Italian Reform: Edward Morrison and Michael Throckmorton, 1532–1538', *Journal of Ecclesiastical History*, 57 (2006), pp. 478–498.

Overell, Anne, *Italian Reform and English Reformation, c.1535-c.1585* (Aldershot: Ashgate, 2008).

Overell, Anne, 'Pole's Piety? The Devotional Reading of Pole and His Friends', *Journal of Ecclesiastical History*, 63 (2012), pp. 458–474.

Parish, Helen, *Clerical Celibacy in the West, c.1100–1700* (Farnham: Ashgate, 2010).

Parish, Helen, *Clerical Marriage and the English Reformation: Precedent, Policy and Practice* (Aldershot: Ashgate, 2000).

Parker, Charles, *Faith on the Margins: Catholics and Catholicism in the Dutch Golden Age* (Cambridge, MA: Harvard University Press, 2008).

Petrina, Alessandra, 'Reginald Pole and the Reception of the *Principe* in Henrician England', in Alessanro Arienzo and Alessandra Petrina, eds, *Machiavellian Encounters in Tudor and Stuart England: Literary and Political Influences from the Reformation to the Restoration* (Farnham: Ashgate, 2013), pp. 13–27.

Pierce, Hazel, 'The King's Cousin: The Life, Career and Welsh Connection of Sir Richard Pole, 1458–1504', *Welsh History Review*, 19 (1998), pp. 187–225.

Pierce, Hazel, 'The Life, Career and Political Significance of Margaret Pole, Countess of Salisbury (1473–1541)', unpublished Ph.D. thesis, University of Wales, Bangor, 1997.

Pierce, Hazel, *Margaret Pole, Countess of Salisbury, 1473–1541: Loyalty, Lineage and Leadership* (Cardiff: University of Wales Press, 2003).

Pierce, Hazel, 'Pole, Margaret', *ODNB*.

Pinto Crespo, Virgilio, *Inquisición y control ideológico en la España del siglo XVI* (Madrid: Taurus, 1982).

Pogson, R[ex] H., 'Cardinal Pole: Papal Legate in England in Mary Tudor's Reign', unpublished Ph.D. dissertation, University of Cambridge, 1972.

Pogson, R[ex] H., 'The Legacy of the Schism: Confusion, Continuity and Change in the Marian Clergy', in Jennifer Loach and Robert Tittler, eds, *The Mid-Tudor Polity, c.1540–1560* (London: Macmillan, 1980), pp. 116–136.

Pogson, R[ex] H., 'Reginald Pole and the Priorities of Government in Mary Tudor's Church', *Historical Journal*, 18 (1975), pp. 3–21.

Pollnitz, Aysha, 'Christian Women or Sovereign Queens? The Schooling of Mary and Elizabeth', in Alice Hunt and Anna Whitelock, eds, *Tudor Queenship: The Reigns of Mary and Elizabeth* (New York: Palgrave Macmillan, 2010), pp. 127–142.

Pollnitz, Aysha, 'Religion and Translation in the Court of Henry VIII: Princess Mary, Katherine Parr an the *Paraphrases* of Erasmus', in Doran and Freeman, *Mary Tudor*, pp. 123–137.

Prestwich, Michael, 'Medieval Biography', *Journal of Interdisciplinary History*, 40 (2010), pp. 325–346.

Questier, Michael C., *Catholicism and Community in Early Modern England: Politics, Aristocratic Patronage and Religion, c.1550–1640* (Cambridge: Cambridge University Press, 2006).

Redworth, Glyn, 'Castro, Alfonso de', *ODNB*.

Redworth, Glyn, *In Defence of the Church Catholic: the Life of Stephen Gardiner* (Oxford: Blackwell, 1990).

Reynolds, Anne, 'The Papal Court in Exile: Clement VII in Orvieto, 1527–28', in Kenneth Gouwens and Sheryl E. Reiss, eds, *The Pontificate of Clement VII: History, Politics, Culture* (Aldershot: Ashgate, 2005), pp. 143–161.

Rodríguez-Salgado, M.J., *The Changing Face of Empire: Charles V, Philip II and Habsburg Authority, 1551–1559* (Cambridge: Cambridge University Press, 1988).

Ross, Charles, *Edward IV* (London: Eyre Methuen, 1974).

Rundle, David, '*Bonae litterae*: The English in Rome', www.bonaelitterae. wordpress.com.

Russell, Elizabeth, 'The Influx of Commoners into the University of Oxford before 1581: An Optical Illusion?', *English Historical Review*, 92 (1977), pp. 721–745.

Russell, Elizabeth, 'Marian Oxford and the Counter-Reformation', in Caroline M. Barron and Christopher Harper-Bill, eds, *The Church in Pre-Reformation Society* (Woodbridge: The Boydell Press, 1985), pp. 212–227.

Scarisbrick, J.J., *Henry VIII* (New Haven and London: Yale University Press, 1997).

Scarisbrick, J.J., *The Reformation and the English People* (Oxford: Oxford University Press, 1984).

Schenk, William, *Reginald Pole, Cardinal of England* (London: Longman, Green and Co., 1950).

Schwartz, Stuart, *All Can Be Saved: Religious Tolerance and Toleration in the Iberian Atlantic World* (New Haven and London: Yale University Press, 2008).

Shagan, Ethan, *Popular Politics and the English Reformation* (Cambridge: Cambridge University Press, 2003).

Simoncelli, Paolo, *Evangelismo italiano del cinquecento: Questione religiose e nicodemismo politico* (Rome: Edizioni di Storia e Letteratura, 1979).

Simoncelli, Paolo, *Il caso Reginald Pole: eresia e santità nelle polemiche religiose del cinquecento* (Rome: Edizioni di Storia e Letteratura, 1977).

Sire, H.J.A., *The Knights of Malta* (New Haven and London: Yale University Press, 1994).

Skidmore, Chris, *Edward VI: The Lost King of England* (London: Weidenfeld & Nicolson, 2007).

Streckfuss, Corinna, 'England's Reconciliation with Rome: A News Event in Early Modern Europe', *Historical Research*, 82 (2009), pp. 62–73.

Taylor, Andrew W., '"*Ad omne virtutum genus*": Mary between Piety, Pedagogy and Praise in Early Tudor Humanism', in Doran and Freeman, *Mary Tudor*, pp. 103–122.

Tellechea Idígoras, José Ignacio, 'Bartolomé Carranza y la restauración católica inglesa (1554–1558)', *CP*, pp. 15–118.

Tellechea Idígoras, José Ignacio, 'Carlos V y Bartolomé Carranza. Un navarro junto al lecho de muerte del Emperador', in Tellechea, *Fray Bartolomé Carranza de Miranda (investigaciones históricas)* (Pamplona: Gobierno de Navarra, Departamento de Educación y Cultura, 2002), pp. 313–377.

Tellechea Idígoras, José Ignacio, 'Contarini, Pole, Morone, denunciados por el Cardenal Francisco de Mendoza (1560). Un documento del proceso de Carranza', *CP*, pp. 285–302.

Tellechea Idígoras, José Ignacio, 'Cuatro sermones inéditos de Carranza en Inglaterra', *CP*, pp. 353–388.

Tellechea Idígoras, José Ignacio, *Paolo IV y Carlos V: la renuncia del Imperio a debate* (Madrid: Fundación Universitaria Española, 2001).

Tellechea Idígoras, José Ignacio, 'Pole, Carranza y Fresneda: cara y cruz de una enemistad', *CP*, pp. 119–197.

Tellechea Idígoras, José Ignacio, 'Pole y Paulo IV: un célebre "Apologia" del Cardenal inglés (1557)', *CP*, pp. 199–211.

Thurston, Herbert, 'The First Englishman to make the Spiritual Exercise, *The Month*, 142 (1923), pp. 336–347.

Wabuda, Susan, 'Latimer, Hugh', *ODNB*.

Wabuda, Susan 'Ridley, Nicholas', *ODNB*.

Whitelock, Anne and Diarmaid MacCulloch, 'Princess Mary's Household and the Succession Crisis, July 1553', *Historical Journal*, 50 (2007), pp. 265–287.

Williams, Penry, 'Elizabethan Oxford', in James McConica, ed., *History of the University of Oxford*, 3 (Oxford: Oxford University Press, 1986), pp. 397–440.

Wizeman, William, *The Theology and Spirituality of Mary Tudor's Church* (Aldershot: Ashgate, 2006).

Woolfson, Jonathan, *Padua and the Tudors: English Students in Italy, 1485–1603* (Cambridge: James Clark, 1998).

Wroe, Anne, *Perkin: A Story of Deception* (London: Jonathan Cape, 2003).

# Index

and Protestants 97–8
and reform and general Council 95,
104–5, 202, 245
and the Nice conference (1538) 75–6
his conflict with King Henry VIII of
England 78
his ill-health and death 115, 116
sends legate to the Emperor Charles V
(1547) 110
sends legate to England (1537) 179–82,
198 *see also* Pole, Reginald, as papal
legate
sends legate to France and the
Habsburgs (1537–9) 74
Paul IV, Pope xi, 242
and Catholic restoration in England
171, 184, 186, 189, 198
and King Henry VIII's divorce 33–4,
35
and Naples 203–4
and papal elections 117–19, 158, 201
and the English Royal Supremacy
47 *see also* Henry VIII, his royal
supremacy
and the Inquisition 92, 93, 100–101,
103, 117–19, 158–9, 164, 227
and the Theatine order 199
death of 235, 236
his conflict with Pole 202–3, 277–8
in Pole's circle 43, 58–9, 202
Paulet, William, marquess of Winchester
245
Pavia, battle of (1525) 16–17, 19, 22, 25, 96
Peacock, Master 185
Pembroke College, Cambridge 184
Pendleton, Henry 220–21
Percy, Henry, earl of Northumberland 3
Pérez, Baltasar, Friar 233
Pérez, Gonzalo 193
Pernau, Louis de 74
Perne, Andrew 184, 187
Peryn (Perin), William, Friar 189
Petit, Guillaume, Bishop 29
Peto, William, Friar 73, 190, 210, 211, 212,
224

Philip II, king of Spain, also I of England
and heresy 162
and the English synod 170
and the Habsburg conflict with France
207–10, 236, 250–51
his household 154
his marriage to Queen Mary I of
England 125, 129–30, 132, 133,
134–5, 203
Phillips, Henry 76
Piacenza 65, 105
Picardy 74
Piedmont 73
Pierce, Hazel 5, 79
Pilgrimage of Grace 58, 60, 61, 64, 67, 69,
70, 72
Pio da Carpi, Alberto 94
Pio da Carpi, Rodolfo, Cardinal 64–5, 67,
69, 70, 74, 75, 117, 202
Pisa 86
Pius IV, Pope 256, 262
Pius V, Pope 225, 230
Plantagenet, royal house of ix, 115, 266
Platonic philosophy 15, 22, 42, 43
Poggio, Giovanni, Cardinal 80, 81, 82, 98
Pogson, R[ex] H. 161–2, 196–7, 198,
215–16
Polanco, Juan de 263
Pole, Arthur 8, 12
Pole, David, bishop of Peterborough 213,
258
Pole, Geoffrey, brother of Reginald 8, 78–9
Pole, Geoffrey, father of Sir Richard Pole 5
Pole, Henry, Baron Montagu 8, 9, 12, 59,
60, 62, 78–9, 83, 115, 127
Pole, John de la, earl of Lincoln 2, 5, 8
Pole, Margaret, countess of Salisbury 1–2,
3, 4–5, 6, 7–9, 59, 60, 72, 78–9
Pole, Owen 6
Pole, Reginald, cardinal archbishop of
Canterbury
and Catholic restoration in England
107, 119, 121–2, 126, 127, 130,
134–5, 138, 140–45, 163–5,
169–213